D1559821

IN THE WAKE OF WAR

CONFLICTING WORLDS
New Dimensions of the American Civil War

T. Michael Parrish, Series Editor

Black troops at Vicksburg

From the photo collection of the Old Court House Museum, Vicksburg, Mississippi

IN THE WAKE OF WAR

Military Occupation, Emancipation,
and Civil War America

ANDREW F. LANG

To Nina—
An exceptional historian. Stay
true to the past.
Best wishes,
Andrew

Louisiana State University Press
Baton Rouge

Published by Louisiana State University Press
Copyright © 2017 by Louisiana State University Press
All rights reserved
Manufactured in the United States of America
First printing

Designer: Michelle A. Neustrom
Typeface: Sentinel
Printer and binder: Sheridan Books, Inc.

Library of Congress Cataloging-in-Publication Data

Names: Lang, Andrew F., 1982– author.
Title: In the wake of war : military occupation, emancipation, and Civil War America /
    Andrew F. Lang.
Description: Baton Rouge : Louisiana State University Press, 2018. | Series: Conflicting worlds:
    new dimensions of the American Civil War | Includes bibliographical references and index.
Identifiers: LCCN 2017008823| ISBN 978-0-8071-6706-9 (cloth : alk. paper) | ISBN 978-0-8071-
    6707-6 (pdf) | ISBN 978-0-8071-6708-3 (epub)
Subjects: LCSH: Reconstruction (U.S. history, 1865–1877) | Southern States—Politics and gov-
    ernment—1865–1950. | United States—Politics and government—1865–1877. | United States—
    History—Civil War, 1861–1865—Occupied territories. | United States—History—Civil War,
    1861–1865—Peace. | Military occupation—Social aspects—Southern States—History—
    19th century. | Civil-military relations—Southern States—History—19th century. | Freed-
    men—Southern States—History—19th century. | Southern States—Race relations—
    History—1865–1950.
Classification: LCC E668 .L269 2018 | DDC 973.8—dc23
LC record available at https://lccn.loc.gov/2017008823

Portions of this book first appeared in "Republicanism, Race, and Reconstruction: The Ethos of
Military Occupation in Civil War America," *Journal of the Civil War Era,* Volume 4, no. 4. Copyright © 2014 by the University of North Carolina Press. Used by permission of the
publisher. www.ncpress.unc.edu

Portions of chapter 5 first appeared in *The Guerrilla Hunters: Irregular Conflicts during
the Civil War,* ed. Brian D. McKnight and Barton A. Myers (Baton Rouge: Louisiana State
University Press, 2017).

For Anne

CONTENTS

ACKNOWLEDGMENTS

Writing this book has been an absolute pleasure, the process of which connected me with a host of wonderful friends, colleagues, and mentors who all encouraged the project from its formative origins. I am humbled by the profound number of people who have left an indelible mark on this book, my scholarly pursuits, and my life in general.

The book profited from generous funding from a variety of sources. I would not have been able to conduct adequate research without financial support from the Historic New Orleans Collection, the William L. Clements Library at the University of Michigan, the Virginia Historical Society, and Rice University. Also, many thanks go to the wonderful staffs at these institutions, as well as to the Bentley Historical Library (University of Michigan); John Nau III Collection, David W. Mullins Library (University of Arkansas Special Collections); Library of Congress; National Archives; Hill Memorial Library (Louisiana State University); Southern Historical Collection (University of North Carolina, Chapel Hill); New York Historical Society; and the United States Army Military Heritage Institute (Carlisle Barracks, Pennsylvania).

I am fortunate to be part of a profession populated with kind, selfless, and genuine people. I especially want to thank my colleagues at Mississippi State University, who have maintained a welcoming, engaged, and supportive academic community. I could not have anticipated a better place in which to launch my professional career. In the ten years that I have been a member of the community of historians, I have had the great privilege of acquainting myself, working with, and benefiting from the expertise of scholars whom I admire greatly, and all of whom have left an indelible impression on this book. Special thanks go to Andrew Baker, John Barr, Stephen Berry, William Blair, Andrew Bledsoe, Peter Carmichael, Bradley Clampitt, Abigail Cooper, Lynda Crist, Rosanne Currarino, Adam Dean, Rand Dotson, Greg Downs, Zach Dresser, Suzanne Scott Gibbs, Lorien Foote, Gaines Foster, Randal Hall, Matthew Hamilton, Luke Harlow, Earl J. Hess, Houston Area Southern Historians, Rebecca Howard, Bethany Johnson, Howard Jones, Kelly Jones, Joe Locke, Brian and Ashley Luskey, Allison Madar, Brian McKnight, Kathryn

Shively Meier, Brian Craig Miller, Barton Myers, Scott Nesbit, Carl and Sarah Paulus, Jason Phillips, Paul Quigley, Aaron Sheehan-Dean (who generously shared parts of his research from the wartime Department of the Gulf collections at the National Archives), Rachel Shelden, Brooks Simpson, Richard Sommers, Whitney Stewart, Mark Summers, Jim Wainwright, Joan Waugh, and Ben Wright. Sincere thanks also go to the referee who reviewed the manuscript and whose valuable comments and critiques made the book stronger.

Two historians deserve special recognition. Gary W. Gallagher, whose scholarship has long inspired and shaped my own historical perspective, has influenced my work in immeasurable ways. I am profoundly grateful for the time and attention Gary has dedicated to my scholarship, offering thorough insight, thoughtful criticism, and generous endorsement of my ideas. T. Michael Parrish has been an unceasing champion of this project, always encouraging me to think big and to make bold contributions. Mike's keen eye for detail, command of sources, and absolute dedication to other people's work are both humbling and appreciated. I am honored now to be co-authoring with him a book on the American Civil War in a global context.

I am especially grateful to Randolph B. "Mike" Campbell, Richard Lowe, and Richard McCaslin, all of whom demonstrated the proper ways to conduct historical research and to approach the past with precision and care. Their encouragement and expectations shaped how I write and teach, and I am fortunate to consider each a colleague and a friend. At Rice University, Ira Gruber, Caleb McDaniel, and Allen Matusow constantly tested my assumptions, broadened my historical awareness, and pushed me to become a deeper thinker and careful writer. Their influence is seen on each page of this book. Finally, one could not ask for a better mentor than John B. Boles. His unceasing dedication to the past, his constant energy, and his perceptive, expansive mind will forever amaze me. John's infectious enthusiasm for history, his respect for the profession, and his commitment to his students and family—which are sometimes inseparable—are characteristics that we all should emulate.

I owe much gratitude to my in-laws, Robert, Karin, Will, and Mary Hierholzer. Their love and respect for history, their dedication to ideas and the life of the mind, and their endless search for fine food, wine, and music have influenced me in the most positive of ways. I always cherish our times together and am grateful that they have welcomed me into their family.

My grandparents, James and Eva Finley and Herb and Edna Lang, have filled me with wonderful memories, supplying unceasing love, endless affection, and gracious support. Randal Finley, Stan and Janette Gesch, and Judy Lang—my uncles and aunts—have also provided laughs and love for which I am thankful. I also greatly value the time spent with Chris, Jim, Gordon, and Howard Hoople as we trekked the battlefields annually at Gettysburg and Antietam. Howard's personal collection of the *Official Records,* which he gave to me when I began graduate school, stand proudly in my house and served as an essential source of research for this book. My brother, Todd, is an upstanding young man, whose thoughtfulness, consideration, and humility have always been the bulwarks of his character. I value my times with him and am grateful for our special bond.

Mere words cannot express how my parents, Jeff and Rhena Lang, have influenced my life and shaped me into the person who I am today. They are, undoubtedly, the sole reason that I have been privileged to pursue the life of an academic. My dad has long taught me the value of pursuing my goals, always encouraging me to locate my potential, never settling for second-best. I have tried to embrace his virtues of hard work and self-sufficiency, for which I am forever grateful. I will always cherish our many trips to the East Coast to visit historical sites and Civil War battlefields, which largely inspired my quest to become a professional historian. My mom has offered constant care, comfort, calm, and love, always thinking of others before herself. Her selflessness is a testament to her character, which I daily strive to follow. My parents' influence is on every page of this book, with me whenever I enter the classroom, and is instilled in me as I prepare to become a parent.

My wife, Anne, has lived with this project for the duration of our relationship. There is no one with whom I have conversed more about this book; no one who has longer endured my bouts of grumpiness and anxieties about the project's worth and whether it would ever get finished; no one who has offered more encouragement and positive reinforcement; and no one who has read and critiqued as many chapter drafts. Indeed, her skills as a professional editor and her eye for cogent writing have made the book better than I ever could have imagined. I dedicate this work to her as a small token of appreciation for her endless love and companionship. As I write these words, we are patiently waiting the arrival of our first child, Margaret. I anticipate that this book will make excellent bedtime reading.

IN THE WAKE OF WAR

Introduction

The Republican Tradition, Military Occupation,
and Civil War History

In 1846, on the eve of the United States' war against Mexico, the *New York Herald* affirmed a long-standing tradition on which American armies would rely in their quest to conquer the lands of the Montezumas. "One of the highest tests of a good citizen," the newspaper declared, "is the readiness or reluctance with which he yields his personal liberty . . . when at his country's call, he leaves his private pursuit and enters the field to fulfill the highest obligation a citizen owes his country." James K. Polk, the rabid expansionist president, agreed, claiming that permanent military establishments "are contrary to the genius of our free institutions"; the nation's manifest destiny must be secured by "our citizen soldiers." Moved by patriotism, the excitement and stimulation of war, and even a sense of duty, thousands of young men left their homes and entered the army in search of martial glory. Celebrated in the popular press and hailed by the commander-in-chief, the romantic image of selfless citizens-turned-soldiers embodied the nation's imagined providential ideals.[1]

Nearly fifteen years later, when the loyal citizenry of the Union waged war against the Confederacy, they too looked to their fellow countrymen as the exemplars and guarantors of the national cause. The secession winter of 1860–61 unleashed a martial response predicated on preserving the United States threatened by southern slaveholding oligarchs. Volunteers who entered Union armies displayed a selfless duty to the public good: private citizens leaving their homes to serve in the military, fight their threatened nation's battles, and, if necessary, die for the cause. George L. Gaskell, a member of a Rhode Island artillery company, informed his sister in March 1862 that crossing the Potomac River into Virginia "was one of the greatest events of my life." He concluded, "I am a man . . . and a *soldier* and if my country needs my life she is welcome."[2]

Union volunteers assumed that the war would be brief, limited in scope, and merely a contest between opposing armies. Stationed within the defenses of Washington, D.C., in May 1861, Henry Wilson Hubbell of the Seventh New York State Militia predicted, "We will all be home within a month, and we may be cured of any ambition for military glory by that time." Disinterested voluntarism and faith in a quick, decisive war informed the principal reason that northern men entered the army: to preserve the Union. Devotion to the American nation filled the ideological fountainhead for enlistment, underscoring why free men believed so deeply in offering their services for its defense. "As soon as I assist in uniting our once happy & prosperous country & firmly planting that glorious old flag in every State in the Union," Joseph Field declared from his camp of instruction in Boston, "then can we enjoy that happiness that it would be impossible to find in the present state of our country."[3]

The idea of Union, of which Joseph Field wrote, evinced by the thousands of men who rushed to war in 1861, and to which most nineteenth-century Americans subscribed, judged the United States a unique nation in which the rule of law was supreme, individual freedom sacrosanct, and the privilege of self-determination implicit. Common rights were protected by judicious governments with a limited scope of authority. The basis of American citizenship, from the founding through the Civil War, was secured by a dedication to and fierce protection of these principles. In these conceptions the United States functioned as the exception to world history in which monarchs ruled by arbitrary fiat, relegating average citizens to lives of servitude to the state. If the young American republic ever failed, so too would its unprecedented experiment in republican government and democratic political participation. At the center of both the Mexican-American and Civil Wars—conflicts waged to expand and preserve the United States' unique political conception—stood the citizen-soldier, the embodiment of a nineteenth-century military tradition predicated on the individual's role in safeguarding the national mission through swift, decisive, and temporary military service.[4]

Seldom at the beginning of the Mexican-American and Civil Wars did these citizen-soldiers consider the complicated prospect of invading, occupying, and subduing hostile peoples and nations. Engaging in an irregular war against violent civilian enemies or, during the Civil War, unfolding the complicated processes of emancipation barely entered the consciousness of these idealistic volunteers. Nor did the possibility of establishing and managing bureaucratic garrisons correspond to the nature of war as understood or imagined by volunteer US soldiers. This book traces a sweeping evolution of the American military tradition, stemming from the confluence of the citizen-soldier ideal and military occupation. To understand volunteer soldiering and occupation during the United States' conflicts with Mexico and the Confederacy and in the Reconstruction South is to appreciate broader conceptions of citizenship; white and black men's relationships to nineteenth-century society, culture, and government; the expectations embraced by citizens-turned-soldiers; and assumptions about the army's proper position in a democratic republic. The nineteenth-century American military tradition underwent striking alterations in these conflicts as provisional volunteers were called upon to enact the unanticipated and unprecedented projects of wartime and peacetime military occupation.

The citizen-soldier tradition grew from the ethos of American republicanism, a culture adopted during the Revolution and consolidated in the early republic. Republicanism defined white Americans' citizenship, individual liberty, and protection of natural rights by government, while limiting the coercive scope of governing institutions. A fierce dedication to private property rights, participatory inclusion in the body politic, and an aversion to venality comprised this web of beliefs. Americans venerated their republican heritage because it functioned as an antithesis to monarchy and oligarchy, the very systems against which the Revolutionary fathers fought. Governments were viewed with both suspicion and reverence because they possessed a dual capacity for inspiring corruption and protecting individual liberty. Thus, the citizen was supreme ruler in this form of government and society; republicanism underscored the privilege and duty of the citizen to govern oneself.[5]

Republican governments safeguarded individual liberty while relying on the citizenry to defend the nation in times of crisis. White males enjoyed the greatest fruits of this tradition. And thus the system, in order to survive, looked to self-sacrificing, voluntary service from its male citizens for support and preservation. Citizen-soldiers were guided by the culture of civic virtue—a conviction that men were not enslaved to the state but rather participated voluntarily in public life—and assumed principal responsibility for shielding the nation in times of emergency. White citizens had a stake in preserving their way of life; the alternative, they feared, presented an existence of suppression and limitation of rights. In order to maintain the unique character of the early American republic, this reasoning held, private individuals would temporarily lay down the tools of their civilian trades, bear arms, and voluntarily defend the republic against enemies both foreign and domestic. Once the crisis was resolved, the soldier, having performed his civic duty, would resume his civilian pursuits. Americans believed *volunteer* service to be crucial to sustaining the form of government that protected their individual freedom.[6]

The citizen-soldier tradition emanated from conceptions of republican citizenship, which, according to political theorist R. Claire Snyder, was constructed on the twin pillars of military service and civic participation. She argues that "individuals *become* republican citizens *only* as they engage together in civic and martial practices." Thus, citizenship was not an amorphous identity granted by birthplace, transferred through bloodlines, or established by legal decree. Instead, it required active, disinterested contributions for the broader public good—militia service or wartime voluntarism, in this instance—that guaranteed associational membership in the body politic. "It is not enough to live within the borders of a nation-state, nor is it enough to have a particular ethnic identity," Snyder warns. "Rather, one's identity as a citizen-soldier requires repeated engagement in civic and martial practices." This requirement charged citizens to participate together in civic rituals, embodying mutual political traits and cultural practices that united the common interest. Citizens, because they enjoyed common liberties, thus shared common military burdens.[7]

The citizen-soldier ideal condemned professional, bureaucratic, and permanent military service. Republicanism looked askance at professional officers, who were considered aristocratic and repressive. Permanent martial duty limited personal autonomy, thereby stripping from an individual one of the central privileges of citizenship. A man's identity as citizen, however, could remain firmly intact if he entered into *temporary* militia service. Citizens-turned-soldiers, therefore, celebrated their voluntariness, understanding that they would return quickly to private life at the completion of their service. Provisional service characterized their relationship to the state, and they exercised the freedom to move in and out of the army, while always retaining the rights and privileges of civilian life. Once citizens entered the military, beliefs about self-government and personal independence also arrived in the ranks. Volunteers demanded, because they were free men, the right to elect officers, to be treated as equals, and to preserve their commitment to individualism. Citizen-soldiers believed that military attempts to regulate their behavior threatened personal independence and liberty and hence were not to be endured by free citizens.[8]

While citizens demanded and oftentimes set the parameters of their volunteer military service, the state responded in good faith, believing in the ability of its citizens to perform disinterested military duty for the public good. George Washington's selfless embodiment of the republican soldier, bolstered by the emerging democratic impulses of the nineteenth century, strengthened societal beliefs in self-government through voluntary defense. Active but temporary military service allowed Americans direct participation in warding off enemies of the state, threats to private property, or coercions against republican institutions. Thus, the citizen-soldier played a crucial role in the formative nation's security. And whereas he demanded the right of self-government in the ranks, he also demarcated the type of service that would be performed. Emphases on temporariness were not taken lightly. Volunteers insisted that they be deployed to the central areas of crisis, allowed to actively battle their nation's enemies, interact minimally with civilians, and be sent home immediately upon resolution of the emergency. Extraneous duty, especially that which reflected any sort of military professionalization, governance, or potentially long-term service, violated the social contracts implicit between volunteer soldiers and their government.[9]

In order for the citizen-soldier ideal to flourish, early Americans needed a "negative" reference by which to compare themselves. American republicans viewed large, permanent armies with great distrust and skepticism, believing them to be the embodiment of European-style military establishments. Long before the first English troops occupied Boston, new republican ideas concerning the problems of standing armies infiltrated the American colonies. Copies of *Cato's Letters,* a blistering indictment of anti-republican tendencies, especially permanent military institutions, flooded the American mainland, warning that professional standing armies thwarted individual liberty and threatened limited governance. Much of the Revolutionary generation assumed that standing armies subordinated the citizen to the power of government. These ideas informed the political climate of Boston, for instance, during the 1760s and 1770s, in which professional red-coated soldiers enforced allegedly tyrannical laws that functioned against the will of the people. The perpetual military presence reminded Americans of their subservient status to the Crown as troops occupied private homes and public dwellings, imposing their will on the community. Indeed, on the eve of independence, Samuel Adams spoke for many colonials when he wrote, "A Standing Army . . . is always dangerous to the Liberties of the People. Soldiers are apt to consider themselves as a Body distinct from the rest of the Citizens. . . . Such a power should be watched with a jealous Eye."[10]

A national conversation arose in the wake of the American Revolution about the postwar responsibilities and presence of the military. One of the great debates during the early national period was over the creation of a standing army, an institution that, some Americans argued, symbolized unchecked power, political instability, and arbitrary class distinctions between officers and enlisted men. Contemporaries maintained that permanent military establishments threatened to corrupt society at large, while also inviting corruption in the ranks, because career soldiers would grow detached from the moral obligations established by the civilized nation. Thus, it is no wonder that the new republic attached itself so strongly to the citizen-soldier ideal in which the individual citizen, rather than a large standing army, assumed paramount responsibility for the defense of liberty.[11]

The new republic nonetheless established an army, which functioned as a small but permanent institution that regulated frontier and coastal defenses and engaged in internal engineering projects. Although recognized as a fixed organization in the developing federal system, the army endured the scrutiny and suspicion of republican societies. Americans accepted their new military establishment, but they condemned military involvement in civil, political, and societal affairs. Republican military culture had long distinguished between the necessity of a large, but temporary, wartime army and the luxury of small independent militias during times of peace. Antebellum Americans feared that standing armies would become unnecessarily involved in politics, divorced from the constraints of civil law, and tempted to use their power coercively. Standing armies were thus viewed as institutions far removed from civilian society, displaying loyalty only to their own leaders and interests. And because of their idle nature, standing armies were assumed to breed corruption, undermining the morality of the soldiers who served in their ranks. Throughout much of the antebellum period, the army was thus relegated to the fringes of American life, where it struggled to create an identity.[12]

The diminutive US Army nonetheless adopted the broader culture of military republicanism, refusing to serve in any capacity that might defy the nation's political order and refraining from fomenting disloyalty against civil governments. Still, countless nineteenth-century Americans continued to look on the regular army with contempt. Believing that a permanent military establishment was a necessary evil, citizens alleged that it possessed the capacity to create class distinctions in an otherwise egalitarian republic. Enlisted men were regarded as good-for-nothing failures in life who had never taken advantage of the fruits of individualism and equality. Volunteers for the regular army, American commentators noted, willingly removed themselves from the capitalist market in which a man had the liberty to forge his own unique identity. Instead, these individuals chose to have their rights and freedoms stripped away, subsumed by the demands of the army.[13]

The regular army came to be associated with the garrisons in which soldiers served. These small, enclosed spaces encapsulated the American public's imagination of the professional army. Consigned to the frontier, removed from civilian life, and ruled by conformity, garrisons symbolized the antithesis of American republicanism, standing in stark contrast to the citizen-soldier tradition. Private civilians were not subject to the harsh discipline that had to be maintained in such static environments, nor were they forced to succumb to the mind-numbing tedium that permeated garrison life. Officers and enlisted men also considered themselves burdened by garrisons' impenetrable environments. Troops often used the term "monotony" to describe their daily existence, underscoring the lack of variety and seclusion from society.[14]

In contrast to the republican citizen-soldier model, garrisons functioned as permanent, professional spaces that restricted freedom and movement. Drill exercises and bureaucratic administration supplied the daily rhythm of garrison life, which soldiers viewed as affronts to the restless, independent American temperament. From his post at Jefferson Barracks, Missouri, Edmund Kirby Smith noted that a peacetime garrison existence induced soldiers to become "automaton like" and "involuntary." Such static conditions reflected broader American concerns that soldiers, because they were removed from the standards of civil society, would revert to practices that contradicted a moral republican character. Drinking especially came to be associated with regular army garrisons, as soldiers sought outlets from the tedium. Yet garrisons rarely offered an opportunity for soldiers to escape from their cloistered military existence. Garrison culture also provoked class tensions between commanding officers and the enlisted soldiers they regulated, complicating relationships between white men who were considered equal in civil society.[15]

Seen as unnatural, limiting environs that dotted the landscape of an otherwise egalitarian republic, garrisons reflected long-held concerns about permanent military establishments. Contemporaries sought to remove the army's presence as far as possible from republican life, protecting civil society from professional military influence. These formative American ideals, grounded in the culture of martial republicanism, grew throughout the early nineteenth century until they collided with an unanticipated military necessity that threatened to undermine long-standing conventions about the volunteer tradition and the fear of standing armies: the problem of military occupation in the United States' conflicts with Mexico and the Confederacy, and in the Reconstruction South. Soldiers perceived in each of these conflicts two fundamental challenges to the nineteenth-century republican military tradition: concerns that the citizen-soldier ideal was incompatible with invasion and occupation and fears that occupying armies were disquietingly similar to the much-reviled standing armies.

* * *

The Civil War era can be considered the dawning age of American wars of occupation, inaugurating a tradition that persisted through the late nineteenth and early twentieth centuries and that continues to the present day.[16] Volunteers who joined the army in the United States' war against Mexico, and loyal citizens who offered service for the Union's war against the Confederacy, initiated a national conversation about the changing nature of American military practice—rooted in occupation—shaping a debate that would continue deep into the Reconstruction years. It is imperative to conceptualize mid-nineteenth-century American military occupation—a post-invasion doctrine that regulated and controlled both passive and hostile civilian enemies by administering conquered territory through martial law and fortified garrisons—as a longitudinal continuum, rather than focusing independently on one of the three great conflicts that occurred between 1846 and 1877. The responses of citizen-soldiers who served in the armies that occupied Mexico, the Confederacy, and the postwar South (and even those of professional soldiers who served long into the Reconstruction years) revealed striking continuity, while also signaling important notes of change across time, space, and conflict.[17]

Approaching military occupation through the eyes of the occupier reveals a war within a war, a conflict fraught with its own unique traits and spirit. Exploring how US soldiers, who reflected the broader society from which they came, interpreted occupation on both ideological and practical grounds reveals an in-the-ranks perspective on the role of American armies in international and domestic wars and crises. Volunteers who invaded Mexico and Union soldiers who served within biracial occupying armies in the wartime Confederacy and postwar South articulated complex beliefs about the military's place, role, and disposition in nineteenth-century America. Across conflicts, American occupiers exhibited a diverse host of opinions, while consistently pronouncing that their form of military service—governing racially "inferior" Mexicans and presiding over black and white southerners during war and peace—was unique and exceptional in the United States' short military history.[18]

Soldiers in all three conflicts drew on long-held understandings of republican culture to reveal an emerging crisis in the nineteenth-century military tradition: negotiating the problematic aftermath of invasion. Launching a grand foray into enemy territory and waging battle on distant fields were immensely complicated endeavors. However, it was an equally complex, largely unprecedented undertaking to govern territories and regulate peoples long after the major armies departed, leaving behind a force of occupation. According to the occupiers, the distinctive, unexpected challenges of martial government fundamentally changed the American tradition of citizen-soldiering. Indeed, the mandates of occupation complicated the ideal of civic virtue, which traditionally operated in *defense* of the nation during times of crisis and not necessarily in active wars of invasion. As the United States assigned its citizen-volunteers to long-term occupation of Mexico, the Confederate South, and the opening scenes of Reconstruction, the occupiers themselves wrestled with the implications of their service.

To appreciate the reaction of US soldiers to occupation, a critical understanding of nineteenth-century military policy, practice, and procedure must be related to the broader cultures in which wars were waged. Occupation was a central component in the conflicts against Mexico and the Confederacy and in securing a lasting peace during Reconstruction. The particular manner in which armies of occupation conducted war and shaped peace exposed and challenged common soldiers' assumptions about the character of American military service. Pursuing a history of military occupation thus reveals how occupation itself brought soldiers face-to-face with a host of critical issues in nineteenth-century America: the relationship between the citizen and government; the balance between republican corporatism and democratic individualism; faith in the exceptional nature of Union; regional, national, and cultural variances in opinion; the status of race and complications of emancipation in a white democracy; the negotiation of gender roles; the limits of free-market capitalism; the boundaries of restricted warfare; the military's simultaneously celebrated and ambivalent place in international affairs and domestic life; and the uncertain scope of the federal state.[19]

Seen within this context, the culture of republicanism reveals great analytical utility in a study of wartime and postwar military occupation, a martial practice so foreign to the era's existing military ethos. Although republicanism as a concept has undergone fierce but necessary scrutiny, when employed within the limited framework of mid-nineteenth-century military culture, the paradigm informs historical practices, discourses, and fears that underscored the army's place in American life. This study thus subscribes to historian Ricardo A. Herrera's contention that "faith in republicanism and a sure knowledge of his place in the nation's life were basic to the identity of the American soldier," guided by "the continuity of republican principles from the American Revolution through the Civil War." Contrasting the unprecedented nature of occupation with the republican tradition, volunteers articulated long-standing anxieties about citizens participating in permanent, bureaucratic military capacities, armies at the vanguard of social and political change, and corruption in the ranks. Republicanism ultimately interprets the citizenry's relationship to the government, army, and society, as well as the wartime and peacetime influences of federal military institutions on civil life.[20]

Citizen-soldiers enacted the principal tenets of military occupation—securing, holding, and guarding territory; enforcing government policies; regulating and defining the limits of civilian combatants; policing cities and towns; and battling guerrillas—from within and without garrisons, which represented the geographic focal point of American occupations and functioned as the locus for the ideological and cultural challenges confronted by occupying soldiers. Whether situated within large occupied cities or created as isolated, fortified outposts, more than one hundred garrisons were established throughout the Confederacy by the Union army during the Civil War. These garrisons were used to concentrate occupation forces, launch raids and expeditions into the countryside, and establish a formidable presence in enemy territory.[21]

The common occupier, however, viewed garrisons as static and constrained spaces that restricted martial movement and sapped the purpose from their service. Garrisons reminded the Union citizen-soldier, as well as soldiers in Mexico and the Reconstruction South, of what he perceived to be his marginalized physical position within the broader wartime landscape. The isolated, stagnant nature of garrison life prompted soldiers to believe that they were left behind, while their comrades in arms served in the campaigning armies, where the truly important service was being rendered. Feeling restless and trapped at what seemed to be the fringes of the war effort, garrison soldiers began to question the validity of their service. As the tangible symbol of occupation, garrisons posed a challenge to the citizen-soldier ideal, forcing US volunteers to consider how their position as military occupiers related to the citizen-soldier heritage and to the nation at large.[22]

Although the occupation of Mexico during the late 1840s produced dynamics similar to the occupations in the Civil War and Reconstruction—namely, citizen-soldiers navigating the challenges of garrison duty and occupying peoples and territories—chapter 1 demonstrates that exploits in the lands of the Montezumas differed in a critical way from the United States' occupations of the Confederacy and postwar South. Perceptions of their Mexican enemies as racial inferiors infused American occupiers of this era with a sense that aggressive occupations and ruthless military engagements against and among civilians were justified. While military occupation had never before been a formal feature of the United States' military tradition, the qualities that informed the American citizen-soldier ideal—democratic individualism, resistance to arbitrary authority, and fierce dedication to national exceptionalism and racial superiority—also supplied the very characteristics that made occupation such a challenging prospect in Mexico. Whether they were stationed in garrisons or deployed on antiguerrilla missions, the unruly and undisciplined conduct of American volunteers convinced the professional military establishment that recalcitrant and needlessly violent amateurs were unfit for international wars of invasion.[23]

The Mexican-American War revealed that governing foreign "others" on international lands proved much more palatable than subjugating fellow white American citizens. Conceptions of who constituted "the enemy" were greatly complicated during the Civil War, when Union troops were called to occupy the land of white southerners, who shared a common language, religion, and heritage. Chapter 2 departs from the perspective of the common soldier, examining from a macro perspective the policies and processes of occupation during the Civil War. Framing the context in which the rest of the book unfolds, the chapter describes the conditions and evolution of occupation, including the regulation of civilians, the processes of emancipation, the uncertainties of civilian combatants, the transition from a limited war to a "hard" war, and the rise of the United States Colored Troops (USCT).

At least one-third of Union soldiers experienced the challenges of wartime military occupation, changing the ways in which they interacted with civilians, testing their perspectives of limited military service, and altering their perceived relationship to the nation. Even if some soldiers fought in battles to claim territory—and many did—the responsibility of actually occupying that territory challenged their hopes for short, temporary service. Chapter 3 explores how Union soldiers imagined armies of occupation as powerful standing armies that regulated the Confederate South's gender, cultural, and racial dynamics. Amidst the oftentimes stagnant and distracting nature of occupation, the conditions of which are surveyed in chapter 4, many soldiers also perpetuated and yielded to informal wartime market economies, which observers identified as the corrupting result of serving in immobile military institutions. However, as chapter 5 explains, the threat of violence always lurked, and occupiers grew anxious at the thought of employing irregular and violent tactics against civilians, guerrillas, and even the natural landscape, actions that pushed the US government to address and enforce the "laws of war."[24]

Above all, because they were reared in the republican tradition, and because the Civil War was a domestic conflict, white Union occupiers feared that their service within the wartime Confederacy had transformed their identities as citizen-soldiers. Though volunteers had performed their civic duty, occupation shattered a shared sense of martial purpose, breaking "the affective bonds that form the necessary prerequisite for attending to what [was held] in common rather than what divides." Indeed, the occupiers noted the perceived shift from selfless volunteer into permanent, powerful arbiters of military government. The principal features of wartime occupation—serving in garrisons and governing peoples and domestic territory—led soldiers to see themselves as the embodiment of a standing, bureaucratic army, which aroused great suspicion and dismay. Such service convinced some Union soldiers that, although perhaps such service was justified by the crisis of war, they had become integrated into an institution that threatened the very republican principles that they had volunteered to defend.[25]

By the midpoint of the Civil War, as Union troops expressed angst at the perceived contradictions between occupation and citizen-soldiering, a new class of occupiers emerged. Chapter 6 interprets how the mass enlistment of African American soldiers into the ranks of US armies prompted white leaders to define service in auxiliary forces along the lines of race. The Emancipation Proclamation declared "that such persons of suitable condition, will be received into the armed service of the United States to garrison forts, positions, stations, and other places, and to man vessels of all sorts in said service." The politics and language of emancipation, articulated by Abraham Lincoln, antislavery rhetoric, myriad Union generals, and the common white soldier, were intended to confine black troops to limited garrisoning roles, including the "dishonorable" duties of occupation. Yet, as chapter 7 argues, black soldiers, the majority of whom garrisoned regions conquered by Union armies, embraced the possibilities of service behind the lines as a potential tool for destabilizing the South's long-standing racial power structure. Rather than viewing garrison service as dishonorable or unpalatable, members of the USCT wielded the power of occupation in a focused effort to reshape society. Long excluded from the United States' republican tradition, black soldiers were not hindered by the limits of national military custom. Instead, they viewed the occupying army as the central vehicle by which to alter the South's entrenched racial hierarchy.[26]

Black occupation complicated existing notions about who participated in and the role of volunteer armies. On the one hand, the Emancipation Proclamation attempted to define, in a conservative fashion, African American soldiers as second-class citizens by relegating them to garrison service. White nineteenth-century Americans viewed volunteer soldiering as a direct prerequisite of male citizenship, determined also by the collective type of military service performed. Because garrisoning was presumed to separate volunteers from the war effort and the martial purpose of confronting enemies on the field of battle, it was thus used to incorporate black men into the army while limiting their inclusion in the body politic. Segregating African American soldiers in the rear of the army suggested that they did not possess the full range of civic aptitude to participate equally in volunteer institutions, an assumption that belied the "citizenship of civic practices." Garrisoning was intended to distinguish black soldiers from white, thereby assuaging white fears about the tension between military occupation and the citizen-soldier tradition.[27]

On the other hand, the manner in which African American soldiers approached their military duties challenged the cultural strictures placed on them by garrison service. Resisting the supposedly static conditions of auxiliary service, and embracing their presence as a force of military occupation, black troops undermined existing assumptions about provisional soldiers serving behind the lines. The fate of emancipation depended on an active domestic army that embedded itself in society, reconfiguring social relationships and political power. The presence of black soldiers in occupied towns and the countryside revealed the revolutionary nature of the black soldiering experience, much more so than enlistment and battlefield performance alone.

African American soldiers converted garrison duty, initially a conservative solution to the stigma felt by white occupiers, into one of the most transformative aspects of the Civil War. Standing as powerful impediments against the Confederate republic's slaveholding promise, black occupiers refused to serve quietly behind the lines. Instead, they used occupation to set the stage for the opening scenes of Reconstruction.[28]

Chapter 8 navigates the conflicting ways in which white and black soldiers interpreted military occupation during the immediate postwar months and years, the former emphasizing a limited martial influence in civil affairs and the latter stressing racial equality and social transformation. What began during the Mexican-American War and grew during the Civil War as a conflict between the citizen-soldier ideal and military occupation evolved into a broader struggle during Reconstruction over the army's civil function in the wake of Confederate defeat. Ultimately, wartime fears and apprehensions articulated by white Union soldiers about the long-term consequences of occupation emerged victorious over the black vision of a powerful postwar occupation. A consensus developed, grounded in the republican ethic and mixed with growing ambivalence about racial equality, that distinguished the army's peacetime position. The evolution of postwar occupation reflected long-standing ideological and cultural aversions to the military's shaping of civil affairs, politics, and social-economic conditions. Chapter 9 features professional soldiers remaining in the postwar army who argued that preserving the Union meant preserving the republican tradition of limited governmental and military institutions. An enduring Union required the disbanding of occupation armies within the United States and bringing the experiment of Military Reconstruction to an end.[29]

This book interprets the conflicts between republicanism, military occupation, and emancipation within a chronological framework that is bound by thematic dimensions. Shaped by the writings of approximately five hundred US soldiers, white and black, volunteer and regular, the study is informed by letters, diaries, government and army reports, the invaluable *Official Records*, contemporary opinion journals, and, in rare instances, memoirs. To sketch as comprehensive a picture as possible, the book evaluates troops who served in all theaters of the Mexican-American War, Civil War, and Reconstruction, and who hailed from diverse regions across the country, revealing the complicated wake of military occupation during the American Civil War era.[30]

1 | Conflicting Cultures and the Mexican-American War

The republican culture informing the citizen-soldier model collided with the professionalizing tendencies of the regular army in 1846 when the United States went to war with Mexico. In this war waged to exert national power and supremacy, consolidate borders, and acquire vast amounts of land, Americans relied on their heritage of martial volunteerism to achieve national war aims. After decades of ideological inculcation of the citizen-soldier ideal, Americans during the 1840s exuded confident, almost cocky expectations about the superiority of the US military compared to their Mexican foes.[1]

As white males rushed to fill volunteer units, Americans celebrated citizen-volunteers on the grounds that they embodied the nation's best interests. They were not hirelings or professionals detached from national goals; instead, their patriotism reflected the essence of republican civic virtue. The very act of volunteering on behalf of the nation confirmed ideals of American nationalism and exceptionalism. Operating within the broader culture of "Manifest Destiny," volunteer troops could be counted on to secure new territory for the United States. Citizen-soldiers accordingly dreamed of earning battlefield glory, securing personal honor, and perpetuating the nation's redemptive character, which in turn preserved individual liberty. Once in the ranks, they enacted their identities as citizens, demanding the right to elect officers and maintain a degree of personal independence; their fierce individualism entered the army with them.[2]

Yet beneath this triumphal veneer, the war against Mexico unveiled a new facet of the American military tradition that collided with the citizen-soldier model. The invasion, acquisition, and governance of territory through military occupation revealed a kind of quasi-war that challenged the nineteenth-century American martial imagination. Citizen-soldiers participated in many of the grand campaigns and battles of the war, accepting the possibility of battlefield death as a necessary risk of their military service. Wartime victories were critically important, but they meant only so much if the acquired lands could not thereafter be governed effectively by the US military. A sizable share of volunteers, many of whom enlisted for the entire war, were thus ordered to oversee the regions already secured by earlier engagements, thereby fostering anxiety about the problematic and uncertain components of occupation. An established tradition of military occupation did not exist, and even the regular army stumbled blindly, searching for effective methods with which to occupy Mexico.[3]

The process and experience of occupying Mexico directly altered the citizen-soldier spirit, prompting far-reaching and fundamental changes to the nation's long-established military practice. Often left behind the front lines of combat to enact the tasks of occupation, American soldiers encountered two paradoxical forces: confrontations with allegedly inferior Mexican civilians and the strictures of military garrisons. First, invasion and martial governance unleashed American conceptions of Mexicans as inferior "others," which lent credence to the belief that occupation justified brutal conduct and harsh governing policies toward civilians. Troops sensed that occupying foreign lands on behalf of the United States and its Anglo-Saxon Protestant civilization would vindicate their conduct. Imbued with this hierarchical worldview, citizen-soldiers embodied the alarming ease with which occupying forces could govern peoples of different nationalities, customs, and religions. The conflict revealed the inherent tension between serving in defense of the nation and serving in an army of invasion in which martial subjugation, defined by race and culture, seemed both necessary and just.[4]

Second, and paradoxically, volunteers interpreted occupied garrisons to be centers of bureaucratic centralization used to regulate the behavior of civilian enemies while also limiting the freedom of citizen-soldiers. Reared within a national context that preached individualism and personal autonomy, volunteers construed military life in general, and occupation duty in particular, as manifest affronts to their liberty. They believed that occupation kept them cloistered far from any glorious contribution to the ennobling events of the war. Citizen-soldiers had volunteered their services to champion the national cause, and they chafed under the strictures of military occupation.[5]

* * *

The very nature of the way in which the United States went to war in 1846 underscored the alteration of the citizen-soldier concept. President James K. Polk and his supporters cloaked their intentions in the rhetoric of national defense and labeled Mexico as the aggressor, calling on volunteers to defend the nation's honor. The rush to arms exhibited the ideal of American civic virtue. Yet such calls to defense were, in large part, merely a façade, masking the true intentions of the administration. Manifest Destiny, an aggressive concept that preached America's providential right to acquire vast continental lands, inspired thousands of men to join the ranks of volunteer units. Faith in American exceptionalism and belief in the inferiority of other nations drove countless citizens into the army.[6]

Citizen-soldiers accepted the necessity of military occupation in order to fulfill the era's obsession with Manifest Destiny. They believed that the war represented a moment to prove the superiority of the American experiment by transforming other peoples, cultures, and regions into the nation's republican image. William P. Rogers, a captain in the First Mississippi Rifles, had heard rumors that the United States sought to conquer Mexico and overthrow its government. Rogers remained uncertain about the moral implications of this proposition, but he did believe that the war created an opportunity for the United States to fundamentally transform an inferior people. It would be "promotive of humanity and the cause of freedom and religion," he wrote, if American arms could "greatly improve the condition of the poor Mexican." Only the United States' influence "will subject one of the most delightful countries on earth to an intelligent people, who will cultivate and improve its soil." Although Mexico professed adherence to a republican form of government, Rogers cautioned, "their laws are more oppressive and more onerous than those of any civilized monarchy," based on blind faith in the Catholic Church, which had entwined itself in the operations of civil government. Rogers spoke on behalf of countless volunteers who merged their identities as citizen-soldiers and agents of cultural change. Nationalism, ethnicity, and religion, combined with the civic ideal of martial volunteerism, collided to create an intricate ideological worldview for American troops.[7]

Soldiers' jingoistic visions could be achieved only if the United States established a substantial military presence on Mexican soil, a prospect that few anticipated or even understood. Indeed, long-term occupation in conquest of foreign territories had rarely before penetrated the nation's citizen-soldier ethos. Yet presumptions about racial and cultural inferiority, as expressed by William Rogers, suggested that this war, unlike previous American conflicts, would utilize occupation in a crucial way. The conflict was far different from the American Revolution or the War of 1812, both of which sought to guard against foreign incursion. In Mexico, by contrast, the American military tradition became inverted. The United States actively waged war in *acquisition* of territory, not only battling the Mexican army, but also engaging civilians, occupying cities, and even testing existing cultural assumptions. Learning the tedious work of occupation proved to be complicated and trying for the citizen-soldier.

One of the most consequential conflicts in United States history, the Mexican-American War inaugurated widespread operations conducted beyond national boundaries. US armies succeeded effortlessly in winning battles and establishing a garrisoned military presence throughout Mexico. Shortly after the war began, in May 1846, General Zachary Taylor captured Matamoros; by August, California and New Mexico had also fallen under American control. Monterey, Saltillo, and Tampico, along with much of northern Mexico, fell by the end of the year. Winfield Scott, in a celebrated campaign, captured Vera Cruz in March 1847 and marched west toward Mexico City, establishing numerous garrisons along the way. He forced the surrender of the capital city in September 1847 and enacted a nine-month occupation prior to the settlement of peace.[8]

Within a two-year period, US armies occupied much of Mexico, establishing precedents in military government and martial law, control of civilian populations, and regulation of soldiers' behavior on foreign soil. From the outset, military authorities encountered the troubling reality of establishing relationships between the army and its conquered foes. Occupation indeed proved complicated and trying, exposing the lack of standards available to American forces by which to measure their conduct. Although much of the American public expressed a frenzied, belligerent attitude toward the war, they paused when considering the responsibilities of a conqueror. Many hoped that the army would guide itself according to nebulous "moral law," acting in accordance with the civilized nations of the world. They argued that the United States could not appear despotic in its rule but rather should be benevolent in its offering of freedom and republicanism to the Mexican people.[9]

Almost immediately after the war began, however, reports surfaced about destructive acts committed by Zachary Taylor's forces on the Rio Grande. Theft, murder, pillaging, random violence against civilians, and the destruction of local property tarnished the image of American forces that entered Mexico in 1846. Volunteers from Texas proved especially difficult to regulate, moved by a frontier spirit of individualism and abject hatred for Mexicans that dated back to the Texas Revolution. The unruly spirit of Taylor's troops emanated not only from lack of discipline but also from a sense of personal revenge and racial superiority. Such impulses were difficult to control, and they were also detrimental to the American war effort. Moderate Mexican civilians, who might have joined the American cause, waged a violent and passionate defense of their territory and homes against the ruthless invaders.[10]

Taylor proved to be ill-suited to execute an effective, ordered war of occupation, failing to maintain a semblance of discipline among his troops. The task fell to Winfield Scott, one of the early republic's great military thinkers, to formulate a systemized application of "moral law" to the occupation effort. Scott's vision offered striking precedents for wartime occupation, military government, and the conduct of republican armies. Future generations of American military theorists adopted his formulations, setting standards of comportment for soldiers in the field. A moral army, Scott declared, could not enter a foreign country devoid of upstanding conduct, especially if that army believed it comprised volunteers from an "exceptional" nation. Scott understood that the Mexican-American War represented a proving ground for the United States in terms of demonstrating both national strength and national character. If the citizen-soldier ideal was worth as much as contemporaries claimed, Scott believed that it needed to be confirmed in an untested environment. Military occupation served as the great challenge.[11]

Scott linked civil affairs with military strategy, twin prospects that had never before been united in the nation's military practice. His awareness stemmed from the reports of destruction along the Rio Grande and in other areas in which US soldiers were accused of unauthorized engagement against private residents. Scott feared that a hostile American army would alienate the Mexican people, unnecessarily transforming the population into an armed resistance that practiced irregular warfare. Thus, he sought to exert complete control over both his army and the local populace, punishing offenses committed by both groups.[12]

Drawing on an extensive historical perspective, Scott formulated his visions of occupation from an intimate appreciation of the Napoleonic era. He believed that maintaining an army indefinitely in a foreign country posed a great challenge to any future American war, as well as to the present conflict with Mexico. He understood that plundering French armies in Spain had needlessly isolated themselves because of their wanton behavior, violence against civilians, and oppressive military regimes. Spanish retaliations against Napoleon's army spawned massive resistance and induced long-term chaos and instability. Scott did not want to replicate this precedent in Mexico; such practices not only perpetuated violence but also alienated the US military from its professed moral ideals.[13]

Scott translated his historical awareness into new policy directives that contained both profound insight and also dramatic implications for future American conflicts: martial law and General Orders No. 20. Understanding that invading armies were oftentimes vulnerable to hostile civilians, Scott sought to mold official strategy based on the supposition that American armies meant no harm to the local populace. The General Orders, issued in February 1847, created military tribunals to try offenses committed by both soldiers and civilians, while establishing working relationships between the army and civil officers, who administered their localities subject to the authority of a military governor. Moreover, Scott did not oblige conquered towns to fund the American occupation; the army paid for the goods that it used and consumed. The General Orders also protected private property, outlawed murder and rape, and demanded a civilized approach to armed conflict. Finally, Scott emphasized the importance of respecting municipal governments, stressing the need for local Mexican authorities, rather than the US military, to direct civil affairs.[14]

In most instances, the army employed General Orders No. 20 as scores of Mexican towns, extending from the eastern coasts through the interior, deep into New Mexico and California, fell under American occupation. Garrisons that dotted the landscape offered departure points for future campaigns, created bases of supply, and functioned as centers of civilian appeasement. Per Scott's dictates, occupying forces enacted martial law and curfews, in addition to curbing the sale of liquor, paying for the needs of the army, and respecting the Catholic faith. Thus occupation and civilian-military compliance functioned as essential components for an American victory; Scott believed that a firm but fair occupation would force the Mexicans to capitulate quickly.[15]

Although General Orders No. 20 functioned precisely as Scott envisioned, his recognition that they needed to be penned at all underscored a realization that citizen-soldiers were less-than-ideal vessels for a war of occupation. It appeared that Scott's awareness of the changing character of American warfare might prevent US armies from mirroring the mistakes of the Napoleonic mold that he so greatly feared. Yet Scott's new policies testified to the profound unfitness of volunteers to conduct professional, bureaucratic operations. Still, they were called upon to regulate and govern territories already won by US arms. The root problem of occupation during the Mexican-American War operated well beyond the dictates of Scott's vision, suggesting that citizen-volunteers, whose conduct was often at odds with General Orders No. 20, tested the limits of occupation in the republican military tradition.

Some contemporaries indeed questioned the wisdom of turning the US Army into a vehicle of pacification and occupation outfitted by unruly volunteers. George Gordon Meade, a West Point graduate and long-time professional soldier in the regular army, revealed the uncertainties of occupation. Although he believed the United States to have a superior military force, certain to win the war, Meade looked beyond the immediate glamour of American arms and predicted what he saw as the troubling implications of martial government. "This plan of armed occupation, I, individually am opposed to," he informed his wife in October 1846 shortly after Monterey fell, "upon the ground of its never having an end." Meade feared the experience of occupation would instill hatred, defiance, and revenge within the Mexican people, "which will compel us to be always prepared by having a large army on this frontier." Demonstrating the full force of American arms on the battlefield, Meade explained, would have a much greater and more decisive impact than garrisons spread across conquered territory. He also feared the exorbitant financial costs and needless commitment of manpower occupation entailed. Wars, he concluded, should be short and decisive, waged in defense of national interests; military occupation undermined these assumptions.[16]

The recognition that volunteers, whom he despised, would be the primary forces of occupation, also filled Meade with trepidation. American military objectives, he believed, would be undermined by volunteers' rowdy conduct on foreign soil. "They are perfectly ignorant of discipline, and most restive under restraint," Meade grumbled. "They are in consequence a most disorderly mass, who will give us, I fear, more trouble than the enemy." Meade further condemned the nation's small professional army as a symptom of relying on the idealized virtue of citizen-soldiers during times of war. Had the United States invaded Mexico with a large professional force, he suggested, capable of "follow[ing] up the results of our victories" and enacting an efficient occupation of Mexico, "the war would have been finished."[17]

Citizen-soldiers' democratic tendencies, political power, and undisciplined character, combined with their oppressive interpretations of Manifest Destiny, illustrated Meade's assessments. Hierarchical perceptions of race and a fierce dedication to individualism informed the ways in which citizen-soldiers conducted themselves on Mexican soil. Decades of inculcation in nineteenth-century conceptions of republicanism, democracy, and national exceptionalism supplied the greatest challenges to the United States' armies of occupation. In General Orders No. 20, Winfield Scott had pinpointed the ways in which volunteer soldiers would behave as an invading and occupying army; the troops performed accordingly.[18]

Although Americans and Mexicans both boasted a republican heritage, US volunteers believed that race created a strong distinction between the legitimacies of both nations' governing systems. Mexicans, citizen-soldiers believed, had ineffectively instituted the republican system and were instead subservient to a state religion; American armies were therefore obligated to invade, occupy, and cleanse the enemy nation. Samuel Ryan Curtis, an officer of Ohio volunteers, disagreed greatly with a restrained approach. "*Subjugation* or *devastation* is my view of the matter," Curtis explained from Matamoros. "The people are semi savage and they must be made to acknowledge our sovereignty or this war will never end."[19]

Curtis's racial outlook reflected the overall character of American occupiers in Mexico. Although some military governors, including Curtis, succeeded in maintaining order and cooperating with Mexican authorities, the occupiers' racist views influenced their martial conduct. Occupation thus functioned in a twofold manner. On the one hand, soldiers instigated numerous acts of violent destruction against Mexican civilians, seeing white supremacy and American military might as proper justifications. On the other hand, troops sometimes employed more moderate approaches, guided by a paternalistic belief that occupation lifted Mexicans out of their impoverished condition. In either event, military occupation unfolded as an active process, always working to achieve both racial and national ends. Even regular army officers, who often displayed more self-control than volunteers, were not immune to these conceptions. Writing from Mexico City toward the end of the war, Daniel Harvey Hill, a West Point–trained artillery lieutenant, believed that the conflict had properly cleansed Mexico. "I look upon the present movement as full of promise for Mexico," he claimed. "May it be the precursor of the down-fall of the present corrupt hierarchy and the [beginning of] universal freedom of conscience," met by annexation of territory and assimilation into American culture.[20]

Using military occupation and the language of Manifest Destiny as justification, US soldiers sought to reorder the Mexican republic according to the standards of white nineteenth-century Americans. Thomas Tennery, a soldier in the Fourth Illinois Volunteers, described Matamoros as an exceedingly obtuse town, due in large part to the local populace's inability to modernize. "Everything appears dull, the houses, the inhabitants little above savages and without energy or business of any importance," he wrote. "This appears to be caused by the want of commerce," Tennery presumed, "with the indolence of the inhabitants and perhaps the want of a settled government that will secure property." In order to effect substantial and necessary change, Tennery determined, "the country must be inhabited by a different race of people." The current occupants of Mexico, "the Spanish and Indian[,] do not make a race of people with patriotism and candor enough to support a republic."[21]

Oftentimes soldiers manifested their racist dogmas through destruction and physical reprisal, rarely concerned about the implications of their actions. From their perspective, any act of violence was justified because the victims, Mexican citizens, were perceived as servile, inferior people. And even the soldiers who might have been uncomfortable at the sight of wanton devastation harbored similar racial outlooks. As historian Mark Neely noted, "racial constructs help explain the unrestrained passions of the unfeeling contempt exemplified by the American volunteer in Mexico." Merely two generations removed from the American Revolution, and the fears and outrage concerning British occupation and invasion of private spaces, volunteers during the Mexican War nevertheless did not see their actions as resembling the very acts that inspired countless Americans to decry the excesses of an occupying army. The reason, of course, was that race justified a limitless occupation, buttressed by a violent democratic expression.[22]

Such behavior produced tense relations between the occupying troops and Mexican civilians, who responded in kind to the violent attacks against their property and fellow citizens. Yet a peculiar problem complicated the interactions between soldier and civilian. The military incursions into Mexico spawned an organic resistance that had long been associated with wars of occupation: guerrilla conflict and irregular combat. The American war against Mexico was not a simple act of conquest. It also revealed the problem of stabilization in which the army was forced to subdue the very civilian resistance produced by the military's invading presence. If US troops were not already motivated to wage a destructive war against civilians and property, the presence and conduct of Mexican guerrillas provided an excuse for American soldiers to perpetuate violent, chaotic retaliation. Clandestine attacks by enemy combatants or guerrillas—the distinctions, to contemporaries, were unclear, confirming the inherent purpose of irregular warfare—upon the occupiers ranged from targeted assassinations in towns to violent assaults on wagon trains and supply lines in the desolate countryside.[23]

American soldiers did not know where the next attack would emanate from, nor could they determine which civilians represented an armed threat. Guerrilla warfare came to be regarded as highly dishonorable, barbaric, and uncivilized. Zachary Taylor believed that "little of reputation can be gained" in guerrilla warfare. Volunteers and regulars alike believed that such modes of martial conduct unmasked Mexicans' primitive identities. Secretary of War William L. Marcy explained that "the guerrilla system is hardly recognized as a legitimate mode of warfare, and should be met with the utmost allowable severity." Thus, soldiers justified any mode of retaliation or revenge, reinforcing their deep-seated beliefs in Mexican inferiority. Members of antiguerrilla units burned villages, killed civilians arbitrarily, and meted out vengeance anywhere they saw fit. US forces ultimately designated the professional Mexican army as a dishonorable institution, even equating it with independent guerrilla bands. Emotions grounded in revenge and retribution clouded an already troubling environment intensified by racial difference.[24]

Although Winfield Scott perceived his conquests in Mexico to be magnanimous, always seeking harmonious relations with civilians, he too looked upon guerrilla warfare with utter contempt. Civilized armies, he believed, could not countenance such conduct. Thus, Scott came to employ merciless retribution against suspected civilian combatants, supported the destruction of towns and property, and hoped to stem resistance through displays of American force. "The system of forming guerrilla parties to annoy us," he assured the Mexican government, "will produce only evils to this country." Scott explained that retaliation would bring little moral pause to his army, "which knows how to protect itself, and how to proceed against such cutthroats." With great fanfare, Scott deliberately wielded his citizen-soldiers against guerrillas, understanding that volunteers possessed the unruly and uninhibited qualities necessary to wage an irregular war. Scott's ironic admission suggested that integrity of the citizen-soldier ideal had been compromised. However, he acted within a deeply rooted American tradition, first announced by George Washington, that amateur soldiers served a valuable purpose in patrolling the countryside and subduing enemy combatants. Volunteers, Scott believed, functioned as ideal candidates for an irregular war because they demanded freedom of mobility, unburdened from the constraints and professionalization of the regular army.[25]

Scott's soldiers responded enthusiastically to his order of no-quarter, which he declared in early 1847 while on the road to Mexico City. The troops believed that an uncivilized mode of warfare necessitated untraditional, even shocking, styles of retribution. Yet irregular conduct, which was often sanctioned by the Mexican government, endorsed by local priests, and embraced by increasing numbers of civilians, signaled to American volunteers that Mexico could not honorably claim a republican heritage. Soldiers presumed that Mexico's unexceptional character invited the very type of uncultured warfare that its citizens perpetrated on American armies. Some troops, who witnessed depredations committed by guerrillas upon local citizens, were stunned that members of the same nation could harm one another. "We will leave behind us here a force to keep the guerrillas from plundering the people and protect them from the rapacity of the Government troops," Major John Corey Henshaw wrote near Puebla. "Whoever before heard of a people asking of the enemy protection against their own Government? What a commentary does this present on the state of affairs in this unfortunate country," he declared. "I think I can see in the introduction of our army into this country, the final annexation of all Mexico to the United States."[26]

Faith in national hierarchy and racial superiority blinded citizen-soldiers to their participation in the irregular war. Thomas Barclay, a soldier in the Second Pennsylvania Volunteers, wrote a lengthy diary exposition highlighting these very problems. Declaring that a war of civilizations between the United States and Mexico had long been inevitable, Barclay justified irregular conduct because "the Anglo Saxon race, that land loving people are on the move." He criticized Mexican governing and religious structures, claiming that their inferior, passé, and corrupt institutions occasioned the bloody conflict, which destined Mexico to be forever changed. "However great a calamity war may be and however much we may regret the sad consequences which follow in its train," Barclay stated, "mankind will [have] no cause to mourn a change of things in this Country." The Mexican people, Barclay reasoned, had long been enslaved by a system that resisted progress and improvement. They were not entirely to blame for their condition; instead, they must be saved from present circumstances, if necessary by destructive, violent force.[27]

Barclay believed that the unrefined culture in which the Mexican people lived inspired the uncivilized manner by which they waged war. "The highways are infested with villains and neither person nor property are safe in travelling," he insisted, undoubtedly recalling the murders of American soldiers that he witnessed earlier in the conflict. The guerrilla war, he explained, arose as a desperate, dishonorable means of preserving territory quickly being overtaken by the United States. Those who stubbornly and violently resisted societal evolution ignored the "forbearance and chivalrous spirit" of the US Army. Thus, Barclay and myriad American observers endorsed a cleansing of the Mexican countryside at the mere presence of civilian combatants.[28]

Corydon Donnavan built on Barclay's assessments, seeing little difference between Mexican rancheros (local farmers) and violent guerrillas. "They are half Spanish and half Indian," Donnavan explained. "They are ever on the alert, and seldom surprised. When not in pursuit of plunder, they roam over the vast plains," herding buffalo and horses. Illustrating a ranchero's daily attire, Donnavan highlighted the presumably indistinguishable characteristics between civilian and irregular combatant, grounded in their simple, backward apparel. "Their costume," he declared, "consists of a pair of tough raw-hide leggings, with sandals of the same material," accompanied by a large blanket draped across the shoulders, and complemented by a large sombrero adorning the head. Although Donnavan submitted that "such is the appearance of the ranchero, in time of peace," wartime accouterments, including a lance and concealed pistols and knives, made him "a member of a troop of banditti." Such warriors were "cowardly as they universally are in the open field," yet also "a formidable foe," who had the ability to withstand fatigue and hunger, strengthened by an insatiable quest for savage violence.[29]

While Donnavan illustrated the presumably lowly and disreputable conditions under which Mexican guerrillas functioned, US volunteers did not consider participation in the guerrilla war to be an affront to their own identities as citizen-soldiers. They believed they served a profound purpose for the army, policing civilians and badgering the enemy. "If justice was done to these highway murderers and robbers," declared a Pennsylvania volunteer, "they ought to be shot, in place of putting them in the guard-house." Winfield Scott subscribed to the same view, oftentimes transforming volunteers into forces of counterinsurgency, rather than advance elements of the army. Indeed, Scott garrisoned nearly one-quarter of his army along the roads to Mexico City in 1847 to engage in counter-guerrilla measures. These soldiers, though, because they had been positioned as forces of occupation behind the lines, largely absent from the grand campaigns and battles of the war, exerted a violent, unruly expression in the face of any perceived enemy.[30]

Irregular warfare possessed a dark and irrevocable underside, spawned by the experience of invasion and occupation and buttressed by the presence of a racially "inferior" enemy. Violent, sporadic actions allowed soldiers to liberate themselves from what they considered the oppressive, limiting character of the army. The guerrilla presence also gave volunteers an excuse to wage war on civilians who might be combatants, to plunder local villages, and to exact revenge against Mexican irregulars who murdered US troops. Northern Mexico as well as Mexico City, in the wake of Taylor's and Scott's respective conquests, especially enveloped these tensions. Ubiquitous reports emanated from both regions that revealed American soldiers' wanton and destructive behavior, rooted in ambivalence regarding "civilized" martial conduct. Ironically, though, American volunteers' chaotic, violent response toward guerrillas and civilians—that distinction, by 1847, had become blurred—undermined the broader war of conquest that required societal stabilization. Thus employing volunteers as arbiters of American policy exposed the inherent tension between the citizen-soldier ethos and the formality of military occupation.[31]

While citizen-soldiers attempted to vindicate their behavior toward civilians, regulars interpreted the implications of volunteer conduct through a much broader lens of experience. They believed, just as George G. Meade had declared at the beginning of the war, that provisional troops, by virtue of their volunteerism, were unfit to conduct an orderly military occupation. They insisted that volunteers instead only perpetuated the chaos of an already unstable environment. Regular soldiers traditionally equated both guerrilla and counterinsurgency warfare with uncivilized martial conduct, which they thought undermined their profession's moral standards. The practice of waging irregular warfare against Native Americans during the antebellum period especially had convinced regulars of the ethical degradation imposed on counterinsurgent forces. Believing that guerrilla warfare molded the American soldier into the image of his depraved opponent, regulars feared the destructive implications of a foreign military ethos that challenged honorable, disciplined restraint.[32]

The American military tradition was fraught with tensions between regulars and volunteers, and the occupation of Mexico further widened the gulf between the two groups. Regulars voiced apprehension about military occupation that would never be fully reconciled by mid-nineteenth-century Americans. They sensed that if the US Army was transformed into an institution of foreign invasion, as it had been in Mexico, it must also take into account the internal cultural elements that composed the army's character, namely the citizen-soldier ideal. A young second lieutenant named Ulysses S. Grant captured this problem early in the war after Matamoros fell. "Some of the volunteers," he wrote, "seem to think it perfectly right to impose upon the people of a conquered City to any extent, and even to murder them where the act can be covered by dark. And how much they seem to enjoy acts of violence too!" Grant implied that invasion, occupation, and the unconventional elements of war, all buttressed by impressions of racial superiority, corrupted the American disposition. An occupying force needed a specific temperament to achieve its objectives; citizen-soldiers, he believed, failed this test.[33]

Regular army officers during the antebellum period, such as Grant, developed a unique culture that informed their beliefs long before and during the war against Mexico. They crafted a professional ethos that stressed honor, duty, and decorum, governed by a sense of political neutrality and systematic regulation; these qualities were nurtured within a peacetime garrison culture. Although they privately endorsed Manifest Destiny and American exceptionalism, careerist officers remained tempered in their public expressions and actions. Regulars instead wedded themselves to the bureaucratic functions of the army and, by extension, national goals. Refusing the temptation of entering Mexico to actively shape, through the power of armed force, political, national, and racial ends, regulars believed that their profession restricted them from interfering with the ambitions set forth by civil authorities. Indeed, they distanced themselves from pursuing personal missions, achieving individual conquests, and engaging in irregular war, in favor of remaining duty-bound to the pragmatic requirements of war. Their peacetime service accordingly erased the era's prominent Jacksonian impulses, allowing regulars to focus on wartime bureaucratic necessity. And when called into battle, regulars performed admirably, vindicating their profession in the eyes of an American public that continued to look askance at a permanent military establishment.[34]

The regular army's professionalization exhibited itself most importantly in the realms of invasion, military occupation, and interactions with civilians. Manifest Destiny signaled national expansion through invasion, bringing peoples and territories under American influence. This process had to be occasioned within long-established institutions and practices, such as garrison culture, that defined the professional army tradition. Thus regulars did not question the wisdom of occupation on ideological or moral grounds; they interpreted it through the lens of national necessity. And they positioned volunteers at the center of their critique. Regulars claimed that if Manifest Destiny served as the basis of American war aims, citizen-soldiers, because they most ardently identified with the concept, were the *least* qualified to enact a war of invasion and conquest. Perhaps volunteers' uncontrollable temperaments made them ideal candidates in irregular battles against guerrillas. But in a war of systematic occupation in which successful invasion and population control were crucial components, volunteers proved detrimental.[35]

Regulars articulated the fundamental paradox of a republican army of occupation: civic virtue, democratic tendencies, and ideological predispositions, which undergirded the citizen-soldier ideal, were the very concepts that destabilized an effective, streamlined, and bureaucratic military governance. Thomas Thorpe commented on the "vandalism of the Volunteers who serve under the banners of the United States," shortly after American armies captured Monterey. "The utmost insecurity prevails; that no one is master of his own property, or even of his own existence, threatened with perfect impunity by the unbridled Volunteers," he wrote. Conversely, the regulars who occupied the city remained "well disciplined, subordinate, and under excellent officers." In language remarkably similar to regulars' worldviews about counterinsurgency warfare during the antebellum period, citizen-soldiers, he concluded, behaved "much like the Camanches in their appearance, ferocity, and customs."[36]

The style of volunteers' behavior shocked the regulars, who projected onto their provisional comrades misgivings about the limits of martial conduct. Thorpe's equation of citizen-soldiers with Native Americans underscored the profound fear that regulars had long harbored about the moral implications of unconventional war. His statement revealed a deep-seated anxiety that certain types of martial conduct could fundamentally transform the American military tradition into an uncivilized, chaotic practice. Officers accordingly judged citizen-soldiers unfit for a war of invasion because such conflicts were not merely about fighting. Instead, active wars necessitated permanent armies that remained in fixed positions for indefinite periods of time, and, in some cases, garrisoned territory for the duration of the conflict. Thus, regulars bemoaned volunteers' transfer of their democratic ideals to the army in which they resisted authority and obligation to order, conflicting with the requirements of invasion and conquest. Even William P. Rogers, the citizen-officer of a Mississippi regiment who celebrated the racial tenets of Manifest Destiny, recognized this conundrum, writing that volunteers did not possess the critical attributes necessary for an effective war of occupation. "One who has never commanded a company of voluntiers can form no idea of the unpleasantness of the life," he explained. "Voluntiers I am satisfied will never do for an invading army—They will do well enough to defend their own firesides, but they can not endure the fatigue incident to an invading army, besides to keep them under proper discipline they should be under excitement."[37]

Rogers captured the underlying irony of volunteer troops occupying foreign lands. The citizen-soldier ideal, he indicated, had been constructed on the basis of defending personal liberty and protecting the nation. The essence of occupation upset these assumptions: the cultural ingredients of the citizen-soldier heritage mixed poorly with the realities of military occupation. Rogers implied that citizen-soldiers could not be relied upon to conduct efficient military governance because they were not imbued with a tradition of such practices. If anything, they were reared in a tradition that *resisted* military occupation and standing armies. Yet they were also instilled with mid-nineteenth-century conceptions of race, national progress, and democracy, all of which inspired the invasions and occupations of Mexico, but which also threatened the very core of an organized American occupation.[38]

* * *

Citizen-soldiers accordingly resisted what they considered the constraints of invasion, believing that the physical embodiment of military occupation—garrisons—were much too evocative of professional military culture. They did not object to occupying Mexico on ideological or moral grounds, nor did they hesitate to actively engage civilians. Rather, their protests were grounded in the belief that army life in general, and garrison duty in particular, endangered their identities as free citizens temporarily functioning as soldiers. Battling guerrillas and waging war against Mexicans offered relief from the otherwise suffocating environment of occupation. Yet once volunteers were placed in garrisons, they initiated a conversation about the role of republican soldiers in a professional, static environment. Ironically, most civil and military authorities alleged that volunteers, *because* of their unruly, democratic tendencies, should be relegated to garrison duty. Within these environments, citizen-soldiers had to negotiate modes of discipline, restraint, and decorum that the regular army had long practiced in garrisons on the American frontier. Citizen-soldiers, therefore, came to equate garrisons and physical occupation as unwelcome checks on their service.[39]

A vast majority of citizen-soldiers during the Mexican-American War faced the burdensome duty of being assigned primarily as garrison forces, relieving regulars to campaign and fight in the war's central battles. Volunteers felt cheated, prevented from enacting their full responsibilities as defenders of the nation. They claimed that remaining in segregated, secondary military classes brought dishonor both to themselves and to their home states. A Pennsylvania volunteer stationed in Mexico City in late 1847 voiced the concerns of many citizen-soldiers, writing, "There is neither honor or prospect in a garrison life.... The question is asked, 'Supposing this war should continue 5 or 8 years, are we to be kept doing garrison duty?'" This inquiry raised the specter not only of martial integrity but also of the problem of permanence. Garrisons, by their very nature, signified immobility and indicated a halting of military aims. Henry Lane, an Indiana volunteer, considered the capture of Monterey "a most brilliant affair," yet "the takeing of that place has not advanced us towards a peace one inch. It is an injury to us."[40]

In order to function properly during wartime, the citizen-soldier ideal required continual progress toward a definitive conclusion. Even camp life, a standard experience in all armies, could at least be construed as temporary, confirmed by a presumption that campaigning would resume in the near future. American volunteers in Mexico subscribed to military occupation as long as it appeared to have an active, violent, and domineering character. Garrisons, however, were permanent spaces, physical reminders of soldiers' immobility and their restricted progress. Formal combat and movement did not exist with the confines of garrisons; rather, soldiers had to learn how to remain stationary, enduring the static rhythms of daily life. In some cases, volunteers blamed their political leaders their restrictive environment. "Well this is the G——d damnest shot of work I ever saw yet," a sentinel sneered from Burita in 1846. "I voted for old Polk G——d d——m him and here I am in mud and rain and misery. I came out here to fight and instead of fighting I have to tread this mud for four hours what a d——d fool I was—I ought to be in Hell."[41]

Over time, garrison culture diminished volunteers' passionate attachment to the war. When they invaded Mexico, acquiring territory and engaging civilians, citizen-soldiers believed that they actively fashioned the vision of Manifest Destiny. But when forced to govern lands and people, volunteers became detached from their ideals. The essence of citizen-soldiering was steeped in fierce ideology; permanent zones of occupation were not. James Coulter, of the Second Pennsylvania Volunteers, articulated this very problem. "I suppose we are destined again to endure the vexation and troubles of a garrison," he be-

moaned, shortly after entering Mexico City. "A garrison," his comrade Thomas
Barclay concluded a month later, "is very dull and tiresome and is injurious to
both the body and mind."[42]

Regulars would have agreed fully with Coulter's and Barclay's assessments. Yet professionals, who had long been reared in the static environment
of garrisons, and who oftentimes refused to be governed by ideology, understood how to function within such a peculiar setting. They accepted the disquieting reality that garrisons were undemocratic institutions, created not for
the purposes of martial egalitarianism but rather for military centralization
and efficiency. Thus, garrisons exposed the army's rigid hierarchies, oftentimes erecting barriers between officers and common soldiers. Citing the professional tradition, historian William B. Skelton explained that "the routines
of garrison life generated almost continual tensions within the ranks and recurrent friction along the officer–enlisted man boundary." Wartime seemed to
inflame such dynamics once volunteers entered the equation. They mandated
equality, resisted when their demands were not met, and became detached
from the nation's war aims. They instead focused on reclaiming their democratic rights, which they believed had been curbed by a confining garrison
culture. Their resistance translated into further breakdowns of discipline and
order, revealing the troubling consequence of volunteers serving as permanent occupiers.[43]

American troops in Mexico like Barclay and Coulter, and especially the
regulars, cited garrison culture as a major problem that influenced the behavior and discipline of citizen-soldiers. Although Winfield Scott envisioned
General Orders No. 20 as a necessary regulation of conduct, volunteers construed the measure as an impediment to their democratic rights. Some volunteers became virulently angry at Scott's measures, believing that they need
not endure the harsh penalties of military discipline. They alleged that Scott
was more interested in protecting the rights and property of Mexican civilians
than he was in assuring the welfare of his own troops.[44]

Citizen-volunteers sought explanations for the source of garrison stagnation. J. B. Duncan, a volunteer in the First Illinois, cited a common problem
endured by many soldiers, which contributed to their behavioral problems.
"We are living a very lazy life," he wrote in April 1847 from Buena Vista, where
his regiment would be stationed for the next six weeks, "nothing to do only
drill a little twice a day . . . and the rest of the time laying on our backs kicking
up our heels or promenading around the [town]." Duncan's illustration sug-

gested that soldiers let down their guard, trapped by the seductive rhythm of life in a quiet Mexican town. Yet the rising tide of monotony and sameness overwhelmed many soldiers who sought ways to alleviate their boredom.[45]

Racial and ethnic prejudices continued to inform volunteer behavior, pushing soldiers to unleash their stifled aggression. Troops sometimes blamed Mexican civilians for infesting American soldiers with laziness, citing what they considered the indolence of local life. Other troops pointed to the indigenous corruption of occupied towns as sources of their unethical behavior. Samuel Ryan Curtis wrote from Matamoros, "about the principle [sic] corners loiter groups of men of all colours and all countries are collected cursing swearing fighting gambling and presenting a most barbarous sight. Volunteers especially are conspicuous in these groups. . . . Murder rapine and vice of all manner of form prevails and predominates here." Stunned by the behavior of his troops, Curtis considered Matamoros "a conquered city [yet] much the receptacle of all the dregs of the United States.—As it now stands, it is a disgrace to our country; for our own citizens are much worse than the Mexicans who are mixed up with them." Similar scenes dotted the occupied landscape, as citizen-soldiers alleviated their boredom through distraction and violence, often meting out vicious aggression against civilians and public spaces. Such conduct produced great tensions between the occupier and the occupied, creating environments of discord, strain, and turmoil. Thus the characteristics that military occupation was supposed to erase ended up functioning as the very attributes that challenged martial governance the most.[46]

In order to keep volunteers in check, officers often employed violent disciplinary methods characteristic of the regular army. Citizen-soldiers despised, above all else, these modes of physical regulation, declaring that as free men they were absolved from arbitrary authority. Nevertheless, discipline during the Mexican-American War assumed a notorious reputation because it revealed how the US Army shaped behavior in ways completely unfamiliar to American republican culture. Discipline became most severe when volunteers slipped into the doldrums of garrison duty, plagued by its stagnant and tempting character. Soldiers embraced their identities as citizens within these environments, neglecting their duties as soldiers and clinging to cherished notions of freedom, movement, and individualism. These qualities, however, often devolved into the very types of poor conduct cited by Samuel Ryan Curtis; officers thus sanctioned severe physical penalties against any suspected perpetrator.[47]

An incident at Saltillo testifies to the severity of wartime garrison discipline. After Zachary Taylor's celebrated victory at Buena Vista in February 1847, parts of his army occupied Saltillo for the next several months. Insubordination, gambling, drinking, sleeping on guard posts, and general belligerence enveloped the garrison as the army remained idle. Officers, especially Robert T. Paine of North Carolina, responded with unusually strict disciplinary measures, both to consolidate their authority and to curb the behavior of troops in the garrison. To demonstrate his power, Paine introduced an intimidating, but also chiefly symbolic, method of punishment that regular army soldiers knew all too well. The "wooden horse," an instrument sustained by two sets of legs and balanced by a log, was a symbol of severe pain and discomfort. Soldiers were forced to straddle the bar for indefinite periods of time, ranging from hours to even days. Convicted troops endured both physical agony and public disgrace. Paine placed the horse in front of the camp of a North Carolina regiment, an unspoken admonishment about their behavior. He never utilized the wooden horse, however. Nearly one hundred soldiers from a nearby Virginia regiment stormed the area and dismantled the reviled icon of undemocratic power, launching a widespread mutiny.[48]

Volunteers' responses to the wooden horse signaled the types of discipline that could occur in a garrison setting. Soldiers were sometimes whipped in public, which reflected the brutal and occasionally limitless modes of garrison violence. Four soldiers stationed at Puebla in May 1847 were convicted of robbery and ordered to remove their shirts. "Amid much writhing," one soldier observed, "the prisoner received 39 [lashes] well and slowly laid on." The demonstration was intended to punish the offenders, setting an example to other soldiers. "There was among all however a general feeling of disgust. . . . Everyone regretted that such a punishment could be inflicted under the laws of our country." Volunteers possessed a fierce streak of defiance and individualism and did not conform after witnessing the flogging. "Instead of reforming," one soldier concluded, "culprits by the exposure are hardened. Spectators forge the crime in sympathy for the sufferers." And thus undisciplined conduct continued unabated, enveloping garrisoned towns in conflict and chaos, as soldiers struggled to assert their democratic privileges by resisting unrepublican authority.[49]

The problem of behavior and discipline in Mexico was an ironic, self-perpetuating phenomenon. The vast majority of volunteers never saw formal combat, the precise reason for which they professed to have volunteered. They instead remained in passive circumstances, called to perform subtle kinds of duty that clashed wildly with their imaginations of war. Rather than campaigning, participating in battles, or even remaining in camp, most citizen-soldiers experienced the war guarding supply lines, garrisoning towns, and serving on the fringes of the wartime landscape. Indeed, military occupation came to be the rule, rather than the exception, that defined volunteer service during the Mexican-American War. This troubling reality intensified the racial tensions that already governed most troops, escalated existing feelings of wronged individualism, and accelerated prevailing desires to prove oneself while in uniform. Soldiers channeled these feelings into a calculated war not on an enemy army but rather on civilians, public spaces, and private property. Many also damaged themselves through ubiquitous alcohol abuse and reckless behavior. Volunteer soldiers sought any means to break out of the restrictive molds of army life associated with garrison duty. The prevalent violence and chaos committed by volunteers can be explained, in large part, by the features of garrison culture.[50]

Senator Jefferson Davis understood all too well the problem of employing volunteers as garrison forces, raising questions about the fitness of citizen-soldiers for wars of invasion and occupation. A noted veteran of the war, Davis, shortly after being elected to the Senate from Mississippi, endorsed the Ten Regiment Bill, a proposal to increase the American occupation presence in Mexico City. Based on the assumption that an augmented military force would compel the Mexican government to discuss peace, the bill authorized ten new regiments to be sent to the war-torn capital. Suspicious Whigs opposed the measure, arguing that President Polk secretly desired a larger, permanent military establishment. Thus, the debate revolved around the kinds of regiments that would be raised.[51]

Davis cherished the American citizen-soldier heritage and celebrated the volunteers' efforts during the war. Yet "to secure a peace," he clarified, "we must show our power to compel submission." A formidable occupation presence, Davis explained, was far different from campaigning and fighting in the field, tasks at which US armies had proven exceptional. Davis then drew a clear dichotomy between garrisoning and campaigning, and explained how the war had altered the assumptions underlying the citizen-soldier ideal. "However necessary it may be to call forth the chivalry of the country to fight its battles, let us not send such men, to be wasted in the mere duties of the sentinel," Davis argued. If the United States had been invaded, he countered,

"I would turn to the great body of the militia . . . for its defense," championing the purity of volunteer service.[52]

Davis's commemoration of the citizen-soldier ideal, although genuine, was also a veiled attempt to explain how volunteers did not possess the capacity for military occupation and garrison duty. The consequences, he believed, could be potentially destructive. Davis made clear that armies of invasion and occupation required a dispassionate temperament, detached from ideological persuasions. "There is a great difference in the material of the volunteers and the regular force," he acknowledged. The former harbored the necessary passion to defend home, hearth, and nation. The latter, Davis claimed, were preferred in foreign wars "because they can be maintained in better discipline. They will maintain a better state of police . . . and [are] therefore more effective," he concluded, "for mere garrison duties." Davis then asked rhetorically if citizen-soldiers would "be content with the performance of the police of a garrison?" Would volunteers be satisfied with "a lower grade in society, and more accustomed to such duties?"[53]

Here, Davis acknowledged that American culture regarded garrisons as ancillary institutions, unfit for citizen-soldiers. Contemporaries had long equated garrisons with the regular army, an institution relegated to the fringes of society. But Davis's distinctions extended far beyond those of the American public. He returned to his contention that the conflict with Mexico, the United States' first (official) war of invasion and occupation, necessitated a specific class of troops. As a soldier trained in the professional West Point tradition, Davis understood that garrisons offered the ideal vehicle by which to enact a successful occupation, as long as they were populated by regulars who comprehended the unnatural environment of garrison life. "It is one thing to beat the enemy and another to hold him in subjection," he continued, "which rests upon the supposition that Mexico is conquered." Davis stipulated that "there is more hostility against us in Mexico now than there was at the beginning of the war. Mexico is not conquered." He argued that "we want this force to hold towns and posts in Mexico—to convince the Mexicans that resistance is idle, and beyond all this, to afford protection to all the citizens of Mexico who are ready to recognize our authority."[54]

While Davis cited the pragmatic obstacles of occupation within the national military tradition, other observers outlined what they believed to be the moral implications of employing volunteers in armies of invasion. Charles T. Porter, a northern commentator writing immediately after the war, claimed that the United States' new-found enthusiasm for wars of invasion had produced a devastating ethical collapse among the republic's soldiers. "This war has introduced crime and vice among us," Porter charged. "Soldiers in a foreign country feel that they are removed from all restraints of civil law," he declared, echoing U. S. Grant's observations at Matamoros, "and whenever the barrier of military discipline can be passed, unrestrained indulgence is sure to be sought." Porter cited the reckless abandon with which volunteers waged their war against Mexicans, fearing that the citizen, upon return to American society, might not discard his identity as soldier: "Having been removed from [civil law] for a time, it is difficult for them to assume again the character of peaceable citizens." Porter ultimately condemned "the lust of conquest and the desire of war for its own sake," which he considered "the greatest curses of any state, and most of all of a republic." The nation's citizen-volunteers, he suggested, had become corrupted by the experience of invasion and occupation.[55]

Jefferson Davis and Charles Porter cited a troubling scenario that Americans would never fully reconcile throughout the rest of the Civil War era: employing volunteers, who were reared in a democratic ethos, in armies of occupation. The citizen-soldier ideal, which had been constructed for a particular purpose and grounded in limited assumptions, now intersected the culture of a changing American military tradition. The ideals of volunteer soldiering—republican virtue and democratic privilege—collided directly with the realities of wartime occupation, which required governing strange peoples in unrestrained, yet also static, environments. The ways that citizen-soldiers navigated these incongruous traditions established a national conversation about the role of the volunteer soldier in a war of invasion. This dialogue did not end in 1848 when American forces withdrew from Mexico. It intensified after the Civil War began in 1861 but would not be addressed directly until Abraham Lincoln's Emancipation Proclamation went into effect in 1863.

2 | Policy, Process, and the Landscape of Union Occupation during the Civil War

The Mexican-American War established a foundation of principles and precedents regarding wartime occupation. Although the United States engaged in a war of extended occupation between 1861 and 1865, contemporaries initially heeded only a few lessons gleaned from the conflict with Mexico. Civilian-military relations dominated conversations among political and military leaders at the outset of the Civil War as observers learned that the conflict itself and the occupation of the Confederacy would be far different from conquering Mexico. Victory for the United States required defeating Confederate armies, convincing white southerners that northern arms posed no threat to civilians, property, and society, and guiding the rebellious states back into the Union. Yet the ways in which civil and military leaders in 1861 imagined the policies and processes of wartime occupation revealed the stunning lack of national experience with military government; policy makers had never seriously considered the complex elements required for an extended domestic war of occupation.

The Union high command thus had to reconcile two crucial differences between the war with Mexico and the impending crisis against the Confederacy: occupying US territory (rather than foreign territory) and regulating the behavior of white American citizens (rather than the behavior of foreign "others"). Wars of occupation were generally waged against nations and peoples who were noticeably "different." It seemed much easier to justify a war of invasion, conquest, and occupation when "the other" possessed what were assumed to be striking traits of inferiority. The Civil War, unlike the conflict with Mexico, presented a different set of circumstances. Although much of the antebellum period witnessed a steadily growing divide between northerners and southerners, members of each faction struggled to plausibly deny that the other was "American." Race especially united North and South, in spite of the divisions sparked by divergent political, cultural, and economic conditions related to slavery.

Once Union armies penetrated the Confederacy, policies enacted behind the lines initially sought to placate white southerners. The US military developed a limited, conciliatory, and pragmatic program that offered magnanimous invitations back into the Union. Careful not to alienate white southern citizens, President Abraham Lincoln and his leading generals trusted that Federal armies could avoid total conquest and complete destruction. Many believed that the conflict should retain a "civilized" character.[1]

The US commanders encountered a startling reality as the war continued indefinitely. Their preferred policy of conciliation began to crumble in the face of defiant resistance from white southerners who, initially unbeknown to the Yankees, harbored deep resentment about the northern invasions. Faced with a perceived threat to their honor and dignity, white southerners, in addition to formal Confederate armies, waged their own form of war against US military forces. This stubborn opposition from southern civilians forced civil and military leaders to revise national policy. By early 1862, Union authorities inaugurated a shift from conciliation to "hard war" in which complex military occupations became the foremost component of US strategy behind the lines. In order to grasp how white and black Union soldiers ultimately interpreted the complicated project of wartime occupation, it is first necessary to examine the processes of that occupation from a top-down policy perspective. Only then can we appreciate how the landscape of occupation informed common soldiers' cultural, ideological, and racial worldviews.[2]

* * *

At the outset of the war, the Union's loyal citizenry assumed that massive US armies, populated by selfless volunteers, would march into the rebellious Confederate states and bend stubborn secessionists to the will of the Federal government. Perhaps only a single battle would be enough to settle the conflict; certainly the threat of armed force would quickly enlighten restive white southerners to their misguided deeds. The government decried most punitive measures to compel southern whites, many of whom the Lincoln administration regarded as potentially loyal, back into the Union. Countless northerners believed that secession had been occasioned by a coterie of slaveholding aristocrats who were determined to erect a new society that catered to their own unique, selfish interests. According to the northern way of thinking, common white southerners, although manipulated by conspiratorial fears of racial unrest, miscegenation, and amalgamation, surely did not support treason or the Confederacy.[3]

Civilian authorities authorized US armies to employ a policy of conciliation in their initial invasions of the Confederacy. Reestablishing loyal state
governments by toppling the secretive cabal of secessionists assumed top
priority; engaging common civilians or tampering with slavery, however, was
strictly forbidden. Secession was seen as a revolutionary act employed by a
radical minority that controlled the levers of southern power. If they could
be removed, the crisis would vanish. Policy makers thus concluded that long-
term military occupation, driven by fundamental social and political reform,
would not be necessary. In fact, the military had rarely ever been employed for
any previous assignments of domestic civil transformation. Although many
loyal northerners believed slavery contradicted free labor principles and democracy, they also believed that interfering with the institution would only
estrange the border states, further threatening the Union.[4]

Abraham Lincoln's first annual message to Congress in December 1861
framed the conciliation policy. He argued that the southern states had never
legally seceded but rather assumed a condition of temporary rebellion. This
logic partially explains why the army was ordered to interact as little as possible with southern civilians, the majority of whom were presumed loyal.
Lincoln feared that the army might become too powerful and overstep its
prescribed authority in the affairs of the southern states, thereby threatening any possibility of reunion and reconciliation. "In considering the policy
to be adopted for suppressing the insurrection," Lincoln explained, "I have
been anxious and careful that the inevitable conflict for this purpose shall
not degenerate into a violent and remorseless revolutionary struggle. I have,
therefore, in every case, thought it proper to keep the integrity of the Union
prominent as the primary object of the contest." The Union, he implied, did
not wage war against peaceful civilians or even the states; the military instead
trained its grievances on enemy armies and the lawless band of secessionists
who had unduly silenced the region's loyal Unionists.[5]

During the first year of the war, numerous Union army commanders es-
poused the conciliation policy, not only instructing their troops about the
government's program but also informing white southerners that they would
receive mild treatment. Benjamin F. Butler declared that soldiers at Fortress
Monroe, Virginia, must respect "the rights of private property and of peaceable citizens." He encouraged any loyal civilian, "at peace with the United
States," to report unruly, plundering soldiers. A month later, Irvin McDowell,
commanding the army that had recently invaded northern Virginia, feared

that reports of depredations committed by his troops "have exasperated the inhabitants and chilled the hopes of the Union men." McDowell accordingly demanded that all of his regiments should "be *restrained* as well as led." Similar refrains echoed across the wartime landscape. Shortly after Nashville, Tennessee, capitulated in February 1862, Don Carlos Buell, commander of the Army of the Ohio, reminded his victorious troops that "we are in arms, not for the purpose of invading the rights of our fellow-countrymen anywhere, but to maintain the integrity of the Union and protect the Constitution under which the people have been prosperous and happy." Buell added that soldiers must respect local property, refrain from entering private residences, and show deference to loyal citizens. Appealing to his men's sense of honor, Buell warned that any violation of restraint or decorum would "bring shame on their comrades and the cause they are engaged in."[6]

Once Federal armies fanned out across the southern countryside, entering towns and cities, the uniformed presence confirmed the government's conciliatory overtures. A host of military proclamations belied the Confederate propaganda that painted northern armies as vandal hordes. Army commanders sought to convey that their armies entered the South merely to preserve order, protect domestic institutions, and ensure the tranquility of civilian life. Ambrose E. Burnside informed the citizens of Roanoke Island, North Carolina, in February 1862 that the Union did not intend "to invade any of your rights, but to assert the authority of the United States, and thus to close with you the desolating war brought upon your State by comparatively a few bad men in your midst." Declaring his faith in southern loyalty, Burnside urged residents to resist secessionist indoctrination, which "impose[d] upon your credulity by telling you of wicked and even diabolical intentions on our part; of our desire to destroy your freedom, demolish your property, liberate your slaves, injure your women, and such like enormities, all of which, we assure you, is not only ridiculous, but utterly and willfully false." Burnside then celebrated the common heritage shared by northerners and southerners, underscoring a mutual faith in God, reverence for the Constitution, and adherence to republican government. Union armies, he concluded, and not the state's secessionists, sought to ensure the perpetuation of these cherished traditions.[7]

The policy of conciliation, although crafted in good faith and reflective of the government's original conceptions of the war, met stiff resistance. White southerners responded to the Union invasions with arrogant contempt, signaling that they were not passive Unionists. Confederate opposition to the growing US military presence manifested itself in civilians shouting verbal taunts and flaunting Confederate symbols, women spitting in the faces of occupying soldiers, and some southerners even joining guerrilla bands who attacked advancing Union armies. Shrewdly aware of the conciliation policy's moderate and lenient tone, southern whites tested the limits of civilian-military relations, challenging the occupiers' resolve.[8]

It became clear by the spring of 1862 that countless white southerners were not soothed by the policy of conciliation. Federal military authorities thus learned that US armies could not simply march into the South, fight a definitive battle, conclude the war, and expect southern whites to flock willingly back to the Union. Major General George B. McClellan, commander of the Army of the Potomac and a leading proponent of conciliatory measures, verified this blunt reality. His failure to capture Richmond in the spring of 1862 exposed the war's indefinite nature, sparking hurried debates about new wartime policies. Indeed, Lincoln responded to the ill-fated Peninsula Campaign and defiant white southern hostility by floating the possibility of emancipation, while his field commanders began to encourage soldiers to confiscate property and any other war materials that might be used to fuel the rebellion. In fact, Union soldiers had long foraged for food and tampered with private property. A newspaper correspondent observed that troops entered abandoned plantations near Beaufort, South Carolina, and engaged "in very wantonness of destructive mischief." "Portraits of distinguished secesh were bayoneted; articles of virtue or value gobbled up; and what could be carried off to camp as spoils . . . was incontinently made off with." A combination of Confederate insolence and Yankee confiscation collapsed the Union's conciliatory policy.[9]

An additional situation also revealed the failure of conciliation. Early in the war thousands of enslaved African Americans began flooding Union lines, forcing army commanders and politicians to recognize and define their humanity. Although at the outbreak of hostilities Lincoln and the majority of moderate Republicans implored their army commanders not to disrupt slavery, the chaotic conditions of invasion and occupation unintentionally shaped the landscape of emancipation. As US armies expanded their scope and influence throughout the occupied Confederacy, enslaved black southerners fled plantations seeking freedom behind the lines. The army was now tasked with an unprecedented role: waging war against the nation's enemies while also negotiating an escalating refugee crisis that reflected the South's collapsing social, economic, and racial hierarchy. Invasion and occupation had now planted the seeds of unexpected revolutionary change.[10]

Black southerners actively secured freedom through their flight to Union armies. As early as May 1861, their self-liberation was recognized and protected by generals in the field. While at Fortress Monroe, Butler refused a request from a local planter to return three escaped slaves who fled to safety at the Union outpost on the Virginia coast. In labeling these runaways as "contraband" and employing them as camp laborers, Butler justified the confiscation of any property—including human property—that could be used to assist the enemy war machine. Butler's unprecedented declaration carried not merely legal implications but also transformed Union military policy. By July, approximately one thousand contraband had abandoned their plantations, finding freedom within the Union army.[11]

With approximately 500,000 enslaved people reaching Federal lines during the war, legislation and official military policies were needed to cope with the massive influx. A pair of laws passed during the first two years of the war codified African Americans' relentless quest for wartime liberation, while also signaling the collapse of conciliation. Building on Butler's order, the First Confiscation Act (1861) declared that property used "in aid of the rebellion" was subject to seizure by the Union military, effectively weakening the Confederate war effort. The Second Confiscation Act (1862) expanded this notion and announced that enslaved people who entered Union lines "shall be forever free of their servitude, and not again held as slaves." Fostered by African Americans' demonstrated capacity for self-emancipation, the Confiscation Acts underscored blacks' willingness to shatter the structures of slavery, increasing the size, scope, and magnitude of the war.[12]

Both the fluidity and the permanence of Union armies ultimately determined freedom's reach. While the formerly enslaved played a crucial role in undermining the peculiar institution's iron grip, and while Congress and the president instituted laws and executive orders that attacked slavery from Washington, Union armies of occupation were the principal institutions that determined the space and setting of wartime freedom. As Lincoln declared in the Emancipation Proclamation, "all persons held as slaves within [rebellious states], are, and henceforward shall be free; and that the Executive government of the United States, including the military and naval authorities thereof, will recognize and maintain the freedom of said persons." The proclamation redefined the assumptions of military occupation, declaring that US forces carried the banner of freedom. Indeed, an established permanent military presence was the key element in safeguarding black liberation while also administering the legal promise of emancipation. As historian Gary W.

Gallagher writes, "Without the projection of United States military power, the Emancipation Proclamation and the Second Confiscation Act represented mere words on paper to both slaves and slaveholders in the Confederacy."[13]

In July 1862, George B. McClellan recognized the stunning reversal of Federal military policy. "This rebellion has now assumed the character of a war," he wrote to Lincoln, "and it should be conducted upon the highest principles known to Christian civilization." Long an advocate of conciliation, McClellan watched with despair as the old policy crumbled. "It should not be at all a war upon population.... Neither confiscation of property, political executions of persons, territorial organization of States, or forcible abolition of slavery should be contemplated for a moment." The conditions of war, however, mandated the very approaches that McClellan deplored. Invading the rebellious South, abandoning conciliation, and adopting emancipation had fundamentally transformed Union occupation policy. US civil and military authorities thus sought a strategy built on conquering territory, regulating civilians, enforcing the destruction of slavery, combating irregular enemies, and challenging formal armies. The Union's civilian and military leaders understood that the enemy's ability and will to fight correlated directly to its capacity to subsist. If Federal armies suffocated large, strategic areas of the southern nation, Confederate civilians and soldiers, in addition to their resources, could be thoroughly fatigued, leading to defeat. Although fraught with challenges, conquering, garrisoning, and occupying Confederate communities would play a crucial role in determining the success or failure of any new wartime policy. Such an approach deprived the Confederacy of essential resources in manpower, food, and labor, thereby weakening the will to resist further occupation.[14]

US armies ultimately adopted the strategy of exhaustion, as it came to be known, blanketing the Confederacy with garrisons manned by scores of Union soldiers. Working in concert with the blockade, which the navy employed to capture strategic cities on the Atlantic and Gulf coasts, Union infantry and cavalry penetrated the southern interior, demanded the surrender of towns, reestablished Federal authority, patrolled the countryside, confiscated war materiel, and maintained an armed presence. No fewer than one hundred southern communities capitulated to Union armies during the war, being transformed into occupied garrisons administered by the US military. Armies did not have to occupy and pacify the entire Confederacy, nor did they have to conquer Richmond. Instead, captured towns could serve as strategic centers of Union control, from which to regulate the countryside through raids and expeditions, reinstate commerce with the North, and provide bases of supply for the mobile field armies. The most prized communities, such as Vicksburg on the Mississippi River, Nashville on the Cumberland River, or Corinth on an important north-south, east-west railroad, were located in advantageous regions that provided efficient transportation and access to commercial markets.[15]

A political dimension also existed. When cities and states capitulated to US forces, loyal governments could be established, inaugurating the process of wartime reconstruction. When Union armies pacified towns, local Unionist citizens exerted their influence under the protection of national arms, hoping to establish loyal governments. Their professed devotion to the Union encouraged the Lincoln administration, which sought loyal southerners to begin a quick and painless process of local and state reconstruction. Although Unionists generally welcomed military protection and complied with military authorities, they also believed that occupation should give way as quickly as possible to local civilian control. For example, Tennessee and Louisiana, both of which fell to Union forces in 1862, each exposed tense relationships between Unionists, army commanders, and military governors, who all harbored different conceptions of power, Federal policy, and especially emancipation. Although loyal governments were established, southern Unionists did not always concede to the United States' definition of a preserved Union that had evolved away from the overtures of conciliation and the racial conditions of the late antebellum era.[16]

The garrisoning strategy slowly but steadily forced the surrender of dozens of crucially important Confederate cities. Although it took nearly four years, the policy of garrisoning through exhaustion occasioned the fall of Alexandria, Nashville, Memphis, New Orleans, Baton Rouge, Norfolk, Little Rock, Pensacola, Vicksburg, Charleston, and Savannah, to name merely a few. Dozens of smaller towns were also garrisoned, establishing Federal authority across great swaths of the Confederacy. Thus, the southern tapestry was dotted with growing islands of blue in a sea of gray violence and chaos. It is crucial to recognize, though, that the Union army did not attempt to unfold its forces permanently across every piece of Confederate territory. Instead, the garrisoning concept worked only when the US forces *concentrated* within a city, using it as a principal zone of occupation from which to launch temporary raids and campaigns, with the intention of weakening civilian resolve.[17]

Some high-ranking generals nonetheless questioned the premise of conquering and holding territory. Their critiques underscored the extent to which nineteenth-century Americans were not accustomed to long-term wars of occupation. Drawing on their formative educations in military theory, some argued that garrisoning wasted precious resources, deprived the armies of manpower, and cost extraordinary amounts of money. As early as 1861, General-in-Chief Winfield Scott warned against a protracted war of occupation, fearing that Union forces might become mired indefinitely in the Confederacy. Scott believed in the possibility of conquering the rebellious South, yet he argued that such a task would take several years and could be accomplished only by an army numbering 300,000 men. But such an invasion would result in an "enormous waste of human life to the North" and create "fifteen devastated Provinces! not to be brought into harmony with their conquerors; but to be held for generations by heavy garrisons," sustained with the exorbitant cost of indefinite maintenance and regulation. Such wars of conquest and occupation were the purview of European kings and mercenary forces—not American presidents and citizen-armies.[18]

In his confessions, Scott implicitly alluded to a central feature of the United States' early republican tradition: the fear of a standing army. Even in the midst of war, and especially in its immediate aftermath, both the American citizenry and government distrusted the concept and utility of a standing army due to its potentially corrupting influence, its seemingly outrageous economic cost, and its tendency to privilege military law at the expense of civil law. Perhaps most important, both a peacetime *and* a wartime standing army would potentially devalue the symbolic and tangible function of the citizen-soldier. These were stunning admissions from the revered general who had conquered Mexico through garrisoning, occupation, and pacification. Scott, though, paused when he recognized the unique circumstance in which the United States found itself in 1861. Although the South was in rebellion, its citizens were still Americans. Scott undoubtedly worried about the implications of the military regulating the lives of citizens; as he said, such scenarios reeked too much of European wars.[19]

The war evolved into the very type of protracted occupation predicted by Scott. The erection of occupied garrisons became vital and necessary components of the North's Civil War strategy. Yet some contemporaries continued to criticize the wisdom of such policies. Whereas Scott shunned long-term occupation on ideological grounds, William T. Sherman approached the concept from a pragmatic standpoint. Sherman sensed, by the midpoint of the war, that Union armies employed far too many troops to garrison the Confederacy. Conquering more and more territory, he worried, necessitated increased numbers of occupation troops, thus depriving campaigning armies of crucial manpower.[20]

Although Sherman endorsed the premise of wartime occupation, he believed that garrisoning should take place only in a few select regions. Undoubtedly influenced by his brief governance of Memphis in the early summer of 1862, Sherman considered control of the Mississippi River crucial to all Union prospects. "I think the Mississippi the great artery of America," he informed his wife, "and whatever power holds it holds the continent." But for Sherman, the river symbolized a deeper, more fundamental problem of occupation. United States armies should focus their attention chiefly on the Mississippi, appreciating its efficient access to the North and its natural barriers, rather than attempting a thorough conquest of the Confederate interior. "Dont expect to overrun Such a Country or subdue such a people in [one] two or five years," he warned his brother John. "It is the task of a century. Although our army is thus far south we cannot stir from our Garrisons." Control of the river, Sherman explained, would allow small army detachments to penetrate quickly into the countryside and disrupt civilian life. "To attempt to hold all the South would demand an army too large even to think of," he cautioned, reminiscent of Winfield Scott's counsels.[21]

Ulysses S. Grant, who envisioned the process of war better than any other Union commander, agreed with Sherman's assessments. Grant closely wedded his strategies to the concepts of occupation and garrisoning, believing that they offered the best means by which to subdue the Confederacy. There simply did not exist, in Grant's mind, a better alternative. He believed, like Sherman, that too much garrisoning would seriously impede the progress of US armies, also confirming Scott's fears from 1861. Yet the presence of Union occupation, embodied by formidable, strategically placed outposts, presented a demoralizing picture to the Confederate people while also serving as useful points of concentration for Federal armies. Grant deemed unrealistic the conquest of *all* rebellious territory.[22]

Thus, by late 1863 through the end the war, Grant subtly adjusted the process of occupation to stake out a line, rather than a region. Instead of straining to occupy an entire state, or even large parts thereof, Union forces would concentrate along lines *through* the states, with outposts often guarded by a river or coastline or secured by close access to a railway. Then, various detachments would leave the garrisons and temporarily raid the countryside, foraging for food, destroying property when necessary, and cleaning out pockets of guerrilla resistance. Grant's vision of occupation, therefore, did not function merely as the fixed process, against which Scott had warned, in which Union armies remained immobile. Occupation, Grant explained, was also a peripatetic event, driven by transitory expeditions and raids. The war could be taken directly to the white southern populace both internally and externally. The raiding plan, which offered a slight moderation to the strategy of exhaustion, relieved the Federals from occupying every corner of the Confederacy. And the plan worked perfectly, subduing parts of Louisiana, Mississippi, and Alabama; western and middle Tennessee; the interior of Georgia (Sherman's March to the Sea in the autumn of 1864 was indeed a raid); and the Shenandoah Valley in Virginia.[23]

The Union high command successfully modified the approach to wartime occupation, assuaging Scott's worries while also accommodating the concept of permanent and strategic garrisoning. Yet just as Scott had warned, US armies required overwhelming numbers of troops to garrison the occupied Confederacy. In order for the strategy of exhaustion to work, an armed presence needed to remain garrisoned at all times, while also raiding the countryside and posing a formidable barrier against any upheaval. Indeed, once a campaigning army conquered a town or region, a sizable occupation force had to stay behind. Wartime occupation, though, was a fluid process, and regiments were not designated exclusively for garrison duty. The Twelfth Connecticut Volunteers, for instance, the first regiment to land at New Orleans in May 1862, occupied the city until October before being assigned to the ongoing campaigns to open the Mississippi River. Another unit then took its place, signaling the permanence of Union occupation, even if it was carried out by a shifting array of regiments.[24]

As the war evolved and Federal armies secured additional Confederate territory, Union occupation required growing numbers of troops to garrison the conquered cities and regions. Forces of collective occupation sometimes even exceeded the size of the United States' principal field armies, underscoring the stunning commitment necessary to garrison the wartime South. A brief glance at official returns from 1863 testifies to this point. In May, Union forces stationed in the Confederacy and loyal border states numbered nearly 500,000 soldiers, approximately 60 percent of whom comprised the major campaigning armies: the armies of the Potomac, the Cumberland, and the Tennessee. Almost 40 percent were stationed in previously conquered regions as occupiers. That nearly half all Union arms occupied the Confederacy two years into the war indicated that civil and military authorities, although somewhat apprehensive, considered military occupation to be a crucial determinant of victory.[25]

United States armies employed at least one-third of their soldiers to garrison strategic positions throughout the war. Oftentimes the figures were much greater, as indicated by the May 1863 returns. Grant, Sherman, and other Union commanders understood that the war was not merely a contest between opposing field armies. It also encompassed the need to protect long supply lines, railroad access, and communication networks; battle insurgents; establish and maintain reconstructed state governments; regulate hostile civilians and squelch secessionist sentiment; provide safe haven for refugees and runaway slaves; construct entrenchments and perform fatigue duties; and sustain commercial ties to northern markets. Grant encountered these truths as early as 1862, shortly after Fort Donelson fell. "I am being so much crippled in my resources that I very much fear that I shall not be able to advance so rapidly as I would like," he confided to his wife, Julia. Aside from the casualties sustained in the fighting, Grant also had to detail two regiments as prison guards, "and if I leave, garrisons will have to be left here, at Clarkesville and Fort Henry. This will weaken me so much that great results cannot be expected." Most victorious Union generals and officers encountered these very dynamics each time Confederate territory yielded to US armies.[26]

Wartime occupation did not function as an ancillary event to the war's major campaigns and battles. Instead, both worked together, each contingent on the other's successes. If Union forces could not successfully campaign across the Confederacy, they could not capture towns, cities, and regions. Incidentally, the major field armies would be stranded precariously if occupation and garrison forces failed to stabilize and hold conquered regions. And the quest for wartime Reconstruction, coupled with the successful enforcement of emancipation, would likely never materialize without an occupation presence.

By 1863 the United States' war of occupation had evolved into a numerical crisis: too few troops existed to remain posted perpetually in conquered regions. The complicated trials of military occupation thus occasioned a revolutionary scenario that would fundamentally reshape the landscape of war. As Union armies penetrated into the Confederacy and droves of enslaved people actively escaped to freedom, civilian and military authorities correctly determined that the enlistment of African American soldiers could provide the additional manpower needed to crush the rebellion. Southern and northern black men poured into the Union army and, by war's end, composed about 10 percent (approximately 180,000) of all US forces. From the issuance of the Emancipation Proclamation through the end of the war and into postbellum occupation, the USCT mostly remained behind the lines, garrisoning important and strategic locales throughout the war-torn South and filling a crucial numerical void.[27]

The enlistment of black soldiers reflected the United States' ability to wage both a war of occupation *and* of active campaigns, confirming its abundance of manpower and resources. Grant and Sherman each recognized this great advantage, even while remaining somewhat unsettled at the prospect of leaving behind so many soldiers in zones of occupation. Yet alternatives did not exist. And in the end, such realities actually aided each general in his conquest of the Confederacy. For example, on the eve of the Atlanta campaign and subsequent marches through Georgia and the Carolinas, Sherman counted 180,087 soldiers "present for duty," dispersed among the armies of the Cumberland, the Tennessee, and the Ohio. Sherman later wrote of these numbers, "The department and army commanders had to maintain strong garrisons in their respective departments, and also to guard their respective lines of supply. I therefore, in my mind aimed to prepare out of these three armies . . . a compact army for active operations in Georgia." Each army commander, as Sherman noted, had to detach enough men to address the exigencies of garrison duty and maintain control over occupied regions. Sherman thus departed for Atlanta with about 100,000 troops, 55 percent of his initial command. Such trends mirrored the process of occupation throughout the wartime landscape.[28]

Logistics and lines of communication helped determine the success or failure of campaigns, including Sherman's march. Although most of the Union's campaigning armies successfully foraged the countryside for food and supplies, they still had to be tied to occupied regions and major garrisons in order to ensure success, highlighting the crucial importance of railroads. Waging an extensive war spread across thousands of miles in enemy territory required substantial infrastructure. Indeed, occupied garrisons were islands of bureaucratic administration and organization, steeped in matters of logistics. "It is safe to say that more than half of the National army was engaged in guarding lines of supplies, or were on leave, sick in hospital or on detail which prevented their bearing arms," Grant explained in his memoirs. "Then, again, large forces were employed where no Confederate army confronted them.

I deem it safe to say that there were no large engagements where the National numbers compensated for the advantage of position and intrenchment occupied by the enemy." Thus, logistical support and maintenance of supply lines, in which occupation forces played a crucial part, facilitated freedom of mobility for the major field armies. The Quartermaster's Department played an undeniably central role, yet it was the common volunteer soldiers, designated from the line regiments, who implemented and sustained logistical lines across the occupied landscape.[29]

On the whole, Union logistical operations, in concert with the process of occupation, worked reasonably well. Yet the continued conquering and acquisition of territory necessitated increased numbers of volunteer soldiers to oversee distended communication and supply lines. Presumed advantages in northern manpower, though, belie any notion of inevitable Union victory. Yes, when compared to the Confederacy, the United States possessed superior numbers of able-bodied, military-age men. Yet such figures need to be placed within the context of the *types* of war waged by both nations. Bureaucratic necessity, maintenance of administrative logistics, and indefinite occupation required great numbers of soldiers to perpetuate the Union's war machine. The Confederacy, however, did not have to conquer and hold enemy territory. When the Army of Northern Virginia invaded the North, Robert E. Lee did not intend permanent occupations of Maryland in 1862 and Pennsylvania in 1863. Yet the Confederate States required a near-total mobilization of their white males to fill their respective field armies. "Northern manpower and material advantages, then, were not so great as they might have seemed," historian Russell F. Weigley writes of this dichotomy. "The Northern reservoir of manpower was not inexhaustible" because "generals faced perplexing problems in waging an offensive war of conquest, in pursuit of rapid victory, without suffering casualties so severe that they would destroy the very resolution which the quest for rapidity of conquest was supposed to sustain."[30]

That it took four long years to conquer, garrison, and occupy large portions of the Confederacy testifies to the resolve of white southerners, both civilians and soldiers, who expended great energy to resist the Union invasions. The Confederacy lasted as long as it did, in large part, because its people simply could not be exhausted. Confederates' popular will to endure was oftentimes reinforced, ironically, by the *presence* of Union occupation. Although US armies manifested themselves across the wartime landscape, their job was made ever more difficult by the restive and sometimes violent demeanor of white southerners. Thus the failure of conciliation compelled civil and military authorities to employ increasingly stringent methods, culminating in the Union's "hard war" policy.[31]

* * *

Focus must now shift to the ground level to appreciate how the particular process of occupation unfolded. Understanding that occupying large, strategic locales and regions served as the basis of wartime policy, how did the armies garrison towns and cities, how were civilians regulated, by what method were raids conducted, and how did the armies apply the hard war philosophy to white southerners? Remarkably, US armies did not have a unified policy by which to guide the garrisoning of towns. Individual commanders oftentimes employed their own methods to meet the immediate challenges of occupation. But their actions tended to reflect a common approach, allowing generalizations to be gleaned.

Occupied garrisons functioned as the locus of Union occupation. Seeking to reshape white attitudes, establish centers of administration, and operate as direct sources of wartime reconstruction, garrisons symbolized absolute Federal authority. While the armies may not have conquered all of the Confederate countryside, they thoroughly dismantled dozens of southern communities, establishing formidable military outposts. Garrisons offered further penetration into the Confederate interior, allowing armies to expand their influence. Although the approach to garrisoning seemed simple, the actual process proved to be quite difficult.

The garrisoning procedure typically followed a general template. Union armies entered southern cities, ordered the mayor to surrender authority, temporarily discontinued local courts, halted newspaper printing, and curbed civilian rights, while simultaneously establishing military rule. The commanding officer rarely worried about the particular legal status of the seceded states, instead believing that any locale occupied by Union armies was subject to martial law. Occupying soldiers then assumed positions throughout the city to ensure order. Southern civilians had two choices: accept the realities of occupation or resist. Most chose the former, realizing the futility of armed defiance in the face of such concentrated Federal force.[32]

When US armies initially entered conquered Confederate towns they encountered rampant chaos, unruly mobs, and threats of unrestrained violence.

Military authority, in most cases, had to be established immediately, signaling that the army now controlled every aspect of civil life. "Affairs in this city," Grant described of Memphis in June 1862, "seem to be in rather bad order, secessionists governing much in their own way." Thus to establish a functioning garrison, commanding generals appointed a post director and provost marshal who formulated rules and regulations, organizing regiments of soldiers to be dispersed throughout the city. Once order had been established internally, remaining troops were deployed outside of town to repair and guard railways, form picket lines along roads, and regulate communications into the city. The commanding general issued further orders protecting private property and requiring all soldiers to remain at their posts. Military police patrolled the city, arresting civilians who violated martial law as well as soldiers who strayed from their required duties. The process of garrisoning and the assembling of Federal authority usually occurred in less than one week.[33]

The dearth of national precedent actually aided army commanders in their occupations of Confederate cities. With the exception of the United States' foray in Mexico, military governors were not bound by a defined tradition of martial law. Civil and military authorities in Washington thus granted wide autonomy to officers to conduct their wartime occupations. Even after the government adopted General Orders No. 100, which codified and streamlined the guidelines of occupation, commanding generals continued to interpret their powers broadly. Circumstance, regional and local necessity, and personal beliefs about the rules of war, rather than strict legal dictate, guided commanders in their approach to garrisoning and occupation. Above all, they focused on strategies to ensure the preservation of order, maintenance of civility, and consolidation of Federal authority.[34]

Army commanders' governance of occupied zones exposed their rejection of conciliation in favor of stringent regulation of white southerners and their institutions. Several examples testify to the varied ways in which commanders wielded their authority. John C. Frémont and David Hunter, both abolitionist generals in command of Union-controlled Missouri and parts of South Carolina respectively, early in the war issued proclamations of emancipation, freeing enslaved African Americans under the US Army's jurisdiction. Although President Lincoln revoked both measures, Frémont and Hunter contended that they had acted lawfully in accordance with the broad nature of martial law. Similarly, Benjamin F. Butler, shortly after entering New Orleans in May 1862, consolidated his authority after William B. Mumford, a local gambler, scaled the local mint and tore down the United States flag. Outraged, Butler demanded Mumford be tried before a military commission, which found him guilty of desecrating the flag and resisting Federal authority. Butler promptly ordered Mumford's execution. In other cities across the occupied landscape, military governors arrested dissident citizens, restricted treasonous speech, and confiscated private property.[35]

Although military governors assumed supreme control and influence in garrisoned communities, the local provost marshal managed the day-to-day affairs. Not necessarily subordinate to a city's overall commander but rather appointed by the provost marshal general of a district or department, local provost marshals governed each garrison's bureaucratic matters. All subjects of wartime import, local business, civilian concerns, and military regulation flowed through the provost marshal's office. Municipal governments were allowed to function yet were also regulated by martial law; the provost marshal directed most forms of local administration. For example, a circular distributed by the provost marshal at Huntsville, Alabama, explained the office's responsibilities: "attend[ing] to such duties as are usually performed by the magistrates and civil officers of towns, as far as consistent with the military occupation of a place." Provost marshals indeed enjoyed a wide latitude of authority and were responsible for granting licenses to trade, regulating and maintaining order and cleanliness, punishing parties guilty of crimes, presiding over property disputes, issuing permits and passes to leave garrisoned towns, and, as the Huntsville circular noted, "enforc[ing] such orders as the post or district commander may find it necessary to issue." Whereas military governors represented the face of occupation, provost marshals symbolized the body of wartime governance, directing every movement and action within the garrisons.[36]

While the army commanders governed cities and provost marshals managed administrative affairs, common soldiers actually carried out the process of wartime occupation. They shouldered a varied and wide-ranging set of duties that reflected the bureaucratic and perfunctory operations required of garrison life. Both officers and enlisted men engaged in sanitary cleanup, policed the town, issued rations and loyalty oaths to civilians, and served as picket guards outside of town. "Perhaps you do not understand what sort of duty this is," Massachusetts soldier William H. Whitney wrote from Baton Rouge. "Pickets are groups of three or four men placed at regular intervals in a line around a place," he illustrated. "These groups are within seeing or hearing distance of one another and one or two are obliged to be on the lookout at a time. This is to prevent a surprise from the enemy as well as to keep citizens or spies from entering without a pass." Each brigade in the occupation force furnished men for daily picket duty, ensuring that an armed presence always existed both in and out of the city.[37]

Other responsibilities mandated that occupying soldiers transform previously peaceful towns into daunting military outposts. Fatigue duty, which consisted of constructing fortifications, erecting breastworks, discharging and stocking transports, repairing railroads, and outfitting units for raids and expeditions, consumed great energy and strength. "The duty consists in unloading vessels laying or repairing plank walks," Charles Blake of the Twelfth Maine wrote from Ship Island, Mississippi, "and may well be called fatigue duty for it does fatigue one greatly." Michigan soldier Elihu P. Chadwick revealed that such labor at DeValls Bluff, Arkansas, "caused a great many of our number to take sick and die it being very hot and a sickly place."[38]

Massachusetts volunteer Charles Francis Adams, Jr., painted a vivid picture of daily life, outlining soldiers' various duties and chores. "Our life is one of rigid garrison duty," he wrote in 1861, "reveille at half past five with breakfast at six; dress parade at seven; a squad drill at eight and a company drill at ten; at twelve dinner and at three a battalion drill which lasts until half past five, when we have an evening dress-parade, which finishes work for those off guard for the day." Soldiers typically enjoyed a quiet evening, retiring early to bed. For those on sentinel or picket duty, though, Adams explained that their responsibilities were far different. "When on guard, which every man is about twice a week, it is rather restless," he explained, "as for twenty-four hours we are on guard two hours and off four, day and night, and properly can't leave."[39]

Based on the power and influence of military governors, provost marshals, and occupying soldiers, wartime garrisons were pillars of Federal authority. Although it required abundant resources, materiel, and manpower to function, the garrisoning strategy worked, consolidating US influence throughout important pockets of the Confederacy. However, occupation continued to meet stiff resistance, not necessarily from white southerners who lived in conquered cities, but rather from those who roamed the untamed countryside far from the authority of Union armies. These contested arenas witnessed the most direct application of the hard war occupation policy.[40]

The US Army ventured out into the landscape surrounding garrisoned towns to conduct repeated raids and expeditions, which served multiple purposes. First, white southerners, who lived in the general vicinities, were always exposed to a recurrent Federal presence. The army did not have to establish a permanent occupation of the entire countryside; instead, consistent incursions confirmed that the Union army did, at least unofficially, control large swaths of Confederate territory. Yet, guerrillas and irregular bands swarmed this "no-man's-land," challenging Federal supremacy and reminding Union soldiers of their precarious, isolated positions. Thus, occupation authorities had to deal carefully with all of the civilians in their midst, never fully confident about who represented a potential threat.[41]

Union occupation authorities sought, above all else, to establish loyalty, to pacify the white southern populace, and to eradicate secessionist sentiment. These aims proved immensely difficult. At first, army commanders punished their troops for unruly behavior and plundering, believing that such displays of good faith would convince white southerners that they did not live under the thumb of military tyrants. This approach, however, failed, undermined by suspicions that local whites secretly aided or harbored guerrillas or vocally endorsed the Confederacy. It became clear that the occupied, in many cases, flouted the occupiers' attempts at appeasement. Thus, when Union patrols departed garrisons and entered the unstable "no-man's-land," they took the war directly to the people. Indeed, the only potential enemy in the immediate area very well may have been civilians.[42]

To punish these suspected rebels, Union raids focused on arrests, confiscation of private property, commandeering of livestock and food, and, sometimes, burning of homes and towns. The Union's armies of occupation had to display their authority, even in the face of persistent defiance. From Nashville, Major General William S. Rosecrans announced in late 1862 the limits of civilian-military relations. All loyal citizens who abstained from any interference with the occupation were granted the full privileges and protections of citizenship, enforced by the army. "Those who are hostile to our Government," however, "repudiating its Constitution and laws, have no rights under them.... The only laws to which they can appeal and which we are bound to observe toward them are the laws of war and the dictates of humanity." Rosecrans characterized guerrillas, and even those suspected of moderately supporting irregular warfare, as "pirates and robbers." Such individuals "are entitled to no rights," characterized instead as lawless enemy combatants.[43]

Such dicta were common by late 1862 and early 1863, outlining the broad and quickly evolving edicts of Federal occupation policy. Army commanders learned not to waste time trying to determine which white southerners might be loyal. Instead, while on expeditions and raids, soldiers were instructed and willingly carried out policies of confiscation and foraging that depleted the countryside of goods, produce, and property. Yet the Union's developing hard war policy was also somewhat restricted and pragmatic. Historian Mark Grimsley, who authored the definitive work on the limits of hard war, suggests that much of the destruction occasioned by occupying armies "had occurred in retaliation, deserved or otherwise, for bushwhacking and other partisan incidents." The growing expanse of a destructive war, he argues, functioned as "a combination of strategic insight[s] and practical circumstances," directed at shattering the white South's spirit. Union armies, therefore, sought to break the Confederacy's ability to wage war, directing their power against property and infrastructure, rather than arbitrary, callous punishment against civilians.[44]

William T. Sherman famously embodied the essence of the Union's shift to hard war, writing "we cannot change the hearts of those people of the South, but we can make war so terrible that they will realize the fact that, however brave and gallant and devoted to their country, still they are mortal and should exhaust all peaceful remedies before they fly to war." He indeed understood that the war, by virtue of indefinite occupation, was not merely a conflict waged by opposing armies on distant fields of battle. The US military must "make old and young, rich and poor, feel the hard hand of war." If the theory of military occupation, Sherman implied, functioned as the direct regulation of civilians' behavior and conduct, then its application must be fluid enough to meet the demands of unforeseen circumstances. Thus, the hard war occupation policy exemplified a broad combination of ideological, strategic, and political imperatives, aimed at dislodging white southerners' faith in secession, dismantling their ability to carry out war, and dissuading their dogmatic attachments to the Confederacy.[45]

Although he sometimes questioned the concept of garrisoning, Sherman begrudgingly accepted its necessity, believing that fortified outposts laid the initial foundation for hard war. If Union armies could not establish a fixed presence in the Confederacy, they could not fan out across the countryside, taking the war to rebel civilians. Indeed, the combination of garrisoning and raiding widened the scope of wartime occupation, making it both a stationary and active process. This was a brilliant tactic and one that ultimately worked. Increasing numbers of white southerners felt the presence of Federal occupation, even if they did not live in occupied garrisons. The integration of garrisoning and mobile occupation placated Winfield Scott's early fears of permanently occupying every inch of Confederate territory. And they worked, on a broader level, to meet unforeseen wartime crises. In its most basic form, military occupation sought to reshape white southern opinion and to reestablish loyalty to the Union. When this proved immensely difficult, and the US armies' need to feed themselves grew desperate, taking the war directly to white southerners seemed to be a reasonable alternative.[46]

Hard war was not total war. Union armies did not blur the lines between soldier and civilian and target the latter as they did the former. Active murdering of civilians and brutalizing their bodies did not characterize the United States' approach to wartime occupation. Although soldiers oftentimes burned private homes, pillaged property, and stole goods, commanders punished their men accordingly, demanding that they abide by a code of civilized conduct. The Civil War was not a European war of occupation in which merciless and unrelenting violence was applied arbitrarily to civilians. Nor did Union army commanders carve the Confederacy into military colonies, erasing borders and dislocating residents. The entire purpose of wartime occupation was to achieve reunion, restoring the rebellious states to their original positions within the nation.[47]

Wartime military occupation, therefore, served multiple purposes: reintroducing Federal authority in the South; establishing loyalty among the populace; reconstructing secessionist state governments; pacifying a hostile countryside; providing lines of communication and logistics for the principal field armies; and carrying out the policy of emancipation, which Abraham Lincoln added as a war aim in 1863. Not one of these goals could be secured if Union armies capriciously scorched the South, murdered disloyal civilians, or created permanent colonies in which all citizens' rights were forever erased. The Union's war of occupation had a fundamental rationale, guided by specific policies and processes. And while it took four long years, the garrisoning of the Confederacy, combined with battlefield victories, forced Confederates to surrender.[48]

Although successful, wartime occupation faced an ironic challenge: the white volunteers in the ranks. The men first responsible for garrisoning and occupying the wartime South came to be some of the occupation strategy's loudest critics. United States troops who had rushed to defend the flag encountered a host of ideological and cultural challenges that shocked their sensibilities and attachment to the cause. Indeed, the greatest challenge to the Union's war of occupation was its perceived challenge to the citizen-soldier ideal. Both the tangible realities and the imagined symbolism of occupying the wartime South revealed to US volunteers that they served in a domestic army tasked with regulating civilians, implementing social change, and exerting authoritative martial influence far from the central theaters of combat. Military occupation during the American Civil War induced great cultural transformations, not the least of which directly altered the very soldiers who populated the garrisons' ranks.

3 | Union Soldiers and the Symbol of a Standing Army of Occupation

Frank Peck enlisted in the Twelfth Connecticut Volunteers in late 1861 and participated in Major General Benjamin F. Butler's celebrated expedition to capture New Orleans. Merely a few days prior to the city's capitulation in late April and early May 1862, Peck wrote his mother and asked, "Do you think any of us are sorry we enlisted? I suspect even you will be reconciled to the fact that you have been deprived of my valuable society for the space of two long months by the result that has been accomplished." Peck had good reason to feel confident, sensing that his service helped occasion the surrender of the Confederacy's largest city. He even mentioned that "I am blessed in my honorable position" within New Orleans. "Our army is a god send to shop keepers and poor people, to the first in giving them customers . . . and to the last in furnishing much employment to those willing to work."[1]

Peck's triumphal attitude changed after a month of service in the Crescent City. He acknowledged that "our life has been very monotonous," particularly once civilian order was restored and local government reinstated under the military's supervision. By the early fall of 1862 he distinguished between his time in New Orleans and what he called "active service," worrying about "our plans and my own hopes and ambitions." Interactions with antagonistic civilians further made Peck ambivalent about the army's capacity to maintain order and stability in the hostile city. "You cant feel as we do," he admitted, "who have for six months been in the midst of people who would rejoice to see every one of us in the bottom of the sea, and who are merely conquered [but] not converted."[2]

Rather than policing restive civilians and managing municipal affairs, Peck yearned to be in a grand battle, to prove himself as a man and to contribute to the national war effort. However, "in the service here I suppose we dont talk half so much about the war as before we enlisted," and "we seldom get excited at any news. . . . Every mans thoughts are occupied with the minutiae of his duties." Although his unit ventured periodically on expeditions into the nearby Lafourche and Teche countryside, Peck remained unimpressed with his duties at New Orleans. Finally, in the autumn of 1862, as his unit dug ditches near the city, Peck spoke for his comrades who claimed this "isnt what I enlisted for." With the exception of a minor foray into Texas in September 1863, Peck and the Twelfth Connecticut remained positioned in southern Louisiana through the spring of 1864. Then they were transferred to Virginia, where Peck finally experienced battle. He was killed leading a charge at the Battle of Chaffin's Farm in September 1864.[3]

Frank Peck's hopes and fears echoed those of other US volunteers during the Civil War who struggled to comprehend their roles as citizen-soldiers in zones of military occupation. Rather than battling their enemies on distant battlefields, some soldiers were assigned the undesirable tasks of policing white and black southerners, garrisoning towns that seemed foreign and strange, laboring in monotonous conditions, and standing idly by as the war exploded around them. The dynamics of military occupation seemed a far cry from the glorious war Union soldiers had thought they were entering. Disillusionment, depressed morale, and the miserable conditions of war influenced nearly every Civil War soldier periodically throughout the conflict. Yet occupation, exemplified by Peck's service in New Orleans, presented a unique blend of trials that forced occupying soldiers to question their preconceived assumptions about the American military tradition.[4]

Peck's expression of unfulfilled martial expectations centered on his role as a volunteer in a Union army of occupation. As an occupier serving in a permanent garrison, he felt alienated not only from the war but also from the citizen-soldier ideal. According to volunteers like Peck, the Union army was not merely a wartime institution. It was also a symbolic reflection of the nation's exceptional values, culture, and republican disposition, personified by the citizens who filled the ranks. The civic virtue intimately attached to wartime military service confirmed one's citizenship and patriotism as volunteers engaged the nation's enemies in formal battle. Ultimately, men expected that their duty would be quick and temporary, resembling nothing of a static, private profession.[5]

For Peck, though, the opposite seemed true. As he described in December 1862, "Do you know what it means to march through and occupy an enemy's country[?] It means . . . to take all the chickens geese and turkeys as you march. To pick every horse you meet, to clear every barn & stable. . . . Frighten the people from their houses to the back country by the stories of your ravages sent on before you, impress every thing that goes on wheels, fill your pockets with letters at every halting place for your amusement till you stop again."

Although he admitted that "the mental and moral growth you are conscious of as you advance is wonderful," Peck's comments framed a broader wartime discourse articulated by Union soldiers who came to believe that occupation fundamentally altered the nation's military customs.[6]

The principal features of domestic occupation—regulating both passive and hostile civilian enemies, administering conquered territory through martial law and fortified garrisons, and transforming society through emancipation—mandated that soldiers act in a military capacity that they viewed with great suspicion. Union soldiers like Peck who served behind the lines came to associate Civil War armies of occupation with a de facto standing army that governed southern civilians, destabilized social conditions, and sought to reshape the South at the point of a bayonet. Antebellum Americans had long feared standing armies, believing they held the potential to be transformed into political institutions, bending civilians to the dictates of military rule and displaying loyalty only to their own interests.[7]

And herein lay the true source of Frank Peck's ambivalence. Occupation thrust citizen-soldiers into uncharted territory in which they used military means to effect civil and structural change in their own nation, even during the midst of rebellion and civil war. Reared in the republican tradition, the occupiers feared their service within the wartime Confederacy had transformed their identities from volunteers to arbiters of military governance who wielded professional, bureaucratic power against those who were after all their fellow citizens, no matter how traitorous and disloyal these were. Volunteerism no longer seemed quick, temporary, and defined by facing the nation's enemies on distant battlefields. It now also meant active invasions into American lands; it meant laboring behind the lines within garrisoned towns; it meant employing the army as a tool of emancipation and social change; it meant administering martial law and regulating civilian behavior; and it ultimately meant waging a war of domestic occupation in which the army governed citizens and private property. The nation's defenders envisioned themselves as a force of military compulsion, which held both symbolic and tangible implications. To preserve the Union through occupation thus meant exercising unprecedented wartime powers that challenged the very principles that northern men had volunteered to defend.[8]

* * *

Military occupation transformed volunteer soldiers into bands of police tasked with providing a semblance of order in garrisoned communities. The occupiers were expected to act as a stabilizing presence to protect private property and ensure peace among civilians and Union military personnel. "Our duty is to 'clean out' disreputable places, to see that soldiers in town are not absent from their regiments without leave, and to attend to moral publicans generally," explained Zenas T. Haines, a private in the Forty-fourth Massachusetts Volunteers, from his post in North Carolina. "A detail of forty men from our regiment was sent into town on provost guard," wrote Alexander Downing of the Eleventh Iowa Volunteers stationed in Vicksburg. "Our orders were to arrest all citizens and soldiers found upon the streets without passes . . . and take them before the [provost marshal] for investigation and punishment."[9]

In their capacity as soldiers, Haines and Downing found it difficult to adopt and enact roles that they considered more suited to civilian actors. In their minds, policing conjured images of local civilian law enforcement, which was held in check by the restraints of civil law. However, the concept of martial police inverted the assumptions of citizen-soldiering. "Some objection is made to the use of the word 'police,' as descriptive of our duties," Haines wrote. "I have used it in the civil and not the military sense of the word." Downing implied that policing white citizens "is not a very pleasant duty, this thing of stopping everyone on the street and requiring him to give an account of himself."[10]

The civil practice of policing and the tradition of citizen-soldiering came together in the Union's war of occupation, forcing volunteers to play both roles. Zenas Haines described policing as "severe, irksome, and often abhorrent. I am rather glad that our present reputation as policemen is not to be the measure of our characters as soldiers." Other troops considered governing American citizens on American soil to challenge their contracts as volunteers. "It is a hard place for the soldier," wrote George Henry Bates, who served in the Nineteenth Connecticut stationed in Arlington, Virginia, because "we act the part of Police," while George O. Jewett, of the Seventeenth Massachusetts, observed from New Bern, North Carolina, "We are the same as police at home." James Kendall Hosmer, an officer in the Fifty-second Massachusetts, derided "the ignoble duty of petty policemen,—pick up the little boys who will sing 'The bonnie blue flag' in the streets, and the naughty ladies who stick out their tongues at the soldiers."[11]

The experience of policing occupied garrisons forced Union soldiers to re-construct the meaning of enemy combatants. While they initially expected the great mass of white southerners (not the aristocratic planters) to greet them with open arms, the Yankees instead arrived to find a populace either vaguely suspicious of their presence or openly aggressive and antagonistic. Soldiers accordingly questioned precisely how civilian enemies should be treated. The traditional battlefield code—kill or be killed—did not apply here. Plus, many potential enemies were women and children, traditional noncombatants, whom soldiers simply could not attack. Instead, soldiers were forced to walk the tightrope of negotiation and martial authority.[12]

As James Hosmer indicated, one of the clearest manifestations of this confusion involved the image of "the southern belle." White southern women, and the peculiar manner in which they engaged Yankee soldiers, forced the Union occupiers to grapple with the limitations of governing civilian enemies, while also navigating apparently inverted gender roles. The major Civil War armies operated generally within an arena of mutually accepted masculine codes, largely due to their remoteness and independence from civilian com-munities. Soldiers in each army agreed that they, as men, perpetuated killing as a means to decide armed conflict. Zones of occupation upset this acknowl-edged truth. The perceived enemies within garrisoned communities or the occupied frontier were not always uniformed Confederate men, but instead unarmed women. This presented a unique challenge for northern volunteers trying to live by the civilized rules of war and the respectability governing gender relations.[13]

Upon meeting Federal soldiers, white southern women sometimes raised their skirts, tossed insults and gibes, blatantly paraded Confederate flag pins or bonnets, and, in New Orleans, emptied chamber pots atop the occupiers' heads. "The girls flirt and stick up their noses at us and the women carry a very haughty air," wrote William T. Shepherd, an artilleryman stationed in Memphis. Women also acted as spies and secretly smuggled medicine and intelligence through the lines. In some instances, they even spat in the faces of Yankee troops. Historians have superbly documented the reasons for such behavior, concluding that white women attempted to combat the mil-itaristic encroachments on their private lives and spaces. The literature on Confederate women has been well documented, yet coverage of the Union soldier's understanding of gender relations under occupation is somewhat ambiguous.[14]

Over the course of the occupation experience, Union troops became markedly disgusted at the verbal abuses hurled by local women. "It is decidedly a secesh town," remarked John Vreeland about Murfreesboro, Tennessee, "shown in a thousand different ways, especially by the women, who are as insulting as possible the immunities of their sex saving them from any molestation." Vreeland sought to treat women as combatants in military zones, yet their identities as noncombatants prevented other Union soldiers from using the martial methods usually deployed to deal with enemies. Instead, they were forced to show restraint, which infuriated their martial temperament. In return, women oftentimes accused the occupiers of cowardice for failing to combat their sneers and taunts.[15]

Union soldiers' attempts to properly confront the hostility expressed by supposedly genteel southern women only resulted in further confusion. The clash of gender cultures produced by wartime occupation shocked Yankee men, who had been reared in a society that painted a radically different picture of women. The so-called "cult of domesticity" informed presumptions of a northern woman's behavior and conduct, framing her role both in the home and in public. Women, this cultural ideal held, were reserved and passive, yet also fiercely moral, consenting to standards of civility and ethics. Northern authors, pamphleteers, and lecturers arranged the region's entire gender balance according to these assumptions. Union troops were undoubtedly exposed to such antebellum concepts, which they likely carried with them into the ranks. Thus the white southern women with whom Yankee soldiers interacted shocked northern sensibilities. "Its enough to make a man disgusted with the sex to see them spare them talk," a Michigan officer wrote from Tennessee. "I suppose they are human or will be in some far distant era in some other sphere." Expecting to encounter the refined and polite southern belle celebrated in popular culture, citizen-soldiers instead often confronted uncouth, antagonistic, and coarse women who exposed northern men's assumptions about nineteenth-century gender dynamics.[16]

Gender relations in occupied communities thus remained ambivalent. One soldier characterized women in Baton Rouge as "for the most part almost violent, threatening to spit in the faces of union officers. . . . Such unsexing was hardly ever before in any cause or country so marked and so universal." Iowan Minos Miller, whose unit occupied Memphis during the winter of 1862, was much more explicit. Miller explained to his mother that "the citizens looked daggers" at the Union soldiers as they marched down a street. "The ladies on

the side walks claped their hands and laughed [at us] but they got their deli-
cacy shocked, if they had any" when one of the Iowa soldiers chastised a young
boy who praised Jefferson Davis. "Go to h——l you d——m little rebble sone of a
b——h," the soldier declared. "If it had been a man," Miller concluded, "he would
have been shot down quicker than lightning." And although Charles G. Blake
of the Thirty-fourth Massachusetts enjoyed the "sight of their pretty selves
as they pass our camp," at Harpers Ferry, Virginia, "you ought to hear [local
women] talk when we search their homes for arms &c. If some of their prayers
should be answered I fear that there is little hope for we poor 34th boys."[17]

Women's purposely antagonistic behavior shaped the evolution of Federal
policies and, more important, shaped the way occupiers negotiated *their own*
identities, both as soldiers and as men. The infamous episodes surrounding
Benjamin F. Butler's occupation of New Orleans offer an ideal example. From
the moment the Yankees landed in the Crescent City, local women mocked
and insulted the soldiers, pushing some troops into outright anger. As one officer walked to church, he passed two ladies on the street and moved to let them
pass. However, as he did so, one woman stopped directly in front of him and
spat in his face. Although angry, the soldier did not know how to respond, except to "take his kerchief and clean his face." He then went to see Butler about
the matter. One of the general's staff asked, "Why didn't you do something?"
"What could I do," responded the abused soldier, "to two women?" "Well," the
staffer suggested, "you ought to have taken your revolver and shot the first *he*
rebel you met." The officer finally admitted to Butler, "General, I can't stand
this. This isn't the first time this thing has been attempted towards me, but
this is the first time it has been accomplished. I want to go home. I came here
to fight the enemies of the country, not to be insulted and disgusted."[18]

Occupation soldiers viewed southern women's resistance as a form of violent defiance, exposing the limits of Yankee power. Women, the soldiers understood from their formative years in the North, were not supposed to exhibit
uncontrolled and passionate boldness, especially in matters of politics or civil
affairs. Yet Confederate women seemed to test this entire assumption, pushing the occupiers to reconcile the concepts of true womanhood *and* enemy
combatants. The soldiers sensed, as one observer wrote, that the rebellion had
unleashed the "furies of women . . . who unsexed themselves to prove their
scorn of 'the Yankees.'" Cyrus Boyd, of the Fifteenth Iowa Volunteers, related
an incident from Holly Springs, Mississippi, in which a woman pled for protection of her property and children. "I told her not to fear as no man would

disturb her," Boyd explained. "This evening this *same* woman was arrested for *shooting* one of our men who was on guard. . . . She cowardly shot him although he was guarding her property." Women, therefore, were no longer *women;* they were combatants, hostile enemies of the Federal government who threatened occupying troops, demonstrated vicious enthusiasm for the southern nation, and defied US authority.[19]

These various exchanges revealed the presence of a gender identity crisis within zones of occupation. Union soldiers expected to engage and kill their enemies. They proved this on the battlefield and willingly extended the definition to encompass civilians who practiced guerrilla warfare. Yet perpetrators of these acts were white southern men, and Yankee occupiers struggled with the implications of including women within the combatant paradigm. Southern women understood precisely the limits of this problem, and slowly, yet consciously, they pushed the occupiers to decide what constituted a war zone and who participated within its realm. Women's explicit protest of military occupation tested the existing social order, upending Union soldiers' expectations of complete military victory by rejecting traditionally accepted notions of defeat. The occupiers could not relish the satisfaction of total triumph because a defiant enemy still remained. Yet this enemy, because she was a woman, could not be properly combated.[20]

* * *

The experiences of carrying out the functions of military police and engaging white southern women suggested to citizen-soldiers that they had become a professional arm of the state. Participation in a standing army of occupation that governed American citizens prompted soldiers to question the long-term implications of domestic military occupation. As his unit prepared for a seven-month garrisoning of Hilton Head, South Carolina, Charles Francis Adams, Jr., wrote in July 1862, "If we succeed in our attempt at subjugation, I see only an immense territory and a savage and ignorant populace to be held down by force, the enigma of slavery to be settled by us somehow, and, most dangerous of all, a spirit of blind, revengeful fanaticism in the North." Adams understood full well that the Confederacy must be defeated in order to preserve the Union, yet he also understood that both wartime and peacetime occupation held serious consequences that would strain the limits of the American tradition. Military occupation, he concluded, "will bankrupt the nation, jeopard all liberty by immense standing armies, debauch the morality of the nation by war, and undermine all our republican foundations to the effect of the immediate destruction of [the Confederacy and its institutions]."[21]

Even professional soldiers, such as Brigadier General Thomas Williams, a veteran of the Old Army and the first occupation commander of Baton Rouge in 1862, sensed the changing nature of American warfare. As an occupier, he explained to his wife, "I'm not only a military commander, but necessarily an administrator of civil affairs, judge, court and jury." As he waded through complicated property claims, financial cases, and the murky boundaries of white southern loyalty, Williams admitted that he never anticipated the "whirl of solicitation, remonstrance and enquiry" required by occupation. Indeed, like the volunteers who defined their military identities according to their civil responsibilities, Williams described his military role as "the servant of the public." In light of his career as a professional officer, the static, bureaucratic demands of Williams's service during the Civil War challenged his assumptions about the appropriate wartime role of the army.[22]

Adams and Williams believed that domestic occupation dangerously linked the army with the state's civil functions. Their apprehensions suggested that the national military tradition had been irrevocably altered, confirming long-held American fears of permanent, standing military establishments. None other than William T. Sherman, one of the Union's great practitioners of occupation policy, who expanded the wartime scope of civilian-military relations, explained how the Civil War revealed a unique moment in the nation's martial heritage. "In Europe whence we derive our principles of war," he explained, "wars are between kings and rulers through hired armies, and not between peoples." Although Sherman endorsed a policy of "directed severity" against civilians who harbored a violent secessionist ideology, his characterization spoke to the ambivalence of men like Adams and Williams, who understood that wars of occupation were indeed "between peoples."[23]

The Civil War mandated that one body of citizen-volunteers subdue and govern another party of citizens, both of whom shared common national bonds. Despite their disgust with rebellious white southerners who defied Federal authority, the occupiers continued to refer to their conquered foes as "citizens," a sacred concept to nineteenth-century Americans who distrusted the unbending power of martial law. Even while Union troops sought the Confederacy's destruction, they could not escape the contradictions of their fellow white Americans being governed by a homegrown military. "Now my quarters are in a house," wrote Lieutenant C. M. Duren from Jacksonville, Florida. "What should you think Father, if a large Army were to come along through Bangor [Maine]—and our Company of noisy soldiers—or a Regt—should take up Quarters in your *Yard*—and the officers should take up quarters in your house[.] It is awfull—War is." Private Clement Abner Boughton, of the Twelfth Wisconsin, agreed, writing from occupied Natchez, Mississippi, "I dont think I should like to be a citizen and [be] invaded by an enemy. Martial law does not a gree with [a] free people."[24]

That their occupied enemies were "a free people" influenced northern soldiers' sense that wartime occupation destabilized society, in large part because of the army's disruptive managerial role in the wartime South. Although occupation purported to maintain stability in the face of mounting chaos, some Union troops attributed restive civilian behavior to the military's presence. George H. Cadman, a private in the Thirty-ninth Ohio, ascribed the rise in social volatility to the presence of a standing army. He related a series of discouraging events from Memphis that exposed his ambivalence about the successes of military occupation. "The citizens do not like us at all," he wrote in June 1863. Several hundred residents, Cadman explained, had petitioned Stephen A. Hurlbut, the commanding general at Memphis, to remove the city's occupying force, "not because of bad conduct, but because we were too strict in the performance of our duty."[25]

Hurlbut denied the request, leading to further unrest between the occupiers and civilians. "There is very little Union feeling in Memphis," Cadman continued. "Nothing but the bayonet keeps it loyal." Even though he acknowledged a need for strict regulation of civilian behavior, he also documented widespread resistance among white southerners. Local citizens, he explained, defied oaths of allegiance and "others turn[ed] up their noses as if the very air the Yankees breathed was poisonous." Cadman described how one woman became so drunk and insulting, picket guards were forced to tie her to a tree until she became sober. "God forbid," he told his wife, "that you should ever live in a country subject to military rule."[26]

Cadman's disillusionment stemmed from a growing anxiety about the inability of military rule to completely pacify and change the ideologies of a conquered people. The republican tradition had long taught that standing armies wielded unbridled power, yet what if even that authority was not enough to quell the rebellious spirit of the Confederacy? Union soldiers suggested that concentrated martial authority generated deep levels of civilian resentment, which could devolve into destabilizing violence and social chaos. "The citizens look at you with a malignant scorn and hatred as you pass along the streets," Michigander David Millspaugh wrote in 1863 from Lexington, Kentucky. They "are very indignant if you question their loyalty and yet they make the state a rendezvous for the lowest and meanest of all creation traitors." George H. Davis, a soldier in the Twenty-sixth Massachusetts, described that "we came very near having a Riot" with civilians in Baton Rouge. "The Citizens turned out to the tune of 20 thousand," he wrote, and "there was quite a Rush with our Boys to get the Secesh flags they waved." Ultimately, Davis's regiment restored order, and the regiment remained on guard throughout the evening.[27]

While some soldiers commented on the stubbornly hostile civilian response to the power of occupying armies, others noticed that some of their fellow volunteers exploited their martial authority in occupied zones. They expressed great unease as their comrades destroyed property, confiscated civilian goods, and exacted vengeance on the southern landscape. Ultimately, Union occupation policy would prescribe such "hard war" measures for use against the Confederacy. While these methods were endorsed by many northern soldiers, others considered such behavior a problematic outgrowth of occupying armies. If standing armies displayed loyalty only to their own interests, this reasoning held, soldiers were corrupted into something other than virtuous volunteers. Benjamin C. Lincoln, who served in the Thirty-ninth Massachusetts, wrote from Poolesville, Maryland, that "the men are wild and lawless [and] are constantly committing depredations on property." They took boots, food, tobacco, "and other stuff much of which was no use to any of the soldiers." Lincoln did not endorse this theft because "I think private property should be respected. Undoubtedly many of the inhabitants are disloyal, but if they are to be deprived of their property, let their disloyalty be proud and their goods legally confiscated."[28]

James W. Denver, a brigadier general of volunteers stationed near Corinth, Mississippi, echoed Lincoln, describing the intellectual and cultural challenges of serving as a volunteer in a standing army. When embarking on expeditions into the countryside, the troops "seem to be possessed with the idea that in order to carry on war men must throw aside civilization and become savages," Denver explained. "We have had some most heart-rending cases, and I do not see how men claiming to be enlightened and educated do such things." Acknowledging that occupation soldiers had become devoid of republican restraint and virtue, Denver described how his troops engaged civilians, destroyed private property, and commandeered livestock. Noticeably worried by these "lawless acts," Denver believed that "it will not be long before the soldier will be sunk in the cowardly plunderer—for men loaded with plunder are always cowards." The more soldiers sought "to sweep the country as with the besom of destruction," he warned, the more they would be detached from the moral behavior required by the citizen-soldier ideal.[29]

Lincoln's and Denver's disquietude arose from a growing suspicion that occupying armies destabilized society, blurring the lines between order and chaos, volunteer and mercenary. Even when acts of destruction were sanctioned, soldiers struggled to reconcile the corrosive nature of occupation with the constraints of national military custom. Preservation of the Union necessitated not only the perpetuation of republican government but also the moral conditions of republican society. Yet Lincoln and Denver suggested that men who entered service as virtuous citizen-soldiers could become corrupted through occupation and their tangled interactions with white southerners. A soldier in the Forty-seventh Indiana, Samuel Kerr, related how his regiment burned an Arkansas town suspected of harboring guerrillas. "It was a sorrowfull sight for me to behold sutch nice Property Burnt," he admitted, commenting on the destruction of furniture, books, carpet. "You may well imagin," he wrote, "how the [residents] felt to see all there property in flames."[30]

Kerr's sentiments did not reflect a wavering commitment to the war effort, nor did he offer sympathy for Confederates. Instead, he revealed *his* reverence for private property, a central staple of republican liberty. Kerr's statement resonated alongside the attitudes of countless Union soldiers who instinctively understood the effects of military power, martial law, and confiscation of property. It was not difficult for these men to envision their own communities at home, also constructed on the basis of private property and civil law, restive and rebellious under the heavy hand of occupying forces. Despite their pronounced cultural differences, a standing army of occupation threatened to undermine the ideological commitment to American republicanism that both North and South held dear.[31]

* * *

For Union soldiers who served behind the lines, the problem of a standing army of occupation extended well beyond interactions with white southerners. Occupation also brought northern volunteers into close proximity with slavery and African Americans. Despite early civil and military policies that prohibited slavery's destruction, the South's premier social and economic institution deteriorated through a lengthy war of invasion and occupation, enslaved southerners' unswerving quest for freedom, and white soldiers' growing commitment to emancipation in a war for Union. Federal armies offered refuge to African Americans who actively pursued freedom, undermining the Confederacy by enforcing emancipation as a military tool in the quest for national preservation.[32]

Soldiers in the ranks helped enact the policy and processes of military emancipation. Zenas T. Haines, who served in the Forty-fourth Massachusetts Volunteers, declared that "there is likely one item of compensation to the Government for holding these posts upon the enemy's soil. It is, indeed, due to the freedmen that we provide these harbors of refuge for those who escape from the rebel lines." New Yorker William H. Root agreed, writing from Bayou Boeuf, Louisiana, "the negroes are now free according to the proclamation," but "their freedom here is conditional with the stay of our troops in this portion of the country." Despite an exhausting raid near New Bern, North Carolina, Charles Hill, of the Fifth Massachusetts, cited the army as the central institution in undermining slavery, "my hatred [of which] has not been lessened by this expedition," he wrote. "If it (the expedition) has not been fruitful in any other direction it has given freedom to a good number of slaves and that is worth something."[33]

Even as these volunteers supported emancipation as a pragmatic means to assist the war effort, other Union soldiers questioned the rapidity with which military occupation brought social dislocation and destabilization to the war-torn South. While detesting the white southern "slave power," believing it spawned an unscrupulous, oligarchic, and aristocratic ruling class, various soldiers worried that the combination of rebellion, invasion, occupation, and emancipation—with a powerful army responding to and directing the course of each—collapsed order and stability. Even as Union armies helped bring about freedom, occupiers questioned what came in the wake of black liberation, sensing that military emancipation thrust freedom onto a people presumably unprepared for the standards of white American liberty.[34]

Part of the problem stemmed from Union soldiers' complex racial worldviews. It is difficult, if not impossible, to ascribe a universal northern posture toward African Americans, yet as historian Reid Mitchell writes, "if there was one attitude, it was an ambivalence compounded of pity, affection, disgust, and hatred." While Union soldiers perceived African Americans through a variegated lens, two constants appeared in their assessments of black southerners: ubiquity and difference. Andrew H. Minnick, of the Sixty-ninth Indiana Volunteers, described the "Nigroes coming through [Memphis] this morning [who were] as thick as bees and as black as tar." The occupiers associated the South with teeming throngs of enslaved peoples who embodied the region's distinct character. "Negroes crowd in swarms to our lines," one soldier wrote from the Atlantic coast, while another described the "odd race of people" who populated Louisiana. Common soldiers, such as New Yorker William H. Nichols, looked upon black southerners with incredulity. "We passed through a contraband camp," he described, "and darkeys of every age, color, and sex flocked to the road to behold us pass. A more varried set of beings I have never before seen."[35]

While negotiating the massive numbers of freedpeople who fled to Union lines, these same Union soldiers also considered armies of occupation to have occasioned an abrupt freedom. Because they had long enjoyed the fruits of republican liberty and democratic privilege, the occupiers struggled to interpret how a formerly enslaved people responded to freedom, the conditions of which had been created by an active army at the vanguard of social change. Two soldiers who served in Louisiana implied that the apparent destabilization caused by occupying armies created vacuums in which freedpeople abused their freedom rather than engaged in a thoughtful process of self-improvement and industry. "They don't care," Lawrence Van Alstyne, an officer in the Ninetieth USCT, wrote in October 1863 in Brashear City. "Someone has always thought for them and will have to think for them for some time to come." Edward Lewis Sturtevant claimed that freedpeople near New Orleans "can hardly be made to work, need strict watch to prevent from stealing. Think liberty means liberty to be idle."[36]

Slavery threatened the core of American exceptionalism, yet so too, Charles Francis Adams, Jr., argued, did emancipation springing from such a sudden, immediate military fashion. A volunteer officer in the First Massachusetts Cavalry, Adams believed black freedom to be long overdue, especially since slavery had sparked the terrible war in which the nation was engaged. "Slavery may perish and no one regret it," he wrote from the Union-occupied South Carolina Sea Islands in April 1862, "but what is to become of the unfortunate African?" Although he endorsed abolition, Adams was unsure how black southerners would become integrated into a white republic. "They are all slavish," he wrote of the freedpeople, "and all that the word slavish implies. They will lie and cheat and steal; they are hypocritical and cunning; they are not brave and they are not fierce." Adams did not blame African Americans for their purportedly depraved characters: "these qualities the white man took out of them generations ago, and in taking them deprived the African of the capacity for freedom."[37]

White northerners, he explained, had long been imbued in the cultures of republicanism, material progress, free labor, and individual liberty; recently enslaved peoples lacked such formative exposure. "My views of the future of those I see about me here are not therefore encouraging," he acknowledged. Adams could not conceive how African Americans might transition from the backward world of slave-based agriculture into a progressive, industrial setting that required self-initiative and economic training. "Will they be educated and encouraged and cared for," he asked, "or will they be challenged to compete in the race, or go to the wall, and finally be swept away as a useless rubbish?"[38]

For Adams, preserving the Union through occupation and emancipation created a paradox. The elimination of slavery was crucial to upholding a true democracy built on egalitarian free-labor. Yet the very people who benefited most from emancipation—African Americans—were presumed unfit for and were even thought to threaten the institutions that defined American uniqueness, especially when that freedom had been shaped so suddenly by the US Army. The experience of occupying the South instilled within Adams a sense that his nation was rapidly changing. He wanted to preserve American republicanism, but a standing army of occupation had created a new nation entirely, leaving Adams uneasy about the massive social transformation wrought by the Union army's occupying presence in the South. Even as he witnessed the fruits of emancipation, he feared that such sweeping change would, in the end, only create more instability and uncertainty.

* * *

Occupying the Confederate South elicited a host of near-irreconcilable contradictions and ironies. Union soldiers celebrated the collapse of slavery, welcomed the destruction of the region's aristocracy, and wielded martial authority against rebellious traitors. Yet many approached their roles as occupiers with apprehension, realizing with discomfort that they had destabilized large swaths of American society, governed fellow citizens as part of a standing army, and occasioned unprecedented social change. Ironically, the experiences of occupation also convinced myriad soldiers that they were not actively contributing to the war effort, deprived from engaging in the principal theaters in which the war would be settled. The sheer monotony and confusion of occupation fostered a gloomy and uninspiring view of republican virtue, which threatened Union soldiers' identities as volunteers. They had enlisted to fight their nation's battles; instead they struggled to navigate the disillusionment of life in occupied garrisons. Thus, they drew clear distinctions between standing armies and campaigning armies, a critique which exposed the unfamiliar place of occupation in the American military tradition.[39]

In July 1862, a discontented John Beatty, who served in the Third Ohio Volunteers, described the static culture of Union military occupation in Tennessee. "Our forces are holding the great scope of country between Memphis and Bridgeport," he wrote, "guarding bridges, railroads, and towns, frittering away the strength of a great army, and wasting our men." Although hundreds of soldiers were placed in strategic positions to exert Federal authority and to stem the tide of guerrilla violence, Beatty scoffed at the stated purpose of wartime occupation. "The climate, and the insane effort to garrison the whole country, consumes our troops," he grumbled, "and we make no progress. May the good Lord be with us, and deliver us from idleness and imbecility." Pleading for liberation from the citizen-soldier's despairing role as an occupier, Beatty called for "common sense[,] which plain people use in the management of their business affairs[,] to the illustrious generals who have our armies in hand!" As US armies spread throughout the Confederacy, erecting fortified garrisons in their wake—"we put down from fifty to one hundred [soldiers], here and there," he commented—growing numbers of troops like John Beatty were required to govern the conquered regions.[40]

Seymour D. Thompson, of the Third Iowa Volunteers, echoed Beatty's critique. Assigned in 1861 to pacify Missouri, his unit was transferred later to Tennessee, where it participated in the battles of Shiloh and Corinth. Over the next two years, Thompson and his fellow soldiers guarded railroads and garrisoned major towns and cities throughout Tennessee and Mississippi. "What had we done to merit less than these comrades of ours?" he recalled. "Had we failed our country in the hour of trial? Had we done so little, suffered so little, and complained so much?" Thompson acknowledged that men in the Third Iowa, as well as other units occupying the region, "read glowing accounts" of distant battles. However, "we almost ceased to be proud of it ourselves.

A soldier would rather die than be behind in honor," he admitted. Thompson did not merely wish to secure honor and battlefield glory for himself and his unit; he also feared that the stagnant tasks of occupying and securing territory dishonored the sacrifices and deaths endured by countless other Union soldiers on distant battlefields. "We began to be ashamed of ourselves," he concluded. "We would have blushed to look our friends in the face; for who thought of us now?"[41]

The immobility of occupied garrisons, the daily routines of police duty, and their perceived failure to quell civilian resistance infused soldiers with a debilitating sense of uselessness, prompting some to question the legitimacy of their contributions to the Union war effort. Michigan artilleryman Luther F. Hale anxiously wrote from Henderson, Kentucky, "Our men are [becoming] verry much dissatisfied. The work which has been done here has been picket [and] scouting." He further expressed great concern about the implications of his regiment's position: "I think I understand well what the consequences will be if we are not [removed from occupation], our men will become demoralised and useless to the government." The soldiers in his command "are willing to serve in any capassity that it may be necessary for them to in an emergency but they want to be equipped for the service for which they enlisted, and as I have said will be of no service to the government unless they are."[42]

Volunteer soldiers took seriously the notion of active, expedient service to the Union cause, which appeared limited by the more mundane duties of occupation. "The men are anxious to fight; to make decisive attacks that shall annihilate the foe," wrote Samuel Root of the Twenty-fourth Massachusetts from New Bern, North Carolina. Other soldiers assumed that their inactivity behind the lines constituted a failure to aid the nation. "I do not think that we are permanently changed, without doing any thing; I should rather be marching round so as to see something, & be of some benefit to my country," wrote Adolphus P. Wolf in 1863 from Memphis, where he had been stationed for several months. George W. Newcomb, who served in the Nineteenth Connecticut, believed that "we are so comfortable situated now" in Alexandria, Virginia, that "some boddy had got to stay here and guard this city, and I dont know but it might as well be us as any boddy, but it still looks as if we wasnt doing any thing for the country."[43]

Questioning their usefulness to the cause and nation and operating far removed from the central theaters of war as a garrisoned standing army contributed to some soldiers' loss of patriotic fervor. Harrison Soule of the Sixth

Michigan Infantry wrote in 1863 from New Orleans that "the soldiers [here] who are in the service of their country but whose patriotism is not quite so ardent as it was two years since . . . now they take up with nigger help." Orrin S. Allen, who served in the 112th New York stationed at Suffolk, Virginia, informed his wife that "you can have no idea of the work the soldiers have done here." By building forts and chopping timber, he said, "our boys see nothing on either side but work, work! We are heartily tired of it, what patriotism they had is nearly crushed out of them by hard labor and useless marches."[44]

In struggling to understand how their roles as occupying forces effectively fulfilled their national obligations, some northern men pitted the twin concepts of the "citizen-soldier" paradigm against one another. Although many had campaigned and fought to secure the territory which they occupied, the actual process of occupation did not conform to notions of volunteer soldiering. Active participation, they believed, rather than idle, indefinite occupation, would more speedily conclude the war, at which point they could return to their lives as private citizens. Some men thus contended that it might be in their best interest to go home if they continued to operate on the periphery of formal war. Charles H. Smith wrote from Beaufort, South Carolina, in 1863, "I thought a while ago we should get a chance [for active service], but it does not look much like it now. . . . I hope we shall strike tents and go home soon." Samuel Kerr of the Forty-seventh Indiana likewise informed his sister that "I want to do my share of fighting and go home and not be laying around [Helena, Arkansas,] doing nothing for that will never close the war." Even in Kentucky, where the presence of the Union army ensured the state's loyalty, one soldier hoped that "when [the] Government has *nothing more* for *me* to do than guard wach a town as that they will *send* me *home* and I will go to tailoring again."[45]

However, instinctively knowing that premature departures from the army would undercut the citizen-soldier tradition more than military occupation, US volunteers yearned to be relocated to the central theaters of war. Only then, they reasoned, could they fulfill their volunteer contracts. A Massachusetts soldier revealed that service in garrisons along the South Carolina coast had "tax[ed] our martial ardor abundantly to keep up with the occasion." He worried that constant policing of the Sea Islands, quick expeditions into the countryside, and weekly unit reviews made him and his comrades appear merely as "peaceful men in this department." John Russell of the Twenty-first Illinois wrote in December 1862, "when we will move is not known," after occupying Nashville for nearly three months. "[The men] begin to pine over the restrictions of camp and long for a more active life." Russell had fought at Corinth and Perryville and was fully accustomed to combat, yet "though I have seen enough of the horrors of the battle field to ever desire to see more of it if it was possible to avoid it . . . I am fully conscious of the dangers attending a battle but feel that I do not fear them."[46]

Union occupiers did not exhibit an idealistic or naïve characterization of the major field armies. They fully grasped the reality of high attrition rates and large casualty lists. Yet their intense focus on virtuous soldiering led them to believe that a movement to the front would make them more productive to the nation. Although military occupation served an important wartime strategy, Yankee troops largely failed to grasp this truth. "Don't think I am tired of the service, it's the lack of service I'm tired of," Harry Beard assured his parents in November 1864. His regiment, the Thirtieth Missouri Volunteers (Union), spent most of its time occupying portions of Mississippi and Arkansas, and Beard tired of the endless monotony. He reasoned that since Union forces had conquered this region long ago, perhaps he should be transferred to regions still teeming with Confederate forces. "If they would send our regiment to Sherman, to Mobile, or anywhere," he wrote, "we would be kept busy [and] I would be better satisfied."[47]

Even Ulysses S. Grant acknowledged the peculiar nature of occupation, sympathizing with the plight of Union soldiers who occupied the Confederacy. In his memoirs, Grant recalled how the fall and "possession" of Corinth, Mississippi, in May 1862, "by the National troops was of strategic importance, but the victory was barren in every other particular. . . . On our side I know officers and men . . . [who] were disappointed at the result. They could not see how the mere occupation of places was to close the war while large and effective rebel armies existed." Grant understood, perhaps better than any wartime contemporary, the cultural temperament of northern citizen-soldiers. The ability to cite the necessities of occupation while empathizing with the common volunteer's worldview revealed Grant's grasp of the Civil War's immense complexity.[48]

John W. De Forest, an officer in the Twelfth Connecticut, echoed Grant and remarked despondently that his regiment remained in New Orleans while other Union troops moved north toward Vicksburg during the fall of 1862. "Singular as it may seem, this is a disappointment," he wrote. "Nearly every officer and the majority of the men would prefer to go up the river, taking the

certainty of hard fare and hard times generally, with a fair likelihood of being killed or wounded, rather than stay here drilling and guard mounting in
peace." De Forest touched on a common theme shared by John M. King, of
the Ninety-second Illinois, who wrote in February 1863, "while thus laying
in camp we [are] all dissatisfied and uneasy. The men preferred anything to
inactivity. . . . We came out to fight and we would rather now go right at it and
have it done with. To lie in camp with nothing to do is one of the most disagreeable things in the world."[49]

In contrast to armies of occupation, the Army of the Potomac held particular allure for men in occupied zones. Symbolizing the republican martial
ideal, the Union's premier military apparatus represented national wartime
purpose, especially for northern soldiers who remained behind lines. Its character and composition designated it as the foremost institution in the fight to
preserve the Union, while Yankee occupiers found themselves consumed with
defining civilian combatants, enforcing emancipation, policing faraway Confederate communities, and performing bureaucratic tasks. James M. Willet of
the Eighth New York Heavy Artillery, which garrisoned parts of Baltimore for
much of the war, acknowledged to his wife that Union soldiers in the Army of
the Potomac were the nation's "best men." Willet drew a clear distinction in
1862 between the principal northern army and his own current position. He
thus insisted that "they ought to send us forward and put a new regiment here
in our place." Nearly two years later, after the Eighth New York was ordered
out of Baltimore, and after fighting at the battles of Spotsylvania Court House
and Cold Harbor, Willet concluded from the Petersburg front, "I shall endear
what service there is for me to do in the Army of the Potomac cheerfully and I
hope patriotically."[50]

Oliver Wilcox Norton, who originally served with the Eighty-third Pennsylvania Volunteers in the Army of the Potomac, enlisted as an officer in the
Eighth USCT that occupied parts of Florida through the spring and summer of
1864. "Any news of special importance is simply out of the question," he wrote
from Jacksonville. "Only a few roving bands of [guerrilla] cavalry remain."
Although Union forces occupied much of Florida, "it seems to be a sort of
dunce block for the government—a place where they send men good for nothing in any other place." "There is no pretense of an enemy," he professed.
"There are not seven hundred rebels in the state." Norton determined that
his regiment languished needlessly in the Gulf backwaters, and he feared the
"demoralizing" effects on his men. "I have wished many times this summer

that I was back in the Army of the Potomac," he lamented. "We would probably knock about more there than here, but it would be to some apparent purpose and we would have the satisfaction of trying to do some good."[51]

Union occupiers echoed Norton's sentiments, idealizing service in the Army of the Potomac as honorable, worthwhile, and productive. Such sentiments underscored the citizen-soldier ideal in which northern men performed defined, focused service to the nation in an effort to conclude the war in a timely manner. The stagnant milieu and uneasy requirements of occupation, however, conflicted with the perceived purposes of the major field armies. Charles O. Musser of the Twenty-ninth Iowa Volunteers embodied these themes. Occupying Helena and Little Rock, Arkansas, for more than two years discouraged Musser, who wrote in February 1863, "I have been writeing what would be called the dark side of soldiering. . . . The boys are geting so that they do not care much for anything. they are all geting tired of the war. they are in for peace in any way or form. if there is not some great movements made between this [winter] and spring, i believe one half of the army will throw down their arms and go home. i have not seen one man but what thinks the same."[52]

Musser struggled to understand why a sizable portion of the Union army had to remain permanently stationed in Arkansas, especially since guerrillas appeared to be their only immediate foe. "A few days ago," he wrote of one incident, "they fired on some [soldiers] and Shot one poor fellow through both thighs." Additional moments of unorganized and sporadic violence, combined with sheer boredom, pushed Musser into complete ambivalence about his current position. Finally, in the summer of 1864, when news of the Overland Campaign reached Arkansas, Musser proclaimed, "I wish I could be transfered to the 'Army of the Potomac.' I would rather go there and run the chances of being Shot than Stay here all Summer. most of the boys would like a change of Department, and if this campaign is to be the decisive one of the war, we would like to partissipate in it."[53]

Distinctions between the Army of the Potomac and armies of occupation underscored the belief that soldiers had not enlisted to garrison and occupy towns, regulate white southerners, and participate in the uncertainties of emancipation. These unexpected scenarios defied the troops' identities as men, volunteer soldiers, and republican citizens, revealing how a domestic war of occupation fundamentally challenged the United States' long-standing military tradition. Republican thought had long warned against the *external* power wielded by standing armies, which Union soldiers feared had damaged the exceptional nature of volunteer institutions. But republicanism also taught that standing armies corrupted soldiers from *within,* undermining their moral, disinterested characters. As they struggled to give meaning to their service behind the lines, the Union's volunteer soldiers exposed deeper implications of the threat posed by wartime occupation to the republican military tradition.

4 | Informal Economies and the Strains of Republican Disinterestedness

"All honor to the volunteer rank and file! The noblest patriotism in the country is to be found there," George H. Hepworth, a chaplain in the Forty-seventh Massachusetts Infantry, wrote in 1864. "They are the most disinterested men we have, and should be held in the warmest regard. The people have vindicated their right to republicanism. The thoughtful, honest, self-sacrificing [Union soldiers] are," Hepworth concluded, "showing the world in how high estimation they hold our . . . free government."[1]

A year earlier, James Harrison Wilson, a brigadier general and member of Ulysses S. Grant's personal staff, exhibited a far less idealistic regard for the common soldier. "I don't like this 'part of the machine,'" Wilson wrote from occupied Memphis, Tennessee, referring to the decrepit condition and undisciplined manner of the volunteer regiments stationed in the city. The source of his disapproval was that "we have too many generals engaged in semi-civil affairs, to the utter neglect of their military duties." Rather than epitomizing Hepworth's ideal of virtuous conduct, Wilson's colleagues were instead actively entangled in Memphis's cotton trade, which governed the bulk of their time and attention. "These distinguished gentlemen should be required to assume command of their men as their first duty, and dispose of civil and trade business afterward," Wilson exclaimed. "They should be held responsible for the discipline, order, and instruction of their troops, and give their first attention to these matters rather than devote their undivided time to cotton, Confederates, and corruption."[2]

Wilson did not simply complain about his generals' behavior. He also worried over the implications of their conduct. "I tell you, sir," he confided to John A. Rawlins, Grant's chief of staff, "the Government of the United States cannot be upheld in purity and honesty by hands that lay aside the sword for instruments of trade and peace. We want soldiers, not traders; generals, not governors and civil agents." Wilson became increasingly exasperated, staggered by the absurd and inexplicable nature of the topic. "A few hundred thousand bayonets led by clear heads and military rules can crush the rebellion, but a million without military generals can do nothing except by main strength and awkwardness." What was worse, he implicitly concluded, was the strong possibility of the soldiers themselves also being corrupted and molded by their leaders' behavior. But in a strange twist of irony, Wilson did not place the blame for such corruption and greed squarely on the troops themselves. Rather, he faulted the environment in which they served. "The system of occupying undisputed territory is all wrong. We must put our armies in the field and compel our generals to lead them against the enemy, and if they fail from ignorance put them aside. I am disgusted with the whole system."[3]

In a war that forced untested US soldiers to negotiate the cultural and ideological challenges of military occupation, Hepworth and Wilson outlined a growing tension within occupying Union armies in which two distinct nineteenth-century American values appeared in conflict: the culture of republican disinterestedness, epitomized by soldiers' voluntary service, and the culture of democratic privilege, which caused white male citizens to chafe under the restrictions required by martial life. The intersection of these principles created a certain tension within the volunteer disposition. On the one hand, white male citizens, guided by a sense of civic virtue—a belief that they were not subservient to the state but rather participated freely in public institutions—were expected to set aside their private interests to secure the common good, defending the nation in times of crisis. Yet on the other hand, these same men embodied a nation that celebrated the democratic prerogatives of individual initiative and economic advancement free from dependence on, and interference from, a central authority. When they volunteered for military service, young northern men brought both characteristics—self-sacrifice and self-interest—with them into the ranks.[4]

Drawn from the broad spectrum of nineteenth-century American society, Union soldiers displayed dedication to democratic individualism, resisted the hierarchical structure of military life, and grew restless under the rigid discipline required by their officers. Volunteers demanded that cherished ideals of democracy and equality be respected and upheld in the ranks. Implicit in their voluntary contracts of service was the notion that their identities as free men and citizens would not be suppressed or restricted by the army. Soldiers expected military life to function as an extension of the society from which they came, where all of the privileges of white-male American citizenship were protected. The volunteer soldier insisted on the right to govern himself and direct his own affairs, just as he did as a private citizen during peacetime. However, the regimented nature of military culture could not fully oblige this insistence on autonomy, resulting in struggles between military order and personal freedom.[5]

Seen within this context, James H. Wilson's disquietude about the thriving Memphis cotton trade highlighted the tension between disinterested service and personal autonomy within zones of military occupation. Soldiers' use of their service in the army to secure individual financial profit was quite common. The inauguration of and involvement in informal economies—that is, markets that were created by and functioned solely because of the upheaval of war and the movement of armies—reflected the strain between volunteer military duty and the liberties enjoyed by free white men in their civilian lives. While boredom, pragmatism, and the desire (and sometimes necessity) to send extra money to families at home influenced some volunteers to pursue financial gain, soldiers also participated in informal economies to recreate some semblance of their prewar domestic lives in which men engaged in business, commerce, and entrepreneurism. The war, they reasoned, should not place arbitrary limits on economic practices cherished by free male citizens. Soldiers believed that the provisional nature of their military service enabled and excused their self-interested pursuits. Thus, the harmony of the citizen-soldier concept was at risk, as some volunteers refused to set aside prerogatives of citizenship, even when the exercise of their rights cast a shadow upon the army's ethical standing.[6]

The stagnant nature of indefinite military occupation played a vital role in shaping men's wartime behavior, including their economic pursuits. Soldiers in occupied zones had few outlets through which to channel pent-up boredom and mounting laziness, reflecting the alleged permanence of garrison life. Occupied zones were also seen to be far removed from the central theaters of the war, detaching occupation troops from their perceived martial obligations. While military service required all soldiers to relinquish aspects of personal independence, the culture of occupation convinced troops that they had become disconnected from all military commitments and identity. Psychiatrist Nathaniel Warner, who wrote in the aftermath of World War II, argued that occupation challenged a soldier's focus, oftentimes reorienting wartime priorities and responsibilities. "As soon as the drab character of occupation duty manifested itself," he explained, "the termination of hostilities [and] the incentives which had appealed to and stimulated the main drives to continue at duty during the war now ceased to apply in force."[7]

Although Union soldiers' participation in informal economies reflected a search to give meaning to their military service, some observers viewed the thriving wartime economic activity in occupied garrisons as the dreaded embodiment of the corrupting tendencies of standing armies. Sustained military life in garrisoned towns, James H. Wilson suggested, lent itself to distracted behavior, which manifested itself in the quest for financial profit at the expense of military responsibility. Garrisons were seen as breeding grounds for conduct that appeared to weaken the disinterested volunteer ideal through distracted self-interest in the form of monetary gain; the soldier was therefore undermined in favor of the citizen.[8]

* * *

The chaos of civil war did not kill market economies, but rather provoked a surge of informal modes of commerce to meet the needs and desires of various parties. The occupied landscape in particular created a host of opportunities for soldiers to trade goods, provide services, and even perpetuate clandestine markets, which grew because of wartime demand. Many occupiers possessed a savvy business acumen, allowing them to emulate their prewar lives as salesmen, merchants, or craftsmen. They ably established unique economic networks enabled only by the disruption of war. Although the US government paid a wage and provided clothing and food, soldiers sought additional, imaginative ways to make extra money either for themselves or to send home to their families.

Numerous factors inspired Union soldiers to pursue financial profit in occupied regions. First, they were bored. Garrisoned communities offered few diversions, tempting soldiers to find creative ways to focus their attention. "The most of the troops are getting paid and money flows freely from their hands," wrote Illinois artilleryman William T. Shepherd from Memphis. Other incentives, though, appeared much more calculated. Despite their military pay, food, and clothing, soldiers generally believed that the government did not do enough to meet their needs. They wondered whether civil authorities purposely neglected their well-being primarily because they were stationed in seemingly forgotten corners of the occupied Confederacy. New Englander Frank Peck wrote in June 1862, following the surrender of New Orleans, that the government "sent on batteries without guns, cavalry without horses, and Paymasters without money." He disparaged the far-off politicians who celebrated the city's capture, even though it was he and his fellow soldiers who had accomplished the feat. Rather than "throwing up their hats," Peck remarked, bureaucrats should consider "how soldiers encamp without tents, or make turtle soup out of salt beef. . . . The nakedness of the men is no pleasant appendix to attach to some of the reports of Congressional Committees." Although he considered his complaints well-founded, Peck admitted, "we are situated now so that it makes very little difference whether the government take any further care or not." Peck knew that his comrades would find alternative means of personal attention and reimbursement.[9]

Pragmatism helped inform the basis of informal economies as soldiers encountered the great expense required to live in garrisoned towns. Officers, who rented rooms and houses from local civilians, paid rent and purchased goods for which their military pay was generally insufficient. In addition, decadent temptations such as alcohol and prostitution required handy cash. "It cost us a great deal to be stationed at Memphis," Oscar Lawrence Jackson wrote in June 1863. "Our mess accounts were large, there being a good market, fine clothing, plenty of whiskey, etc." Jackson recounted how many of his comrades had been "ruined," wasting their money on "such indulgences." Courtland Stanton, of the Twenty-first Connecticut, agreed, explaining that Norfolk, Virginia, was equally pricey. "I wish we were in the field," he admitted. "It is so expensive to live in the city, if one keeps any kind of an appearance."[10]

As they took up residence in the Confederacy, northern men observed the South's stagnant, unsophisticated economy, finding it ripe for entrepreneurial activity. Marred by slavery's shameful influence, the region seemed unmoving, devoid of energy and economic development. The war only aggravated these long-festering commercial wounds. Cities were desolate, towns were abandoned, and the countryside was a dying vestige of a once-imposing agricultural dominion. As he walked through New Orleans, one week after the city capitulated in May 1862, Michigander Harrison Soule noticed that all businesses were closed, "look[ing] like one large Sunday to pass through day after day." Although he linked the failing Confederate economy to the war, Soule also attributed the collapse of day-to-day business to the outmoded conditions of southern commerce. When he moved upriver by June, Soule looked at Baton Rouge with stunned amazement. "The buildings and business places are mostly closed in this City," he reported, "so there is no inducement to go to town for a few little comforts." While a few stores remained open, they "keep hardly anything and [resemble] an old Barn."[11]

Other soldiers, such as the Twelfth Wisconsin's Clement Boughton, noticed the economic potential of the war-torn South. "I am very much pleased with the looks of the country through which we marched," he wrote in 1862 about north-central Alabama's streams, springs, and even a few foundries. Boughton indicted the locals, however, because "they do not look as they ever done a very [exciting] business" with their available resources. The solution was simple. "If they had the enterprise of the north it would become noted for its commerce." Boughton envisioned water power for factories, which could manufacture cotton at unimaginable rates, liberating the region from its sluggish economic depravity. But alas, "as long as men of the south could get their living by negro labor they would not set their heads to work to make any improvements," Boughton lamented. The lands below Mason and Dixon's line could become efficient and diverse only if "[slave] labor would be dispenced with as Yankees of the north did."[12]

The South seemed disposed for an economic transformation guided by the ambitions of Yankee ingenuity. Enterprising Union soldiers looked at the region's stagnant economy as a blessing rather than a curse. Henry C. Gilbert, a regimental officer detached in the rear of the Army of the Cumberland, cited the lack of business in middle Tennessee—"Nobody has anything to sell & nobody any thing to buy with"—the implications of which were not lost on young northern men. They understood that indigent, helpless white southerners, who had never been moved by the entrepreneurial spirit, would pose little market competition. Civilians were weighed down by worthless Confederate money, desperate for food and clothing. Union soldiers thus first encountered the potential of informal economies shortly after a town or region fell to the forces of occupation. Impoverished civilians swarmed garrisoned communities, hoping to receive some sort of relief.[13]

The occupiers blurred the distinction between civilian enemies and potential clients. They traded and negotiated prices with residents of garrisoned towns, bartering with passersby while posted on picket duty. "People come in here from the country every day," wrote Robert Stuart Finley, an Illinois soldier stationed at Fort Donelson, Tennessee. Nearly a month after the Union army secured the strategic river garrison, civilians entered the lines, offering to take loyalty oaths. "Some of them come in wagons 30 & 40 miles & bring corn meal & butter & eggs which they trade for coffee with the soldiers," Finley explained. He was satisfied with the market that developed, especially after his regiment was treated to a barrel of sauerkraut, which sold "out briskly at 10 cts a plate full." Other goods and produce were exchanged at acceptable rates, which Finley considered "Pretty dear for the 'Sunny South.'"[14]

White southerners eagerly sought economic protection from the occupiers. As the war further shattered the Confederate economy, Union occupation offered alternative means of subsistence. "Refugees and Deserters are coming every few days," Benjamin T. Wright, of the Tenth Connecticut, wrote from Jacksonville, Florida. "The people in the country are in a miserable condition [and] are heart[ily] sick of the war, in fact they are completely destitute." Wright described how occupation authorities allowed civilians to enter the lines once a week "and bring what they have to sell such as sweet potatoes venison &c." In return, the army sold goods from the commissary stores, effectively fulfilling the needs of both parties. "The trading is done under the supervision of the Provost Marshal," Wright concluded, suggesting the legitimate and accepted means of commerce.[15]

Sometimes, though, soldiers suspected that they were deceived when negotiating with white southerners. In order to keep their practices discreet, troops near Norfolk, Virginia, sneaked into town during the evening to engage in trade. "I cant imagine why they will go nights," wondered Courtland G. Stanton of the Twenty-first Connecticut, who considered, "they could trade so much better in the day time." "But they will eventually learn better," he concluded, "for I have heard quite a number of them complaining . . . that they got cheated making change in the dark."[16]

While boredom, pragmatism, disrupted southern markets, and interactions with Confederate refugees inspired Union soldiers to test the potential of wartime economics, the isolated, permanent nature of occupied garrisons strongly shaped the conditions of informal economies. Joseph Waldo Denny, a soldier in the Twenty-fifth Massachusetts Volunteers, explained the transformation of his regiment's conduct shortly after it occupied New Bern, North Carolina, in the spring of 1862. Life in the city, Denny explained, imitated the comforts of home during the prewar days. The companies were lodged in "some of the best houses, and from the gardens were able to procure many esculents, some of which were almost ripened for the table." The soldiers also enjoyed an abundance of produce and a variety of meats, all of which brought pleasant changes from their lives campaigning in the field. In addition, the regiment had only to act as the daily provost guard, performing to the satisfaction of their commanding general, Ambrose E. Burnside. It appeared that New Bern would offer an ideal respite from the war, a needed rest for weary troops.[17]

Denny acknowledged, however, a troubling problem that emerged as the occupation grew more indefinite. "Long continued duty in a city was not desirable for a soldier," he declared. "Its effect was very disastrous to a wholesome *esprit*

du corps." The longer the soldiers spent in the city, the more they were surrounded by "the inertia and temptations incident to a town garrison." Denny's
comrades were enveloped in a setting that resembled their civilian lives but
which also mandated temporary detachment from the comforts of home.
For now, their identity as soldiers had to govern their focus and conduct. Yet
Denny believed that "men [could be] ruined in character or morality" if they
succumbed to the enticements available within garrisoned towns. "Army life
pours a flood of light upon men," he concluded, "and we see them as they are—
see them as they give full swing to natural propensities."[18]

Denny equated occupied garrisons with immorality and corruption because they lulled soldiers into a false sense of security, tempting them with
the trappings of home life. Other occupiers likewise explained that garrisons
fostered laziness and idleness, traits that further inspired distracted behavior. Illinoisan Rankin P. McPheeters, who served at DeValls Bluff, Arkansas,
during the spring of 1864, noted that "a large army laying idle, as long as we
have been becomes demoralized in spite of rigid discipline. . . . Licentiousness
and every other evil vice of which man is heir to, is prevailing here to an alarming extent." Volunteers sought constant forward movement, a validation that
indicated the war's conclusion. Yet garrisoning large swaths of the Confederate South, by definition, required soldiers to remain stationary, making illu-
sory any sense of progress. And thus the occupiers grew discomfited with their
idleness, fearing a detrimental effect not only on Union military fortunes, but
also on their identities as young northern men.[19]

As early as 1861, Union soldiers noted the effects of idleness upon themselves and their armies. Wilder Dwight, of the Second Massachusetts Volunteers, labeled Harpers Ferry, Virginia, a "lazy military department which
awaits new life." Although celebrating the effortless seizure of the town,
Dwight and his men yearned to push ahead, "getting ready for better things,
I hope." But a month later, he observed that "the hard work, hot weather, and
soldier's fare begin to tell upon the men, and they are not as well satisfied
as they were." Dwight noted that the soldiers were also affected by disorder
and lowered standards of discipline. "The result is," he concluded, "that the
regiment seems to lack willingness, obedience, enthusiasm, and vigor." In
August 1862, Valentine C. Rudolph, who served in the Thirty-ninth Illinois
Volunteers, remarked, "The garrison [Fortress Monroe, Virginia] looks like
holiday soldiers. They have not seen such hard times as the 'veterans' of the
field." Even future president Benjamin Harrison described his service in mid-

dle Tennessee during the autumn of 1863 as the "lazy, spiritless life of a garrison soldier." And J. Henry Blakeman, stationed on the Florida coast in 1864, admitted "feeling rather lazy as a natural consequence of staying five or six months in the extreme south."[20]

When stationed in wartime garrisons, Union occupiers' principal enemy was not musket-wielding Confederates, whizzing bullets, or bursting shell, but rather an invisible adversary of languor and apathy. The boredom from which soldiers suffered carried grave consequences. Immobility fomented not only a lack of interest in the war, but also fears that an overdue stay in the stagnant South might transform industrious northern men into the embodiments of lethargy that had long cursed the region's economic potential. Life along the North Carolina coast was, for William Augustus Walker, "growing terribly monotonous." He encountered "literally nothing to do," which "would be jolly for a lazy man, but I am not a lazy man & prefer a little activity." Samuel Root, who served in the Twenty-fourth Massachusetts, long stationed at New Bern, North Carolina, further outlined the occupier's dilemma. "The soldiers are uneasy at laying still so long & pine for action, no matter what or where it would keep them busy and healthy," he wrote in September 1862. "They have not much to do, they are in danger of becoming lazy."[21]

Walker and Root implied that laziness seemed to breed a life devoid of principled purpose. Union volunteers had grown up in an era that preached that white men could seek improvement and pursue self-interest; the quest to craft one's identity based on work reigned supreme throughout the antebellum North. Individual achievement came through vigor and resolve, made possible by resisting the natural temptations of a lazy life. "Ambitious strivers made their own success," one historian wrote recently of this cultural dynamic, "idle loungers made their own failure." In a fiercely democratic nation governed by the power of the individual, northern men instinctively resisted any constraint placed in the paths of their self-interest and self-worth. Occupying soldiers feared the result of laziness and idleness within their garrisons, worrying that continued stagnation would diminish their identity as energetic free men of enterprise.[22]

The ubiquity of laziness in wartime garrisons was also a symptom of dependence on military pay. Soldiers who relied on the timely disbursement of their monthly army salaries usually found the government's efficiency inadequate. Indeed, Union soldiers sometimes received their wages six months after they were promised. Although military authorities sought to revive the economic life of occupied cities, delayed soldier payments often caused the local economies to collapse. "We have had a long time or season of perfect stagnation in all kinds of business," wrote T. F. Browne, an army purchasing agent from New Orleans in 1864. "The troops have not been paid off for eight months," and more than "eighteen millions of dollars are now due." Once the paymasters arrived in the city, Browne wrote hopefully, soldiers would "spend money freely and the Shoemakers and Tailors will be once more busy and in funds. I anticipate a good trade then."[23]

The mid-nineteenth-century cultures of "self-making" and masculine autonomy, however, taught northern men to eschew dependence. The increasingly bureaucratic conditions of army life, and the resulting limitations to personal freedom in occupied garrisons—exhibited in the pay crisis at New Orleans—convinced some volunteers that the disruption of war might forever hinder their ability to advance economically. Luther Fairbanks, a Massachusetts volunteer stationed at New Orleans, worried that *not* pursuing work while temporarily in military service would render his skills useless in peacetime. "We [try to] work the same as we used to work at the Otis Co.," he remarked. "I always used to work no doubteth well." However, he admitted that "it has not help[ed] me in the least going to work for *Uncle Sam.* he is not an easy task master [and] I am afraid when he discharges his workmen he will turn out a good many lazy men into the world again." John C. Kinney, who also occupied the Crescent City, believed he was "wasting time which should be fitting me for my profession." Isolated on the Sea Islands of South Carolina, Samuel Root sensed his personal autonomy, and his ability to maintain a self-sufficient life, slipping away. "Give me neither poverty nor riches," he informed his wife, "[but] some business or situation where I can be independent on my own Exertions."[24]

* * *

Fearful that garrison life would undermine, if not extinguish, their skills as clerks, laborers, and budding capitalists, and finding themselves with time on their hands, occupying soldiers shrugged off the restrictive yoke of military culture to resume their antebellum quest of "self-making." Informal commerce begun by soldiers integrated peacetime economic practices such as offering goods and services in exchange for money, owing debts, and negotiating market fluctuations. The occupiers initiated and participated in both simple and complex modes of commerce. Simple forms of commerce included acquiring and selling minor goods, such as paper or tobacco, coupled with providing services, such as haircuts, taking a fellow soldier's place on picket duty, or buying and selling with southern civilians. Complex modes of commerce included monopolies within garrisoned towns, which caused prices to soar, making a single soldier, or small alliances of troops, quite wealthy. Or soldiers inserted themselves into larger markets, such as the cotton trade, which held regional, national, and international economic implications. Regardless of the commerce in which they engaged, soldiers usually maintained low profiles, trying not to draw attention to their activities.[25]

The needs of civilians, the wants of fellow troops, and the potential of untapped markets in the occupied Confederacy summoned the common Union soldier to work. The entrepreneurial spirit, gleaned from their days as private citizens in the North, infused volunteers with an optimistic vision of economic profit. These markets existed solely because of the war, threatening to evaporate once peace ensued. John M. Steward of the First Maine Heavy Artillery, stationed at the garrisons protecting Washington, D.C., learned how to use his military income "to a good advantage." He reported that he earned an extra ten dollars in only three days because there "is a good many of the boys that get short and sell thing verry cheap which I will buy and find no trouble in selling them for a few dollars more than I gave." He proudly explained how he purchased a pistol for six dollars and an overcoat for one dollar, which he then resold for eleven dollars and two dollars and fifty cents, respectively. Troops such as Steward acted quickly, finding ways to expand markets to meet the widest demand. Soldiers considered their new commerce to be legitimate, even though they attempted to conceal their activities. They did not advertise nor did they actively promote their practices. Informal economies were instead governed by reputation, purchasing power, and the ability to meet demand.[26]

Though informal, and at times irregular, economic arrangements in occupied zones were governed by the immutable market laws of supply and demand. Southern civilians especially involved themselves in buying, selling, and trading with soldiers. The disrupted condition of the Confederate economy, coupled with a depreciating currency and dearth of important staple products, forced residents of occupied areas into business relations with their occupiers. While stationed at Carrollton, Arkansas, Benjamin McIntyre, of the Nineteenth Iowa, described the intricate trade maintained by local civilians and Union soldiers. "Salt is much needed," McIntyre reported, because "families having [a] large number of hogs cannot Kill them for the want of it." The locals offered "tobacco, Sorghum, socks, & various other things which they are very willing to barter for coffee, sugar, [and] Salt." Two months later, while in southern Missouri, McIntyre revealed that women would arrive in camp, looking to trade, purchase, or sell goods. Often, though, "they charge exhorbitant prices," suggesting that soldiers who could not pay had to forgo the sought-after items.[27]

The solution seemed simple: corner the market on a particular good or service, earn a substantial profit, and achieve financial independence. The eight months in which Orrin S. Allen, a private in the 112th New York Volunteers, spent at Suffolk, Virginia, offered ample opportunity to create a profitable business. He routinely expressed "how disgusted I have become with these fellows who are stumbling over each other to get [promoted] to the office[r corps]," and thus sought alternative avenues of personal distinction. Occupied Suffolk presented Allen with an ideal environment in which to earn a commercial reputation in the garrisoned community. In January 1863, after receiving his pay, he visited numerous sutler's stores and even the camps of soldiers who privately sold merchandise. "The business is not as nigh as good as it was," he reported. "Too much competition, some of the officers buy [goods] and turn them over to the government and pocket a pricey sum in the operation," he continued. Although discouraged, Allen sought to match, and even exceed, the transactions conducted by the officers, "but it takes smart moneying," he informed his wife. "Only think," he fancied, "today the Sutler came round, some of the fellows have run up half their wages. . . . Oh what a thing of temptations does the soldiers money expose him to!" He proudly explained how he resisted the urge to purchase needless trinkets, instead saving his cash for a potential business venture. He surveyed the situation at Suffolk, analyzed the market, and learned how to overcome his business competitors.[28]

Nearly a month later, Allen sent his wife twenty dollars, even though the army paid him only sixteen dollars a month. "You ask if I sent more pay then I got," he wrote, "I did . . . but did not steal the $4. I worked for it but there is too much competition now, every nigger and boy is running around camp taking the money from the [soldiers]." Allen learned about the high demand for apples, so he bought a bushel, "took out the injured ones and sold the rest for 50 cts more then [the] cost." He then made applesauce from those that were left over, which he also sold. Soldiers in the 112th, probably including Allen, confiscated apples while on picket duty, which increased potential supply. In addition, he made a list of items most valued by soldiers, including food, paper, and writing utensils, of which he made "packages" for sale. It was much easier for fellow troops to buy their goods in one trip, he reasoned, rather than travel across the garrison to visit different dealers and sutlers. Allen purchased all of these goods himself, assembled them in one bundle, marked up the price slightly, and, in the first few days, "have sold 40 packages profit $2.00." Soldiers indeed valued convenience over price.[29]

Allen was not finished. Upon selling out his original supply, he went to the town's train station to purchase more packages. It turned out that the sutler with whom Allen competed was about to leave Suffolk because his cost of business had become too great. Thus, to Allen's surprise, he "will sell me 200 packages at 17 cts each, I pay 20 now." Although his principal source of competition was now removed, Allen faced another problem. The goods he purchased, which encompassed his "packages," were now inspected by the garrison's customhouse. "It is very hard getting goods of any kind through," he wrote. "Every box and package of goods that is sent to or from this place is subject to the closest scrutiny." Recognizing that soldiers were allowed access only to certain items that met the authorities' approval, Allen could have dropped his business venture, but the new regulations increased demand for his services.[30]

Allen's business thrived, and by the end of March 1863, he boasted selling "44 packages, 6 portfolios, some envelopes and a few quires of paper, profits about $3." He had developed a reputation as Suffolk's premier wholesaler, and "they think it curious I can 'Smell Money.'" The troops could not understand how or why Allen constantly evaded detection, especially since most other soldiers "are fined $5 if they sell a few apples. Some of them told me today their wages were stopped, to pay the fine." Though he did not explicitly state it, Allen alluded to the reason he was never caught. "It does me good to see the guards salute as I pass," he wrote, "instead of ordering to 'halt' as they should. . . . They have strict orders to stop all private soldiers and examine their passes, but they scarce ever ask for mine." Allen's reputation was presumably so pervasive, coupled with services that only he could provide, that he enjoyed high standing in a garrisoned community otherwise governed by strict discipline. Over the next few months, Allen expanded his business, in which he bought and resold shoes, jewelry, and paper. In one instance, he even traded his pistol for a watch, which he also later sold. He consistently reported profits, estimating that his net gains totaled twenty-four dollars per month, which meant that he earned between nine and eleven dollars in addition to his wages from the government.[31]

Allen's sentiments and habits changed drastically as the war crept along. In 1864, when Union armies prepared for another grueling spring campaign, Allen and the men of the 112th New York left their coastal paradise for Ulysses S. Grant's swelling ranks in Virginia. Allen was now part of the active war, far removed from the slothful garrisons he once inhabited. "We expect to see sharp fighting this spring," he predicted in April, "but I do not feel anxiety about it." "If it is my lot to be sacrificed for the cost of freedom," he declared, "I am ready." Six weeks later, after surviving the bloody debacle at Cold Harbor, Allen remained resolute. "If it were consistent with my duties, to my country I should like to be with you," he informed his wife, "but no domestic pleasures could bribe me to neglect the interest of the Nation in this time of peril. Should I be spared till my term of service expires I shall feel that my duty as a soldier is done." Orrin S. Allen's civil war had come full circle. While serving in a garrison, the demands of war felt far off, and Allen turned his attention to personal profit. When back on the front lines, he temporarily discarded all of his financial ambitions, moved instead by the pressing demands of the war's principal front. No longer did he define his service as a quest for personal profit, no longer did he use his blue uniform to line the pockets of his civilian life. He survived the conflict and soon returned home to New York.[32]

While soldiers such as Orrin S. Allen developed unique ways of facilitating simple economies—the successful of which became lucrative and monopolistic businesses—others invested themselves into larger, burgeoning markets. As the war dragged on, commercial economies became increasingly complex. "Our boyes are all making money," Rankin P. McPheeters wrote from DeValls Bluff, Arkansas, "peddling trading &c.," with local civilians, as well as dabbling in the larger markets at Little Rock. The emerging complexity of wartime markets shaped the conditions of war in occupied regions. Blue-clad soldiers acclimated themselves to the wartime landscape's diverse economic climates, tapping into a region's particular market specialty.[33]

Trade in livestock, for example, directly manipulated the Union war effort from the Trans-Mississippi frontier to Georgia. The occupiers in Missouri learned that horse trading garnered power and money. Union troops joined with rebel civilians near St. Louis, establishing a "ready, safe, and reliable market" in which locals, concealing themselves as government contractors, entered Yankee camps and bought horses that were seized by soldiers on scouting expeditions. Knowing that they could turn quick profits upon returning to their garrisons, the troops sometimes even confiscated horses from local Unionists, disregarding the implications of white southern loyalty, and selling their prizes to the highest bidder. A concerned officer observed that the occupiers and traders had erected "a very profitable monopoly." "It is utterly impossible for me to protect loyal citizens in their just rights and to maintain discipline among troops," he lamented.[34]

The consequences of cattle trading with local Indian groups in nearby Kansas seemed even more pronounced. Government agents had long conducted licensed business with the Indians, and while cattle exchanges were permitted within army lines, informal trade often took place outside formal military supervision. "The stock was passed around my remotely separated stations," General Samuel Ryan Curtis explained, "and invited rebel raids to follow remote cattle routes." Desirous that his troops at Fort Leavenworth safeguard the legal trade, and protect government agents in their commercial ventures, Curtis sensed that the men under his command also joined in the clandestine trafficking. Curtis averred that his men "seek to profit by it," becoming "demoralized and diverted from our pressing foes, the bushwhackers."[35]

Secret trade in horses and cattle revealed a soldiery willing to manipulate the circumstances of war in their favor, oftentimes at the expense of the Union they were charged to defend. Nothing demonstrated this dynamic better, or more notoriously, than the cotton trade. Touching nearly every region of the occupied Confederacy, the cotton exchange presented great opportunity for speculation and enormous profits for anyone willing to risk both personal investment and safety. Northern demand for cotton, coupled with southern demand for reliable commercial trade and capital, created vast networks of negotiation and transaction. Although the US and Confederate governments desperately sought the benefits provided by mutual participation in the cotton trade, both nations soon realized the inherent problem in such an arrangement: an enemy's goods, used by the opposing side, to finance and wage war. Yet, the trade in contraband cotton proved much too seductive to be left untapped.[36]

Abraham Lincoln spearheaded efforts at the beginning of the war to acquire southern cotton. While he endorsed the Federal blockade of the Confederate coastline, the president also respected the power and influence that cotton, the king of all antebellum exports, commanded both at home and abroad. Northeastern textile mills—and by extension, the voting public—craved white gold, while Great Britain seemed prepared to intervene on the Confederacy's behalf if American cotton could not travel freely across the Atlantic. In addition, Lincoln believed that suppressed unionism would flourish in regions of the loyal South if civilians were allowed to trade their principal commodity. Thus, Congress authorized the Treasury Department in July 1861 to distribute licenses to agents charged with buying and selling cotton throughout the occupied Confederacy. For Lincoln, an orderly cotton trade rekindled commerce between the North and South, paving a hopeful road of reunification.[37]

Yet such idealistic notions proved hollow. By the autumn of 1862, cotton became so scarce (due to the stiffening Union blockade and southern embargo) that prices skyrocketed to unprecedented, lucrative levels. Indeed, cotton could be acquired for ten cents a pound and then sold for at least seventy cents in northern and international markets, securing its highest rate of return at any point during the nineteenth century. Inspired by greedy visions of a quick profit, northern speculators flooded the South seeking black-market trade permits, alliances with generals, and coalitions with money-starved white southerners. And while Lincoln continued to endorse the trade, in spite of its mounting corruption, some elements of the northern public feared the debasing influence of trade with the rebellious South. Wartime northerners associated cotton with the nefarious designs of slaveholding aristocrats who had long craved quick, unfair profits. The cotton trade emulated the evils of slaveholding. Some feared that speculators, through their ravenous hunger for money, arbitrarily and immorally sustained the southern slave power. Preservation of the Union, charged some critics of the trade, meant dismantling the slaveholding class's grip on the national economy while also upholding the moral boundaries demanded of republican citizens.[38]

Northern discontent stemmed in part from the army's role in facilitating Federal policy. Union forces stationed in the Mississippi Valley were entrenched in speculation, as civilian fortune hunters sought both cheap cotton and protection from army officers. By the summer of 1862, the cotton trade had proven so rewarding that the government even urged the army to assist buyers, protect storehouses, aid in shipments, and seize cotton from southerners. The US military was no longer an institution tasked solely with defending the nation against violent rebels; it was now a managerial bureaucracy complicit in shady civilian profit. Disgusted by what he considered a corrupted partnership, Ulysses S. Grant limited the trade in January 1863 along Union-occupied portions of the Mississippi River. The restrictions, however, inspired the opposite effect. Memphis, Helena (Arkansas), and ultimately Vicksburg deteriorated into dens of corruption as speculators bribed officers and soldiers, effectively transforming the region into a giant black market.[39]

The provost marshal at Vicksburg reported to Grant that some of the garrison's occupiers "really violate the spirit of the orders prohibiting trade in cotton," and he worried that if "minor offenses are now tolerated, open violation of orders will soon occur." He likened the soldiers to "mischievous school boys" who insisted on "going as far as possible without being caught." The provost marshal recommended that these troops, "and all others of like character, be ordered to leave the Department immediately, not to return under the penalty of arrest and imprisonment." His concern was not merely law-breaking behavior, but also the larger effect of such conduct on the moral condition of the republic's citizen-soldiers. Understanding the great danger of other occupiers emulating these practices, the provost marshal pleaded that Grant limit the trade even further.[40]

The provost marshal's report suggested that the common soldier had assumed an active, rather than passive, role in shaping the wartime cotton economy. But how would soldiers, who seemed far less economically experienced than shrewd civilian speculators, emerge as the central actors in this budding enterprise? Positioned on the front lines of occupation, exposed to roving opportunists, and surrounded by abundant cotton, some rank-and-file troops exploited the privileged access to white gold afforded by their military service. While venturing on expeditions into the southern countryside, some soldiers used their military salaries to purchase cotton from southern civilians, then sold the cotton directly on the open market. Or, the occupiers would simply accept payoffs, turning a blind eye while speculators acquired their desired share. "Soldiers on picket are bribed, officers are bribed," Stephen A. Hurlbut, the occupation commander of Memphis, grumbled in March 1863. "Men are looking for opportunities to make money," he affirmed. "Honesty is the exception and peculation the rule wherever the army is brought into contact with trade."[41]

Soldiers governed by an acute sense of market dynamics and a thirst for profit were themselves a crucial commodity in perpetuating the cotton trade. Because they were at the forefront of the occupied landscape and because they were well-versed in the doctrines of supply and demand, blue-clad northerners understood precisely how the trade worked and leveraged their military position to turn a profit. In war, just as in peace, the enticement of financial gain exerted an equally strong pull on industrious Union soldiers-turned-businessmen. While the occupiers may not have masterminded large-scale trade schemes, they served as essential cogs in the cotton machine. With their talent for trade and markets, honed during their civilian lives in the industrious North, Yankee men were frequently sought out for their access and aptitude for business.

J. R. Paul, who served in Ormsby Mitchel's division of the Army of the Ohio, which occupied northern Alabama in the spring of 1862, explained to Samuel Sharp, a potential northern speculator, how soldiers opened access to the lucrative trade. Paul advised "what a fine chance there is to make money in buying cotton," exemplified by one Cleveland dealer who acquired sixty bales near Nashville, shipped the goods to New York, and stood to profit four thousand dollars. The transaction, Paul counseled, took place only because he introduced the businessman to General Mitchel, who pledged stealthy transportation and use of the railroads. Paul urged Sharp to join the enterprise, especially since soldiers were integral in opening access to the trade. "You would have to let some one here do the buying and then some one that is acquainted with the army could do the work," Paul instructed, "and all you could do would be just to see to it a little, and have it shipped in some other person's name until it got to Nashville."[42]

Although not stated explicitly, it is safe to assume Paul's ulterior motive: a substantial kickback in return for his assistance. He fully admitted as much. "If I was out of [the] army and had funds, with the knowledge I have of the matter, I could make more money at buying cotton." Writing later to his brother, Paul claimed that "Sharp has missed it badly. If he had made the arrangement and come down here I could put him in the way to make $10,000 or $20,000." Although prevented from reaping massive rewards from the cotton exchange, soldiers such as J. R. Paul still padded their own fortunes by leveraging their skills, privileged access, and martial authority. "The cotton speculators are quite clamorous for aid in getting their cotton away," declared a brigadier general in Tennessee, "and [they] offer to pay liberally for the service."[43]

J. R. Paul's observations and experiences reflected a broader problem. Some common soldiers came to believe that officers exploited their privileged positions within the military hierarchy to reap the rewards of the cotton trade, unfairly enjoying the spoils of war and arbitrarily pushing the common soldier out of competition. Guided by their ambition, some officers could not resist the temptations of acquiring quick wealth through exchanges in cotton. Enlisted men, however, sensed that officers conspired to eliminate competition, blocking market access from those whom they commanded. This dynamic established a hierarchical tension in which white men who were equal in civilian life did not enjoy equal access to wartime markets. Relations between officers and enlisted men thus strained, undermining claims that informal economies were extensions of antebellum free labor. Henry R. Gardner, who served in Baton Rouge, claimed that "Officers[,] to fill their own pockets, will make laws, by which the market price of everything is raised so that a private's $13.00 dont go a great ways." Convinced that the new commander at Baton Rouge, Philip St. George Cooke, arrived merely "to make his share on the Cotton speculations," Gardner surmised, "It seems as if every Post Commander here [makes] a good pile, and then [gives] way to someone else. One thing sure," he concluded, "someone high in power must wink at these speculations, or they never could be carried on."[44]

Henry Gardner scorned what he considered undeserved officer privilege within the Union army's democratic culture. Another volunteer acknowledged that officers' quests for wartime profits created tension in the ranks. "There is a great deal of selfishness out here in the army," he claimed; "it is not all pure blue patriotism that leads men out to the war." One did not have to travel further than the headquarters of Benjamin F. Butler, the first occupation commander at New Orleans, to see the embodiment of this claim. The brusque Massachusetts general fed his rapacious appetite for financial rewards on the plentiful cotton in his Department of the Gulf. Butler did not attempt to hide his money-making schemes, using his position to earn both himself and his brother hundreds of thousands of dollars from contraband cotton. And the men in the ranks looked with scorn at Butler's efforts, some wanting to abandon the war effort altogether. One observer recognized the general's "great ability, great energy, shrewdness and activity, and industry," yet also admitted that those very qualities undermined morale among Butler's men. "He can never acquire a character here for disinterestedness," the correspondent claimed. "Many officers and soldiers want to go home, not wishing to risk their lives to make fortunes for others."[45]

The varied conflicts arising from the Union army's entrenchment in wartime cotton trading framed the context in which an exasperated James H. Wilson—Ulysses S. Grant's personal adviser—lamented Union soldiers who dedicated their "undivided time to cotton, Confederates, and corruption." Citing the static nature of military occupation as the prime culprit in facilitating informal commerce—"The system of occupying undisputed territory is all wrong," he maintained—Wilson's frustration reflected civil and military authorities' desperate attempts to curb soldiers' economic tendencies. Because they exploited the conditions of war in their own favor, restrictions on the occupiers' industrious, yet unethical maneuvering would have to be authored.[46]

Writing from Memphis in August 1862, William T. Sherman declared that soldiers, because they received a government salary, "cannot charge a fee for any official act" that propagated both simple and complex commerce. As defenders of the Union, Sherman implied, volunteers sacrificed their quest for personal profit: it was "not only a crime but a disgrace to the whole country." Later the following year, serious about limiting soldiers' participation in wartime economies, Sherman confided privately, "I have announced in orders that any officer of my command who makes a cent of profit by selling permits, passes, &c., or by any species of trade and speculation, is corrupt and criminal." Similar orders issued in the Department of the Gulf forbade soldiers "to engage, in any manner whatever, directly or indirectly, in the purchase or sale of the products of the country . . . or material of the army of the purpose of speculation." Echoing Sherman's sentiments, the orders clarified that "the appropriation of the property of the country to private use or personal emolument demoralizes the army and dishonors the service."[47]

Additional orders issued at Nashville required sutlers to receive permits to sell goods; no one else, "unless he is a resident trader," would be allowed to engage in business. Soldiers would be punished, and their units' officers held accountable, if they were "found shipping, selling, or attempting to sell goods, either directly or indirectly, in violation of the above orders." At Huntsville, Alabama, and Morganza, Louisiana, even as late as 1864 and 1865 respectively, civilians not connected to the government would be arrested if they were caught loitering around camps or interacting with the soldiers, for fear that goods would be smuggled out of the lines. Interestingly, these latter two directives were passed *after* the army issued its most sweeping restrictions in 1863 governing the conduct of armies in the field and in zones of occupation: General Orders No. 100, or Lieber's Code. Section II, Article 46, explicitly forbade soldiers engaging in informal economies: "Neither officers nor soldiers are allowed to make use of their position or power in the hostile country for private gain, not even for commercial transactions otherwise legitimate. Offenses to the contrary committed by commissioned officers will be punished with cashiering or such other punishment as the nature of the offense may require; if by soldiers, they shall be punished according to the nature of the offense."[48]

These restrictions were inspired by occupation commanders who were disgusted at the conduct of their soldiers who participated in informal economies. Even despite the limits placed on the troops' economic ambitions, "a perpetual flood of fraud, false swearing, and contraband goods runs through this city," Stephen A. Hurlbut, the commanding general at Memphis, wrote in November 1863, "interfering with all proper military control and guided and managed by designing men for their own purposes." Ironically, Hurlbut built a notorious reputation for his corrupt occupation of the city. Gambling, drinking, prostitution, and especially intricate rings of cotton extortion escalated under his leadership, oftentimes at his own direction. Yet even Hurlbut, the man responsible for much of his soldiers' inattention to detail and military discipline, could not help being troubled with the occupiers' neglect of order and restraint. "Pickets, in whom the ultimate virtue of a line consists, are bribed and corrupted, and no vigilance that I can use can prevent it," he lamented. In spite of numerous general orders and restrictions from the civil and military governments, Hurlbut realized that soldiers in occupied zones would not give up their pursuit of financial profit. "I trust [such actions of restriction] will have no effect," he concluded. And he was correct. Soldiers continued to join northern merchants in the illicit cotton trade, and a major in the Eighth Missouri Volunteers (Union) even resigned his commission in order to focus his full attention on the "mercantile business" of illegal cotton trading in Memphis.[49]

* * *

As occupation commanders continued to restrict their soldiers' involvement in informal economies, Charles A. Dana, a Union investigating agent and confidant to President Lincoln and Secretary of War Edwin M. Stanton, attempted to define the worrying implications of wartime commerce. He implored Stanton to remove cotton speculators from occupied regions "as a measure of military necessity. The mania for sudden fortunes made in cotton," he asserted, "has to an alarming extent corrupted and demoralized the army. Every colonel, captain, or quartermaster is in secret partnership with some operator in cotton; every soldier dreams of adding a bale of cotton to his monthly pay." Calling these practices "evil," Dana recommended that "no private purchaser of cotton shall be allowed in any part of the occupied region." Ulysses S. Grant agreed, commenting that he was "very much opposed to any trade whatever until the rebellion in this part of the country is entirely crushed out." Trading with white southerners, Grant implied, and even experimenting in entrepreneurism, were perfectly acceptable practices in which northerners could partake, as long as they suspended such inclinations while in the military. Henry Seaman, a conscientious Illinois soldier stationed at Helena, Arkansas, concurred, writing simply that "speculating is unbecoming to a soldier, and is apt to infringe upon military duty." It was not acceptable, these three men suggested, for soldiers to neglect their duties and use their military position to profit from their voluntary service to the nation.[50]

Dana, Grant, and Seaman critiqued informal economies on two principal fronts: demoralization of the army and corruption of the citizen-soldier ideal. Both phenomena found expressions in various forms in the problematic atmosphere of wartime occupation. Northern critics equated wartime commerce with the collapse of disinterested military service, as soldiers used their place in a volunteer army to advance their own personal interests. This problem was rooted in the conditions of military occupation. When northern males selflessly left their private lives to serve and defend the nation, they imagined grand campaigns and heroic battlefield exploits. When they instead found themselves assigned to garrisons, soldiers realized the mundane, inglorious duties of occupation did not conform to their imagined vison of military service. Believing that they were detached from the war, they turned their energies toward personal profit and gain.

The pursuit of personal economic ambitions was seen to depress and undermine the virtue of a citizen-army. When Charles A. Dana wrote that the cotton trade had "corrupted and demoralized the army," he touched on long-held societal fears concerning the nature of standing armies and their tendency toward unrestrained ambition. The nature of informal economies during the Civil War reflected the antebellum creed of self-sufficiency but also functioned as an ethos in which military power and access secured disparate financial advantage. From the earliest days of the nation's founding through the late prewar era, American culture distinguished between healthy autonomy and harmful uninhibited ambition. Those soldiers steeped in the cotton trade, however, were governed by intemperate ambition, obsessed with earning profits based on access to markets opened only because of war and military service.[51]

Looking askance at what they saw as their comrades' unbridled ambition, some Union soldiers criticized those who propagated complex economies at the expense of their military duty. These men claimed that their fellow troops had become so consumed by the prospect of wartime profit that they desired to see the war, and thus their businesses, continue indefinitely. "But you will ask," Samuel Root wrote his wife in April 1863 from Hilton Head, South Carolina, "when is this war to end." Although uncertain about the conflict's definitive conclusion, Root acknowledged that "there seems to be a leakage in all the great movements that paralyzes the effort of our best Generals & discourages real patriots in all grades of the army." Contrary to the republican notion of temporary military duty and the quest for a swift end to fighting, Root moaned, "to make money seems the object of many let the wants of the country be never so pressing." Lamenting the same conditions from New Orleans in 1864, Major General David Hunter admitted to Grant, "Cotton and politics, instead of the war, appear to have engrossed the army." "The vital interests of the contest are laid aside," he wrote with discouragement, "and the lives of our men are sacrificed in the interests of cotton speculators."[52]

The confluence of wartime occupation and informal economies stemmed from a paradoxical relationship. Soldiers came of age in an era that valued both democratic individualism and a strong dedication to republican virtue. In civilian life these traditional American traits went hand-in-hand, but garrison life placed them in opposition to each other. In order to function effectively, Union soldiers needed to maintain martial discipline. Yet the malaise of occupation culture lulled volunteers into a sense of remoteness from the war, which prompted them to revert back to the individualism of their civilian lives. Private citizens during peacetime could find outlets for their individualistic impulses in healthy pursuits, such as enterprise or education. Bereft of the opportunities they had enjoyed as civilians during peacetime, the occupiers expressed their individualism through illicit wartime commerce and trade. Such activity confirmed the worst fears of those who equated armies of occupation with standing armies. As garrison soldiers used their wartime authority and access to turn a profit, they embodied the corruption endemic to permanent military institutions, thereby threatening the ideal of virtuous volunteer military service. The internal, economic antagonists of military occupation, however, did not pose the only hazard to citizen-soldiers. A clandestine, external foe also roamed beyond garrisons, threatening the lives of Union troops throughout the occupied South.

5 | The Irregular War, Guerrilla Violence, and Counterinsurgency

After battling guerrillas in western Virginia for much of 1861, men in the Ninth Ohio Volunteers were accustomed to the stealthy, violent conditions of irregular warfare. Thus it is little surprising how the Ohioans responded to the murder of their general, Robert L. McCook, in August 1862, shortly after the regiment's transfer to north Alabama. Injured in an earlier engagement, McCook was being transported in an ambulance when his command halted temporarily near the edge of a clearing. A mounted guerrilla band emerged suddenly from an adjacent woodlot, ambushed the Union soldiers, and fatally shot the prostrate general. Seeking immediate retribution, "very much enraged, and before they could be stopped," McCook's troops "burned and destroyed some four or five farm-houses." But their vengeful acts did not stop there. "They broke over all restraints," recalled a fellow Ohioan, "and could not be controlled" as they laid waste to nearby plantations, private dwellings, and even "shot a rebel lieutenant who was on furlough."[1]

The murder of General McCook and the Ninth Ohio's subsequent reprisal exposed the unrestrained culture of war within arenas of military occupation. Relegated to garrisons or patrolling the southern countryside, volunteers came face to face with an enemy who did not engage in formal combat, who refused a soldier's uniform, and who attacked with clandestine ferocity. The Union's occupation of the Confederacy spawned a widespread guerrilla resistance which thrust unsuspecting volunteers into a conflicted chaos seemingly removed from the nineteenth-century American martial imagination. Isolated in a sea of irregular warfare, northern volunteers learned that honorable military practices did not exist in zones of occupation.[2]

Guerrillas and combatants dressed as private citizens reflected a very different kind of war from what Union soldiers expected. This was not a war conducted on distant fields of battle in which organized ranks of uniformed soldiers engaged one another. On the contrary, the irregular war raged in the streets of towns and in the desolate countryside where traditional rules of engagement and "civilized" combat rarely occurred. Unorganized violence flourished, forcing Union soldiers to adopt powerful modes of recourse, changing the occupiers in the process. Soon they no longer waited to be attacked; they no longer acted confused about the nature of their enemy. Instead, they craved revenge, which they sometimes poured on their aggressors in a grisly fashion.

The sporadic, furtive violence of guerrilla warfare forced US volunteers to alter their conceptions of the citizen-soldier ideal. Symbolized by the Ninth Ohio's fateful actions in north Alabama, identifying a faceless enemy and waging a war of counterinsurgency required targeting elements of society traditionally removed from previous American conflicts: civilians, landscapes, towns, and private property. This irregular conflict unleashed waves of punishment against both occupier and occupied, often shattering the limits of civility and restraint, and creating the sense of an endless war. As historian Michael Fellman has written, "guerrillas broke all the conventions of honorable war and led the occupying forces into a deepening cycle of attack and counterattack, revenge and retaliation, in a war that blurred all distinctions between the civilian and the military, thus deepening war and brutalizing combatants."[3]

The Civil War's irregular conflict was not a minor sideshow to the "real" war fought by the conventional armies. It functioned instead as the battlefield of military occupation, pitting the power of the occupier against the resistance of the occupied. And it reflected the broader, complex trials of waging a war of invasion, which undermined all notions of a quick, decisive, romantic struggle. The unforeseen conditions of wartime occupation—governing rebellious civilians, administering martial law, unfolding the process of emancipation, serving in what they defined as standing armies, participating in the social dislocation wrought by the military's presence, and ensuring the loyalty of wayward states—had already collided with the citizen-soldier ideal. Fearing that their roles as occupiers accelerated a detachment from republican values, Union volunteers equated armies of occupation with formal, permanent military institutions. Acting as agents of counterinsurgency exacerbated these tensions, fostering further anxiety among northern men about the changing nature of American military culture.[4]

Although they became willing participants in this conflict, Union soldiers also became deeply troubled by the implications of their antiguerrilla conduct and actions. Waging a war of counterinsurgency ultimately required adopting guerrilla tactics, thus revealing the fundamental tension underlying the entire irregular war. Perceiving that wars of occupation transformed volunteers into the very embodiment of violence that they combated, Union soldiers believed that their virtue as individual men, provisional soldiers, and a collective army had been irrevocably altered. Dealing with a direct outgrowth of wartime occupation, US volunteers thus struggled to define the consequences of irregular warfare upon the republican military tradition. They sensed that the moral nature of volunteer service had been discarded, rendering the American citizen-soldier little more than a guerrilla.

* * *

Guerrilla warfare represented an organic response both to the tangible and to the imagined nature of Union military occupation, offering an unorganized alternative to the more traditional war fought on the fields of Shiloh, Antietam, and Gettysburg. Guerrillas unleashed murder and thievery; destruction of bridges, towns, railroads, and supply lines; intimidation of Unionists and African Americans; and even the capturing and kidnapping of civilians and enemy soldiers. Exposure to the insurgent, sinister dynamics of guerrilla conduct pushed Union occupiers to redefine their preconceived notions about the enemy in particular and the war in general.[5]

Soldiers encountered sparse guerrilla activity in the wake of the initial forays into the South. During the spring of 1862, although minor attacks annoyed Union rearguards, full-scale assaults rarely occurred. This tepid resistance convinced the invading troops that occupation might be relatively peaceful. However, as the Yankee presence grew, and it became clear to white southerners that their unwelcome guests would not soon depart, guerrilla resistance mounted and spiraled out of control. Much of the occupied Confederacy erupted into a muddled, disorderly war in which small bands of irregular forces rode the countryside and harassed the occupying soldiers in their midst. Flouting the conventional and "proper" rules of civilized warfare, guerrillas convinced Union soldiers of their precarious and dangerous positions. "There is not a Garrison in Tennessee where a man can go beyond the sight of the flagstaff without being shot or captured," William T. Sherman wrote during the late summer of 1862. It became quite difficult to combat these forces: they operated at night, disguised themselves in civilian clothes, and employed hit-and-run tactics expressly to inspire fear and terror.[6]

Union occupiers believed that the guerrilla war distorted traditional conceptions of "the enemy." Insurgents behind the lines hardly resembled and functioned as the gray-clad soldiers in the principal Confederate armies. Writing from Nashville, John M. King, whose unit occupied middle Tennessee for much of 1863, characterized this problem. "The citizens were all rebel in sympathy and to guard those magazines and store houses was no easy task. Rebel spies and bushwhackers were going in and coming out [of the city] dressed as farmers, women, negroes, and the like, crawling through the guard line under the cover of darkness, getting ammunition and supplies to shoot our men from behind a tree or under a bush."[7]

King's description outlined the challenge of defining a civilian combatant. Acting largely independent of any formal guidelines, Yankee soldiers often followed the definitions established by their commanding officers. Guerrilla warfare, General William S. Rosecrans declared, embodied "bands of armed men [who] are let loose upon the country with the instincts and the means for the exercise of lawless power and with few if any restraints of military rule." John Pope, who commanded the Army of Virginia in July 1862, similarly indicted those "lawless bands of individuals not forming part of the organized forces of the enemy" who rejected "the garb of soldiers, who, seeking and obtaining safety on pretext of being peaceful citizens," harass the Union army, murder United States soldiers, devastate railroads and bridges, "and commit outrages disgraceful to civilized people and revolting to humanity."[8]

The blurry distinctions between civilian and guerrilla spread paranoia among the occupiers who believed that both groups conspired as a single body to dislodge the Yankee presence. Charles Harding Cox, whose Seventieth Indiana Volunteers protected the rail lines in Tennessee, commented, "Our career as railroad guards was tended with a great deal more danger . . . as we were scattered in small squads in a strong secesh country, where guerrilla bands were thick as hail, and the citizens would aid them against us any moment." In Rolla, Missouri, Henry J. Seaman related how one of his commanding officers in the Thirteenth Illinois led a small detachment that "captured every man woman and child that was capable of conveying intelligence to the [local guerrillas]." Union soldiers also sensed that they were constantly watched, believing that the shadowy guerrilla bands outnumbered them and threatened to kill anyone who dared to leave a garrison. "Last night there was considerable confusion in camp as the gurillas attacked our Pickets," wrote an Indiana soldier stationed in eastern Arkansas. "We do not know on going to Bed any night but what we may be aroused up during the night to fight the devils as they are hovering around us day and night watching an oportunity to surprise us."[9]

Guerrillas operated with a frightening combination of viciousness and unpredictability; Yankee soldiers continuously remained on edge, wondering when the next attack, murder, or theft might occur. "I have felt very uneasy about [our current location at Fort Donelson, Tennessee] on account of the trouble along the river," wrote Jerome Spilman of the Fifth Iowa Cavalry. "At this place we know not what a day may bring forth. Gurilla bands are roving all over the country.... We sleep on our arms every night." Courtland G. Stanton of the Twenty-first Connecticut similarly believed his position at Suffolk, Virginia, to be quite dangerous: "The people are all Secesh & the country is full of Guerilas." Although his unit had recently constructed a fort, Stanton believed that they were only minimally safe. "Picket duty here," he explained to his wife, "is such as you have heard of where the pickets have to keep themselves hid and are liable to get poped over it any time."[10]

Indeed, guerrillas indiscriminately hanged soldiers, burned their remains, and left their bodies behind as physical reminders of the occupiers' unwanted presence. Northern volunteers were often killed in a deliberate, yet random style fixed on intimidating the Union rank-and-file. Frank Twitchell revealed the varied ways his comrades died in Louisiana, describing their disfigured bodies. "The guerrilas captured a transport and burned it with 15 officers and a few soldiers[;] "what was done with them is more than wee know." A few days later, Twitchell better understood. "An officer of the 128th NY went across the river to look for some cotton that was hiden in the woods, he was found the other day hung by the neck to a tree." Twitchell concluded that "those Officers on the boat may of shared the same fate," ultimately learning that several soldiers ventured a "little ways from the camp after some brush to make brooms [and] they found a human skeleton laying in the weeds very likely it was one of our own men shot [by] the guerrilas."[11]

Rather than falling honorably in formal combat, the occupiers believed, their comrades had been slain indiscriminately by lawless bands of assassins. Iowan Charles O. Musser distinguished between various modes of wartime death, judging that guerrilla warfare near Helena, Arkansas, produced "not so much bloodshed as murder." Being "killed in battle and [dying] of sickness," Musser wrote in 1863, were far different from succumbing to the arbitrary will of guerrillas. Countless Union soldiers, such as Musser, had entered the army prepared to die on the field of battle—not to be murdered in the southern backwoods. The lack of honor and dignity attached to this form of passing underscored how US volunteers reasoned that they should not have to bear random acts of violence.[12]

While stationed in remote areas, protected only by small garrisons, and enduring the haphazard, arbitrary, and terrifying encounters with guerrillas, occupation soldiers questioned the honor and legitimacy of their clandestine foes. Guerrilla warfare epitomized anything but the grand battlefield encounters in which the war would be determined between troops clothed in the blue and gray. Instead, the guerrilla presence inspired an ambiguous outlook about the conflict. A Connecticut major wrote from Louisiana that his regiment had battled guerrillas continuously. "Nearly every day we have [fought] them to a fair engagement distant from our support," he recollected. However, "on each occasion we obtained only dissolving views of them. . . . They are activated by no motive but plunder, they fight only from ambuscade and war indiscriminately, upon friend and foe."[13]

It seemed that guerrillas existed merely to perpetuate chaos and spread violence. Union soldiers learned that they could not fight a fair, open battle against irregular bands in which a decisive outcome might be achieved. This led many occupiers to conclude that guerrillas were, in the words of John Vreeland of the Nineteenth Illinois, "only equalled by the Cowardly Mexicans." Other soldiers similarly categorized guerrillas as dishonorable cultural inferiors. "The expeditions sent out to break up guerrilla dens & seize & bring in there effects are always attended with a good deal of fatigue, & sometimes, but rarely, with skirmishing," explained an officer in the Department of the Gulf, "which is generally after the Indian fashion of skulking thro' the woods & bushes thus approaching their object or lying in wait. The general weapon of the Guerrillas is a double barreled gun loaded with buckshot. His appearance & his qualities those of a white Indian." Even Union general William S. Rosecrans argued that guerrillas "scalping their victims is all that is wanting to make their warfare like that which seventy or eighty years ago was waged by the Indians against the white race."[14]

In labeling guerrillas as inferior racial and cultural groups, Union soldiers classified as dishonorable the entire experience of irregular warfare. The essence of wartime military occupation and its accompanying violent resistance from white southerners resembled a destabilized environment in which chaos and disarray ruled supreme. Such attributes disturbed northern men who attached themselves intimately to societal order and balance. By employing scornful tropes of presumably inferior races and cultures, Union soldiers suggested that guerrilla defiance resembled dislocated Mexican regimes and loose-knit Indian nations always on the verge of collapse. Guerrillas, in the minds of the occupiers, represented the ignoble and fragmented components of these societies.[15]

Union soldiers' descriptions of fierce Indians creeping through dense forests beyond the bushes established their definitions—or perhaps imaginations— of a clandestine enemy. Likewise, the "uncivilized" character of guerrilla conduct came to be associated with the remote, untamed fringes of the southern landscape, as northern volunteers connected primitive warfare with the region's wild spaces. Irregular combatants used the natural environment to perpetuate grisly attacks upon unsuspecting soldiers, reorienting both the face and the landscape of war. Union soldiers thus linked the South's unimproved terrains, thick gnarled woods, and twisted underbrush with the crude manner in which its people waged battle.[16]

The occupiers produced a discourse unique to the irregular war, employing environmental rhetoric merged with traditional military expression. This language fused guerrillas with the natural environment, which transformed the local geography into an active, violent setting. "Having been shot at from the brush," an Illinois soldier wrote from Mississippi, the "infantry always thinks the enemy is just out of gunshot of them." The brush extended indefinitely, concealing the prowling guerrilla, offering impenetrable safety. Officer Stephen F. Fleharty described riding in a supply train in north-central Tennessee, "thundering along through a wild uncivilized region, when as we approached a dense wood it suddenly stopped, and bang! bang! bang! went firearms in the woods near by." Equating the remote lands with the guerrillas who inhabited the woods, Fleharty and his comrades later were "busy at work felling trees that might protect an attacking party."[17]

The unruly environment and the wild enemy it concealed became synonymous, each symbolizing the South's violent, archaic character. Union soldiers often did not distinguish between their adversaries and the landscape, instead seeing man and nature as a single object. The dearth of improved land seemed to sprout and nourish guerrillas, providing sustenance for their violent conditions. "The country looks desolate about this place," Michigander David Millspaugh wrote from Nashville; "the thick scrubby cedar grows along the road offering a good place for rebs to hide and prowl about." William Whitney, a volunteer in the Thirty-eighth Massachusetts, described how the guerrillas' "mode of action is to hide in the bushes when they hear of the approach of travelers and jumping out suddenly presenting a pistol.... Such is the state of the country."[18]

Linking the untamed backwoods with irregular combatants, finding their comrades' mutilated bodies, and enduring fear, stress, and worry about being murdered collectively transformed Union occupiers' understanding of a meaningful conflict. According to loyal volunteers, guerrillas merged their identities as civilians and combatants through peculiar incarnations of savage Indians and feral landscapes. Thus the disarrayed milieu of irregular warfare strained the occupiers' own blurring line between private civilian and combatant. The citizen-soldier ideal necessitated that those who threatened the nation must be killed or defeated, determined by a code of ethical wartime conduct.

However, guerrillas completely repudiated the basic requirements and assumptions of the citizen-soldier concept. Their identity as civilians-turned-combatants relied on murder and secrecy evident in their disregard for moral law and military custom. Union occupiers had to adapt to this model themselves or else be killed. But they struggled with the implications of this dilemma, primarily because they retained so much of their *own* civilian identities. In their minds, guerrillas did not function as formal soldiers but rather as rebellious and dangerous civilians. In peacetime society private citizens naturally would remove themselves from the presence of such uncouth individuals. And civilians certainly were not granted the legal or moral recourse to act in such a warlike manner.

The experience of occupation thrust these contradictory elements directly at Union soldiers, challenging them to decide how best to wage a war of counterinsurgency. Killing functioned as a universally acknowledged component of warfare; blurring the lines between civilian, combatant, and arbitrary murder did not. Their immediate enemies thrived *exclusively* on this brand of lawlessness, yet methods of conventional warfare failed to work within the occupation environment. Ultimately, the Union's citizen-volunteers would have to adopt guerrilla tactics, which transformed the common soldier's relationship to the army and to American society.[19]

* * *

As Charles Wright Wills and his comrades in the Seventh Illinois Cavalry rode through northern Alabama, confiscating cotton and enforcing the Union's authority, he outlined the citizen-soldier's emerging role as a force of counterinsurgency. "It makes the chivalry howl," he rejoiced in August 1862, "which is glorious music in our ears." Yet Wills tempered his enthusiasm when he recalled "the murders of Bob McCook, a dozen of men in this command, and hundreds in the army" who allegedly died at the hands of guerrillas. "We are satisfied that citizens do ten-elevenths of such work," he estimated, "and nothing less than the removal of every citizen beyond our lines . . . will satisfy us."[20]

Several months later, while guarding the railroads near Holly Springs, Mississippi, Wills's perspective had darkened, but not due to guerrilla violence. Instead, he struggled to accept the counterinsurgent tactics employed by his fellow occupation soldiers. Although he hardly sympathized with rebellious Confederates, Wills admitted that "'tis shocking and enough to make one's blood boil to see the manner in which some of our folks have treated them." Disgusted at the sight of his comrades destroying private property in the name of vengeance, Wills declared that "the army is becoming awfully depraved. How the civilized home folks will ever be able to live with them after the war, is, I think something of a question. If we don't degenerate into a nation of thieves," he wrote, "'twill not be for lack of example set by a fair portion of our army."[21]

Charles Wills outlined one of the great challenges of military occupation in the citizen-soldier tradition. Expecting a war governed by restraint and civilized conduct, he instead saw firsthand how insurgencies defied traditional assumptions of warfare. The enemy had changed his tactics, arbitrarily killing Union soldiers beyond the bounds of mutually accepted combat. The common Union soldier, therefore, would have to change *his* approach to war. But for Wills, the implications were stark: the long-term virtue of the common citizen-soldier was at stake. Could volunteer soldiers wage a war of counterinsurgency while also safeguarding the exceptional nature of the American citizen-soldier ideal?

Although Union soldiers strove to fulfill the obligations of the volunteer tradition, they believed that guerrillas could not be fully eradicated. Their enemies refused to fight in an honorable and open manner, straining available means of retaliation. However, instead of skulking in fear and struggling to abide by more muted approaches to war, the occupiers embarked on a campaign of destructiveness and violence, hoping to punish the perpetrators of irregular warfare. Union soldiers justified an overwhelming response against guerrillas, stretching the limits of restraint and widening the gulf between wartime civility and annihilation. Officers learned that their men could not be persuaded to withhold their anger; thus, they sanctioned, sometimes unofficially, wide-ranging tactics to counter the guerrilla presence. The occupation war was now reshaped, defined by vengeance and measured by devastation, altered by a profound shift in the citizen-soldier's mentality.[22]

Writing from Memphis in the summer of 1862, William T. Sherman summarized the evolving convictions of countless Union troops. "The Government of the United States may now safely proceed on the proper Rule that all in the South are Enemies of all in the North," he declared, "and not only are they unfriendly, but all who can procure arms now bear them as organized Regiments or Guerrillas." While one can debate the accuracy of Sherman's claim, he himself believed it to be true, as did many soldiers, thus dictating how they would conduct a war of counterinsurgency. Since all white southerners were potentially complicit in inflicting harm on US armies, and all were considered impediments to the restoration of the Union, nothing short of annihilation would settle the issue. Of course widespread extermination never occurred, but that misses the point. The *mind* and *practice* of the citizen-soldier were irrevocably altered in the realization that new methods of reprisal were now justified.[23]

The occupiers channeled their retribution through two distinct modes of recourse. First, they attacked the southern landscape, targeting local environs, towns, buildings, and private homes. Second, they trained their sights directly on irregular combatants, the physical embodiment of insurgent brutality. Union armies of occupation conducted this new war through patrols and scouting expeditions, deploying small squads to move swiftly and efficiently across the southern countryside. Using fortified garrisons as bases of operation, counterinsurgent forces often moved at night, ambushing guerrilla dens and surprising communities suspected of harboring irregular warriors. These approaches were not unique. They were the same ones employed by the guerrillas themselves.[24]

A key distinction needs to be drawn between the nature of reprisals and the ways in which Union occupiers understood their new roles in the irregular war. Desires for retaliation certainly inspired the evolution of counterinsurgency warfare. Yet it is crucial to recognize the constraints placed on the conduct of Union armies. Although most soldiers and commanders sought to extend "the hard hand of war" against guerrillas and sympathetic civilians, appropriate calculations were made on the acceptable limits of wartime retribution. Rather than murdering or imprisoning whole communities, Union authorities instead countered the guerrilla presence by burning private dwellings thought to be the sources of civilian violence, or even banishing and dislocating citizens from entire towns. The targets of such actions were particular citizens suspected of harboring, funding, or operating as guerrillas. These pragmatic policies nonetheless conditioned the troops in the art of waging war against the countryside and ununiformed civilians.[25]

Edward F. Noyes, an Ohio soldier, summarized the emerging tension. "As I go through this traitor country," he wrote, "two impulses are struggling in my heart, one to lay waste as we go—like destroying angels, to kill & burn and make the way of the transgressors hard—the other is to wage a civilized warfare." Union policy makers and military authorities initially sought the latter path, but the troops chose differently. "In view of the atrocities of the rebels," Noyes concluded, "our boys only wait for the word, to make the land desolate."[26]

Lieutenant Colonel John A. Keith of the Twenty-first Indiana Volunteers expanded on Noyes's wavering but ultimate acceptance of attacking the physical landscape in retribution for guerrilla warfare. Stationed in southeastern Louisiana, Keith received orders to take a detachment of troops into Terrebonne Parish to "arrest and punish" those guilty of killing wounded Union soldiers. The dead soldiers "were robbed of everything . . . [their] bodies after being brutally and disgustingly abused, being kicked and beaten, the face of [one soldier] scarcely retaining the semblance of a human being." Keith, along with 240 members of the Twenty-first Indiana, arrested several citizens of Houma, learning that the primary culprit was a prominent attorney and newspaper editor who plotted the murders of other local citizens. Keith demanded that other residents come forward who could provide information. He then declared that "the foul and unnatural murder of two American soldiers, repugnant alike to the instincts of humanity and the practice of civilized warfare," had caused the perpetual occupation of the town. "The atrocious nature of the crime itself," he continued, "the indecent, shameless and un-Christianlike burial and robbery of the dead . . . have forever disgraced the town of Houma."[27]

Since the citizens of Houma opted to embrace an uncivilized mode of warfare, Keith implied, Union occupiers were justified to respond in kind. After Keith ordered Houma's citizens to rebury the dead soldiers, he left a flag atop the courthouse as a reminder that "terrible consequences" would befall the town and its population if the graves were disturbed or future attacks attempted. Indeed, local residents were given forty-eight hours to identify and turn in the culprits. If they failed to comply, Keith warned, "not a vestige of the town of Houma shall be left to identify its former location, and the plantations in the parish of Terrebonne shall suffer in a like degree." Southern civilians and the physical landscape were no longer passive actors in the drama of wartime occupation. All were now brought into the purview of Union occupation, used as symbols of retribution and vengeance.[28]

Houma, Louisiana, escaped the destruction of the US military; other southern communities were not so fortunate. As the guerrilla threat continued unabated, Union armies unleashed the very tactics threatened by Keith. Occupiers exacted devastation to southern towns with meticulous commitment. Addison McPheeters, Jr., of the Twenty-first Illinois Volunteers, commented that "the boys are raising hell in Nashville every night, I would not care if they would burn it to ashes, it is no [uncommon] thing to see houses burning here." McPheeters explained that such occurrences are "the best way to put down the rebellion, burn them out, damn them." Charles Wright Wills, a fellow Illinoisan, agreed. "This little town had when the war commenced some 40 house," he wrote from Middleton, Tennessee, in June 1863. "Now it boasts of not more than 12 or 15. . . . This country has literally been scraped, swept and scoured."[29]

Such tactics were crucial to reconstruct what McPheeters and Wills considered an archaic, rebellious society. Union soldiers believed that a reunited nation must be rid of the physical emblems of violent resistance. Guided by an acute sense of national cleansing, Major James A. Connolly, of the 123rd Illinois, declared in 1864, "We'll burn every house, barn, church . . . and nothing but the most complete desolation will be found in our track." If civilians, Connolly continued, "play the guerrilla against us, neither youth nor age, nor sex will be respected. Everything must be destroyed." Irregular violence symbolized what Union soldiers considered to be outmoded relics of the southern culture of honor. Everything in the southern world, from its agricultural staples, to its rural lands, to its embrace of guerrillas, must be extinguished. The postwar Union needed a singular identity, they believed, one drawn in the northern image.[30]

Citizen-soldiers realized that national rejuvenation could come only through great destruction and violence. Rather than expressing shock or confusion in the wake of clandestine attacks, the occupiers devastated properties suspected of harboring guerrilla assailants. As he traveled on a railroad transport to Huntsville, Alabama, John Beatty described how guerrillas attacked the train, wounding multiple Yankees and slashing telegraph lines. Informing the residents of nearby Paint Rock "that this bushwhacking must cease," Beatty "then set fire to the town, took three citizens with me, returned to the train, and proceeded to Huntsville." Irregular enemy combatants, Beatty explained, did not have a place in formal warfare: "If they wanted to fight they should enter the army, meet us like honorable men, and not, assassin-like, fire at us from the woods and run." He pledged thenceforth to hold all citizens responsible for similar conduct, "mak[ing] them more uncomfortable than they would be in hell."[31]

While Union soldiers made a deliberate decision to target both the southern countryside and local towns, they also trained their vengeance on the bodies and physical presence of their guerrilla adversaries. The choice to integrate a corporeal element into the irregular war created an intimate, yet deeply violent bond between the rivals. Guerrillas had long disgraced the occupiers' bodies through mutilation, hanging, and disfigurement. Union soldiers now responded in like manner, applying methods that they believed would smother the guerrilla threat, redefining a war that lacked structure and clarity.

The guerrilla conflict had always been an acutely personal affair. Thus, Union volunteers justified modes of unconventional recourse against the enemies' bodies, refusing to acknowledge irregulars to be official soldiers deserving of honorable treatment. Capturing an officer from a guerrilla company roaming the countryside near Bayou Boeuf, Louisiana, "evidently for the purpose of shooting down our soldiers," one officer issued a directive outlining the rebel's destiny. The guerrilla would "be shot to death . . . as a warning to all men not soldiers to remain peaceably at their homes, if they desire the protection of the Government of the 'United States.'" His crime was simple, his verdict a warning to other potential civilian combatants: "And the fate of this man shall be the fate of every man found with arms in his hands not belonging to the so-called Army of the Confederate States of America." An honorable man, in the minds of Union occupiers, would enlist in the military and fight his nation's battles in uniform. If he chose an alternative course, he would meet a fate similar to the very type of war he perpetrated.[32]

The occupiers implemented a similar variety of violent procedures, which ranged from hangings, executions, beatings, chases through the woods, and even knocking on *suspected* guerrillas' doors and pulling the trigger. If northern men's bodies were targeted, killed, and mutilated in a shameful fashion, then their aggressors would endure the same destiny. Union soldiers sought to demonstrate that they too could play the game of irregular warfare, while reducing their enemy to nothing more than a skeleton. Simple killing and burial were unsatisfactory, practiced only by the uniformed, principal armies. A new code governed the irregular war, with competitions of power directing its course.[33]

Oftentimes, soldiers were instructed to avoid capturing and imprisoning guerrillas. One officer ordered his troops, who picketed the lines outside of New Orleans, "if attacked by such infernal rascals to bring no prisoners in, only their dead carcasses, of those that they are successful in securing." A Michigan colonel stationed in middle Tennessee replied to similar orders in July 1863, "I propose to bring some of the scoundrels to grief if I can. I have no doubt they intend the same thing by me." Over the next few months, his regiment captured numerous bushwhackers, most of whom were sent to Nashville for imprisonment. Yet the colonel kept "two or three to hang when we want a little fun."[34]

Union occupiers indeed used hanging as an effective, symbolic means of retribution. Charles O. Musser explained to his father that although reports of such executions rarely appeared in northern newspapers, "that is no sign that it is not done." In fact, Musser acknowledged that when captured, guerrillas were often hanged. As early as August 1861, the occupation commander at Cape Girardeau, Missouri, declared that if local guerrillas made war on the local population or army, "I will hang them, and take a bitter revenge on you in other respects." And the practice continued nearly four years later following the murders of three Union troops at Powder Springs, Georgia. The guerrilla perpetrators were caught and ordered to "be either shot or hung in retaliation."[35]

No-quarter retaliation provided soldiers with significant martial leverage. Mirroring guerrilla tactics allowed the Yankees to exert a degree of power and control that they believed had been undermined by irregular warfare. A Massachusetts soldier disagreed with imprisoning guerrillas, calling on his officers "to take everyone they catch and shoot them." And Taylor Peirce's comrades in Missouri did exactly that. "We gather up [the guerrillas] as we go along and shoot them," he wrote in February 1863. "They are a set of murderers and are not fit to encumber society." One local resident allegedly fired at Peirce's officers, and was eventually apprehended and shot near his house. "When we came along he was lying by the side of the road and his wife was crying over him," Peirce wrote. "It looks hard to me to see a man shot and his wife and children left alone but these men are the ones that keep up the cruelties that are continually being practiced in this part of Missouri."[36]

The male image emerged as the central target in this sphere of violence.

Yet some modes of recourse, while grounded in masculine humiliation, represented basic forms of peace, innocence, and even a sense of playful restraint. Considering guerrillas and their tactics to be acts of purposeful emasculation, the occupiers fashioned ways to make their enemies endure the shame of their conduct. As the Ninety-second New York Volunteers picketed the cold, dark shores of the Neuse River in coastal North Carolina, they experienced nightly battles with guerrillas. The cavalrymen "hated them cordially, and were disposed to show them but little mercy." The irregular combatants often dressed in civilian clothes, professing to be "unionists, neutrals, or 'know nothings,'" often shooting "our men in cold blood." After a scouting mission departed to rout a guerrilla band, the rebel leader challenged one of the occupation officers to a fight. The two parties squared off in the woods, riding, yelling, and shooting in a violent rampage.[37]

When the fighting ceased, men on both sides lay killed or wounded, while some of the guerrillas were captured and taken to the Union garrison at New Bern. "One prisoner was marched through the city," an observer noted, "with a woman's skirt on, and on his back a placard with the words, 'guerrilla caught dressed in woman's clothes.'" The soldiers simply could have killed their prized catch, leaving his body to rot in the woods enveloped only by the peace of nature. Many Union occupiers had, after all, experienced their final moments alone and isolated. But the spectacle of uncensored public humiliation to guerrillas' masculinity in the broad daylight of southern society seemed much too tempting to resist. Cloaking the male body in women's attire, in this instance, was far superior to wasting a bullet.[38]

The corpus of Union reprisals extended far beyond gendered humiliation. Perhaps the most peculiar tactic in the war against Confederate guerrillas was not a variation in military strategy or conduct. Rather, it was a change in language, an alteration of an imagined mentality. Union soldiers transformed expeditions and battles against guerrillas into a symbolic hunt, reminiscent of their prewar days in pursuit of deer, quail, or other wild game. Converting guerrillas into a faceless foe, devoid of personality or humanity, allowed the occupiers to pursue their adversaries without concern for moral bearing. Instead, the hunt for guerrillas evolved into a game, a competition to see who could acquire the best prize. The environment of occupation, which threatened the core of northern masculinity, permitted the occupiers to exhibit the virtues of manly contest. There were no rules, no limitations, and no referees. Only raw instinct guided the soldier against his prey.[39]

The guerrilla body, indeed the "dead carcasses" of deceased opponents, became the trophy in this competition. The soldiers carefully gauged the score, always noting the number of dead opponents compared to survived comrades. "Captain Bishop with some 25 men of Companies A and G did a splendid thing last Thursday night," Charles Wills exclaimed. "He surprised Saulstreet and 20 of his gang ... killed three wounded and captured five and six sound prisoners, without losing one of our men or getting scratched. Three of the wounded guerrillas have since died." The hunt had commenced.[40]

Cloaking the battle against guerrillas in familiar prewar language allowed the occupiers to distance themselves from the horrors of irregular war. But their rhetoric also revealed the troubling extent to which they had become desensitized to shocking conduct. Characterizing their opponents merely as animals implicitly sanctioned a mode of warfare that stripped the humanity away from both the hunter and the hunted. "I have just returned from a grand guerrilla hunt of over a week," Connecticut officer Frank Peck reported from New Orleans. The pursuit, though, proved difficult because "they never fight openly" and often "skedaddled" when the hunters appeared.[41]

Yet such hunts offered a uniquely challenging element: the crafty and clever intellects of the prey. The human, intellectual component indeed added a distinct challenge. Henry C. Gilbert, a colonel in the Nineteenth Michigan Volunteers, described a guerrilla pursuit in Tennessee. "Our hunting still goes on," he wrote in March 1864, "'the hunting of men.' Over 40 of the guerrillas have been shot since Feb." The search parties, he reported, "go on foot & hunt men as they would deer. . . . It is awful but there is an excitement about it that places it far above anything recorded by Cumming and Gerard the Lion Hunter. Their game were mere brutes without intelligence. Here we hunt men with brains." Gilbert exhibited an acute sense of pride, celebrating the sport's great difficulty, and praising his victims' shrewdness and quickness. The thrill of securing a human trophy appeared all the more satisfying.[42]

The hunting paradigm functioned not only as a metaphor or an imagined discourse, but also morphed into official military policy. A circular distributed throughout central Missouri instructed Union forces on how to blend into the local landscape. "The brush and low grounds that would be likely to afford cover for guerrillas must be closely examined," the directive stated; "to move secretly, the men will be marched across the prairies in the night." The environmental dimensions of guerrilla warfare had come full circle. United States soldiers who had once been victims of the wild landscape now became part of untamed bush. "While on the hunt no talking or other loud noises will be made," the order charged, "except signals, which should be the imitation of some forest bird or animal." If northern troops employed these instructions carefully, "it [would] not be possible for bands of guerrillas to remain concealed in any portion of this district." Thus, the guerrilla-turned-prey signified an object to be killed, not captured. In a war stripped of honor and control, the language of hunting—employed either by guerrillas or Union soldiers— assumed a hierarchical structure, with a superior assailant tracking a less powerful foe, who always fled for his life.[43]

* * *

The hunt for men testified to Union authorities' increasing concern that the guerrilla war had spiraled dangerously out of control. Soldiers in service to the republic, some reasoned, did not adopt irregular, brutal tactics, but rather adhered to the standards of civilized warfare. An inspector general from the US Army, writing from St. Louis in March 1864, perhaps best summarized the implications of the occupiers' violent retributions. "It has been the custom in many parts of the department for officers and soldiers, when operating against guerrillas, to immediately put to death all who fall into their hands," he disclosed, "even after they have thrown down their arms and asked for mercy." The inspector reported that most officers prohibited taking prisoners, explaining that these unyielding tactics prolonged the nature of irregular warfare by inducing the enemy to "to fight to desperation." He concluded that the guerrilla war would continue as long as occupation continued, "where murder, highway robbery, pillage, and other kindred crimes are now of almost daily occurrence."[44]

The inspector further outlined his concerns about the tactics adopted by local counterinsurgency forces. Acknowledging that "bushwhackers undoubtedly deserve the most severe chastisement for the atrocities they have committed," he nonetheless wondered if imprisonment and military tribunals— traditional modes of recourse—would provide "the opportunity to prove their innocence before being executed." The inspector's disquietude emerged not out of sympathy for suspected guerrillas, but from a deep-seated anxiety that the republic's citizen-soldiers had themselves morphed into bodies of unrestrained, chaotic violence. "The existing practice," he conceded, "enables evil-disposed soldiers to rob and murder loyal and inoffensive citizens under the plea that they were acting as bushwhackers, and it unquestionably tends to demoralize the troops."[45]

Ironically, the inspector general's report appeared one year *after* civil and military authorities sought to address the consequences of Union soldiers' participation in the irregular war. In the spring of 1863, General-in-Chief Henry W. Halleck enlisted Francis Lieber, a German-born political philosopher, historian, and expert on international military conduct, to codify the United States' counterinsurgency doctrine. In a pamphlet entitled "Guerrilla Parties Considered with Reference to the Laws and Usages of War," Lieber defined nearly a dozen forms of irregular combat, concluding that the nature of guerrilla warfare presented the greatest threat to an effective military governance. Lieber considered all forms of guerrilla warfare and the individuals who perpetrated it to be illegitimate, which civilized nations should not utilize or acknowledge. Though he argued that "guerrillamen" should be captured and tried as war criminals, and sometimes even subject to decisive modes of recourse, Lieber understood that theoretical applications of irregular warfare were "much diminished by the fact that the soldier generally decides these cases for himself."[46]

Lieber's pamphlet culminated in General Orders No. 100, a codified system of conduct for armies of occupation. Published in April 1863, the code incorporated the nebulous laws of war into systematized legal theory. Hoping to define the Union's war of occupation in moral and humanitarian terms, Lieber's Code instructed the proper ways to conduct martial law, to protect civilians' rights and private property, and to accommodate prisoners of war. The code grew out of Lieber's concern about the implications of wartime destruction, targeting of civilians, and seemingly wanton rampage perpetrated by Union armies. Inspired to introduce a level of moral consideration to wartime occupation, Lieber believed that "men who take up arms against one another in public war do not cease on this account to be moral beings, responsible to one another and to God."[47]

The insistence on morality and restraint functioned at the heart of Lieber's quest. He authorized wide latitude for Union armies as they swept across the South, employing "those measures which are indispensable for securing the ends of the war." Lieber merely wanted to curb what he considered unnecessary or unauthorized pillaging, destruction, or killing. The definitions of such terms, though, were left to the discretions of soldiers and field commanders. In fact, General Orders No. 100 suggested that protection of enemy civilians and property were exceptions to the rule. Above all, Lieber's Code was hazy on its particular guidelines. On the one hand, armies of occupation were instructed to practice civilized restraint, while on the other, they given substantial leeway to measure their destruction of hostile environments and people.[48]

Although seemingly ambiguous, and at times contradictory, General Orders No. 100 held deeper significance. Lieber's writings conveyed a sense of discomfort with the apparent cultural degradation of the Union's citizen-armies as they became mired in the long-term occupation of the Confederacy. Military occupation created unprecedented challenges, including waging an expansive war of counterinsurgency against hostile southern civilians. Lieber's Code implied that the United States simply did not have a grounded experience in wars of occupation or a martial culture dedicated to regulating the behavior of white citizens. Indeed, large, static, invading armies, even in wartime, were believed to spawn depravity and violence and to fragment society. Occupation sought to restore peace and loyalty to rebellious regions, yet sometimes the exact opposite occurred. White southerners resisted and blue-clad troops pushed back until explosive chaos ensued.

General Orders No. 100, then, served as the US government's attempt to articulate a national position on the ethical integrity of the republic's soldiers. Lieber's Code suggested that the *troops* were to blame if they committed acts of destruction or violently engaged enemy combatants, while the *nation* would be exonerated. Those Union occupiers who defied the orders would be interpreted as men who failed to abide by the official ethical standards of the Union. Lieber therefore sought to return a degree of virtue and restraint to military institutions that might become detached frommoral direction. The United States must win this war, he concluded, or else all efforts to rededicate the nation to a system of moral wartime conduct would be irrelevant. Thus, Lieber's Code was less an inflexible legal decree and more a commentary on maintaining the honorable standards of a citizen army.[49]

Lieber's Code gave voice to the broader anxieties of Union soldiers who feared that counterinsurgency warfare had fundamentally transformed the American citizen-soldier tradition. They came to consider that their conduct, while necessary, also contained damaging consequences. Guerrilla attacks outside of New Orleans, for example, pushed local occupation commanders to order the destruction of nearby Donaldsonville, Louisiana. F. A. Roe, a naval lieutenant on the USS *Katahdin,* implored his commanding officers to halt what he considered the needless leveling of the town. "I am desirous of encountering enemies and of injuring them in every manly manner," he protested, "but I cannot further prostitute the dignity of my profession." Roe believed that "it is disgraceful and humiliating to me to be ordered on guard duty of soldiers employed in pillaging ladies' dresses and petticoats, and I respectfully request that I may be relieved from such service."[50]

Likewise, Charles Henry Moulton, a private in the Sixth Michigan Volunteers believed that occupation and guerrilla warfare altered the character of northern volunteers. In the wake of a recent expedition and guerrilla hunt through the swamps near New Orleans, Moulton wrote, "I am getting so I dont care for anything. let a man be in the army," he warned, "and he is more like a Savage than a man." As early as October 1862, he suggested that the irregular war had taken its toll on his fellow Michiganders occupying southern Louisiana. Their violent responses functioned as the great agents in their changed attitudes. "Our men is all sick and tired of the war," he moaned, "and are discouraged." The war seemed "as though it would never get done," primarily because guerrillas appeared to be self-perpetuating, never fully eradicated. Thus, Union soldiers, Moulton concluded with troubled expression, became hardened and distant, adopting a callous regard for civilized conduct and human dignity.[51]

Conceptions of participating in an army both surrounded and inculcated by haphazard violence infected Union soldiers' perspectives of themselves. Like Moulton, Charles O. Musser, a volunteer in the Twenty-ninth Iowa, admitted in February 1863 that he served in "what would be called the dark side of soldiering." After waging war against guerrillas for several months, he recognized that "the boys are geting so that they do not care much for anything." Indeed, the constant firing upon Union pickets and the hit-and-run tactics employed by clandestine foes inspired deep-seated hatred for all white southerners. "We are in for fighting to the last rather than give way to traitors and rebels," he declared in April, and "we will kill, 'burn,' and destroy every thing before us to gain our end. I never want to come home untill the war is ended." Musser's brand of demoralization culminated not with a desire to leave the army, but rather to lay waste to the people and region he associated with irregular war. "I have no pity, no mercy," he acknowledged. "I would rather put a minne ball through the brain of one of them renegades than the . . . [regular army] rebel down here."[52]

The transformation of soldiers to "savages" who sought unmitigated vengeance against communities and enemy combatants, caused some Yankees to believe that they had transformed Union armies into destabilizing institutions. Military occupation aimed to restore peace and calm to rebellious regions, yet according to Sergeant Major Stephen F. Fleharty, invading armies only spawned guerrilla resistance. "A bitter feeling of hostility is naturally engendered," he wrote as a result of the incursions into Tennessee, "and we find the citizens ever willing to aid the armed rebels in all their designs against us." Anti-Union sentiment and guerrilla conduct accordingly pushed volunteers into extreme forms of retaliation, fueling a self-perpetuating cycle of violence.[53]

Northern citizen-soldiers considered that their perceptions of volunteer service, their understanding of the enemy, and the nature of their military art had been changed by the irregular war. As the inspector general in St. Louis suggested, little distinguished guerrilla from occupier. The ethos of occupation brought them both together, merging their identities as collective agents of violence. Robert Gould Shaw, the white colonel of the famed Fifty-fourth Massachusetts Volunteers, perhaps best articulated the blurring line between citizen-soldier and guerrilla. Shaw pledged himself to civilized warfare, trusting that belligerents on both sides must remain wedded to controlled, moral conduct. Guerrilla warfare, he believed, unleashed Union soldiers to perform acts of peculiar violence against people, property, and the environment. "Besides my own distaste for this barbarous sort of warfare," he acknowledged, the guerrilla conflict was fraught with disrepute and disgrace, sinking the citizen-soldier "into a plunderer or robber."[54]

Shaw observed that the abnormal culture of occupation spawned an equally strange mode of warfare, which he considered unprofessional and simplistic. He criticized his colleague in the Department of the South, James Montgomery, for adopting irregular tactics to combat the insurgent presence. "He is a guerrilla-man," Shaw scoffed. "He is an Indian in his mode of warfare. . . . I can't say I admire it. It isn't like a fair stand up such as our Potomac Army is accustomed to." Distinguishing between his former service in the Union's principal field army, and the guerrilla war in South Carolina and Georgia, Shaw denounced Montgomery's tactics. His willingness to burn and destroy "wherever he goes with great gusto, & looks as if he had quite a taste for hanging people & throat-cutting whenever a suitable subject offers."[55]

Disgusted not only by Montgomery's tactics, Shaw also worried about the broader implications of his comrade's conduct. Denigrating him a "bushwhacker," Shaw believed that Montgomery reflected the larger body of soldiers who relished wanton destruction and unnecessary violence. Montgomery evidently had been converted by the dictates of counterinsurgent operations, claiming that Union soldiers were no longer bound by traditional modes of warfare. "That makes it none the less revolting to wreak our vengeance on the innocent and defenseless," Shaw grumbled in June 1863 following the burning of Darien, Georgia, which he believed degraded the character of citizen-armies. Referring to it as a "dirty piece of business," Shaw noticed the stark differences between occupying the Department of the South and serving in the field with the Army of the Potomac. "For myself, I have gone through the war so far without dishonour," he acknowledged, yet the very acts of committing war upon civilians, hanging guerrilla enemies, or skulking through the woods, Shaw believed, were all devoid of "pluck or courage."[56]

If, though, the army had fought honorably for possession of territory, such as it did in Virginia, "there might have been some reason for Montgomery's acting as he did; but as the case stands, I can't see any justification." Outlining the spirit of the citizen-soldier ideal, Shaw suggested that "if it were the order of our government to overrun the South with fire and sword, I might look at it in a different light." But "as the case stands, we are no better than 'Semmes,' who attacks and destroys defenceless vessels, and haven't even the poor excuse of gaining anything by it." He concluded, writing, "After going through the hard campaigning and hard fighting in Virginia, this makes me very much ashamed of myself."[57]

Robert Gould Shaw witnessed both the regular and the irregular war during his time in the service. He was exposed to the massive eastern armies that confronted one another on the formal field of battle, generally devoid of contact with civilians, focused on deciding the fate of the nation. He considered himself a citizen-soldier in this conflict, performing his civic duty and accepting the possibility of an honorable death. Guided by a sense of moral integrity that accompanied his identity as a volunteer, Shaw applied control and discipline. As a participant in the irregular war, though, Shaw witnessed what he perceived to be the deterioration of the citizen-soldier's moral character. The ethos of war in the occupied Confederacy, he learned, was far different from that in the eastern theater. Although disgusted with Montgomery's contention that "we are outlawed, and therefore not bound by the rules of regular warfare," Shaw could not deny the sentiment's truth. The irregular war, populated by vicious guerrillas, vengeful soldiers, and suspicious civilians, enveloped all participants into its violent fold, changing everyone in the process.[58]

The American Civil War and even its aftermath were nowhere near as destructive as other nineteenth-century conflicts, in, for example, Napoleonic Europe or dynastic China. The tolls of human death and environmental annihilation fell far short of these international episodes. However, Robert Gould Shaw highlighted a curious feature when he attempted to interpret the problematic nature of the Civil War's irregular conflict. Underscoring both the impact of individual experience and the collective national identity, Shaw implied that focusing on numbers of dead soldiers or civilians missed a startling reality about the changing character of American warfare. Indeed, he witnessed far more deaths on the fields at Antietam than he did in the destruction of Darien, Georgia. Yet, as indicated by his adverse reaction to the latter, Shaw emphasized the fast-evolving integrity of the citizen-soldier ideal in occupied zones.[59]

Americans believed that they lived in an exceptional nation in which free citizens were obligated to protect and defend the republic that safeguarded their liberty. So when Shaw perceived that citizen-soldiers might discard the obligations of morality and honor, engaging in modes of warfare reflective of guerrilla tactics, he considered the ethic of republican citizenship to be threatened. This idea revealed the fundamental tension underlying the entire irregular war. Although Union occupiers actually behaved with considerable restraint, especially when compared to other nineteenth-century civil conflicts, Shaw presumed that their *participation* in counterinsurgency warfare had pushed them into an inescapable arena of perceived immorality, far removed from the romanticized citizen-soldier tradition.

Part of the problem stemmed from the character of their enemy: white southerners. Yankee troops hated their Confederate and irregular foes, believing that the rebellious South had to be remade into a loyal northern image. United States armies, though, did not set the entire region ablaze or imprison and murder millions of civilians. Yet for each home that was burned, each community that was destroyed, and each guerrilla who was hunted, Union soldiers feared the symbolism of what they considered violent conduct against American environs and white American citizens.[60]

And herein lay one of the ironic tragedies of military occupation, counterinsurgency, and guerrilla combat during the American Civil War. Union citizen-soldiers who participated in irregular conflict underwent a striking alteration in their intellectual conceptions of war, their definitions of the enemy, and their understandings of traditional, civilized conduct. Occupiers learned that war was not a restricted event in which only formal armies battled for the fate of nations. Instead, occupation sometimes necessitated making war on civilians, destroying private homes, and wrecking the landscape. Union soldiers thus recognized that their particular war was directed against *white* civilians, *private* property, and *American* environs—ingredients central to the concept of national exceptionalism. Contemporaries could not escape the unsettling reality that white citizen-soldiers conducted war against white citizens, all of whom claimed a common national heritage, and who might again inhabit the same nation. The white citizen-soldier had long voiced his discontent with the ideological, cultural, and military dimensions of wartime occupation. In 1863, President Abraham Lincoln definitively addressed the disaffected positions of his occupiers garrisoned behind the lines.[61]

6 | Lincoln's Proclamation and the White Racial Assumptions of Wartime Occupation

By the time Garland H. White's letter reached Secretary of State William H. Seward in May 1862, the Federal government had long been inundated with similar missives. As an African American minister, White was "called upon By my peopl to tender . . . thir willingness to serve as soldiers in the southern parts during the summer season or longer if required." Abolitionists had likewise petitioned Abraham Lincoln since the earliest days of the war, imploring the president to raise regiments of black men like Garland White, many of whom had been enslaved and who sought to strike a decisive blow for their race's freedom. When he wrote Seward, White acknowledged that he was "formerly the Servant of Robert Toombs of Georgia," now a general in the Confederate Army. White made no special appeal; his request was "not for speculation or self interest[,] but for our love for the north & the government at large." He sought only Union victory and "restoration of peace [which] will prove an eternal overthrow of the institution of slavery."[1]

Echoing the basic foundations of the republican military ethic in which private civilians offered their services to the government during times of crisis, Garland White's petition rang loud with symbolism. African American men had long been marginalized by the citizen-soldier tradition, which recognized only white men as participants. But in a war so clearly defined by the fate of race and nation, White's request for military service portended great change to American institutions. As Frederick Douglass famously declared in 1863, "Once let the black man get upon his person the brass letters U.S.; let him get an eagle on his button, and a musket on his shoulder and bullets in his pocket, and there is no power on the earth . . . which can deny that he has earned the right of citizenship in the United States." For White and Douglass, black military service during the Civil War had the potential to undermine, shatter, and reorganize the American racial landscape. Yet in May 1862, when White penned his letter, President Lincoln opposed enlisting black men, a position he had defended since the beginning of the conflict.[2]

Meanwhile, as the Union war effort evolved into a complicated war of occupation, disillusioned white volunteers believed that their occupying duties had detached them from the citizen-soldier tradition. They equated wartime occupation and the garrisons in which they served with the troubling symbolism of a standing army, which they believed reordered society at the bayonet's point, concentrated sources of temptation and corruption, fostered laziness and idleness, and provided the departure point from which to wage a chaotic war of counterinsurgency. The ideological, cultural, and military crises of wartime occupation were not the only problems faced by Union armies in late 1862 and early 1863. Too many troops were deployed as garrison forces, depriving field armies of precious manpower; many regiments' terms of enlistment were about to expire; thousands of soldiers were absent without leave; and the flow of volunteers had slowed to a near halt. As occupation grew to encompass more and more of the conflict, prominent Americans reacted not only to the Union's manpower demands but also to the apparent conflicts between garrison culture and the citizen-soldier ideal. Within this disquieting military context, much of the white North began to reconsider its views on black soldiers. President Abraham Lincoln, along with other policy makers, high-ranking military authorities, and white soldiers together attempted to solve the crisis of wartime occupation through the use of African American soldiers, many of whom had been formerly enslaved.[3]

The Emancipation Proclamation offered one of the first official policy pronouncements about black troops, mirroring white America's cultural definitions of volunteer military service. "And I further declare and make known," the proclamation read, "that such persons of suitable condition, will be received into the armed service of the United States to garrison forts, positions, stations, and other places, and to man vessels of all sorts in said service." Lincoln's phrasing addressed white soldiers' grievances about garrisoning by assigning black soldiers to take over these duties, thereby weaving a distinct racial component into the web of wartime occupation. Upon enlistment, the vast majority of the USCT were relegated behind the lines in garrison units, comprising by the end of the war nearly 10 percent (178,975) of all Union forces. They populated 166 regiments, 145 of which were infantry, in addition to serving in the navy. More than 100 (64 percent) USCT units exclusively performed garrison duty, reflecting much of the loyal northern citizenry's perception of black regiments as a second-tier military force. A minority of other USCT regiments witnessed and participated in formal combat and field operations, yet very few were engaged in more than one battle or skirmish. Lincoln's language of emancipation assigned African American soldiers to garrison duty in order to free white troops from such service so they—white soldiers—could take part in the central and decisive theaters of the war, thus allowing them to fulfill the citizen-soldier ideal. Emancipation and black soldiering, as envisioned by the white wartime generation, and especially Lincoln, were limited by distinctions between "genuine" citizen-soldiers and "second-class" auxiliary forces. By 1863, military occupiers were no longer solely aggrieved white volunteers; their ranks now included a sizable black element.[4]

Black military service has received justifiable praise, grounded in heroic battlefield exploits, the successful political quest for equal military pay, and the origins of African American male citizenship. Such due admiration effectively undermines the wartime generation's racist assumptions that black men were too docile and unwilling to engage in combat.[5] The collision of wartime occupation and emancipation, however, complicates this triumphal narrative. By casting African American soldiers' primary wartime role as garrison troops, Lincoln's proclamation held great implications for the scope of wartime emancipation, the question of biracial citizenship, and the assumptions underlying the American citizen-soldier tradition. Situated as it was within nineteenth-century American martial culture, wartime occupation, and Lincoln's brand of antislavery politics, the famed Emancipation Proclamation must undergo fresh scrutiny. By taking seriously the military context and constraining language in which Lincoln wrote the proclamation's call for black troops, and the subsequent manner in which African American men were enrolled into the army and deployed as soldiers, we see that the road to black male citizenship was uneven at best and unpaved at worst.[6]

When viewing the black military experience through the complex lens of garrisoning, occupation, and citizen-soldiering, the very assumptions of nineteenth-century military citizenship are obscured. According to white contemporaries, the problem of military occupation during the Civil War era revealed that the act of volunteerism was not in itself enough to confirm American male citizenship upon volunteers either white or black. Instead, white volunteers revealed through their wartime discourses and actions that occupation and garrisoning were fundamentally antithetical (in their minds) to the citizen-soldier tradition, which was also defined by the *type* and *condition* of service that the volunteer performed.

The Emancipation Proclamation placed African American men in a military context—garrisons—in which American society believed white citizen-soldiers did not belong. "This realization," historian Carole Emberton recently wrote about the problematic limits of black military service, "should cause us to question not *if* military service made blacks into citizens but instead what *kind* of citizens it made." While the proclamation's enrollment of African American soldiers did not stifle black men's claims to citizenship—and indeed justified such claims—Lincoln's phrasing, and the consequent wartime roles undertaken by most USCT, suggested to white Americans that black men were second-class citizens, defined by second-class wartime roles in garrisons. While formal black enlistment was a revolutionary, unprecedented doctrine, overturning decades of legal and political exclusions, the entrance of formerly enslaved men into a free, volunteer institution—the army—was immediately limited by the environment in which they served. If garrisoning undermined white men's civic virtue and the premise on which the entire citizen-soldier tradition was based, the Emancipation Proclamation's assignment of the USCT to this undesirable form of volunteer military service implied that black men were not entitled to demand the full range of civic privileges enjoyed by white men.[7]

The proclamation's casual and inconspicuous, but also profoundly symbolic, phrasing about black soldiers should caution us about looking at the Civil Rights Act of 1866 and the Fourteenth Amendment of 1868—both of which conferred legal black male citizenship—and working backward to locate their wartime origins in the African American military experience. Instead, a much more troublesome origins story is written in the language of emancipation and the crisis of wartime garrisoning: separate but equal. If Civil War armies, and the soldiers in the ranks, reflected the societies from which they came, black garrisoning both mirrored and foreshadowed the second-class conditions of black freedom in mid-nineteenth-century America. Garrisoning placed black men outside the mainstream of volunteer military culture, establishing a tenuous relationship to broader civic and political life. And when white observers duly acknowledged African American soldiers' manhood and brave battlefield performances on the levees at Milliken's Bend, the riverbanks of Port Hudson, the beaches of Fort Wagner, and in the trenches of Petersburg, and when a majority of white northerners fiercely defended the policy of emancipation, the garrisoning stigma remained fixed, underscoring the new racial hierarchy within Union armies. While this bleak narrative of emancipation still highlights the grand evolution from slavery to freedom, it also asks, what kind of freedom? What kind of Union? Such inquiries framed most problems in Civil War America, including the unforeseen crisis of wartime military occupation, which Lincoln's proclamation attempted to solve.[8]

* * *

By the summer of 1862, Union armies in the West were bogged down in stalemate, while those in the East had suffered numerous defeats at the hands of a determined Confederate foe. Moreover, thousands of runaway slaves populated US military camps, forcing local commanders and politicians to recognize their presence and humanity. Faced with manpower shortages, battlefield reverses, the complications of occupation, and increasing masses of freedpeople within army lines, Lincoln turned to emancipation as a matter of military necessity, hoping to use this policy to further his primary purpose of preserving the Union. On September 22, 1862, Lincoln issued a preliminary proclamation of emancipation that took effect on January 1, 1863, thereby enshrining the United States' official, legal commitment to abolition. In addition to its bold assertions of universal freedom, the proclamation charged the Union army with enforcing black freedom and also invited African American males to enlist in the military of the United States. This dramatic pronouncement fundamentally widened the conflict's scope. No longer would the war for Union be waged only by white soldiers; black men would now share in the nation's martial struggles.[9]

However, the proclamation was not purely an idealistic statement of the Union's commitment to freedom. There were more utilitarian motives at play. Alongside the language of emancipation, Lincoln incorporated statements relating to occupation, using the proclamation to actively divide black soldiers from white. White Union troops, who had long served in occupied zones, believed that they held second-class positions within the military and desperately sought removal from a mode of service that they thought contradicted the lofty ideals of citizen-soldiering. While military occupation served as a central component to the Union's war, Lincoln's careful wording reveals his acute awareness of the unpopularity of garrison service among the white troops. He was forced to determine how to incorporate black men—considered inferior by most white northerners—into the military, while also accommodating the racism prevalent in the Union ranks. Many white Union soldiers had long been hostile to notions of emancipation and black soldiering. So, Lincoln's phrasing in the proclamation made a way for his troops to accept the revolutionary inclusion of black men within their ranks. The term "garrison," which Lincoln used to describe the main form of service to be performed by black troops, held intensely negative cultural connotations. It now acquired an explicit racial undertone. As William W. Freehling writes of the Emancipation Proclamation, "'Garrisoning' leached racial equality from black soldiering, relegating blacks to guarding behind the lines while whites strode to the front."[10]

Formerly enslaved black men would now be welcomed as soldiers into the Union army, but only under limits established by white American military culture. The nature of garrisoning determined that African American soldiers would be immobile, laboring behind the lines and potentially neutering their claim to equality with white volunteers. The language of emancipation clearly defined the black role; it implicitly shaped the white role as well. The proclamation presumably freed white troops to focus *exclusively* on the principal elements of the war, rather than the perceived distractions of occupation. Conversely, black soldiers, although they now held muskets and donned the accoutrements of war, were diverted into modes of service strikingly reminiscent of their pre-enlistment days as "contraband of war."[11]

The presumably limited ways in which black soldiers would be utilized in US armies revealed Lincoln's understanding of the assumed contradictions between citizen-soldiering and garrison duty. The president's modest phrasing implicitly told white soldiers that their distasteful duties as occupying forces were now over. Because of their perceived social standing as second-class persons, newly enlisted black men would now assume second-class military assignments. Although the Emancipation Proclamation loudly announced black freedom, it also limited the scope of how that freedom could be enacted within the ranks of republican citizen-armies. In this instance, race played an exclusionary role within the citizen-soldier ideal, segregating white from black through definitions of military service. Lincoln envisioned that the Union's military assignments for the remainder of the Civil War would be determined according to race.[12]

The Emancipation Proclamation's black garrisoning paradigm appeared within the context of four contemporary tensions—conflicts in the American military tradition, debates on the Militia Act of 1862, the problem of equality in Lincoln's antislavery politics, and the nebulous definitions of national citizenship—all of which informed the scope and implications of service performed by the USCT. First, Lincoln's use of the term "garrison" carried heavy weight for his audience. The garrison was a widely understood nineteenth-century military concept, historically associated with service performed by the regular army—not by volunteer citizen-soldiers. Relegated to the fringes of antebellum society and suffocated by the lack of individual liberty, soldiers in garrisons epitomized the antithesis of the volunteer character. A regular soldier's life was often defined by physical labor, such as constructing forts and repairing roads; regulars bemoaned such tasks for undermining their military training and aptitude. But "the old soldier will tell you," Alexander Hays wrote just before the Civil War, "that the most irksome period of his service, are the days of garrison duty, a monotonous round of parades, and drills, fife playing, and stacking." Regular soldiers often decried their colorless military lives, claiming that their seclusion from society thwarted intellectual and martial growth.[13]

The conditions of garrison culture gave rise to a rigid, hierarchical relationship between officers and enlisted men, an arrangement that caused friction in the all-white armies of occupation during the first years of the Civil War. Limitations on democratic privilege, arbitrary punishment, and leaders perceived as over-bearing, pompous, and domineering shaped the character of garrison life. For white wartime volunteers who demanded fair, equitable treatment, the military hierarchy necessary to maintain a garrison came as something of a shock. Officers, who needed to establish their authority, were put in difficult positions. Garrisons prevented officers from displaying their martial prowess on the field of combat, offering few occasions to lead on the battlefield and to distinguish themselves from the common soldier. Both antebellum garrisons and wartime zones of occupation alike produced officers who forced their will on those they commanded in an effort to assert their authority, committing acts which enlisted men oftentimes interpreted as unfair and arbitrary.[14]

In the face of their volunteer soldiers' democratic impulses, officers were challenged by the difficulty of sustaining a strict hierarchical arrangement. Common soldiers interpreted the intense methods of punishment and control that defined garrison life as direct affronts to their identities as free citizens. Garrisons, they believed, should be an extension of civil society; officers disagreed. Severe disciplinary procedures were accordingly implemented, in hopes of inspiring respect and deference. But such methods only amplified the gulf between officers and the men they commanded. Enlisted men resisted a system that they deemed threatening to their individual rights. Regular army garrisons throughout the antebellum United States, coupled with those in occupied regions during the Civil War, came to represent contested spaces of power, authority, and stratification. By 1863, African American men, most of whom had only recently been emancipated, enrolled into USCT units that were subject to the same tensions of control and dominance that governed antebellum and wartime garrisons. Only this time, race emerged as a means to liberate white volunteers from the existing hierarchy, rigid discipline, hard labor, and detachment from the war in garrison life, based on the assumption that black men in blue uniforms were second-class, auxiliary soldiers who were used to laboring for hard masters under restrictive conditions.[15]

Contemporary assumptions about garrisoning also framed debates on the Militia Act, which took place during the summer of 1862, the same time that Lincoln settled on the policy of emancipation. As the Union war effort reached crisis proportions, Congress deliberated whether African Americans should be enrolled into the military, ultimately overturning the Militia Act of 1792, which permitted only white male citizens to serve as soldiers. Senators justified amending the law on several grounds. First, both white *and* black had an obligation to defend the nation during times of war, suggesting African Americans had a significant role to play in the body politic. Second, some in Congress sympathized with white soldiers' grievances that occupation duty and hard garrison labor undermined their fighting spirit and the reasons for which they volunteered. The revised Militia Act of 1862 thus authorized the president "to receive into the service of the United States, for the purpose of constructing intrenchments, or performing camp service or any other labor, or any military or naval service for which they may be found competent, persons of African descent." The law removed the stipulation that only white citizens could enroll in the military, instead calling for all "able-bodied male citizens," a revolutionary implication for black civil rights. However, the law left open *how* the president would employ African American troops, which Lincoln filled with the garrison paradigm, thereby limiting black claims to full equality.[16]

Lincoln's call for black garrisoning sprang from his own personal interpretation of emancipation, race, and equality, an internal struggle rooted in the contrast between the evils of slavery and the unsettling prospect of a biracial democracy. As an antebellum politician and early spokesman for the Republican Party, Lincoln declared that white and black were not equal. Even if emancipation were to occur, he famously posed in his Peoria Address of 1854, "What next? Free them, and make them politically and socially, our equals? My own feelings will not admit of this." Yet Lincoln's faith in natural law—that all men were endowed with rights that could not be stripped away by worldly institutions—informed his moderate antislavery position. Slavery was wrong, Lincoln argued, because it denied the inalienable rights of life, liberty, and the pursuit of happiness; it was wrong because it deprived men of the fruits of their labor; it was wrong because it offered unfair economic and political advantage to slaveholders in an otherwise democratic republic. Falling somewhere between the extremes of radical abolitionism and virulent white supremacy, Lincoln's views on race and slavery were, as historian George M. Fredrickson estimates, "much closer to racism as conformity than to racism as pathology."[17]

Abraham Lincoln's worldview during the Civil War acknowledged the sin of slavery and endorsed the necessity of emancipation, while doubting the prospect of black social and political equality. Lincoln pursued an aggressive policy of military emancipation beginning in 1862, justifying his actions through wartime necessity to suppress the rebellion, yet he seemed not to move radically toward making racial egalitarianism a reality. He instead vacillated, sometimes inching closer to the prospect, while at other times retreating swiftly. The war ultimately demonstrated Lincoln's ambivalence that emancipation signaled equality. His equivocation can be seen in the implicit relationship between his support for colonization—the attempt to deport newly freed African Americans abroad to their "native" lands in hopes of evading racial strife at home—and his advocacy of black garrisoning.[18]

Long an adherent of colonization during the antebellum period, Lincoln also endorsed the concept during the early years of the war, even including a provision for the measure in the preliminary draft of the proclamation. For Lincoln, the appeal of colonization was the promise of bringing freedom to the enslaved while also keeping them separate from white America. He defined his position before a delegation of African American leaders who visited the White House in August 1862, declaring, "It is better for us both, therefore, to be separated." The pairing of racial separation and colonization remained with Lincoln through much of the war. By proposing numerous colonization schemes, including constitutional amendments in 1862, Lincoln sought to deflect the impending surge of free blacks into the economic and civic mainstream that would follow in the wake of emancipation. Lincoln also argued in favor of isothermalism, the notion that African Americans were better fitted for tropical climates. Thus, colonies in Central America and the Caribbean provided ideal locales for the migration of freed blacks, while preserving the North's white majority. "If gradual emancipation and deportation be adopted," the president declared in his December 1862 message to Congress, "[freed-people's] old masters will give them wages at least until new laborers can be procured; and the freed men, in turn, will gladly give their labor for the wages, till new homes can be found for them, in congenial climes, and with people of their own blood and race."[19]

For Lincoln, colonization offered a conservative solution to a radical problem. The various proposals ultimately failed, some never materializing and others collapsing with catastrophic results for the few freedpeople who participated. Although Lincoln discarded any serious colonization *policies* after the Emancipation Proclamation went into effect, he never fully expelled the *idea* until well into 1864, suggesting that he remained unconvinced about the possibility of genuine racial equality. It is thus important to recognize that Lincoln's most aggressive attempts at colonization came during the same period in which he considered and proclaimed the inclusion of African American soldiers into the Union army.[20]

The final proclamation contained two notable changes from the preliminary version: the colonization provision had been eliminated and African American males were invited to join the army. With colonization out of the picture, Lincoln tempered the radical notion of black soldiering by indicating that free, volunteer institutions—such as the army—would be segregated along racial lines, using service categories to make the separation a reality. Staunch abolitionist Wendell Phillips noted that, through the words of the proclamation, the president had simultaneously discarded colonization and linked it with black soldiering. According to Phillips, the president was asking, "Will you [freedmen] go away if I venture to free you?" "May I colonize you among the sickly deserts or the vast jungles of South America?" "Let me colonize you in the forts of the Union, and put rifles in your hands." While he had ultimately retreated from international colonization, Lincoln used garrisoning to enact a domestic colonization scheme, implying that black soldiers were better suited for the tropical, disease-ridden climates of the South that had decimated white soldiers. According to the proclamation, USCT regiments would now be effectively colonized in garrisons on the fringes of American military culture, and black men, although now free, would be relegated to the margins of American life.[21]

Ideas about nineteenth-century American citizenship offered the final contemporary influence for Lincoln's decision on black garrisoning. In the months preceding the issuance of the final proclamation, Attorney General Edward Bates prepared a formal statement on the status and definition of national citizenship. Bates's opinion ultimately framed the Emancipation Proclamation's major contention that once free, African Americans could not be re-enslaved, declaring "every person born in the country is, at the moment of birth," a citizen. Bates opined unequivocally that free black people were born citizens, implying that the formerly enslaved were entitled to the same rights and responsibilities of national citizenship. Natural-born citizenship established a sacred bond between the individual and the government, in which the former was compelled with "the duty of allegiance" and the latter with "the right to protection." These were "correlative obligations," Bates concluded, "the one the price of the other."[22]

The citizenry's obligation to the government framed the context in which African American men poured into Union armies beginning in 1863. Military service had long been a prerogative of republican citizenship, and freedmen were obliged to volunteer for the military, a notion that complemented the assumptions in the Militia Act, and which underscored Lincoln's invitation of black military service. Indeed, Bates's opinion coincided with the Militia Act's recognition that "able-bodied male citizens," regardless of color, were eligible for the military. By incorporating black men into institutions of the broader body politic, Bates's opinion gave Lincoln the legal justification he needed to issue his proclamation, which implicitly recognized that African Americans were indeed citizens.[23]

Yet as the attorney general admitted, the scope and application of citizenship lacked formal definition and procedure. Bates interpreted citizenship as a concept rooted in natural law, one not to be artificially or universally deprived. He further recognized that as citizens, African American men could be equally integrated into the national polity while also being separated into second-class positions within the nation's institutions. Bates personally disagreed with notions of classes and distinctions of citizenship because "if there be grades and classes of citizens, still, the lowest individual of the lowest possible class is a citizen, and as such fills the requirement of the Constitution." Bates may not have subscribed to the theory of second-class citizenship, but President Lincoln did, and the consequences of this belief posed direct implications for the status of black volunteers both in the army and in society at large.[24] Ironically, while Lincoln accepted the notion of African American citizenship, he was not an unwavering believer in black equality, as evinced by his support for colonization and the relegation of black troops to garrison service.

While the president agreed with Bates's premise that African American men were indeed citizens, thus qualifying them for volunteer military service under the new Militia Act, the Emancipation Proclamation's garrisoning clause revealed Lincoln's belief in an alternate concept of citizenship: the associational notion that citizens could be organized and defined by status within the institutions in which they participated. On the eve of the final proclamation's release, Abraham Lincoln's worldview reflected early nineteenth-century notions of civic citizenship, a concept rooted in the laws of association. Antebellum Americans derived their status as citizens from the institutions to which they belonged, including churches, clubs, parties, or municipalities. "Each association had rules of membership: one was either in or out," writes historian Michael Vorenberg. "Thus citizenship was as much about exclusion of others as membership for oneself."[25]

In his call for African American troops, Lincoln used garrisoning as a way to establish racial separation within one of the era's most cherished associations of citizens: volunteer armies. Military service roles, now largely delineated by race, were used to create separate domains within an otherwise "egalitarian" army. Black soldiers would now fill the military roles that white troops scorned as beneath their status as citizen-soldiers. Based on their presumed positions as second-class citizens, the USCT were, according to the president, fit for hard labor, hierarchical discipline, and permanent, seemingly indefinite service, assumptions suggesting that they were incapable of waging war on the same plane as white soldiers. The Emancipation Proclamation, therefore, recognized black citizenship, but limited its claim based on cultural assumptions about volunteer military service, the problem of wartime occupation, and the hazy, fluid question of inclusion in national associations. While both white and black wore the same uniform, they were assigned to service roles that carried vastly different levels of prestige. White volunteers believed that occupying and garrisoning ran counter to the citizen-soldier tradition, and Lincoln used the concept of black garrison duty to appease these grumbles by accepting black men as citizens who had a duty to serve while simultaneously relegating them to what white soldiers perceived to be the margins of military culture.

Lincoln described emancipation and African American soldiering as crucial for Union success, but he usually moderated his sentiments according to his interpretation of black garrisoning. Shortly after the Emancipation Proclamation went into effect, he wrote to one of his generals, "We were not succeeding—at best, were progressing too slowly—without it [black garrisoning]. . . . We must also take some benefit from it, if practicable. . . . I therefore will thank you for your well considered opinion whether Fortress-Monroe, and York-Town, one or both, could not, in whole or in part, be garrisoned by colored troops, leaving the white forces now necessary at those places, to be employed elsewhere." Lincoln further developed these sentiments when he informed Andrew Johnson, the military governor of Tennessee, that "the colored population is the great *available* and yet *unavailed* of, force for restoring the Union. The bare sight of fifty thousand armed, and drilled black soldiers on the banks of the Mississippi, would end the rebellion at once."[26]

Integrating the language of emancipation into the garrisoning concept allowed Lincoln to explain to white America how black soldiers should largely be used, in spite of a handful of exceptional moments in which they proved themselves on the front lines of battle. Black troops "act upon motives," he explained to Illinois politician James C. Conkling. "If they stake their lives for us, they must be prompted by the strongest motive—even the promise of freedom. And the promise being made, must be kept." Lincoln well understood what was at stake for African Americans: a Union victory ensured freedom, while defeat threatened a return to slavery. Although he happily received reports of black men fighting on distant fields of battle, he hesitated to remove black Union troops from the limitations of garrisoning. Lincoln wrote in the same letter to Conkling, "I thought that whatever negroes can be got to do as soldiers, leaves just so much less for white soldiers to do, in saving the Union."[27]

Lincoln clarified his argument in greater detail to Ulysses S. Grant, shortly after Vicksburg fell in July 1863. The president understood that the massive gains made in the Mississippi Valley might well be lost without a substantial occupation presence to guard rail lines, regulate depots, garrison strategic locales, and battle guerrillas. Moreover, he believed that battle-hardened white veterans should be absolved of such responsibilities (which they detested) and sent to more decisive theaters. Lincoln described to Grant the racial components of garrison service as he saw it. "I have no reason to doubt that you are doing what you reasonably can [to raise black regiments]," Lincoln expressed. "I believe it is a resource which, if vigorously applied now, will soon close the contest. It works doubly, weakening the enemy and strengthening us. We were not fully ripe for it until the river was opened. Now, I think at least a hundred thousand can, and ought to be rapidly organized along it's [*sic*] shores, relieving all the white troops to serve elsewhere." Lincoln's suggestion came two months *after* African American soldiers played a crucial role at the battle of Milliken's Bend, successfully fighting off numerous Confederate advances. It was abundantly clear to any observer that black men who donned the Union blue would fight. However, the new racial arrangements of garrisoning were too seductive not to be exploited during the Union's war of occupation. Indeed, Grant responded by garrisoning portions of the Mississippi Valley with black troops: "I did not want white men to do any work that can possibly be avoided during the hot months." By March 1865, 18,299 African American soldiers garrisoned various locales along the Mississippi River.[28]

Throughout the war Lincoln positioned race and garrisoning at the center of military occupation. In December 1863, during his third annual message to Congress, he praised the more than 100,000 African American men who volunteered for military service. These soldiers, Lincoln added, give "the double advantage of taking so much labor from the insurgent cause, and supplying the places which otherwise must be filled with so many white men." By the winter of 1863–64, though, black troops had been tried on the fields of battle and judged with newfound respect. And the president accordingly commended their efforts. "So far as tested, it is difficult to say they are not as good soldiers as any. No servile insurrection, or tendency to violence of cruelty, has marked the measures of emancipation and arming of the blacks." These latter notions surprised white society and partly mollified their concerns about African American soldiery.[29]

In spite of his celebration of African American combat valor, Lincoln remained wedded to the concept of black garrisoning. He acknowledged during a private interview in August 1864 that emancipation would be crucial in determining the outcome of the war. The enslaved people of the South, he explained, had to be used *against* the Confederacy in order to supply a Union victory. He then noted how the conflict had quickly evolved into a war of occupation. The Civil War, Lincoln recognized, was not exclusively a series of encounters between two opposing armies on distant battlefields. It was, on the contrary, a struggle between two peoples, two mobilized nations. Occupation assumed a consequential role in guiding the war to a successful conclusion, and black soldiers played a central part in that quest. "Abandon all the posts now possessed by black men surrender all these advantages to the enemy," Lincoln argued, "& we would be compelled to abandon the war in 3 weeks. We have to hold territory." Similar to his 1863 message to Congress, Lincoln did not ignore "the black warriors of Port Hudson and Olustee," yet he made clear that "no human power can subdue this rebellion without using the Emancipation lever as I have done."[30]

While he remained committed to the implications of black garrisoning, two events near the end of the war both complicated and complemented Lincoln's position. The first came when he advocated suffrage rights for African American soldiers. In a March 1864 letter to Michael Hahn, Louisiana's wartime Reconstruction governor, Lincoln explained that soldiering conferred certain privileges, echoing a hallmark of republican citizenship. "I barely suggest for your private consideration whether some of the colored people may not be let in," Lincoln wrote, referencing the inclusion of black political rights in Louisiana's pending state constitution, "as, for instance, the very intelligent and especially those who have fought gallantly in our ranks." While the constitutional convention voted not to tender black suffrage, Lincoln again spoke in favor of the measure on April 11, 1865, his final public remarks before the fateful journey to Ford's Theater. Again referencing Louisiana's readmission to the Union, Lincoln declared, "I would myself prefer that [voting rights] were now conferred on the very intelligent, and on those who serve our cause as soldiers."[31]

Although this stance might seem to contradict Lincoln's deep-seated belief that African Americans were unfit for the full rights and privileges of citizenship, he nonetheless applauded the contributions of black soldiers, recognizing their legitimate claim to at least some of the fruits of citizenship, while also acknowledging that these limited rights could be bestowed only by the individual states. In a way, Lincoln's stance on African American voting echoed his belief in black garrisoning, each of which reflected the president's conviction that black men, as second-class citizens, could not be naturally and fully integrated into a national body of white citizens.[32]

Another episode of confusion regarding the place of black soldiers came from General Benjamin F. Butler's controversial recollections published nearly thirty years after the war. Butler related a conversation that he and Lincoln supposedly had in the spring of 1865 about the possibility of racial tensions arising once black soldiers demobilized from the army. Recounting Lincoln's fears of a potential race war, Butler claimed that the president advocated deporting black veterans who might pose a threat to racial harmony. While the general acknowledged the impracticality of the president's proposal, Butler did recommend taking the USCT, whose contracts of service would remain active for more than a year, to Panama to construct a canal across the coveted isthmus. Lincoln, Butler remembered, privately endorsed the plan. Many historians have discounted the validity of Butler's testimony due mainly to Lincoln's explicit rejection of black colonization earlier in the war.[33]

If, however, the conversation took place, it reveals the continuity in Lincoln's interpretation of black soldiering. Lincoln believed that men in the USCT were indeed citizens, but they were citizens with a limited claim to full national inclusion. The Butler testimony would confirm that black garrisoning unfolded the classification of second-class citizenship in which African American soldiers would be deployed abroad to perform service that fell outside the citizen-soldier tradition. In Panama, the USCT would engage in hard labor, operate in a professional, static environment, and risk not being mustered out of service at the expiration of their contracts. Such a role would have been unthinkable to ask of white volunteers whose political power and national influence enshrined their rights as first-class citizen-soldiers.

* * *

Union generals who led armies of occupation that stretched from New Orleans, up the Mississippi River to Memphis, through Tennessee, and all the way to the South Carolina coast, implemented the race-based garrisoning philosophy outlined in the Emancipation Proclamation. Their approach generally mirrored Lincoln's garrisoning vision: the USCT would concentrate in humid, unhealthy regions thought to be ideal for men of African descent; black military service would encompass labor and fatigue assignments; the occupation duties of African American soldiers would release white soldiers to fight at the front; and military discipline would be regulated according to the army's new racial hierarchy. Thus, before they even entered the service, USCT regiments were already defined by the Union's culture of wartime occupation.

Long concerned about northern white men's ability to withstand the hot, humid southern climate, an apprehension confirmed by countless wartime diseases and noncombat deaths, military authorities believed black men more suited to serve in the South's tropical environment. After all, this reasoning held, formerly enslaved men had long labored on steamy riverbank plantations, supposedly acclimating themselves to a mode of military service for which white soldiers were unfit. Nearly a year before the army began enrolling USCT regiments, Major General David Hunter, an abolitionist who commanded the Department of the South, wrote, "in the peculiarities of this climate and country they will prove invaluable auxiliaries," who would release "an equal number of white men and regiments from the weary and often pestilential, though indispensable, duty of manning the works along the Southern sea-coast." Edward F. Hall, a white New Hampshire volunteer, explained how members of a nearby Maine regiment contracted "the Swamp fever" while digging ditches in muddy, stagnant, hot conditions in South Carolina. Rather than use white volunteers to labor in such "malarious" environments, Hall advocated the use of black men: "they are strong robust and healthy—used to work—and are perfectly at home in the climate." While Hall did not advocate arming African American men, General-in-Chief Henry W. Halleck saw the benefit of black garrison soldiers. "It is the policy of the government to use the negroes of the South," he informed Ulysses S. Grant in May 1863, "for the defence of forts, depots, &c." Some USCT regiments, Halleck continued, "can be used on the Mississippi during the sickly season, [affording] much relief to our armies."[34]

When David Hunter expressed his belief that African American soldiers would "prove invaluable auxiliaries," he touched on an international discourse that maintained that black troops across the broader Atlantic world were ideally used for service in tropical and semitropical climates. In garrisons, Hunter continued, future USCT units would be "fully equal to the similar regiments so long and successfully used by the British authorities in the West India Islands." The *New York Times,* one week after the Emancipation Proclamation went into effect, also explained that "Negro troops have already been used for many years by the British in garrisoning their [Caribbean holdings], and no doubt is entertained by the British military authorities of their trustworthiness in active service."[35]

Justifying the placement of black troops in southern climates on international precedent, William Winthrop, the American diplomat to Malta, informed Assistant Secretary of State Frederick Seward that "in hot climates, and for garrison duty, not better soldiers can be found than the blacks." Referencing military precedents set by England, Spain, Portugal, Turkey, and "the Brazils," Winthrop maintained that African American soldiers were crucial not only to wage war against the Confederacy, but also to establish the United States as a premier military nation. Much as with Lincoln's alleged conversation with Benjamin Butler about using the USCT in Panama, Winthrop looked beyond the Civil War to see the implications of a permanent, separate black army. In order to protect US interests in North America, Winthrop advocated "a colored army of at least 75, to 80,000 men, [which] would enable us to expel the French from Mexico whenever we make the attempt, and at the same time to meet the black regiments of England." Winthrop projected the wartime garrisoning philosophy—employing the USCT in stationary forts throughout the tropical South—into a future peace, "necessary for the preservation of our whole Country," in which black soldiers would remain stationed permanently on American rivers, coastlines, and harbors. Contemporary distinctions once again had been made between the types of service for which white citizen-soldiers and black auxiliary soldiers were fit, reflecting the international implications of an inconspicuous clause in Lincoln's proclamation.[36]

In contrast to Winthrop's vision of black troops protecting the homeland in exotic locales, USCT regiments were first assigned to more menial, strenuous labor duties, which in fact characterized much of their garrison service. Military labor served a critical component of the Union's war of occupation, and military leaders believed the USCT were best suited to this job. Loading and unloading transports, building fortifications, and digging trenches had wreaked havoc among white soldiers, many of whom succumbed to the debilitating ravages of fatigue duties. Ulysses S. Grant, responding to Halleck's appeal for black troops, explained in July 1863 that the garrisoning of Vicksburg "will necessarily progress slowly for I do not want the White men to do any work that can possibly be avoided during the hot months." Upon enlisting, most African American soldiers went to work rather than training in the art of soldiering. "The Government makes use of mules, horses, uneducated and educated white men, in the defense of its institutions," Major General Nathaniel P. Banks, commander of the Department of the Gulf, penned in an official order. "Why should not the negro contribute whatever is in his power for the cause in which he is as deeply interested as other men?" Encapsulating the essence of the race-based garrisoning philosophy, defined by separation, hard labor, and isothermalism, Banks concluded that African American military service "is not established upon any dogma of equality or other theory, but as a practical and sensible matter of business."[37]

Regardless of one's race, labor and fatigue duty were hard, dangerous, and unhealthy assignments. Yet black soldiers were given the brunt of the toil. In 1863, once the Mississippi Valley was firmly in Union control, newly raised black regiments were dispersed as labor battalions, relieving white troops in the hot, sticky Delta summer. The Fiftieth USCT, for instance, organized at Vicksburg and populated by former slaves primarily from nearby Natchez, was tasked with moving ordnance materiel and unloading river transports while working in deplorable conditions; most white troops who had captured the prized Mississippi River fortress were sent to other theaters. Those who remained behind watched as black men's bodies strained under the weight of fatigue responsibilities. Similarly, the commander of the Twenty-first USCT described how his men at Seabrook, South Carolina, worked literally around the clock "drawing sand; loading wood; water and pumping out vessels assisting the crews of the vessel. The duty performed is the hardest kind." Such trends continued through most occupied regions well into 1864.[38]

The physical burdens of military labor imposed a symbolic stigma on USCT regiments. Some Union generals, such as William T. Sherman, believed the fatigue duties assigned to African American soldiers were perfectly in line with the assumption of second-class service for black troops contained in Lincoln's proclamation. In July 1864, long after USCT soldiers demonstrated their bravery on the battlefield, Sherman remained wedded to the principles of black garrisoning. Attempting to disabuse the notion that "I am opposed to the organization of colored regiments," Sherman outlined what he considered their necessity. There was a distinction, Sherman claimed, between black soldiers and white "volunteers who are fighting"; it was thus "unjust," he argued, "to place them [white soldiers] on a par" with freed slaves who donned blue uniforms. Indeed, "the negro is in a transition state, and is not the equal of the white man," Sherman averred.[39]

Although he still endorsed the raising of African American regiments, Sherman nonetheless delineated service duties along the basis of race, just as Lincoln had done in his garrisoning paradigm. "I prefer some negroes as pioneers, teamsters, cooks, and servants," he continued, nodding to the role of the black soldier-as-laborer, "others gradually to experiment in the art of the soldier, beginning with the duties of local garrison." While Sherman's notorious letter is often discounted as the bluster of a reactionary racist, his musings underscore the extent to which wartime occupation, in the minds of white mid-nineteenth-century contemporaries, was the duty most suited for the newly enlisted freedmen. For Sherman, and all who endorsed the garrisoning concept, military garrisons were a hindrance to white volunteer service, a distraction for white volunteers trying to fulfill the citizen-soldier ideal.[40]

Employment of black soldiers as a labor force carried tangible, destructive implications, well beyond Sherman's racism. The USCT regiments assumed a disproportionate share of fatigue duty, oftentimes affording respite for white soldiers, thereby permanently racializing service behind the lines. An officer in the Twenty-third USCT reported that his soldiers had "been engaged in building forts for a week past & the labors of the men have been severe & arduous, but the colored men perform more work than white soldiers." Julian E. Bryant, a white abolitionist in command of the Forty-sixth USCT, wrote from Vicksburg in January 1864, "For the past three months the colored regiments here have been constantly at work upon the fortifications, doing common laborers duty at the landings, loading and unloading boats and barges, or policing the streets of the town, while white regiments are laying idle in camp, or are occupied only in soldierly duties." David Branson, an officer in the Sixty-second USCT, wrote that his men at Morganza, Louisiana, "have been worked from 8 to 10 hours daily on the fortifications," while "no white troops have been worked . . . during said period except those held as prisoners."[41]

Black military labor thus clouded the distinctions between freedom and slavery. While donning the Union blue meant forever discarding the tattered rags of enslavement, some white observers struggled to see the distinction. "They have been slaves and are just learning to be men," wrote James C. Beecher, a colonel of a USCT regiment at Folly Island, South Carolina. "When they are set to menial work doing for white regiments what those Regiments are entitled to do for themselves," he exclaimed, "it simply throws them back where they were before and reduces them to the position of slaves again." Thomas J. Morgan, an officer in the Fourteenth USCT, agreed, writing from his post at Gallatin, Tennessee. "It is degrading to single out Col[ored] Troops for fatigue duty while white troops stand idly by," he explained. "Such treatment savors too much of the old regime." An inspection of the Port Hudson and Morganza, Louisiana, garrisons in August 1864 revealed that "all the fatigue duty on fortifications is performed by colored troops and prisoners sentenced to hard labor. This duty is reported to be incessant to the exclusion of all opportunities for drill or inspection. The difficulty of making soldiers of these men, in the face of the constant practical assertion of their unfitness for anything but that labor . . . is self evident." Because they were defined largely by second-class labor duties, USCT regiments were often deprived of adequate military training and drill, provided with ineffective weapons, disadvantaged with unsuitable food, shelter, and clothing, and, most notoriously, earned less pay than white regiments.[42]

Hard garrison labor translated into disproportionate disease, injury, and death to African American soldiers. While the theory of isothermalism and the experience of slavery led some white onlookers to believe that black men were naturally suited for strenuous toil in semitropical climates, USCT soldiers fell to the rigors of auxiliary service in greater numbers than white soldiers. Because black troops were concentrated in areas prone to disease, especially the Mississippi River Valley, and due to slavery's adverse influence in stemming African American immunity, 18.5 percent of all USCT soldiers died while in the army, compared to 13.5 percent of white soldiers, even though the latter engaged in far more military combat. An inspection report of the Sixty-second, Sixty-fifth, and Sixty-seventh USCT regiments, all of which were raised at St. Louis and served in 1864 near Port Hudson and Morganza, might serve as a representative documentation of the black garrison experience. The three units lost, on average, 44 percent of soldiers to disease-related deaths, which authorities attributed to inordinate fatigue labor in the summer heat, inadequate health examinations, and lack of vegetables. In the entire Union army, which comprised more than two thousand regiments, the Sixty-fifth USCT endured the most deaths caused by disease, while suffering zero combat casualties. "The morbidity and mortality rates of the 65th," writes medical historian Margaret Humphreys, "may have been extreme but only by matter of degree. Their experience was echoed throughout the ranks of black troops."[43]

In addition to heavy labor, the garrisoning philosophy prescribed sundry other duties for African American soldiers. In 1863, Lincoln and Secretary of War Edwin M. Stanton instructed Adjutant General Lorenzo Thomas to raise black regiments in the Mississippi Valley. Thomas approached his task with the pragmatism of a professional soldier, rather than as a proponent of racial equality, seeking to create a robust black occupation of Union holdings from New Orleans to Memphis. In so doing, he exemplified contemporary white perceptions of black military roles. "The negro Regiments could give protection to these plantations [on which freedpeople labored for the US Army], and also operate effectively against the guerrillas," Thomas remarked. "They could garrison positions, and thus additional regiments could be sent to the front." And, black troops, "knowing where cotton is secreted, should be encouraged to bring it to the banks of the river, where it could be taken possession of by a government agent." Thomas, like much of the white North, saw the logical benefit in raising regiments of black soldiers to contribute to a massive war effort, one in desperate need of supplementary manpower.[44]

Although Thomas's appeal was modest—much like Lincoln's garrisoning clause—his recommendations for African American soldiers responded directly to the ideological, cultural, and military problems associated with white occupation: stationary garrisoning, guerrilla warfare, and informal economies. Thomas did not consider the necessities of occupation unimportant— he was, after all, charged with maintaining Union control of the Mississippi Valley—but his vision assumed that black soldiers who performed occupying duties would not suffer from the same crisis that had infected the ranks of white occupiers tasked with these same duties. Indeed, because they were marginalized within the citizen-soldier tradition, black troops were presumed fit to guard positions, engage in the chaos of counterinsurgency, and use their martial positions to propagate the Union's cotton trade. Wartime occupation, therefore, could be practiced only by a class of soldiers who were outside the republican military ethic, so as not to undermine it.

Ulysses S. Grant agreed with Thomas's premise that the USCT served a purpose much greater than mere military labor. Implementing the garrisoning policy in the Mississippi Valley, Grant informed Lincoln, "I have given the subject of arming the negro my hearty support." He later added, "This, with emancipation, is the heavyest blow yet to the Confederacy. . . . By arming the negro, we have added a powerful ally. They will make good soldiers and taking them from the enemy weaken him in the same proportion they strengthen us. I am therefore most decidedly in favor of pushing this policy to the enlistment of a force sufficient to hold all the South falling into our hands and to aid in capturing more." Grant insisted that garrisoning in the Mississippi Valley should be constructed along racial lines. For example, shortly after Vicksburg fell, he was "particularly desirous of organizing a regiment of Heavy Artillerists from the negroes to garrison this place, and shall do so as soon as possible." And, to ensure that the valley would remain secure, Grant instructed Sherman in March 1864 to "use the negroes, or negro troops, more particularly for guarding plantations and for the defense of the West bank of the river." Grant remained consistent in his belief that African American soldiers served as ideal occupation forces and wrote with satisfaction one month later, "the district of Vicksburg [contains] such a large proportion of colored troops." Although he did not repudiate the employment of black troops in combat, welcoming USCT participation in the 1864 Virginia campaigns, Grant continued to endorse the black garrisoning philosophy.[45]

Other officers built on Lorenzo Thomas's contention that African American soldiers were well suited for guerrilla warfare. Unlike white volunteers, who judged insurgent conflicts to be uncivilized, black troops were considered ideal for the often chaotic work of guarding railroads, protecting plantations, and securing supply lines from roving Confederate partisans. "The able-bodied men, formed into regiments and posted in the rear of the settlements, would afford ample protection to the cultivators of the soil, besides rendering the navigation of the Mississippi perfectly safe from guerrilla attacks, which are now so annoying to our transports," wrote one general. Others argued that black men, because they were raised in the South, possessed intimate knowledge of the land, one of the principal elements of clandestine warfare. Thomas Wentworth Higginson, a Boston abolitionist who raised the war's first regiment of black troops in South Carolina, believed his men "peculiarly fitted for offensive operations, and especially for partisan warfare; they have so much dash and such abundant resources, combined with such an Indian-like knowledge of the country and its ways," he wrote in 1862. A paternalistic pride in his troops' unique skill set guided Higginson's belief that black soldiers could effectively practice occupation warfare.[46]

While USCT units were deployed in the more active aspects of wartime occupation, such as raiding expeditions and counterinsurgency warfare, the black soldiering experience continued to be largely associated with the stigma of garrison service, which reflected white assumptions about black behavior and discipline. Symbolizing a static world of immobility and truncated liberty, garrisons served as fraught entry points into black freedom, often continuing to uphold the familiar forces of racial distinction and harsh discipline black troops had known in the days before their freedom. White citizen-soldiers, with their heritage of liberty, chafed at the rigidity and hierarchy of military culture and argued that their status as free white men made them inherently equal to their officers. As African American males poured into USCT regiments, the ranks swelled with men newly freed from bondage, who were only just beginning to transition from the plantation to the garrison. The distinction between slave and soldier was sometimes blurred as white garrison leaders leaned on stereotypes of black character and capabilities.[47]

Drawing on two contradictory assumptions—that black men were docile and submissive, while also unruly and violent—white military authorities debated whether African Americans could make self-controlled, disciplined soldiers. Ulysses S. Grant welcomed black enlistment because "the negro troops are easier to preserve discipline among than our white troops, and I doubt not will prove equally good garrison duty." Grant's conviction underscored the presumption that African American soldiers would serve as an ideal occupation force because their previously limited lives under slavery conditioned in them a detached obedience which was ideal for the fixed nature of garrisoning. Grant long grumbled about the lax discipline that accompanied inactive soldiers, believing that acute attention to detail and conduct were crucial for an effective military occupation. In contrast, the democratic tendencies of white troops, Grant believed, inspired self-indulgence in occupied garrisons. Thomas Wentworth Higginson agreed, writing, "I have never yet heard a doubt expressed among the officers as to the *superiority* of these men to white troops in aptitude for drill and discipline, because of their imitativeness and docility, and the pride they take in the service."[48]

According to Grant and Higginson, garrisons accommodated black men's allegedly submissive nature, but also were considered to inflame USCT soldiers' supposed violent tendencies. A lifetime of bondage, some whites thought, might stimulate a sense of retribution and warlike thirst to murder former masters. Francis H. Pierpont, the commander at Alexandria, Virginia, thus argued that "discipline is the first requisite for troops of any color," especially when they were placed as forces of occupation and sent on expeditions into the countryside. But the six hundred African American soldiers sent to northern Virginia in 1864 apparently posed a problem. "These colored troops are new recruits just from bondage. Their own welfare requires discipline," he explained. Concerned about "the positive insolence of these colored soldiers, undisciplined as they are, to the white citizen," he confided to Secretary of War Edwin M. Stanton, "I know you would not leave your wife and daughters in a community of armed negroes, undisciplined and just liberated from bondage, with no other armed protection." Pierpont feared the potential depredations committed by black soldiers would dislodge the growing unionist sentiment in the region, inspiring "terrible apprehensions that must haunt [the white citizens] by the presence of these troops."[49]

Such misguided notions revealed paradoxical assumptions about the presumed racial contradictions of garrison service. Occupied garrisons were considered to place unbearable constraints on white liberty, while simultaneously serving as ideal schools of instruction for black men's entrance into freedom. By their very nature, garrisons reflected restraint and hierarchy, control and obedience, labor and work. As republican citizens, white volunteers resisted, and often failed to abide by, such martial qualities, which checked their claim to liberty. Yet, due to lives of enslavement, black soldiers had to relearn their understandings of obedience, respect for authority, and work, all of which garrison life would presumably teach. Thomas Wentworth Higginson empha-sized discipline based on justice, respect for military decorum and hierarchy, and the importance of guard duty, which taught authority. "I see that the pride which military life creates may cause the plantation trickeries to diminish," he wrote. And as *Harper's Weekly* opined, "there is no present way of making [freedmen] earn their living except by making them garrison our forts." Equal combinations of drill and manual labor, according to Daniel Ullman, a white commander of black troops in Louisiana, "will be best accomplished by es-tablishing the better regiments on the same footing and permanence as the Regular Army."[50]

While envisioned as entrées into freedom, garrisons maintained a rigid hierarchical structure, established both by military culture and race, which rationalized white punishment and discipline against black troops. Common soldiers long endured the severe conditions of military discipline, but when a racial component was added to garrison life, the result, according to historian Joseph T. Glatthaar, "was too reminiscent of the relationship of master and slave." Punishments such as bondage, riding the wooden horse, and whipping reflected some white officers' contentions that even the most trivial offense merited harsh discipline, an ugly derivative of the garrison-as-education concept. Garrisons grew mired in tension between white officers desperate to demonstrate their leadership by maintaining racial dominance and black soldiers desperate to shed the lingering yoke of slavery.[51] Indeed, by imple-menting the garrisoning policy as outlined in the Emancipation Proclama-tion, military authorities had constructed a racialized military hierarchy that treated African American men as second-class soldiers and citizens.

* * *

Although Abraham Lincoln and leading military commanders assumed that African American troops would relieve white soldiers from occupation duty, events proved otherwise. The Union's war of occupation grew with such inten-sity that it required both black *and* white soldiers to garrison the conquered Confederacy. While black troops comprised the majority of the Union military presence in some areas (reaching up to 65 percent in the Mississippi Valley in 1865), white troops continued to serve in many garrisons.[52] As a result, white soldiers had to negotiate a new tension added to the already-fraught prospect of garrison life: rationalizing their military service alongside black troops.

The racializing of garrison service was intended to differentiate between citizen-soldiers and auxiliary forces, yet a mixed-race occupation presence undermined such assumptions. Wielding the language of emancipation, white occupation troops thus launched a campaign to distinguish themselves from newly enlisted African American soldiers.[53]

White Union soldiers responded to Lincoln's call for black troops with rhetoric similar to the Emancipation Proclamation's garrisoning clause. They read the president's words through their own experience of military occupation, welcoming African American soldiers to serve as principal auxiliary forces. Minos Miller, a member of the Thirty-sixth Iowa Volunteers, which garrisoned Helena and Little Rock, Arkansas, for nearly two years, exclaimed on January 9, 1863, "We are rejoicing to day over . . . old Abes proclamation[.] we got the news last night at 8 oclock that all the negroes was free and them that was able for servis was to be armed and set to guarding foarts. I think now the union is safe and all will be over by the forth of Jul[y]. I feel like fighting now for we something to fight for. I say on to Vicksburg or any other place we are needed." Charles Hill, of the Fifth Massachusetts, agreed. "There are colored men here who would make splendid soldiers," he wrote in April 1863 from New Bern, North Carolina, "and I long to see the time when they will be used . . . to hold these places in the warm months." More than a year later, long after USCT regiments confirmed their battle valor, Pennsylvanian John C. Myers, in language remarkably similar to the proclamation, revealed how the garrisoning stigma remained fixed on black soldiers. "A Regiment of Colored troops passed up the river to-day en route for the Shenandoah Valley," he wrote from the Virginia theater in October 1864, "to have and to hold the places captured by our Generals, henceforth and forever."[54]

A majority of black soldiers served behind the lines, thereby causing a crisis among white volunteers who were also serving behind the lines: the prospect of serving as equals with formerly enslaved men in a role that was seen to fall decidedly outside the citizen-soldier tradition. White troops thus turned to racial discourse to highlight and preserve their place in the Union army's social hierarchy. "I saw a *Nigger* Brigade this morning," Charles Harding Cox of the Seventieth Indiana wrote in August 1863 from Nashville; "they made a splendid appearance (for niggers) and will *probably* fight." However, "I do not believe it right to make soldiers of them and class & rank with our *white* soldiers. It makes them feel and act as our equals." To avoid any pretense of equality, white soldiers had to distinguish themselves from black soldiers.

After all, they wore the same uniform, shouldered the same muskets, served under the same flag, and, most troublingly, garrisoned the same regions. White troops thus claimed black soldiers to be temporary imposters within the American military tradition. Commenting on African American soldiers at Savannah, Georgia, in 1865, Silas Doolittle, who served in the Seventy-fifth New York, scoffed, "You ought to see the style they put on, with their white gloves, a 'la militaire[.]' I think it is an insult to U.S. soldiers to put the uniform on Orang-ou-tangs."[55]

The language of inequality sometimes translated into physical action. Through acts of violence, discrimination, and defiance, whites attempted to convey the power of their racial privilege even within the constricting confines of garrisons. To justify the biracial garrison presence, white soldiers sought to assert the superiority of their racial identity. At Port Hudson, they defied the authority of black patrolmen; at Folly Island, South Carolina, white officers verbally abused black soldiers who guarded the town; at Ship Island, Mississippi, a Maine regiment refused to participate in drill exercises with soldiers of the Corps d'Afrique; near Point Lookout, North Carolina, New Hampshire cavalrymen attacked a company of black troops returning from picket duty; and at Morganza, Louisiana, white soldiers rested in the shade of trees while black troops labored and guarded the vicinity.[56]

Some attempts at asserting white dominance built on the belief that USCT regiments were naturally fit for immobile service, which required strict discipline and obedience, traits which white volunteers disdained. Henry Brown, of the Fifteenth New Hampshire, wrote that the African American troops guarding New Orleans "are a fine looking set of men and make excellent soldiers," willingly submitting to their officers and offering "a good pattern for white soldiers, also in discipline." In responding to inquiries about the martial capacity of black troops, a white volunteer officer acknowledged their docility, patience, and fidelity. When comparing both races he said, "the phases of the character of the white touches the stars and descends to the lowest depths. The black character occupies the inner circle. Their status is mediocrity, and this uniformity and mediocrity," he concluded, "for military fatigue duty, I think answers best."[57]

The second-class distinctions of black men in blue uniforms, the officer implied, somehow had to be maintained. Harrison Soule, an officer in the Sixth Michigan Volunteers, articulated this principle in January 1864. "All the reports about the exploits of the colored troops their darring marches through the swamps [of southeast Louisiana] &c are no dout true," Soule wrote from the Mississippi Valley, "they have no doubt performed all and possibly more than they have credit for." He nevertheless concluded, "A nigger makes a good enough Soldier for garrison and guard duty but for Field Service a Hundred [white] men is worth a Thousand of them." Soule allowed that African American soldiers could perhaps confront guerrillas, mainly since white soldiers despised counterinsurgency warfare. But, "they are only fit to help us in the capacity of Laborers and watchmen they cant be trusted when there is the least danger." Soule's worldview, it seems, had been fundamentally altered by emancipation, African American enlistment, and the prospect of racial equality, confirmed in his acknowledgment of black battlefield valor. He clung, however, to any tangible distinction that might forestall the potential collapse of the American racial hierarchy. The garrisoning concept thus offered white soldiers like Soule a powerful, comfortable reminder of racial and social distinctions in a nation rapidly transforming through the maelstrom of war.[58]

Soule's emphasis on labor as a principal duty for African American soldiers underscored other white volunteers' attempts to classify USCT regiments as second-class institutions. Long disgusted by the menial drudgeries of garrisoning, white soldiers welcomed black troops to carry the army's toilsome burden. Following their participation in the siege of Vicksburg, Benjamin F. McIntyre's Nineteenth Iowa Infantry moved to Port Hudson, augmenting the garrison's biracial presence. "To say they had not a soldierly appearance would be doing them great injustice," McIntyre remarked in August 1863 about the numerous African American regiments at the river fortress, "and I cannot say they are not brave, for the three charges they made here in one day loosing half their number would stamp it a false hood."[59]

Combat, however, contradicted the proper military roles for black troops, at least according to McIntyre. Writing several months later from Brownsville, Texas, which the Union occupied for nearly eight months, he noted "several Corps d'Afrique regiments that came over with us have been employed in unloading vessels, assisting the Pioneers in constructing pontoon bridges, and various other arduous duties that would have compelled our own boys to have performed had no negro regiments been in the service to the government." "They are the laborers of the Army," he continued in April 1864; "there was daily labor for hundreds of men and which of necessity must have been performed by soldiers had not we had negroes with us." Black soldiers, McIntyre implied, were not only well suited for auxiliary service, but also served to release white volunteers from the stigma of menial garrison duties. "Streets are to be swept and cleaned daily [as well as fortifications erected] and this is work of a very disagreeable character and for one I thank the originators of the Corps d'Afrique for taking from us such labor as belong to menials."[60]

Daniel W. Sawtelle of the Eighth Maine Volunteers explained that military labor threatened both white men's health *and* their identity as free men. "They are getting up another regt of blacks here," Sawtelle wrote from Beaufort, South Carolina. Like Soule and McIntyre, Sawtelle acknowledged African American soldiers' ability to fight, but he also considered that it would be difficult to "make negroes fight their own masters." Sawtelle thus concluded that "I am willing for one but I don't want to be made a nigger of anyway. I come out here to fight not work" doing garrison duty. He articulated the diverging military roles assumed for each race, roles that had been envisioned in the Emancipation Proclamation and by Union generals. For Sawtelle, fighting in the field was far different from laboring behind the lines, the work for which black soldiers had been enlisted.[61]

Union soldiers' attempts to define African American troops by their supplementary service reflected a deep ambivalence about a biracial army, especially once both groups served together behind the lines. The ideological and cultural crises of wartime occupation now assumed even greater dimensions. White soldiers, although promised relief from auxiliary garrisons by a racially defined assemblage of supplementary troops, now shared the duties of occupation with formerly enslaved men who had entered national institutions. The language of emancipation continued to organize African American soldiers as second-class citizens who were subject to second-class military treatment. Indeed, the majority of USCT regiments were garrisoned behind the lines, offering a tenuous entry into lives of liberation, grounded in violent discipline, hard labor, and stationary service. Yet as men who had long tested the constraints of slavery and racial discrimination, black soldiers did not sit passively in the face of the control and dominance imposed by their military service. Their quest to undermine the implications of garrison service fundamentally altered both the character of military occupation and the entire Civil War.

7 | Racial Authority, Cultural Change, and Black Wartime Military Occupation

Long before Corporal James Henry Gooding petitioned Abraham Lincoln in September 1863, the Fifty-fourth Massachusetts Volunteers had captured the nation's imagination earlier that summer in their epic, fatal assault upon Fort Wagner, South Carolina. When Gooding and other freeborn northerners, alongside formerly enslaved comrades, stormed the beaches outside Charleston Harbor, they defied long-held assumptions about the unfitness of black men to serve equally in volunteer citizen-armies. Indeed, Fort Wagner and other battlefield actions throughout the year challenged Lincoln's theory that African American soldiers were best suited for duty behind the lines. Yet Gooding himself acknowledged the nearly unbendable strength of the garrison stigma, a force that continued to organize and relegate the Fifty-fourth and most black units into supplementary roles. Taking his case to the president, Gooding decried the unfair treatment endured by black garrison troops. "Are we *Soldiers,* or are we LABOURERS?" he demanded. "We are fully armed, and equipped, have done all the various Duties, pertaining to a Soldiers life." He questioned why he and other black soldiers, who had sacrificed just as much as white men, were paid less. And he also expressed doubts about the policy of distinguishing military service along racial lines.[1]

Gooding's appeal ultimately sought to clarify the meaning of "citizen-soldier," a concept greatly complicated by the Union's war of occupation, and which Lincoln's proclamation sought to clarify. That many of his comrades were born free northerners, Gooding asserted, validated their claim to the full rights, privileges, and responsibilities of citizen-volunteers. Ironically, he employed language that echoed Lincoln's garrisoning philosophy, which pitted free men against formerly enslaved men. "We of this Regt. were not enlisted under any 'contraband' act," Gooding declared. "Having the advantage of *thinking,* and acting for ourselves, so far as the Laws would allow us," he cautioned, "we do not consider ourselves fit subjects" for auxiliary treatment. Gooding thus concluded that the Fifty-fourth should be regarded "as american SOLDIERS, not as menial hirelings." Differences in pay, service, and conduct, he informed the president, symbolized the stark, unfair ways in which the government classified and treated its citizen-soldiers along lines of race.[2]

James F. Jones, an African American soldier and hospital ward master in the Fourteenth Rhode Island Heavy Artillery (Colored), adopted a different perspective on black garrisoning. Also freeborn, he and his black artillerymen arrived in New Orleans in the spring of 1864, and would remain there for the duration of the conflict. "We could see signs of smothered hate and prejudice to both our color and present character as Union soldiers," Jones explained. The white regiments also stationed in the Crescent City, he continued, "thought to deride us and disrespect us as soldiers because we were colored." However, Jones and his fellow soldiers were not overcome by such insults. The Fourteenth Rhode Island comprised free northern black men who traveled south to occupy conquered regions of the Confederacy, and they savored the significance and symbolism of the moment. "For once in his life," Jones wrote, "your humble correspondent walked fearlessly and boldly through the streets of a southern city! And he did this without being required to take off his cap at every step, or give all the side walks to those lordly princes of the sunny south, the planter's sons! Oh, chivalry! how hast thou lost thy potent power and charms!"[3]

Both Gooding and Jones exemplify how African American soldiers protested and shaped their roles in Union armies. Rather than acting as passive residents in a world of military oppression, black men in blue uniforms used the upheaval of war to undercut the racial assumptions of garrisoning. Although the Emancipation Proclamation sought a conservative solution to the problem of white citizen-soldier occupation, contained potentially damaging consequences for the fate of second-class black citizenship, and curbed black soldiers' wartime contributions by placing them in the back of the army, it also inadvertently positioned USCT regiments on the frontlines of occupation, an unprecedented transformation in American military history. As Jones explained, military occupation served as the ideal vehicle by which to collapse the South's slave-based racial hierarchy. African American occupiers represented a unique moment within the broader tradition of occupation: few periods in human history had witnessed occupying forces of men who came from the very regions they were sent to control. Black soldiers, the majority of whom garrisoned lands conquered by Union armies, used occupation to their advantage, unbalancing traditional southern power dynamics. They defied the status quo and impressed their newfound martial authority on the very society guilty of enslaving them. Reflecting the stunning impact of emancipation, their actions redefined the limited, conservative nature of garrisoning as articulated in Lincoln's proclamation.

The addition of African American soldiers to Union armies complicated the existing ideological and cultural dimensions of wartime occupation. The extent to which black troops sought to reshape the South actually revealed the limits of white volunteers' grievances about occupation in the citizen-soldier tradition. White critiques of wartime occupation echoed the traditional aversion of using the army to reorder society, which some argued undermined the nation's republican heritage. But because it *was* a domestic war of occupation, waged on the crumbling lands of slavery, black soldiers had the most to lose by not applying themselves in an active military capacity. They demonstrated the potential for provisional soldiers to serve with zeal in an occupying role, employing their martial power to collapse the South's slaveholding hierarchy. African American soldiers thus envisioned the military to be *the* essential tool for social and political transformation, and they exercised their position as occupiers in three fundamental ways: using garrison service to challenge local power and social structures; asserting newfound roles of freedom and authority through raiding expeditions and counterinsurgency warfare; and destroying the remnants of slavery wherever occupying Union armies traveled. That a majority of USCT regiments remained behind the lines was, ironically, one of the most revolutionary implications of the black military experience.[4]

* * *

The Confederate South was not occupied exclusively by an invading army of white northerners. Garrisoned communities came to be governed in large measure by black southerners-turned-soldiers who were largely homegrown and enlisted and deployed to regions once ruled by the slaveholding elite. African American soldiers used their presence within occupied garrisons to liberate themselves from the previous strictures of racial bondage, while also bending white southerners to their will. Standing picket, challenging passersby, and demanding passes elevated black soldiers to unprecedented positions of authority within garrisoned towns. African American troops did not sit passively in occupied zones; instead, they embraced the opportunities of occupation, enforcing their conceptions of liberty and challenging planter legitimacy. As one soldier marched by a cluster of Confederate prisoners at the end of the war, he noticed his former master among the group. "Hello, massa," the soldier exclaimed, "bottom rail on top dis time!" Indeed it was. *This* was the potential and promise of black occupation.[5]

Joseph T. Wilson, an African American soldier and later historian of the black soldier experience, quoted Thomas J. Morgan, a white officer in the Fourteenth USCT, to catalog the varied ways in which African American occupiers exerted their martial will on southern communities. Morgan arrived to organize the regiment at Gallatin, Tennessee, finding "several hundred negro men in camp" who "were a motley crowd,—old young, middle aged. Some wore the United States uniform, but most of them had on the clothes in which they had left the plantations, or had worn during periods of hard service as laborers in the army." He recognized the challenge before him: the men had not passed a medical exam, never been formally trained or drilled, and their weapons, if they had any at all, were old and battered. "The colored men knew nothing of the duties of a soldier," he explained in November 1863, "except a little they had picked up as camp-followers."[6]

Over the subsequent weeks, Morgan drilled the new troops and instructed them on the import of discipline and soldierly virtue. By January, the Fourteenth USCT reflected a marked change in appearance and attitude. Although a few white troops garrisoned Gallatin, the bulk of the occupation force comprised black soldiers, who "acted as pickets, and no citizen was allowed to pass our lines either into the village or out, without a proper permit." Local residents who were found without documentation were sent promptly to headquarters. "Thus many proud Southern slave-holders," he recounted, "found themselves marched through the street, guarded by those who three months before had been slaves." The black troops especially noticed the fundamental change that had occurred, injecting themselves into unprecedented societal roles. "The negroes often laughed over these changed relations," Morgan commented, "as they sat around their camp fires, or chatted together while off duty."[7]

African American soldiers indeed savored the opportunity to occupy Confederate towns and wield their authority among white southerners. Rufus Sibb Jones, of the Eighth USCT, part of the occupying forces at Jacksonville, Florida, was troubled by the inordinate amount of fatigue labor that his regiment performed. Yet he reported with satisfaction that "it must be humiliating to those who once lived in style and owned slaves, to see their property and that of others occupied as hospitals by Negro soldiers." Jones further revealed how the white southern class system had been broken by war: "It often happens here that the mistress and servant eat together in Sutler stores." A black soldier from Maryland, who served in the Seventh USCT, also at Jacksonville, appreciated the troubled countenances of local civilians. "The people here are less a people than any I have seen; they do not seem to understand anything but they are the most God-forsaken looking animals on earth, and all miserable accordingly. They look mean; they live *meanly,* act *meanly,* and they don't mean anything but *mean.* . . . To think that these fellows voted Florida out of the Union without the aid of the primitive inhabitants—alligators—is simply preposterous."[8]

John C. Brock, a commissary sergeant in the Forty-third USCT, celebrated "how horrible it must have been to the rebels that their 'sacred soil' should have been polluted by the footsteps of colored Union soldiers!" The local residents, he observed in Alexandria, Virginia, "looked at us with astonishment, as if we were some great monsters risen up out of the ground. They looked bewildered," he related, "yet it seemed to be too true and apparent to them that they really beheld nearly 10,000 colored soldiers filing by, armed to the teeth, with bayonets bristling in the sun." Brock described that, while his men welcomed the shocked looks upon the countenances of white Virginians, the striking symbolism of the moment was not lost on his black comrades. "I tell you our boys seemed to fully appreciate the importance of marching through a secesh town. On, on we came, regiment after regiment, pouring in, as it seemed to their bewildered optics, by countless thousands—with colors flying and the bands playing." "I must say," Brock continued, "that the 43d looked truly grand." The regiment was assigned to guard the rail lines near the old battlefields at Manassas. "We have been regularly drilled for picket duty both day and night since we came here," Brock wrote. "The boys halt a man very quick, and if he does not answer quick, he gets a ball sent through him."[9]

The sudden shifts in power and authority described by Jones and Brock indeed shocked white southerners as they witnessed the manifestation of their worst nightmare: black soldiers with muskets, marching in organized ranks, policing towns, all with consent from the very government that once sanctioned their enslavement. The reactions of southern whites testified to the effectiveness of African American occupation. "Yankee men are the order of the day," Mary Semmes wrote about Alexandria, Virginia. "We have a negro here as Capt in the quarter master's department and who goes around in great style. It is thought that we will have negro soldiers to guard the town so that the white soldiers may go in the field." She concluded that their existence was "perfectly intolerable."[10]

Harriet Ellen Moore confided to her diary that yielding to the will of Federal armies was humiliating; acquiescing to what she saw as an inferior race was nothing short of crushing, debasing, and nauseating. "A brigade of *negroes* uniformed and equipped paraded our streets to day. Oh how humiliating. What have we come to?" she wondered from Nashville. "I would willingly live on bread & water in the south, where there is liberty and society such as we once enjoyed than to dwell in luxury among people who consider 'niggers' their superiors and raise them up in our midst to kill and destroy." Such fears extended into states that had not even seceded. Residents of Baltimore, Maryland, pleaded to the governor "that a *negro regiment* which they threaten to . . . quarter in our neighborhood may not be allowed to come. Our people are in a state of utter Consternation at the prospect of such a thing." A white woman in occupied Vicksburg summarized all of these sentiments after she encountered "a *negro officer* and a Yankee! hitherto two of the crowning hating pieces of creation."[11]

James Rumley, who lived in Beaufort, North Carolina, and whose remarkable diaries offer a candid white-southern critique of Union occupation, opined endlessly about the fears and tribulations associated with black garrisoning. "We have seen our entire slave population turned loose in our midst," he wrote, echoing the anxieties of countless Confederates who witnessed emancipation take shape. "Nothing during our captivity has shocked the feelings of some of our people more than the act of the military authorities here, converting the court room of our Court House . . . into a negro Recruiting office!" Recognizing the stunning change in local power dynamics, Rumley alleged that "the presence of a negro garrison in Beaufort creates immense dissatisfaction among all classes of white citizens. Never during the darkest hours of the dark war have the whites realized such a sense of degradation as they now feel, and never have they felt so keenly the loss of liberty." For Rumley, black military occupation carried far greater implications than service in the field. Garrisoning, much like slavery, brought white and black in close contact, and the intimacy of occupation exposed the rapid alterations in social and political relations. That formerly enslaved men now wearing the Federal uniform, and stationed in a once-thriving slaveholding community, confirmed to Rumley "one of the results of subjugation, that the north would insist on placing the negroes on an equality with the white man at the ballot box."[12]

White Union soldiers also realized the effectiveness of black occupation as a blow to southern morale. Thomas Wentworth Higginson observed that the First South Carolina Volunteers, shortly after they captured Jacksonville, Florida, in 1864, "were to endure another test, as to their demeanor as victors." The town was populated with "five hundred citizens, nearly all white, at the mercy of their former slaves." The Massachusetts abolitionist explained that "to some of these whites it was the last crowning humiliation, and they were, or professed to be, in perpetual fear." Indeed, as he recalled after the war, "it was the only military service which they had ever shared within the town, and it moreover gave a sense of self-respect to be keeping the peace of their own streets."[13]

Other white troops agreed with Higginson's assessment that the crucible of war had irrevocably altered black soldiers' relationship to the South. A white colonel in the Ninety-second USCT explained the symbolic success of an expedition near Morganza, Louisiana, in September 1864. "The people along the road of this raid and the one previous seemed terror stricken at the sight of black troops," he wrote, and "if every raid is answered by black troops, you will Soon not hear of one this side of the Atchafalaya River, yet they behaved in a soldierly manner and were at all times under strict discipline." An officer in the Thirty-fifth USCT, writing from Jacksonville, Florida, advised, "You had better believe the citizens are mad because the town is to be occupied by colored troops." Local residents "hate the sight of the blacks it hurts them to think that these fellows who were once their slaves can walk about the town as big as any body now." Henry Gilbert, who served in the Nineteenth Michigan, rejoiced at the effect black soldiers had on the "rebel community" of Murfreesboro, Tennessee. He vowed to staff his picket lines with black soldiers who would intimidate local whites from trading with the army. "Wont it hurt them?" Gilbert exclaimed. "Many of them will prefer to turn round & go back," he wrote, concluding, "They shall take one dose of human rights all round & see how it will affect them."[14]

The presence of African American soldiers provoked fierce hatred among white southerners, who watched with fear as their slaveholding republic crumbled. The tension that gripped white communities garrisoned by black troops sometimes erupted into ferocious, clandestine attacks from citizens desperate to reclaim the fading racial promise of the Confederate nation. Foreshadowing potential violence between soldier and civilian, an officer in the Thirty-fifth USCT commented that whites "hate all the blacks but the black soldier worst of all." He recounted an incident in which residents of

Jacksonville "met a couple of black soldiers on the sidewalk last night[.] they could not pass each other with out a quarrel and in the end one of the blacks got cut so badly with a knife that he is not expected to live." The officer predicted an "open war between them after we leave."[15]

Attacks against black occupiers signaled the ultimate reprisals to emancipation and a biracial Union army. While not common, the covert slaying of black US soldiers reflected the viciousness of occupied garrisons and symbolized the retaliation for alleged slave insurrection, underscoring the problematic aftermath of emancipation. The hanging of African American soldiers represented one form of white revenge. In the wake of the assaults on Port Hudson, Louisiana, "two of the colored soldiers of this command have been recently hanged," while others were "badly beaten and otherwise ill-treated." Union picket guards found another soldier near Memphis, "about twenty-five years of age, evidently murdered, shirt bloody, marks of blows on neck and back and head," left to die "by rebel citizens for enlisting in government service." The murder of black soldiers, and the public display of their bodies, sought to reclaim white racial control in communities torn asunder by war, occupation, and emancipation. Even when the Confederate War Department opted not to sanctify the policy of executing black soldiers, informal efforts at the local level spoke to white southerners' innate quest to reestablish the antebellum barriers between enslaved and free.[16]

A clash between a black regiment and a white resident at Norfolk, Virginia, during the summer of 1863 reflected the desire of white southerners to delegitimize USCT military occupiers. As Alanson Sanborn, a white officer in the First USCT, marched his black troops through the streets of Norfolk— streets on which some men in the regiment likely had been paraded as slaves— David M. Wright, a local doctor, impeded the procession. As the troops marched closer, Wright allegedly declared, "'My God, did ever I expect my country to come to this? Did ever I expect to see such a regiment on the streets of the city of Norfolk'?" Sanborn approached with a drawn sword, preparing "to slap [Wright] on the cheek," when the doctor called the officer a coward. As both men proceeded to wrestle, Wright pulled a pistol and shot Sanborn in the head, killing him instantly. Later in the year, a Federal court martial convicted Wright of murder, sentencing him to death by hanging. Despite its small scale and historical obscurity, the murder of an officer of African American soldiers in broad daylight underscored the profound, unsettling influence of black occupation.[17]

While the Alanson Sanborn–David Wright affair may appear minor, especially within the context of the massive civil war in which it took place, it is remarkably significant in its long-term symbolism. Indeed, the event may contain far greater implications than even the massacre at Fort Pillow, Tennessee, in which Nathan Bedford Forrest's cavalry slayed scores of black Union soldiers attempting to surrender their Mississippi River garrison. Sanborn's murder occurred within the intimate confines of a southern community which had long been organized along particular social relationships and racial assumptions. Slavery served as the greatest and most visible means of societal division, a safe reminder of white authority and black subservience. Localism—the cultural elimination of outside influence—further reinforced and stabilized antebellum southern towns from outside encroachment. Yet the advent of war shattered the protective insulation of communities such as Norfolk, undermining white southerners' tenuous hold on their social reality. The Civil War created a vacuum into which flooded armies, emancipation, social upheaval, and occupation, all of which converged to create a new world that made little sense to some and provided an opportunity for others. And thus David Wright—who grasped for a community that no longer existed—confronted Alanson Sanborn—who embodied that community's future—ending in conflict and bloodshed, seemingly the only certainties within a revolutionary struggle.

Their fight in the streets of Norfolk was based principally on the pillars of emancipation and military occupation, the former a death blow to the South's racial hierarchy and the latter an indication that local control no longer existed. And because Sanborn's soldiers were black, they represented an amalgamation of both realities, prompting Wright to banish the presence of the perceived threat through any means necessary. Justifying his action, Wright explained that he intended "not to be arrested and marched off under a guard of negroes," which he associated with Sanborn's leadership. Wright alleged "a provocation for his act in the presence of the colored troops, whom he deem[ed] to have been brought into Norfolk to provoke and insult the inhabitants." A witness to Wright's arrest recorded the provost marshal asking whether he—Wright—"had anything to say," to which Wright responded that "he was excited when he did the deed."[18]

While David Wright's quest to overthrow the black military occupation of Norfolk ended in the murder of a Union soldier, its imagery resonated with prominent Confederates. Rather than ignoring, downplaying, or clarifying the episode, President Jefferson Davis and Secretary of War James A. Seddon defended the act wholly, recognizing the implications of USCT regiments occupying southern communities. Before Wright's execution, Davis yearned to "do anything in my power to rescue him from an enemy regardless alike of the laws and customs of civilized people in their dealings with us." Seddon acknowledged his "deep sympathy" for Wright's "natural indignation . . . at the shameful spectacle" of black military authority, while praising the "prompt vindication of his honor against the indignity offered him." Like Wright, Davis and Seddon associated Alanson Sanborn with the troubled fate of the Confederacy, the destiny of its culture of honor, and its promise of white supremacy. Perhaps more than any other factor, the rise of African American occupation taught white southerners that active, violent resistance, even if it meant the slow but steady hanging of a black man here, and the shooting of a white Unionist there, might eventually redeem the South. The Sanborn-Wright affair quite possibly was one of the first seeds planted in the larger drama of violence that would engulf southern communities for years to come as black and white residents struggled to exert newfound authority on the one hand and to eliminate racial obstruction on the other.[19]

Black soldiers also shaped the culture of violence within garrisons, demonstrating how military occupation reflected the broader collapse of antebellum race relations. Occupied zones long functioned as arenas of irregular conflict, and some USCT regiments applied a particular mode of unconventional warfare to meet the clandestine threats posed by the likes of David Wright. Because certain white southerners purposely refused to place limits on how they contested black soldiers—oftentimes black troops received no quarter simply because of their skin color—African American occupiers were forced to respond in like manner, testing the strength of wartime civility in the occupied Confederacy. For example, an officer in the Twenty-eighth USCT recounted an incident when soldiers in his regiment guarded a group of Confederate prisoners of war, many of whom "being the old Masters of some the Darkies." The officer explained how the soldiers were formerly enslaved in Kentucky and took "greate pride in pointing them [the former masters] out to us. I assure you it is gauling to the feelings of [the] prisoners to be guarded by Niggers. Yesterday was [their] first day of duty, one of the prisoners threw a stone at one of them [and he was] shot dead on the spot."[20]

Rather than negotiating new racial and social arrangements, other soldiers in Vicksburg sought to redress past grievances by killing a citizen "in open day in the streets." The episode prompted authorities to issue a general order decrying such methods. "The recent murder of a citizen by colored soldiers," it read, "should arouse the attention of every officer serving with the troops to be absolute necessity of preventing their soldiers from attempting a redress of their own grievances." Local commanders understood not only the precarious environment of occupation, but also the tenuous relationship between black soldiers and white civilians. "If the spirit which led to this act of violence is not at once repressed, consequences of the most terrible nature must follow." Both white and black undertook acts of vengeance in an attempt either to restore the racial hierarchy of the old South or to remake the South into something entirely new.[21]

While many USCT used their garrisoned positions to assert freedom and enforce a new social order in the South, their use of irregular tactics to combat white violence and to resist the broader culture of white supremacy was deemed by some onlookers to be unbefitting of provisional soldiers. Within this context, the concerns of Francis H. Pierpont, the occupation commander at Alexandria, Virginia, come into greater focus. Since "colored troops are new recruits just from bondage," Pierpont alleged that their interactions with white southerners resulted from a lack of discipline. He sympathized with local civilians whose "great objection is the positive insolence of these colored soldiers. . . . It is at the risk of the life of the citizen that we make any complaint of their bad conduct." The response to the confrontation between black soldiers and a white civilian at Vicksburg confirmed Pierpont's opinion. "But if in teaching the colored man that he is free, and that, in becoming a soldier, he has become the equal of his former master, we forget to teach him the first duty of the soldier, that of obedience to the law," read a general order; "if we encourage him in rushing for his arms and coolly murdering citizens for every fancied insult, nothing but disgrace and dishonor can befall all connected with the organization."[22]

Both Pierpont and the general orders from Vicksburg failed to recognize that African American soldiers' seemingly "undisciplined" conduct sprang from a desire for active resistance against white southern domination. What was for Pierpont and white officers in Vicksburg a sign of unruly, belligerent, destabilizing conduct was actually the effort of some black troops to consolidate and hold their newfound authority. Unforeseen implications of Abraham Lincoln's garrisoning prescription in the Emancipation Proclamation thus emerged. By placing most black soldiers in the rear of the army, they were forced to confront white southerners on violent, unprecedented terms, occasionally resulting in chaos and random killing. While African American troops were instrumental in defying slaveholding power, their actions created ironic, tragic consequences. White southern violence, which had a long, devastating history, could be resisted only by black soldiers willing to employ similarly intense methods.

The intersection of racial violence and occupation complicates triumphal narratives about the black military experience. African American soldiers indeed stood as impediments to white southern power and hierarchy, symbolizing a society undergoing rapid transformation. Yet their martial presence concentrated the wrath of those who would stop at nothing short of murder to ensure the preservation of white southern life; some black troops responded in kind to demonstrate that they were no longer an enslaved, subservient class. While emancipation and the USCT redefined and reprioritized conceptions of liberty, they also unleashed a power struggle between white southerners and black soldiers who competed for the fate of freedom, a freedom that became militarized and embroiled in a vicious, troubling dichotomy. To meet the flood of white violence, black soldiers employed equally aggressive tactics to safeguard their independence and manhood. Yet their actions were also interpreted—sometimes by white officers in the Union army—as signs of a bellicose and uncontrollable class of formerly enslaved men. African American soldiers were thus trapped between southern white violence, which could be met only with violence, and northern white stereotypes, which considered black men naturally warlike.[23]

* * *

The paths of violence and "militarized freedom," which were learned within the confines of occupied garrisons, set the stage for an expansion of black liberty in the post-emancipation South. Soldiers of the USCT employed their martial efforts to greatest effect on raids, expeditions, and counterinsurgency warfare, all of which continued to destabilize the Confederate South's political and social hierarchies. Such approaches hardly resembled the static conditions of garrisoning, instead functioning as active, mobile occupations. Indeed, Union armies had long used garrisons as departure points to deploy raids into the southern countryside, confiscating and destroying Confederate war-making resources, enforcing emancipation, and dislodging guerrilla resistance. Black occupiers viewed these tactics through a political lens, sensing an opportunity to transform their homelands. If white southerners feared the sight of black soldiers marching freely on the streets of garrisoned communities, how much more did the sight of USCT fanning out across the South signal the death knell of the antebellum order.[24]

As formerly enslaved southerners, African American soldiers excelled at raiding due to their intimate knowledge of the local country and landscape. Endorsing an active black military occupation, Brigadier General Edward M. McCook opined that "their keen sense of locality, and familiarity with their native regions make them invaluable as scouts and for flying expeditions in the interior of the Enemy's Country." At first glance, McCook's expectations of black military service may appear paternalistic, limiting, and even condescending. Yet he believed that the USCT could contribute to occupation in unique ways that white soldiers could not. "With a few regiments of picked, well mounted [men]," he wrote, "I am persuaded I could penetrate farther into the rebel country." And keen to black soldiers' political objectives in occupying the South, McCook sensed that "the active sympathies [of] the appearance of black troops would naturally excite [much] among the preponderating slave population . . . upsetting the abnormal fabric of the rebellion." Such scenarios would indeed do more "than any white troops have as yet attempted or accomplished."[25]

Raids along the Atlantic coast and in the Mississippi River Valley testify to the broader experience of black expeditions throughout the occupied Confederacy. Like Edward McCook, white officers in South Carolina attributed successful expeditions to the distinctive culture created by African American occupiers. "These [men] are better than white soldiers for this service," wrote Rufus Saxton, commander of the Department of the South, "on account of the greater facility with which they can effect landings through the marshes and thick woods which line the banks of streams." Thomas Wentworth Higginson, colonel of the First South Carolina Volunteers, claimed that the "superiority" of black expeditions "lies simply in the fact that they know the country, while white troops do not," and "instead of leaving their homes and families to fight they are fighting for their homes and families, and they show the resolution and the sagacity which a personal purpose gives." Thus, on a raid that departed Beaufort in January 1863 and extended south along the St. Mary's River into Florida, the First South Carolina successfully engaged rebel cavalry, confiscated iron, brick, and lumber, and enforced the recently issued Emancipation Proclamation.[26]

Even William T. Sherman, who was largely skeptical about the capacity of African American soldiers, relied on their raiding abilities as part of his Meridian, Mississippi, expedition in 1864. Still wedded to his narrow assumptions of black military service, Sherman withdrew white troops from Vicksburg, who would be used in the campaign's principal offensives, and replaced them with USCT regiments. Most of the black soldiers hailed from the Mississippi Valley and had joined the army at points along the river between Memphis and Natchez. They were ordered to patrol the inlets, creeks, and swamps that crisscrossed the Yazoo and Mississippi rivers, stabilizing the region and displacing Confederate resistance. "Such expeditions will suit the habits of [black] troops," Sherman wrote with a tinge of racism, due to their knowledge of the local surroundings. Black soldiers' acquaintance with the local landscapes of South Carolina and Mississippi indeed proved instrumental in wartime expeditions.[27]

The active nature of raiding facilitated a distinct sense of freedom. James W. Anderson, a black soldier in the Thirty-first USCT, knew that a march in hostile country near Richmond, Virginia, made him and his comrades "true soldiers." In a ten-day expedition that traversed "the most fertile country that there is in Virginia," Anderson cataloged the rich lands and plentiful goods that his unit confiscated. "We helped ourselves to anything that we saw and wanted in the shape of poultry, meat, tobacco, corn, horses," emptying their haversacks of army-issued food, "replacing it with turkeys, chickens, ducks, sweet potatoes." The instability of war that had wrecked the southern countryside presented an opportunity for the Thirty-first USCT, some of whom likely had been enslaved on nearby plantations. The act of confiscating food was not done purely out of the rowdy behavior typical of many volunteer soldiers. Instead, as Anderson acknowledged, "the boys were living high," an indication that they had separated themselves from the unfree conditions in which they had previously lived.[28]

Raids and expeditions also familiarized African American occupiers with antiguerrilla warfare. Guerrillas, and the unconventional tactics they used to contest occupation, reflected white southern embitterment about military invasion and the war's inversion of traditional racial structures. Symbolizing the last vestige of a militarized South, guerrillas often checked black civilians' pursuit of freedom and blocked their access to Union armies. In August 1863, a Federal officer reported the crumbling conditions of slavery near St. Louis, noting that "many of [the enslaved] have escaped from their masters farms to adjacent military stations." Yet "they dare not travel by land, lest they be murdered on the road. The guerrillas have shown a singular and inhuman ferocity towards them." Black soldiers responded with equally aggressive actions to counter such irregular warfare; raiding expeditions sought to destabilize insurgent activities and safeguard routes to liberation. A soldier in the Thirteenth USCT believed that his comrades were "the bravest set of men on the Western Continent. They think nothing of routing the guerrillas that roam at large in the wilds of Tennessee."[29]

Three episodes illustrate black occupiers' conceptions of counterinsurgency warfare. First, raids along the swampy rivers in Georgia and South Carolina conducted by freeborn northerners and formerly enslaved men during the summer of 1863 raised questions about African American soldiers' enthusiastic embrace of irregular tactics. Debate centered primarily on James Montgomery's Second South Carolina Volunteers, Robert Gould Shaw's Fifty-fourth Massachusetts Infantry, and Thomas Wentworth Higginson's First South Carolina Volunteers. Montgomery incorporated vicious tactics into his counterinsurgency raids, plundering southern communities and bringing what William T. Sherman later called "the hard hand of war" to local rebels. Departing in early June on an expedition along the Combahee River in South Carolina, Montgomery's men leveled affluent rice plantations, destroying property, flooding fields, and torching estates. The Second South Carolina's tactics elicited concerns among some observers, who voiced anxieties about the broader implications of black soldiers' conduct during antiguerrilla campaigns. While Higginson sometimes approved of unconventional approaches, he disavowed razing private property, acknowledging that Montgomery's "concepts of foraging were rather more Western and liberal than his."[30]

On June 10, scarcely a week after the Combahee expedition, Shaw's Fifty-fourth Massachusetts joined Montgomery's regiment aboard a steamship on the Altamaha River. Arriving at the sleepy, deserted town of Darien, Georgia, Montgomery commanded his men to loot private dwellings, after which he ordered the town to be burned. Amidst Shaw's vehement objections to torching Darien, and his protests against the wanton pillaging and destruction of Montgomery's soldiers, he approved of his men confiscating goods that served a military purpose. Nonetheless, dreading dishonor and shame heaped upon his troops, Shaw, in articulating the citizen-soldier ideal, feared that aggressive, partisan warfare transformed volunteers into sullied, violent ruffians. It was "revolting," he commented in the wake of the expedition, "to wreak our vengeance on the innocent and defenseless." Shaw distinguished between the "ex-slave contraband regiments," like Montgomery's Second South Carolina, and his own Fifty-fourth Massachusetts, composed largely of free northern black men, believing that the undisciplined character of the former threatened the integrity of the latter. Shaw denounced "this barbarous sort of warfare," because "I am not sure that it will not harm very much the reputation of black troops and of those connected with them." Northern abolitionists, like Shaw, worried that such irregular tactics would prevent black men from learning the civilized limits of freedom, instead "re-developing all [their] savage instincts."[31]

Robert Gould Shaw interpreted the Darien affair through the lens of a white citizen-soldier, assuming that an army of occupation, composed primarily of volunteers, ought to place safeguards on its conduct and interactions with civilians. Those soldiers who failed to abide by civilized standards, especially in a domestic war, undermined the republican military tradition. However, Shaw's association of the Second South Carolina Volunteers—formerly enslaved men whom he believed had scorned the privileges of freedom—with an undisciplined and rowdy mob bent on mindless annihilation, exposed his limited grasp of the fast-changing nature of the citizen-soldier ideal. While white soldiers like Shaw had long considered pillaging and destruction of property as antithetical to American exceptionalism, they failed to see how those same tactics informed an emerging *black* citizen-soldier tradition. For African American men, a domestic war of occupation presented the opportunity to cleanse the South of its slaveholding character, to eliminate the symbols of white supremacy, and to crase the artifacts of plantation life. Military conduct that might have appeared to undermine the virtue of white citizen-soldiers was employed by black soldiers who believed it necessary for securing the racial gains created by emancipation.[32]

While Shaw struggled to grasp his soldiers' conceptions of raiding and counterinsurgency warfare, Colonel Edward A. Wild, who conducted a famed expedition across the marshlands of eastern North Carolina in December 1863, seemed to understand the emerging culture of black occupation. Wild's raid comprised nearly two thousand men from the First and Second USCT, First and Second North Carolina Colored, Fifty-fifth Massachusetts Infantry (Colored), and a small collection of white regiments, hoping to regain control of the Dismal Swamp Canal, annihilate local guerrillas, and recruit formerly enslaved men into the Union army. Because they served in an occupation capacity, Wild's soldiers operated independently from conventional wartime standards. Wild reported that his men lived off the land, "judiciously discriminating in favor of the worst rebels." A wartime correspondent for the *New York Times* traveling with the expedition confirmed that the "inhabitants being almost exclusively 'Secesh,' the colored boys were allowed to forage at will along the road." The men foraged not only for food. The region contained large, wealthy plantations and an abundance of slaves, whom the African American occupiers invited into their lines. Oftentimes, groups of black soldiers entered the mansions and found locked behind closed doors numerous enslaved people who were promptly set free, the white planters taken prisoner, and scores of personal property confiscated.[33]

The raid was marked by relentless interaction with guerrillas who swarmed the Dismal Swamp region. "The guerrillas pestered us," Wild wrote. "They crept on our pickets at night, waylaid our expeditions and our cavalry scouts, firing upon us whenever they could." Wild's men responded with force. They burned houses and barns, consumed livestock, and captured family members of local guerrillas. In one instance, Wild ordered the hanging of one of the bushwhackers, Daniel Bright, as a sign of ultimate retribution. African American occupiers initiated a powerful and effective response to the guerrilla presence. They "adopted a more rigorous style of warfare," which knew few bounds. As a result, some of the guerrillas became disaffected, "some wishing to quit the business," and even considered joining the regular Confederate army. As the raid progressed, however, violence persisted. "They are virtually bandits," Wild wrote, and "can only harass us by stealing, murdering, and burning." Thus that "enemy I would now engage to exterminate in two months by means of my colored infantry." Black soldiers on the raid reflected Wild's assertion that the active guerrilla presence prevented the region from enjoying peace and stability, hampering enslaved families from escaping to Union lines.[34]

African American soldiers on Wild's raid successfully executed irregular violence against their guerrilla adversary. Milton M. Holland, a sergeant in the Fifth USCT, wrote shortly after the expedition of an episode in which he and his comrades "faced the cowardly foe when they were hid in the swamp firing upon them. They stood like men, and when ordered to charge, went in with a yell, and came out victorious." Holland expressed utter contempt for guerrillas. One of their fellow soldiers was captured and hanged by the southern bandits; the black troops responded in equal manner. "We hold one of their 'fair daughters,'" Holland reported, in return for the guerrillas' behavior. Their murdered comrade "was found with a note pinned to his flesh," and Holland promised that "before this war ends we will pin their sentences to them with Uncle Sam's leaden pills." He then celebrated the symbolism of Daniel Bright's execution, writing simply "we hung [the] guerrilla dead, by the neck."[35]

A final episode occurred during the summer of 1864 in the Mississippi River Valley, a region particularly prone to guerrilla attacks on free black laborers. When Union armies occupied Louisiana during the spring and summer of 1862, thus inaugurating the process of wartime Reconstruction, military supervisors transformed confiscated plantations into experiments of free labor. Formerly enslaved people now worked for wages, symbolizing the destruction of unfree toil. While this arrangement was fraught with corruption and debilitating working conditions, the free-labor plantation system multiplied throughout the Mississippi Valley concomitant with the United States' expanded military purview of the region. The dissolution of local white rule coincided with the rise of guerrilla resistance, which retaliated against the establishment of free black labor. Plantations were rarely immune to guerrilla raids, inspiring fierce retaliation from the occupiers. Black soldiers, who ultimately comprised a majority of Union occupation forces in the valley, interpreted counterinsurgency as a rebuke to guerrillas and as a central means of protecting free laborers. Their antiguerrilla tactics sought to cleanse the region of its clandestine violence.[36]

An incident near Lake Providence, Louisiana, testifies to white guerrilla violence against river plantations and the subsequent retaliation from African American soldiers. In August 1864, in an act characteristic of the violent instability along the sugar planting districts, two hundred guerrillas stormed the plantations at Goodrich's Landing, murdering both white and black laborers. As was the case in much of Louisiana, local civilians had petitioned Confederate military authorities to permit the roving guerrillas to harass Union-operated plantations. The Third USCT Cavalry was detached on a "retaliatory visit" to locate and destroy the mounted partisans. Upon reaching the guerrillas' rendezvous at Floyd and Pinhook, the black cavalrymen were ordered to set fire to each town, after which they captured and killed several guerrillas. Their actions confirmed William T. Sherman's belief that manning the valley with black troops "will effectually prevent the smaller bands of guerrillas from approaching the river plantations." The protection of black laborers was paramount in the quest to rid the South of any obstruction posed by guerrillas who harassed Union-controlled plantations. Launching counterinsurgency raids and expeditions that targeted towns sympathetic to local irregulars weakened guerrilla attacks throughout the region, safeguarding free labor.[37]

* * *

The war African American troops waged on the streets of garrisoned towns, on raids in the countryside, and on counterinsurgent missions remade the South at the point of a bayonet. Their approach expanded the citizen-soldier's role into an active political tool that could be used to reshape society. Far from indicating that their military conduct made them unfit for freedom, black soldiers dynamically influenced occupation to confirm and safeguard that freedom. "We are now determined to hold every step which has been offered to us as citizens of the United States," wrote Joseph E. Williams, a soldier in the Thirty-fifth USCT. "We must learn deeply to realize the duty, the moral and political necessity for the benefit of our race," he continued. "Every consideration of honor, of interest, and of duty to God and man, requires that we should be true to our trust." At the root of it all, Williams implied, rested the remnants of slavery, a dying institution that could be combated only through a destructive occupation.[38]

Garrisoning towns from the Mississippi River Valley to the Atlantic coast, raiding lands once dominated by oppressive planters, embarking on expeditions to eliminate merciless guerrillas, and occupying southern communities, all converged into the central project of black occupation: eliminating slavery, through any means necessary, from the American landscape. Active and sometimes irregular military tactics most efficiently and effectively challenged the remnants of the Confederacy's slaveholding presence. Some African American soldiers even engaged white civilians, turning them into enemy combatants. In battling slavery and its proponents, however, black soldiers did not perform with wanton bellicosity and carelessness. They acted out of perceived necessity, clearing new fields of hope on which the seeds of freedom could sprout, giving sustenance to the process of emancipation.

The results of Edward A. Wild's raid through North Carolina illustrate black soldiers' focus on destroying slavery. Milton Holland, who served in the Fifth USCT, estimated that "thousands of slaves belonging to rebel masters were liberated," confirmed in Wild's official report that the raid freed 2,500 enslaved people. Burning plantations, capturing white civilians, freeing slaves who literally were chained in closets, and ridding the countryside of guerrillas unlocked the gates of freedom. At one point, the expedition passed through the neighborhood of one of the black soldiers. He "came running to the General in breathless haste [and] wished permission to go to the house of his former master, a half a mile from the road, and get his son." Similar episodes marked the character of the raid. "On arriving at [any given] house, the front windows and doors would invariably be found closed, when the men would rush at once to the rear, and overrun the premises like so many ants," claiming goods, supplies, white prisoners, and especially enslaved people.[39]

In helping to liberate their enslaved families and friends from bondage, African American troops identified white southerners, regardless of whether they were enlisted soldiers, civilians, or guerrillas, with state-sanctioned slavery. This was the fundamental assumption behind Wild's expedition, and this mindset also characterized the actions of other black soldiers throughout the occupied Confederacy. All white southerners were viewed as hostile. In St. Bernard Parish, Louisiana, several soldiers from the First Louisiana Native Guards entered local plantations, allegedly for purposes of recruiting. Arriving in August 1863, the soldiers put guards over various houses, "threatening to shoot any white person attempting to leave the houses and there seizing horse carts & mules for the purpose of transporting men women & children from the plantations to the city of New Orleans." The Native Guard troops liberated seventy-five black people. A few days later, more black soldiers arrived at the front door of a prominent planter, "loaded their muskets in front of his door and demanded some colored women whom they called their wives."[40]

Black soldiers thus served as an army of liberation. James F. Jones, of the Fourteenth Rhode Island Heavy Artillery, related how civilians near New Orleans received his unit with "every demonstration of joy and gladness." The 'contrabands,'" he wrote, "look for more certain help, and a more speedy termination of the war, at the hands of the colored soldiers than from any other source; hence their delight at seeing us." Likewise, as a detachment of soldiers from the Eighth Louisiana Infantry (Union, African Descent, later the Forty-seventh USCT), traversed the swamps and bayous that crisscrossed the Mississippi Valley, they came upon a relatively hidden plantation populated by slaves who were "over worked and had but little to eat." An officer reported that the enslaved men's "greatest desire appeared to be, to get with the Union army, and were willing and even anxious to go with it [in] any capacity they could be useful." Although the men believed that service in the army offered the best mode of refuge, they expressed their fear "of being worked [only] on the canals." The troops in the Eighth Louisiana provided "our promise and assurance that they were to be soldiers, and that all would be done for their families that could, be they all come willingly." Several of the enslaved men responded to the request, put down their tools, and walked away with the black Union soldiers, almost certainly to be enfolded into the very force of liberation that had just liberated them.[41]

By removing their families from bondage and embodying the promise of emancipation, these black soldiers in North Carolina, Louisiana, and the Mississippi Valley systematically dismantled the structures of slavery. Other soldiers attacked the institution by targeting one of the foremost symbols of slavery: the white master. During an expedition in the Virginia Tidewater in May 1864, soldiers in the First USCT embarked on a foraging raid to nearby plantations. George W. Hatton, a sergeant in the regiment, described how the war brought forth great change and wrecked the institution of slavery. "But behold what has been revealed in the past three or four years; why the colored men have ascended upon a platform of equality, and the slave can now apply the lash to the tender flesh of his master, for this day I am now an eyewitness of the fact." Many of the soldiers who filled the ranks of the First USCT were originally enslaved by the region's local planters. The soldiers "captured a Mr. Clayton, a noted reb in this part of the country," who had a reputation of meting out the "most unmerciful whipping[s] to enslaved women." When Clayton was brought into the black soldiers' camp, William Harris, another soldier in the First USCT and formerly enslaved to Clayton, was ordered to undress the white captive. "Mr. Harris played his part conspicuously, bringing the blood from his loins at every stroke, and not forgetting to remind the gentlemen of the days gone by." The women whom Clayton used to beat were also present, and they proceeded to "giving him some fifteen or twenty well-directed strokes ... [and] reminded him that they were no longer his." "Oh, that I had the tongue to express my feelings," George Hatton wrote of the episode, "while standing upon the banks of the James River, on the soil of Virginia, the mother state of slavery, as a witness of such a sudden reverse!"[42]

Rearranging and collapsing the old master-slave relationship embodied the central feature in these black occupiers' quest to reshape the South. Similarly, the Thirty-sixth USCT, most of whom had been formerly enslaved men, transferred in early 1864 to Point Lookout, a military prison in Maryland, where they guarded Confederate POWs, some of whom had been the masters of the men in the black regiment. Guards from the Thirty-sixth were instructed to prevent the rebel prisoners from congregating in large numbers and to thwart them from relieving themselves in unauthorized areas of the camp. If these orders were violated, the black sentinels conveyed three warnings, after which they were granted permission to shoot their captives. Disgusted at the sight of armed African Americans, some of the white southern captives refused to obey orders given by the black soldiers. In numerous instances, soldiers shot Confederate prisoners who ignored or defied commands. "The Prisoners were repeatedly ordered to desist in the course they were persuing," wrote one officer; "their only reply was that they would not receive from or be ordered by Damned Nigers." Perhaps even more than in combat, the tension felt between white prisoners and black guards underscored the stunning social transformation wrought by emancipation and African American enlistment. Joined together in close, intimate proximity, both white and black could experience a new tenor of racial authority, a process long characterized by plantation violence against the latter, which had now morphed into military violence against the former.[43]

If Wild's North Carolina raid, the incursions onto St. Bernard Parish's plantations, the whipping of a Virginia slave master, and the shooting of prisoners in Maryland indicated sweeping alterations created by the black military presence, other African American soldiers targeted smaller, yet highly symbolic relics of the slaveholding South. For example, troops on an expedition through the rich planting districts of the Chesapeake Bay strayed from their command, appearing to forage for livestock and food. Yet the soldiers instead besieged a wooden apparatus fixed in the ground and secured with a sturdy crossbeam. "It was a whipping post," a white officer revealed, "& they were in a perfect fury as they cut it down. It seemed as though they were cutting an animate enemy & revenging upon him the accumulated wrongs of two centuries." Similar episodes saw soldiers burning slave pens, destroying vestiges of bondage that had long gripped the region, and contesting the very notions of enslaved and master.[44]

In addition to attacking physical artifacts of slavery, USCT soldiers in North Carolina directed their sights to local law enforcement, a body long charged with regulating behavior and movement among enslaved southerners. Local slave patrols, which prowled the roads and backwoods in search of runaways, commanded great power and authority both before and during the war, serving as the last line of defense against self-emancipation. During a ninety-mile expedition, Edward Wild's African Brigade learned that "upwards of thirty colored prisoners" languished in a local courthouse awaiting trial for attempting to escape to Union lines. Joseph E. Williams explained that although the soldiers failed to chop down the prison doors, "the key was sent for, threatening the sheriff with vengeance in case of refusal, in the form of a can of tar and feathers." Upon opening the prison doors, the soldiers liberated the black prisoners, yet "the thirty was a fabulous number," Williams acknowledged, "which had diminished to three live colored men; their lives were saved."[45]

Some white officers confirmed the unique ways black soldiers used military occupation to destroy slavery and shape their broader world of freedom. Thomas J. Morgan, commander of the Fourteenth USCT, which occupied much of middle and east Tennessee, declared that a "Reg't of a thousand, stalwart, determined black men, well armed, clothed, and decently drilled, is a fact comprehensible by the *dullest;* and no sophistry of traitors, nor prejudice of bigots, can recist its influence." Acknowledging that even the most vocal antislavery activists might sometimes be ignored, Morgan admitted that a "well trained Reg't is the crystalization of all anti-slavery philosophy, and bears too plainly upon its face the power of recistence." Edward M. McCook, a brigadier general of cavalry, recognized the "aptitude of the negroes for Military service." Serving nearly two years in Kentucky, Mississippi, and Alabama "has tended to impress me with both the wisdom and necessity of fighting the rebellion with its own weapons and knocking away its main support by destroying slavery."[46]

Such testimony bears witness to the stunning numbers of enslaved people freed by raiding expeditions conducted by African American units. Wild's North Carolina raid alone freed 2,500 black southerners, one of the largest mass liberations during the entire war. At other times, much smaller groups were liberated, such as the "27 slaves on the Heyward plantation," who returned to Beaufort, South Carolina, with a company of Thomas Wentworth Higginson's black volunteers. On an August 1864 raid through Key West, Florida, conducted by the Second USCT, "the expedition brought in 115 contrabands," in addition to materiel, livestock, and cotton. And, while traversing the countryside near Morganza, Louisiana, the Ninety-second USCT acquired "about 150 contrabands." In April 1865, as the Eighth USCT marched into Petersburg, Virginia, the last major Confederate citadel, they were greeted with a "most cheering and hearty welcome from the colored inhabitants of the city whom their presence had made free."[47]

While it is difficult, if not impossible, to tally a comprehensive number of enslaved people liberated by African American soldiers, the magnitude of military emancipation, which began long before black enlistment, expanded exponentially by the presence of active, mobile USCT regiments. In the wake of Wild's raid, Milton Holland articulated the enthusiasm with which his comrades in the Fifth USCT approached this particular potentiality of occupation. "The colored man makes no distinction in regards to persons," he declared, "so I may say all belonging to slaveholders were liberated." Holland continued: "The boys are generally well, and satisfied that though they are deprived of all the comforts of home, and laboring under great disadvantages . . . still trust that when they do return they will be crowned with honors, and a happier home prepared for them, when they will be free from the abuses of northern and southern fire-eaters."[48]

For Milton Holland, service in the US military was not defined by the limitations of garrisoning; the army instead presented an opportunity to clear a path for a new national and racial landscape. As a freeborn northerner, Holland had already begun to probe what the aftermath of emancipation would look like. Seemingly untroubled by the implications of using the army to engage in social change, Holland, emblematic of much of the black military experience, viewed the Union's armed forces as the fountainhead of a new American freedom to be enjoyed by black southerners *and* northerners. Indeed, the culture of African American occupation departed greatly from traditional understandings about the army's place within the republican military tradition. While white and black soldiers jointly occupied the Confederacy, USC troops like Holland demonstrated unprecedented enthusiasm for using the army to transform civil society. White occupiers, however, continued to express great trepidation about the effects and consequences of domestic occupation. As the war ground to a halt in the spring of 1865, these dual visions of military occupation, based respectively in race and republicanism, competed for prominence in the postwar environment.

8 | Republicanism, Race, and the Problem of Postwar Occupation

Several months after he received Robert E. Lee's surrender at Appomattox Court House, Ulysses S. Grant surveyed the conditions of the postwar South. Returning in December 1865 from a late autumn tour of the conquered rebel states, Grant reported that, while Confederate armies no longer existed, Union forces should remain stationed across the southern landscape to maintain order and oversee the reimplementation of civil government. In a marked departure from his stance of conciliation and ambivalence about a robust military occupation in the immediate wake of the war, Grant endorsed a continued Federal military presence, informing President Andrew Johnson that "small garrisons throughout the states [are] necessary until such time as labor returns to its proper channel and civil authority is fully established." Although Grant acknowledged "a universal acquiescence in the authority of the General Government," he sensed that "the white and the black mutually require the protection" of the US Army.[1]

Despite his insistence that former Confederates had accepted the war's verdict—the deaths of secession and slavery "having been settled forever, by the highest tribunal, arms, that man can resort to"—Grant could not ignore the troubling reports of violence and discrimination committed against freedpeople and the unwillingness of white southerners to relinquish the intransigent spirit that powered their ill-fated rebellion. The army was, therefore, the only institution capable of regulating the rocky transitions from war to peace, slavery to freedom, and martial authority to civil authority. Indeed, the military managed the process of postwar reconstruction, involving itself in the economy, labor relations, military tribunals, and public education, while also monitoring elections, maintaining peace, and assisting civil authorities enforce the law. These were crucial and unique obligations for an institution that had once been relegated to the margins of American society. Now, the army was called to implement and direct Federal Reconstruction policy, to ensure southern loyalty, and to enforce the promise of emancipation.[2]

Grant's prescriptions came at a moment in which the armies that had battled for the Union were being demobilized at a rapid pace. With the fall of the

Confederate nation, northern volunteers clamored to be sent home, arguing that they had fulfilled their contracts as citizen-soldiers. On May 1, 1865, US armies totaled more than 1 million men; by December, when Grant penned his memo, fewer than 100,000 soldiers remained in the former Confederacy, a number that dwindled for much of the next year. The regular army, an institution buoyed by the advent of "peace," would ultimately be charged with Reconstruction duties. Despite these numbers, recent interpretations of Grant's call for a continued military presence suggest that the Civil War never ended at Appomattox. This reasoning holds that the US Army maintained its sanctioned war powers long after Confederate surrender because the rebellious southern states had yet to be readmitted into the Union, thus forestalling peace. The army therefore assumed a robust and active occupation of the South. Capitulation of Confederate armies was merely a "turning point" in a broader conflict that lasted until the early 1870s when the recalcitrant southern states legally rejoined the nation, finally preserving the Union.[3]

While this argument seems to confirm Grant's position in late 1865, it misses one of the central themes of the early postwar years. The Union army indeed retained its war powers in the wake of Confederate surrender, governing the rebellious South with unprecedented martial authority. Yet the army charged with maintaining order and guiding the wayward states back into the Union was a very different institution from the one that defeated Confederate armies between 1861 and 1865. It was no longer a massive army of temporary volunteers. Now, a mere skeleton of its former muscular self, the postwar army took on a mainly bureaucratic, professional character, the antithesis of the citizen-soldier tradition from which wartime military forces were derived. Adopting newfound responsibilities that it had never before assumed, the Reconstruction army dismissed its volunteers, who in turn gladly withdrew from additional martial commitments.[4]

That the US Army was no longer drawn from the citizen-soldier tradition further complicates the continued-war theory. The concomitant forces of demobilization and professionalization underscored the triumph of the republican military ideal, a principle long articulated by white northern volunteers. Their appeals to be mustered out of the army upon Confederate surrender revealed that, for the Union's citizen-soldiers, the war had ended. By volunteering to defend the nation, extinguishing secession, and crushing rebel armies—and, in many cases, expanding the scope of their service to garrison, occupy, and enforce martial law throughout the war-torn South—they had fulfilled their responsibilities as citizens to preserve the Union. They wished to go home now that the supreme threat to democracy, in their minds, had been eliminated. If the war indeed continued after 1865, why were not these same soldiers waging the conflict? Why were they so eager to leave if the battle was only half won?[5]

Answers to these questions resided in lingering republican suspicions of a standing army, an institution that many Union soldiers feared would be the natural outgrowth of any attempt at large-scale domestic occupation. While their foes were rebellious, violent, slaveholding aristocrats who threatened national unity, Union soldiers still viewed vanquished Confederates as Americans, especially now that the fighting had ceased. Eager to excuse themselves from duties of military government and martial law wielded against fellow, albeit defiant, citizens, Union soldiers viewed 1865 as a return to normalcy occasioned by the cessation of formal hostilities. They had no frame of reference for the idea of a strong military force continuing to wield its power across the domestic landscape. While a small US Army continued to administer the social, political, and economic conditions of the postwar South, demobilization confirmed the ideals of Union. Indeed, the government's ability and willingness to send soldiers home after the war was won underscored the very reasons for which the war had been waged. Preservation of the Union meant not only conquering secession and abolishing slavery but also returning to the limited, restrained principles of constitutional republicanism, to which a standing army of volunteers presented a dire threat. While this danger may seem archaic to modern sensibilities, which indict the government and army for denying themselves the necessary tools and manpower to construct a new, sturdier postwar edifice of equality and opportunity, it was a very real fear for most white nineteenth-century Americans.[6]

The seeming abhorrence of standing armies, however, clashed with the necessities of race articulated by the USCT, who were eager to continue using their martial power to consolidate and protect the gains of emancipation. Although enlisted into the military under the conservative garrisoning prescriptions of the Emancipation Proclamation, African American soldiers had used wartime occupation to forge a durable foundation of freedom. They now envisioned a continuation of that authoritative military role during the early postwar years, caring little about the republican implications of peacetime occupation. To some in the USCT, Union victory signaled the beginning of a fundamental transformation of the South in which the military would permanently weaken planter influence, protect communities of freedpeople, and safeguard the promise of free labor. While the postwar army indeed performed these duties, demobilization spread the military's influence too thin, allowing former Confederates to fill critical voids, reinstate their authority, and erect racial barriers eerily reminiscent of slavery. As they had during the war, black troops thus sought to combat pugnacious white southerners with equal force.[7]

However, military leaders such as Ulysses S. Grant came to view black troops and their desire for an active, commanding occupation as leading to the destabilization of the South, uprooting social stability and impeding sectional (and white) reunion. Although disgusted by reports of white violence against freedpeople—a principal reason behind his advocacy of postwar occupation— Grant also indicted USCT regiments for disrupting a lasting peace. African American soldiers, white northern moderates claimed, embodied the alarming, chaotic nature of a standing army. In his December 1865 statement, Grant explained that "the good of the country, and economy, requires that the force kept in the interior where there are many freedmen . . . should all be White troops." African American soldiers, "lately slaves," Grant cautioned, "demoralizes labor both by their advice and furnishing in their camps a resort for the Freedmen for long distances around." Because most USCT had been formerly enslaved, he concluded, "there is danger of collisions" between black soldiers and white planters. Only professional white troops, "who generally excited no opposition," could facilitate a peaceful, stable occupation. And thus republicanism and race, the two elements that had long defined military occupation during the Civil War era, competed for meaning and primacy in the new postwar environment. The implications of each would go a long way in shaping the Union that had just been preserved.[8]

* * *

The Union's white citizen-soldiers were instrumental in defining the army's postwar role as they opposed a robust, continued military occupation. Soldiers' opinions reflected an acute understanding of the cultural contracts they had made with the nation: they had volunteered and fought to preserve the Union, which in turn guaranteed and protected their liberties as free men. To thousands of northern volunteers, the surrenders at Appomattox and Durham Station signaled the end of the war and marked the end of their military service. Any consideration of postwar work was simply out of the question, as continued service after the cessation of hostilities was thought to violate the citizen-soldier ideal. Postwar occupation, which they believed could last indefinitely, was a job for the regular army, and perhaps civil authorities, but not for citizen-volunteers, who yearned for home and a return to private life. These men did not think of themselves as professional soldiers; they did not seek to operate in the same bureaucratic capacity in which many had served grudgingly as wartime occupiers. The rapid demobilization of volunteer units echoed this citizen-soldier ideal, forging a sharp divide from the war that was just waged. By November 1865, 801,000 volunteers had been mustered out of the army, leaving only 11,043 citizen-soldiers in the service.[9]

As they waited to be sent home, white volunteers who remained in the defeated South between 1865 and 1866 voiced a consensual view of their relationship to the nation, army, and society, defining the citizen-soldier perspective on postwar military occupation. Their rhetoric centered on the definitions of surrender to which they linked the capitulation of Confederate armies with preservation of the Union and the dawn of peace. "Today we truly live in the Land of the free and our home shall be among the Brave," Edward Rolfe wrote from Montgomery, Alabama, on July 4, 1865: "The Enemy of Human Liberty and a Nations Glory is conquered." Iowan Charles O. Musser declared that his unit's postwar service in Texas was "an outrage and a wrong that if we *are men,* we will resent it." Believing the war to be over, and his sojourn on the Gulf Coast inconsequential, Musser professed, "We offered our services to our country to help put down the rebellion. That object has been accomplished, and our time is out, and we are no longer needed." Upon receiving word of the surrenders in Virginia and North Carolina, Madison Bowler, an officer in the 113th USCT, recorded the celebrations at Little Rock, which included "bonfires, rockets, noise, and bad whiskey. The war is virtually to an end," he announced. "Peace *must follow soon.* What a grand glorious result of four years of strife!" Bowler thus concluded, "I do not consider myself under the least obligation to the Gov't."[10]

Other Union soldiers specifically equated the surrender of Lee's Army of Northern Virginia with the end of the war. Although Grant did not engage in peace negotiations at Appomattox—a task designated for civil authorities, indicating a technical, legal continuation of the conflict—northern volunteers still linked the capitulation of the supreme rebel army with the death of the Confederate nation. Lee's army had long functioned as the premier symbol of Confederate nationhood; its demise relieved the paramount threat to the

Union. Self-described "anti-rebel" Wilbur Fisk, of the Second Vermont Volunteers, announced "the war being over" in May 1865, citing "the complete overthrow of Gen. Lee and his rebel host." With the army's surrender, "the great serpent of secession whose poisonous fangs had been struck at the nation's life, was about to lose its power for evil forevermore." Augustus D. Ayling, who served in the Twenty-ninth Massachusetts Volunteers, believed that Lee's surrender would induce additional capitulations throughout the Confederacy. Now "that the war is over, for with Lee and his Army of Northern Virginia out of it," Ayling wrote from Richmond, "there will not be much fight left in the other armies." Rhode Islander Elisha Hunt Rhodes, whose regiment in the Army of Potomac had battled Lee for most of the war, wrote from Appomattox on that fateful April 9, "Thank God Lee has surrendered, and the war will soon end. . . . I have seen the end of the Rebellion."[11]

The surrender of Confederate armies, according to these Union soldiers, preserved the United States' democratic promise. Volunteers believed that defeated white southerners, as republican citizens, would accept the war's verdict and again submit peacefully to a nation underwritten by the rule of law. A shared sense of Americanism and pride in reunification would obviate the bitterness of fratricidal conflict, eliminating the need for military rule. Maintaining his ambivalence about postwar occupation, Charles O. Musser assumed that "the olive branch will flourish, and the old Banner of freedom will wave over a once more united people. And *we* will let foreign nations know that *our* flag cannot be insulted with impunity by any one. *We* will let them know that man is capable of Self-Government." John F. Brobst, of the Twenty-fifth Wisconsin, articulated similar opinions, claiming to "have no more fears or doubts as to how this rebellion will terminate. Our country is surely safe now." The twin fates of secession and slavery had been determined by a bloody trial of arms, which eliminated the plague of sectionalism. Overpowering Confederate armies, Brobst thus averred, would dissuade future acts of national defiance. "There is not a doubt in regard to the ability of great and good government to crush all rebellions that may spring up through petty politicians and fire eaters."[12]

While naïvely optimistic, these views underscored the extent to which volunteers believed in the complete triumph of Union armies in the spring of 1865. Victory signaled not only preservation of the republic and the death of rebellion, but also spurred the transition from volunteer soldier to private citizen. As the Twenty-eighth Wisconsin headed to Texas in June 1865,

Thomas N. Stevens could not understand why he and his comrades were needed in a remote corner of the South, especially now that the Confederacy did not exist. "This *staying about* in a place like this is *hard work* for us citizen soldiers," he grumbled. "If there was fighting to be done we would be more contented, but to be kept here doing nothing except guard & fatigue duty, when we want to be going home, it grinds us." Although still physically in uniform, troops like Stevens now identified principally as civilians. Indeed, while Elisha Hunt Rhodes admitted that he would concede to orders to remain in the army, "now that the war is over I feel that I should like to become a citizen again," later adding, "I am ready to go home now that our work is done." Like Rhodes, Benjamin Sanborn, stationed in Mobile with the Twentieth Wisconsin, began thinking more "as a civilian than as a soldier," informing his wife of the various improvements he had planned for their house. M. S. Crowell, of the Eighth Minnesota, similarly admitted an obligation to be with his family now that his military commitment had ended. "I am very anxious to see home," he lamented from Fort Smith, Arkansas, "and do not feel that I am doing quite right remaining so long away."[13]

Although some Union volunteers believed that Confederate surrender marked the war's end, others acknowledged the army's necessary presence to maintain regional stability. They argued, however, that any postwar occupation assignments, any quest to rebuild the war-ravaged South, and any program to retain an active army fell beyond the scope of the citizen-soldier's obligations to his country. J. Henry Blakeman and his comrades in the Seventeenth Connecticut were tasked with repairing the railroads near Jacksonville, Florida, which he considered "rather an insult to oblige [us] to perform such labor now [that our] time of service has expired." Blakeman admitted that the troops refused to exert too much energy on this project, especially in light of the past three years of campaigning and fighting. Service in the defeated South, he lamented, was an "unnecessary detention." Other soldiers, such as Jethro Hatch of the Thirty-sixth Illinois, admitted that officers might well desire to remain in the service, an aspiration consistent with the professionalizing tendencies of postwar duty. But considering that he had "to give up all thoughts of civil life and its enjoyments" while remaining in Nashville, Hatch opposed the government "trying to keep a large army in the field just to give our generals a command."[14]

Responding to rumors that the Federal government sought to create a standing army of occupation, one in which his regiment might serve, Wilbur

Fisk echoed Blakeman's and Hatch's opposition to permanent military service. "In such an event," Fisk explained, "the prospect opens before us of being
sent to Savannah, New Orleans, Texas or some other place, and put into a dull
garrison, where we shall have to do our stupid round of duty for our full 'sentence.'" In rhetoric strikingly reminiscent of white soldiers' critiques of wartime occupation, Fisk implied that a postwar army would be a very different
creation, serve in a different capacity, and assume a different culture from the
armies that defeated the Confederacy. He struggled to countenance further
work in the weeks and months after Confederate surrender, citing a sharp
break between war and peace. While not necessarily opposed to postwar occupation in principle, he did oppose the unprecedented implication of using
volunteers for military service during peace. Predicting the maintenance of a
formidable regular army, Fisk believed that "the Government can get all the
men they will need without asking any one to stay who does not choose to do
so." Explaining that the postwar army would comprise professionals, USCT
regiments, and any other willing volunteers, Fisk concluded, "The regular
army will be increased and the volunteers dispensed with. Good policy, as well
as justice, would seem to require this."[15]

The Federal government responded in kind to soldiers like Wilbur Fisk.
The lingering presence of volunteers in the defeated South was, however,
an ironic symptom of the massive demobilization project. In a process that
took nearly a year to complete, the Federal government bowed to the potent
political power of millions of citizen-soldiers, acceding to their appeals for a
speedy return to civilian life. In so doing, the government also acknowledged
the emerging limitations of postwar occupation. Although charged with maintaining stability, regulating the Freedmen's Bureau, managing labor relations
between planters and the formerly enslaved, superseding civil authority, and
checking the influence of former Confederates, the US Army saw its power
and wartime influence contract significantly with the purging of volunteer
units. Relegated to strategic posts, towns, and cities, the military could no longer manage hefty swaths of the South. Indeed, by September and October 1866,
little more than seventeen thousand soldiers, the vast majority of whom comprised regular army and USCT units, were stationed in eighty-five posts across
the entire region. While the army remained committed to the early years
of Reconstruction, it mainly assumed a supervisory, administrative role.[16]

The protracted course of demobilization kept some volunteers on duty
long enough to experience the requisite duties of postwar occupation. These

soldiers performed a variety of functions that helped guide the chaos of Confederate defeat into a semblance of order. They assisted in issuing loyalty oaths, mediated property disputes, aided in the construction of civil government, and maintained the peace by policing towns and guarding roads. Soldiers who served in three principal capacities—managing relations between freedpeople and white planters, preserving peace, and transitioning former rebels into loyal citizens—underscored the civilian-military nature of postwar occupation.[17]

First, while slavery collapsed in occupied portions of the wartime South, the institution thrived in areas of the late Confederacy never touched by the military. The army, as it had during the war, was thus instrumental in offering haven and protection to freed-people while also utilizing its war powers to shatter the remnants of slavery. Most important, the military after 1865 sought to prevent planters from reestablishing old labor regimes and racial hierarchies. Madison Bowler, an officer in the 113th USCT, had "to scare some of the planters into permitting their (late) slaves to exercise and enjoy the full rights of freemen." Compelled to rip the remaining threads of slaveholding injustice from the southern tapestry, Bowler forced local planters in the Mississippi Valley to reunite families that had long been separated. "I try to give them their rights so long withheld," he explained, "and to assist them every way I can."[18]

Guided by a sense of racial paternalism, a pair of soldiers from Maine, serving in South Carolina, believed that labor contracts could be procured *only* through the army's participation. Hannibal Augustus Johnson explained in July 1865, "Negroes are [so] glad, for they can not trust to have a contract made by their late masters." "Any thing made of them [planters] they [freedpeople] agree to willingly, and we are giving them justice, for they never have had a chance with a white man, until now, and we are bound to see them protected." Henry Gay admitted that the army's relationship to freedpeople "is not much like the soldiering that we had last year." Convinced that the formerly enslaved believed "the white men have not any right to come on the plantations," Gay objected to sorting out disputes. "Niggars are so ignorant that they will not sign the papers unless a soldier goes and makes them do it," he remarked; "the men here can not do any thing with them." Struggling to steer contract negotiations between both parties, Gay sighed, "I do not like to be a soldier in the peaceable time. Thare is not any fun in it."[19]

Second, the army attempted to stem the tide of violence and chaos that engulfed the post–Civil War South. Union soldiers were all too familiar with the type of war spawned by the presence of military occupation. The guerrilla conflict, which engulfed most occupied regions during the war, remained a fixture of the postwar landscape. Clinging to established cultures of honor and violence, vigilantes and guerrillas overran a land devoid of civil law, destabilizing regions already torn asunder by war and social upheaval. Now emboldened by the shame and humiliation of defeat, white southerners viewed both blue-clad occupiers and the reality of emancipation as despotic, dire threats to their society. Although small and spread perilously thin, the army sought to fill critical voids, enforce martial law, and administer justice. Two Union occupiers in Arkansas scrutinized this conflict. James Sykes, stationed in the eastern part of the state, wrote bluntly, "We are in a hostile country." Danford D. Cole, of the Twelfth Michigan Volunteers, confirmed from nearby Washington that "there is lots of d——d old rebs here and some of them are pretty saucy." Some of his comrades even struggled to negotiate the intimate, personal culture of violence that seemed emboldened by Confederate defeat. "Some of the boys in the reg are dissatisfied and talk of bolting," he described, but "if the war is played out the thing must be settled up and in some places it needs troops to keep the d——d rebs in their place."[20]

Obligations to promote order and stability translated into the reestablishment of civil authority, as the army guided white southerners back into the Union as loyal citizens, in addition to providing aid and relief to civilians in need. Some soldiers embraced the opportunity to act as agents of change, seeing a moment to reconstruct the Union now that they had preserved it. In their minds, US armies had protected the right of self-government and destroyed slavery; it was now incumbent on white southerners to accept the realities of a changed world. H. Matson, of the Third Minnesota Volunteers, remained in Arkansas "to guide, help, and protect [former Confederates] . . . in all the rights of citizen-ship." Assisting to restore law and order, he helped "the people [start] anew in the peaceful avocations of life." Matson believed that Union soldiers, protectors of the integrity and perpetuation of republican institutions, were the most qualified to reintroduce southerners into the American tradition. "It was in this work that our soldiers," he remarked, "showed without exception, that trait of character which entitles them to the name of exemplary citizens as well as exemplary soldiers."[21]

Matson's hopeful, optimistic position on the army's postwar role conflicted with a broader discourse articulated by other volunteers who questioned the implications of peacetime occupation. While grasping the necessity of a continued military presence in the South, white soldiers also came to express the same unease voiced by those who had occupied the Confederacy during the war. Such continuity of expression revealed the profound level at which US volunteers questioned the idea of the army's sustained involvement in military government, maintenance of societal stability, and regulation of civilian affairs. Their standpoint did not emanate merely out of annoyance at remaining in the army. They instead trained their critiques at what they considered to be dangerous effects of peacetime military service. Imbued in the republican military tradition and steeped in the meaning of American citizenship, some occupying soldiers interpreted Union victory as the triumph of democracy. Disagreeing with Matson's reading of the postwar scene, they believed that *because* self-government had been preserved, white southerners were expected to return to the nation and dedicate themselves to the perpetuation of American ideals. It was not a peacetime army's responsibility, soldiers believed, to ensure white southern conformity, which had been occasioned by a triumph of arms between 1861 and 1865.

Testimony from six contemporaries outlined the citizen-soldier critique of postwar military occupation, an appraisal born during the war and framed around distrust of a standing army. Mathew Woodruff, a sergeant in the Twenty-first Missouri Volunteers, embodied this system of beliefs. Enlisting in 1861 and fighting throughout the western theater, he served in the postwar occupation forces at Mobile, Alabama. A self-described pragmatist, Woodruff believed that the war had settled all of the nation's divisive issues; he was thus opposed to an indefinite occupation of the postwar South. By November 1865 Woodruff had grown weary of his continued service on the Gulf Coast. Commenting on the recent congressional elections, Woodruff hoped for "*Loyal* candidates" to represent a changed South. Although he hated secession and celebrated the defeat of the Confederacy, he offered a profound point about the elections. "There was an Order Issued to Keep all Soldiers in camp during the day," he commented, "which I think was verry beneficial from the fact that Politicians of either side can not say, that the Election in Mobile was controlled by Yankee Bayonets." Woodruff implied that self-government, which he believed had been preserved on the field of battle, could not be artificially enforced by the military. The very essence of republicanism, in his view, was tied directly to the will of the people, not the muzzle of a rifle. "I am verry anxious indeed to hear the Returns of the Election," he explained, "thinking it will have some bearing in regard to the Mustering out of the troops in this Dept."

A free, fair, and open election, Woodruff suggested, would legitimize the war and honor the deaths of countless northern men who strove to secure the promise of democracy. Conversely, a sustained military occupation would betray the spirit of Union victory.[22]

Brevet Major General Alvin C. Voris, of the Sixty-seventh Ohio Volunteers, echoed Woodruff's position, writing from Virginia in the weeks and months following the Confederate surrender. Voris, a devoted Republican and opponent of slavery, dedicated significant thought to the state of the postwar South and its changed racial structure. He perceived a series of unsettled issues that lingered in the immediate aftermath of hostilities. Charged with commanding a sizable subdistrict consisting of counties that stretched from Albemarle eastward to Henrico, Voris relished the opportunity to preserve order and regulate oaths of loyalty. Seeking to use his influence to protect the rights of recently freed African Americans, Voris "hope[d] to be able to do some good . . . to a poor class of heretofore abused people. I had rather have the satisfaction of having done them permanent & substantial good than have the honor of fighting a battle."[23]

Voris genuinely believed that "I am doing good here," acting as "a sort of middle man between the former poor, helpless slave and his owner." By late June 1865, he became dejected, however, sensing the dedication of white planters to resurrecting the antebellum racial and labor order. This troubling situation, he wrote, "occasions much perplexity," primarily because "I must confess to verry vague ideas as to what ought to be done." As he assessed the mounting tension and unbalanced relationships between white landowner and black laborer, Voris remarked, "efforts made by military authorities to regulate the domestic relations and internal affairs of a community must be looked on as being an assumption and should not be resorted to only as a matter of necessity." He struggled to divorce the republican tenets of Union from the nation's newly constructed racial dynamics. On the one hand, genuine self-government must prevail, Voris believed, in the absence of a standing army guiding, or even dictating, local, civil affairs. But on the other hand, Voris instinctively knew that freedpeople's rights would soon be trampled without dedicated, focused military support.[24]

Voris's intellectual conflict was rooted in the citizen-soldier's conception of the army's, or even the Federal government's, role in peacetime. His uncertainty weighed the destinies of freedpeople against the limits of military influence, underscoring one of the central tensions of the immediate postwar period. One or the other set of interests would have to give way to the other. "The General Government never has regulated the details of social life & obligation," he wrote, concerned that his position as a force of military occupation would require such obligations. Even if the military was not actively formulating laws, it would still be enforcing the government's will on newly "loyal" citizens of the nation, violating the cherished republican tenet of self-determination.[25]

As Voris suggested, the army struggled to prevent chaos, which manifested itself through massacres, theft, murder, and consolidation of the Black Codes, which reinstituted the old southern racial order. Soldiers were given few official guidelines on how to engage the restive civilians under their control. Even General Orders No. 100, which attempted to codify and organize the manner in which conquering armies treated occupied civilians during the war, had little effect during peacetime. Martial law existed throughout much of the postwar South but sometimes offered little protection for freedpeople against defiant white southerners. Finally, the Constitution was silent on any issue pertaining to secession, civil war, and reconstruction. Thus, it is no wonder why citizen-soldiers who remained in the South for no more than a year after the war (and in most cases a much shorter time) voiced serious concerns about the implications of their continued service. Precedents and traditions did not exist for this moment of American military history, causing them to think and write deeply about these issues.[26]

These confusing dynamics echoed the wartime and postwar beliefs that a standing army might complicate societal matters, inadvertently contributing to the instability of the South. Even as early as 1862, Henry Adams, an American civilian working in London, predicted the dilemmas of postwar occupation. "Firmly convinced as I am that there can be no peace on our continent so long as the Southern people exist," he wrote to Charles Francis Adams, Jr., "I don't much care whether they are destroyed by emancipation, or . . . a vigorous system of guerrilla war." Adams believed that absolute annihilation of the southern economy, political system, and ideology must be occasioned in order for peace to be secured; the ingredients of secession must be torn completely from the nation's identity. If not, he warned, the United States would be compelled to use military force during peacetime in its attempt to reshape the South.[27]

Adams, however, recognized a difficult, potentially unanswerable problem. How would the United States erase the *ideology* that inspired secession, the very dogma that Voris sensed in his interactions with southern planters? "We must not let them as an independent state get the monopoly of cotton again," he advised, alluding to the southern staple crop as a key source of ideological separatism. If the South retained its antebellum identity the nation as a whole was "sure to be in perpetual anarchy within," which would "compel us to support a standing army no less large than if we conquer them and hold them so, and with infinite means of wounding and scattering dissension among us." The nation, in the process, very well might lose cherished aspects of its exceptionalist identity, moving closer to a European style of reconstruction, one grounded in chaos and instability. Indeed, Adams believed that his time in England fostered a unique understanding of European systems. He concluded that permanent military establishments could dislodge the possibility of a successful reunion, rendering the United States, like Europe, in a perpetual condition of insecurity. But like Voris, Adams sought complete destruction of the old southern order. The conflict between republican tradition and transformational reconstruction proved to be a significant problem for many Americans.[28]

The experiences of John C. Gill of the 114th Ohio Volunteers, who served in Texas as part of the Union's largest postwar occupying force, affirmed Henry Adams's predicament. Gill noticed that local residents of Houston, whom he initially thought welcomed peace and reunion, resisted US authority in disturbing, violent ways. Relating a common occurrence throughout the postwar South, Gill remarked that "occasionally we meet . . . rabid rebels. . . . Everyone carries a large bowie knife and revolver." Local citizens, he explained, murdered a soldier from a nearby Iowa regiment "before we had been in the city fifteen minutes." After his regiment transferred one month later to nearby Millican, Gill revealed that organized gangs patrolled the outskirts of Federal occupation, "threaten[ing] to kill every officer if they have to pick them off one by one." Gill implied that white southern resistance, indeed the lingering guerrilla war that had not faded in the wake of formal hostilities, appeared revitalized by Confederate defeat and the continued Union occupation. The violent setting in which he served reflected a society without law and order, despite the army's successful regulation of parts of the region.[29]

Thus by the late summer and early fall of 1865, occupiers sensed the resurgence of a particular southern ideology, born from the Confederate experience, that sought to dislocate the Yankee presence in the South. It was one thing to destroy the Confederate army on the field of battle, forcing a termination of hostilities in 1865. It was another matter to eliminate the forces that had inspired secession and war. H. C. Forbes, a lieutenant colonel in the Seventh Illinois Cavalry, stationed at Okolona, Mississippi, expressed great concern at the manner in which white citizens unfairly treated former slaves. "We are in the midst of a remote, populous, sensitive district," he began, "without instructions to guide, or orders to administer." Forbes received daily reports that revealed planters abusing their laborers, oftentimes enacting cruel and unjust practices. Black migrants, Forbes explained, then became demoralized, notwithstanding continuous efforts by the military to negotiate fair labor contracts. Nevertheless, he cited the ultimate problem: rise of the Black Codes, effectively reinstituting the old southern racial order.[30]

Forbes was at a loss, searching for ways to solve this problem. "To announce their freedom is not to make them free," he wrote dejectedly. "As Federal soldiers, we can neither recognize slavery nor its equivalent and are left helpless lookers on." Yet, he suggested that perhaps the Federal government and military could involve themselves in this situation, with courts enforcing the law and proper instructions on free labor bestowed to black people. Ultimately, "careful policing of the entire area of the slave States by mounted soldiery in support of the jurisdiction of the courts" might assure the protection of labor and rights. And herein lay Forbes's predicament. He instinctively knew that the military would have to play a substantial role in regulating and protecting civilian behavior, a proposition far removed from the American tradition of independence and self-determination. "I presume that so comprehensive a measure will not be taken until some great and fatal mischief has indicated its necessity," he wrote. His concluding sentence revealed his thoughts on the proper role of the army, doubtlessly shaped by the confusing and depressing milieu of postwar occupation: "I would rather face an old-fashioned war-time skirmish line any time than the inevitable morning eruption of lean and hungry widows that besiege me at sun up and ply me until night with supplications that refuse to be silenced." The American military tradition was swiftly changing, and Forbes recognized that he stood directly at the center of its alteration.[31]

John William DeForest, a former captain in the Twelfth Connecticut Volunteers, further identified the crisis faced by the postwar military. At the beginning of 1866, DeForest, still an officer in the army, joined the Freedmen's Bureau in Greenville, South Carolina, assisting formerly enslaved people enter the world of freedom. Shortly after his arrival, DeForest witnessed aggressive efforts made by local whites to curb black rights; these whites often resorted to violence in hopes of resurrecting the antebellum political and social order. Disgusted with the rampant chaos in his district, DeForest concluded that the war had changed little in the white southern mind. In fact, the experience of defeat, he suggested, only exacerbated long-held racial beliefs, grounded in violence and control: whites "simply kill [free blacks] in the exercise of their ordinary pugnacity." Violence thus served as the white South's chosen means of defiance against emancipation.[32]

Despite his loathing of local whites and his desire to promote African American equality, DeForest still acknowledged the problems posed by peacetime occupation. "It was a dubious and critical matter to handle," he explained. "On the one hand, I wanted to make sure that [freedpeople] should not fall a victim to any burst of popular fury, and that the bushwhackers who had outraged [them] should be brought to condign punishment. On the other hand I so interpreted my orders as to believe that my first and great duty lay in raising the blacks and restoring the whites of my district to a confidence in civil law, thus fitting both as rapidly as possible to assume the duties of citizenship." DeForest, comforted that this responsibility did not undermine the presumed role of the peacetime army, gladly used his identity as a citizen-soldier to guide other citizens back in the Union's fold. There was, however, a problem. "If the military power were to rule them forever," he warned, in language that echoed Henry Adams, "if it were to settle all their difficulties without demanding of them any exercise of judgment and self-control, how could they ever be, in any profound and lasting sense, 'reconstructed?'"[33]

DeForest thus summarized the ultimate dilemma faced by white citizen-soldiers during the early postwar months. Volunteers viewed the military's role with suspicion and misgiving, even as they acknowledged that occupation played an integral role in Reconstruction. Their articulation of republicanism, their idealistic faith in self-government, and their fears of a standing army assuming a central part in peacetime affairs stood in stark contrast to the military's continuing role. Such misgivings were further confirmed when the vast majority of volunteer regiments had been mustered out of the service, leaving a force of little more than seventeen thousand soldiers by October 1866. As Grant declared earlier in the year, "A small military force is required in all states heretofore in rebellion and it cannot be foreseen that this force will not be required for some time to come." Yet, also admitting that "white Volunteers have become dissatisfied and claim that the contract with them has been violated by retaining them after the war," Grant consented that "they are no longer of use and might as well be discharged at once." These volunteer soldiers were citizens, not permanent government agents, and they wielded strong political leverage that forced policy makers to heed their demand for demobilization. Acknowledging that the post-1865 nation was hardly different from the one previously consumed by four years of war, the Federal government never entertained the idea that volunteers would be compelled to contribute to a long-term project of postwar occupation.[34]

Demobilization and the citizen-soldier critique of occupation represented a broader quest to establish an antimilitaristic postwar nation. Both the volunteer protests against remaining in service and the Federal government's radical downsizing of the army indicated that Union victory would not yield a new American state defined by unfettered and unrestricted military authority. "Whatever the war had done to America," historian Mark Wahlgren Summers writes, "it had not turned it into a garrison state." While it may be tempting to read Ulysses S. Grant's December 1865 memo as a call for widespread, active occupations of the former Confederacy, his recommendations were set within a postwar culture averse to an expansive military establishment. Demobilization was thus a purposeful process of maintaining an army and a fiscal state that were as small as possible to effect the limited, but necessary, functions of government. The triumph of Federal armies indeed *preserved* the Union's republican principles, rather than creating something entirely new. *Harper's Weekly*, a mainstream pulse of mid-nineteenth-century public opinion, declared as much in 1867: "The army of the people with which *Washington* secured our national existence, and that with which *Grant* maintained it, dissolved in the moment of victory." Echoing the concomitant foundations of the republican military tradition and the citizen-soldier ideal, *Harper's* opined that "when the people are the army, their liberties are pretty safe. It is the standing army which is the enemy of Liberty." In the months following the cessation of hostilities in 1865, white citizen-soldiers made it clear that a transformational reconstruction of the South through military means did not mandate a fundamental transformation of the Union.[35]

* * *

While white Union soldiers debated the ideological implications of peacetime occupation, African American troops, as they had during the war, continued to believe that the army could and should be used to reshape the racial and social landscapes of the postwar South. They understood that their positions as occupying soldiers during the first two years of Reconstruction could stem rising tides of white southern violence. Black soldiers sought to exercise their martial influence to protect freedpeople, giving little thought to the republican implications of a peacetime standing army that directed the course of social and political affairs. The black military experience had indeed changed in marked ways since the issuance of the Emancipation Proclamation in 1863. Although USCT regiments had enlisted under the conservative assumptions of garrisoning—a purposeful way to segregate African American soldiers along lines of race and duty, limiting their claim to the citizen-soldier ideal—black troops transformed the culture of military service behind the lines. Wielding the power of a standing army of occupation to safeguard the promises of emancipation, black soldiers acted to effect revolutionary change directly from the point of a bayonet.[36]

As white troops poured out of a demobilizing army, USCT regiments, most of which had two years remaining on their service contracts, encompassed a larger, more dynamic share of the postwar occupying forces. By the autumn of 1865, black units comprised 36 percent of the US Army. With the exception of the all-black XXV Corps, which entered and occupied Richmond in April, and subsequently transferred to Texas later in the spring, African American soldiers retained a conspicuous presence across the defeated Confederacy. Embodying the collapse of the southern slaveholding republic, black occupiers daily reminded the region's shattered ruling class that war and defeat had occasioned pivotal upheavals in social relations. White southerners lashed out with ferocity against emancipation, attempting to defy the humiliation of defeat and to rebuild their system of racial subordination. African American occupiers responded in like manner, employing an active force of arms to combat violent injustice brandished against themselves and freedpeople. Far from acting as a merely supervisory, regulatory force, and sometimes employing violent action, black soldiers presented a more dynamic view of the ways military force could be used to forge a new, reconditioned Union.[37]

Regiments of the USCT were surrounded by the chaotic volatility that marred the first year of "peace." As white southern society attained relative stability in the wake of defeat, many former Confederates began resurrecting tactics of racial terror. Some never discarded their weapons of rebellion, striking out at African Americans who sought to create new, independent lives.

Indeed, the immediate post-emancipation world was one of hope and uncertainty in which freedpeople built autonomous communities that strained against the bonds of white violence. In December 1865, Calvin Holly, a black soldier from Mississippi, described how "Rebbles are going a bout in many places through the State and robbing the colered peple of arms money and all they have and in many places killing." Reflecting on the quest of white southern self-reconstruction, Holly surmised that "they are doing all they can to prevent free labor, and reasstablish a kind of secondary slavery." Suffering the destruction of what little property they owned, forced into unfair labor contracts, bound by the restrictive "Black Codes," and attacked merely for declaring that they were free, freedpeople likely probed the question long on the minds of most mid-nineteenth-century Americans: what *was* the aftermath of emancipation?[38]

Expanding on Holly's concerns, James H. Payne, a sergeant in the Twenty-seventh USCT, described the rehabilitation of North Carolina's white ruling class. Acknowledging that the war's verdict unleashed "trouble and destitution, as well as hatred and revenge, [which] await our poor people in these Southern States," Payne leveled a serious charge against one of the most cherished ideals in American life: democracy. Lambasting Andrew Johnson's program of self-reconstruction, the process by which former Confederates regained prominent political standing in efforts to bring their states back into the Union, Payne "regretted that the President has left so much to be decided by the choice of prejudiced loyal white men of the South." Although African Americans played a crucial role in shaping the Union's wartime triumph, "after the victory is obtained," Payne continued, "[the black man] can have no voice in making the laws which are to govern his future destiny in this country. No, but he must sit in a state of perfect dormancy, as though he were under slavery's cruel power still."[39]

For Payne, white violence sustained white democracy. Attacks on African Americans did not occur by mere haphazard chance, but rather were the product of a calculated campaign to cleanse the South of biracial freedom, opportunity, and competition. White democracy had long thrived on the foundation of black enslavement, a promise that the Confederate nation had failed to consolidate, but which postwar white southerners were desperate to restore. Calvin Holly thus wondered if there existed "power enough in the arm of the Government to give Justice," suggesting that "it is not incompatible with the public interest to pass some laws that will give protection to the colered men."

A black minister from Georgia went beyond Holly's prescriptions for legal remedy, advocating stout military force to combat white violence. "I trust you will order a Strong garrison of Colored Soldiers to remain here," he implored Secretary of War Edwin M. Stanton. "The fact is, when colored Soldiers are about [local whites] are afraid to kick colored women, and abuse colored people on the Streets." The promise of emancipation and true biracial democracy, the minister hinted, hung in the balance, guarded by one of the Civil War era's most controversial institutions: the occupied garrison of USCT soldiers.[40]

As Payne, Holly, and the minister indicated, African American freedom had to be safeguarded through active, formidable means. Combating the violent excesses of white democracy mandated an equal show of strength that only military force could provide. As they had during the war, USCT soldiers thus used occupation to shelter black freedom. Indeed, the African American definition of postwar occupation required energetic military interventions to ensure the gains of emancipation. Some troops detested the ugly realities that trailed in the wake of the destruction of the slave system, and they sought to serve as protectors in places where their people struggled to negotiate with local whites. Although N. B. Sterrett, a sergeant in the Thirty-ninth USCT, savored the opportunity to occupy Kinston, North Carolina, he desired to be transferred. Hearing rumors of violence against blacks elsewhere in the state, he wrote, "We are needed in other places of more importance." From the Twenty-eighth USCT's encampment at Corpus Christi, Texas, Garland H. White echoed Sterrett's sentiments. Responding to the Black Codes, White contended that occupation, and even military coercion, were necessary in order to rid the South of racial discrimination. And he volunteered to remain in the postwar occupation force. "The Government has a right to the services of men, when and where it [needs them]," he wrote, "and we calmly submit to it."[41]

Seen as the most radical manifestations of emancipation and Confederate defeat, black troops who policed conquered southern towns inspired fierce reprisals from local whites. Encounters between soldier and civilian often escalated into violent confrontations, rendering both parties bruised and bloodied. Yet far from dissuading African American occupiers, such episodes emboldened their resolve. Some soldiers recognized that postwar occupation offered a chance to use their martial influence to reshape the South, erasing the ideologies undergirding white supremacy. Although military authorities never formulated an effective policy to combat the violence perpetuated against black soldiers and civilians, African American troops were not passive bystanders in the occupied South. Instead, they openly demonstrated their martial influence, oftentimes taking matters into their own hands. They did not hesitate to aim and shoot their rifles, attack restive civilians, enter private homes, execute the laws, or protect free laborers. African American soldiers understood that their presence necessitated active involvement in postwar society. To them, occupation was not something to endure but rather to direct.[42]

Black occupation sometimes meant transgressing orders, military decorum, and restraint to seek reprisal for racial crimes committed against freedpeople. African American soldiers thus found themselves in a problematic scenario. On the one hand, they could remain idle, waiting for the army to be summoned by civil authorities to arrest the offenders. Such an idle approach, however, could only encourage further white violence. On the other hand, black troops could meet white lawlessness with aggression, a strategy that might achieve a relative balance of power, but also could contribute to charges of unwarranted belligerence and lack of martial discipline. Soldiers in the Forty-fourth USCT took it upon themselves to arrest lawbreaking residents in Huntsville, Alabama, "presuming to exercise such authority on [those] guilty of disobedience of lawful orders." The regiment's officers were later reprimanded for not controlling their enlisted men. Similarly, on a dark night in July 1865, troops in the Ninety-eighth USCT eluded a picket guard, escaping from camp and traveling to a plantation near New Iberia, Louisiana. There, they fired upon several members of the local family. Though no one was hurt, three of the guilty soldiers were arrested. In Wilmington, North Carolina, "soldiers are in the habit of leaving their posts and roaming through the country," a report from the Twenty-seventh USCT indicated. Seeking to defend freedpeople who had been maltreated by landowners, "soldiers assume responsibility of redressing their wrongs, and administering justice between the Freedmen and his former master."[43]

While white authorities condemned the actions of black troops in each of these episodes, William B. Johnson, a soldier in the Third USCT, explained the rationale behind such measures. "The rebs here seem to die very hard at the idea of having black troops to guard them, but they have been very quiet," he wrote from Jacksonville, Florida. "How true is the saying that we know not what a day may bring forth! Great changes are being wrought." Although slow, steady, and oftentimes violent, black occupation sparked revolutionary transformations in the southern social order. "We have dress parade downtown in the public square," George Thomas, a former Kentucky slave, and, in July 1865, a corporal in the Twelfth USC Heavy Artillery, wrote from Bowling Green, "and as we are drilled *very well,* the former slaveholders open their eyes, astonished that their former Kentucky *working stock* are capable of being on an equal footing with them." Echoing Johnson and Thomas, A. J. Willard, a white lieutenant colonel, who oversaw a military subdistrict near Charleston, South Carolina, advocated on behalf of many black civilians who looked to USCT occupation forces for protection, soon after the Black Codes went into effect. He wrote, "The freedpeople were looking forward to the arrival of Colored Troops with the expectation that their advent would enlarge their privileges, and obtain the realization of their expectations of obtaining possession of the lands of the country."[44]

The very presence of black soldiers inculcated trust toward the US government among recently freed slaves. Of all government agents, Willard suggested, African American troops most desired to guard the well-being of freedpeople. "The services they are called upon to perform, being so obviously directed to the advancement of the true interests of the people of color," he explained, "are rendered freely and cheerfully without reluctance, while [white] volunteer Troops being anxious to return to their homes, feel that this service is a burden, and in many instances an imposition." John Ely, the chief superintendent of the Freedmen's Bureau for the District of Kentucky, concurred with Willard's appraisal. "The presence of [black troops] caused a marked change for the better in the sentiments of the people toward the Bureau," he wrote, "and gave confidence to many good men (white people) who accept the present condition of affairs." Although some black soldiers and civilians had been murdered in neighboring counties, freedpeople across the region, Ely concluded, "are in the main well employed, at fair wages," due in large part to the relative stability offered by black occupation troops.[45]

Carl Schurz, an antislavery advocate, dedicated Republican, and former Union army general, toured the Deep South during the summer of 1865 and also reported what he considered to be the invaluable impact of black occupation. Although Schurz suspected that former secessionists attempted to reinsert themselves into local politics, he informed President Johnson, "There is far less disorder in Mississippi than in Alabama," because it was "more perfectly garrisoned than any of those [states] that I have visited." Schurz attributed the success of occupation exclusively to the region's black troops. Like John Ely, he considered white soldiers an ineffective occupation force because of their inattention to military responsibility and desire to go home.

In contrast, he praised black soldiers' focus, coupled with their "pride and a strict observance of their instructions." In comparing white and black soldiers, Schurz explained that African American troops had a lot to lose by an ineffective postwar occupation. In spite of the chaotic dislocation in the postwar South, Schurz believed that societal stability, and change, could be shaped by a robust, black military occupation. "There is nothing," he concluded, referring to the symbolism of black garrisons, "that will make [African American freedom] more evident than the bodily presence of a negro with a musket on his shoulder."[46]

Schurz was correct, probably more than he knew, yet in ways that unsettled the very nature of black occupation. Few emotions wrought by Confederate defeat inspired such outrage and defiance from white southerners as the presence of African American troops—a presence galling during the war, and even more infuriating in peace. In addition to committing violence against black soldiers, former Confederates alleged that USCT units attacked white civilians, used their authority to steal goods and destroy property, and convinced freedpeople that the government would provide land and means of subsistence, jeopardizing labor relationships between planters and the formerly enslaved. Some whites even suggested that black troops conspired with freedpeople to initiate Haitian-style race wars. White southerners believed that the Federal government purposely garrisoned the former Confederacy with African American troops as a means of punishing the crime of secession and capitalizing on victory. Warning that violent collisions would inevitably result from a continued occupation by black soldiers, William H. Holden, governor of North Carolina, advocated that "a body of white troops be stationed at points where there are large numbers of colored troops." A correspondent from Knoxville, Tennessee, informed President Johnson of purported attacks on white citizens from black soldiers, who even killed milk cows. "The conduct of these negro soldiers is such that while they remain we cannot expect to have good order," he declared. "I am perfectly satisfied that if they could be removed, we would have peace and good order at once and thereby put down much prejudice against the negro."[47]

White southerners thus embarked on a campaign of rhetoric and ideology to rid the region of African American soldiers, using the language of republicanism to question the legitimacy of black military occupation. As USCT regiments came to form a sizable portion of Federal forces, southern whites hoped to demonstrate that black occupiers embodied the instabilities wrought

by a standing army. More fundamentally, white opposition grew from a startling conviction that their region had changed dramatically. Black independence, asserted provocatively through military power, represented the most
salient anxieties of a slave society. If such fears caught on widely, the occupying troops might well be sent home or be reassigned, effectively eliminating at
least one of the great social transformations wrought by the war.[48]

Hugh P. Kennedy, a civilian in Louisiana, accused black soldiers garrisoned near Port Hudson of "keep[ing] up a vexatious & perilous agitation.
They hope by exasperating the white & colored population belonging to the
country to maintain a constant disquietude," thereby thwarting peace and
reunion. Observing affairs from Jackson, Mississippi, Provisional Governor
William L. Sharkey charged that "Negro troops do more harm than good when
scattered through the Country." Planters in Mississippi indeed claimed that
black troops promised freedpeople of the government's intention to confiscate and distribute lands of former slave owners. "The consequence is they
are becoming careless, & impudent," read a petition to the state legislature,
"for they are told by the soldiers that they are as good as the whites." Fearful
that the continued presence of USCT regiments would destabilize the region,
the planters warned "that if the negro troops are not removed . . . trouble of the
direst kind will befal us." "Get the negro Soldiery removed from our midst & no
danger will follow," they demanded. "Let the Soldiery remain—& our negroes
will refuse to hire will grow more & more insolent": conditions which might
well foment a race war.[49]

Former Confederates reasoned that if the president, who also was a virulent racist, could be convinced that black occupation instigated the chaotic
violence that had engulfed the South, the military as a whole might pull out,
leaving former Confederates to self-reconstruct their region. Indeed, Johnson had long advocated a conservative program of self-reconstruction; negative accusations against black soldiers only served to confirm his belief that
the army should play, at most, a regulatory role. If African American troops
continued to "disrupt" the postwar scene, Johnson concluded, they should be
mustered out of service as quickly as possible. "In regard to the Troops now
stationed in Mississippi which seems to be producing dissatisfaction to a
great extent," Johnson replied to Sharkey, "the Government does not intend
to irritate or humiliate the People of the South but will be magnanimous and
remove the cause of your complaint at the earliest period it is practicable to do
so." The president fully accepted white southerners' accounts and agreed that

black soldiers propagated acts of violence against helpless victims, even as he ignored pleas from unionists and steadfast Republicans, such as Carl Schurz, who contradicted the former Confederates' claims.[50]

While Johnson's sympathy for the plight of some white southerners grew from his racist worldview, high-ranking army officers also critiqued black military occupation, appraising what they considered the destabilizing influence of USCT regiments. Although General George H. Thomas assured the president "that there is the least foundation for fearing an insurrection among the negroes," other officers, in assessing the implications of continued black occupation, harped on Thomas's claim that "it is exceedingly repugnant to the Southerners to have negro soldiers in their midst." A colonel in the Forty-fourth USCT, whose troops had attempted to arrest civilians at Huntsville, Alabama, decried "the lawlessness of all enlisted men in many respects [which] renders their rule absolutely necessary." Another officer accused soldiers in Louisville, Kentucky, of "fir[ing] indiscriminately through the Town, endangering the lives of citizens." "I have adopted every measure in my power to prevent it," he explained, "& it cannot be expected that I could arm a lot of slaves among their former masters & bring them down to strict military discipline all at once." Major General George G. Meade did not believe African American soldiers would stoke a rebellion among the formerly enslaved; he assumed "that the colored troops fraternize more with the laboring population" which "may produce some evil by tempting the laborers to leave their work, and visit the camps." Rather than further weakening the social order, Meade advocated, in language reminiscent of the Emancipation Proclamation, transferring USCT units "to the seaboard, where they can be usefully employed garrisoning the fortifications, and where they will be measurably removed from contact with the whites."[51]

Even the general-in-chief of the army, Ulysses S. Grant, distressed by the tensions between white southerners and black occupiers, struggled to find a solution to the racial imbalance. Although an ardent supporter of black troops during the war, Grant approached the postwar period with caution, searching for an efficient route to national reunion. He accordingly wrestled with the ironies of Reconstruction. On the one hand, he desired that white southerners accept the realities of defeat, including emancipation, believing that their compliance would speed national healing. On the other hand, he could not escape news about the unsettling violence against African Americans and understood the necessity of a substantial military occupation. Grant attempted to solve the problem, in part, by sending some USCT regiments "as far West as possible," explaining that they "will do very well on the Plains," while agreeing with Meade that others should "garrison the sea coast entirely."[52]

Grant continued to believe, however, that *too* strong of a black occupation might perpetuate social and political chaos. "To him," writes historian Brooks D. Simpson, "truth of the charges [from white southerners] was irrelevant; the mere presence of black troops was destabilizing and inhibited reconciliation, which justified their removal." In March 1866, Grant endorsed "the withdrawel of Colored troops from the interior of the Southern states to avoid unnecessary irritation and the demoralization of labor." He advised George Thomas to replace black regiments "with White troops or so far as you can abandon the occupation of the interior without endangering the rights of loyal Whites and Freedmen." Yet in May, a bloody massacre at Memphis seemed to change Grant's mind. When bands of local white police attacked black veterans and slaughtered African American civilians, Grant lambasted the "scene of murder, arson, rape & robery in which the victims were all helpless and unresisting negroes stamping lasting disgrace upon the civil authorities that permitted them." The Memphis massacre, which challenged the most basic foundations of emancipation, exposed mounting white resentment about the collapse of the South's racial and social hierarchies, engendered in large part by USCT occupation.[53]

In the wake of the Memphis massacre, Grant articulated numerous positions that would determine the course of postwar occupation. Recognizing that the South's quest to maintain a region based on racial and social control did not die at Appomattox, he promoted a continued occupation of the rebellious states, fearful of what might happen to African Americans and loyal Unionists without the army's protection. But by the spring of 1866 Grant was also one of the leading proponents of demobilization for both white *and* black volunteer regiments. "How long," he asked Edwin Stanton, "will existing laws authorize the retention of [USCT units] even [if] they are content to remain?" While he endorsed keeping black soldiers in the regular army, Grant made it clear that their regiments would be assigned to duty in the West. The fate of military reconstruction and occupation in the former Confederacy would therefore be left to a small army composed of white professionals, a force that Grant also believed should be quickly removed. Thus, throughout the rest of 1866, the vast majority of USCT units were transferred from the interior of the South to coastal fortifications or the western frontier, or else mustered out altogether. By early 1867, no more African American soldiers remained in the South.[54]

The failure of black occupation during Reconstruction reflected a long-established trait of the nineteenth-century American military character. Quests for postwar stability emanated from a strong desire for peace, but also from a position that the army must maintain order, not spread unrest. Although race and black soldiering were perceived as primary factors in postwar tension and volatility, they were also linked to the nature of military occupation in which the army was seen as the culprit of civil destabilization. Ironically, American republicanism, an ideology that transcended the sectional divide, united northern and southern critiques of African American occupation. Whether described by the governor of Georgia as "unfavorable to the public peace and tranquility," or, as one of Grant's staff officers noted, "it is easy to recommend that the black troops be removed from the Southern districts . . . satisfactorily to the resident population," the culture of African American occupation had been pushed out of the national mainstream. Such perspectives considered black soldiers to be instigators of the instability and violence of standing armies, which displayed loyalty only to themselves and thwarted democratic expression. While African American troops sought to use the army to destroy the lingering vestiges of the old southern order, their influence was checked by an indissoluble dedication among whites to nineteenth-century principles that prioritized national reunion, self-government, and a limited postwar role for the army.[55]

Black soldiering, which in 1863, had been proposed as a conservative solution to the problem of white citizen-soldier occupation, had, by 1866, transformed into a seemingly radical threat to national reunion. African American soldiers themselves had occasioned this change, transforming their roles as garrison laborers into active champions of military authority. Enthusiastic occupiers, black troops used their positions behind the lines to create change in the regions where many had grown up enslaved. That very zeal, however, contributed to the demise of black military occupation, reflecting the triumph of republicanism over race. Indeed, the early postwar years indicated that the Union would not emerge as an authoritarian military state that relied on the use of citizen-soldiers in peacetime to impose societal change. Nor would the Union maintain a large European-style standing army that destabilized domestic life and undermined democracy. And, perhaps most destructive and catastrophic for freedpeople, the Union would not countenance an army of homegrown soldiers directing the course of racial and social affairs in the conquered Confederacy. Despite appeals from Freedmen's Bureau agents who pled for military protection, despite black laborers now at the mercy of former slaveholders, and despite the resurrection of the South's old white ruling class, the demobilization of USCT regiments reflected broader national commitments to antimilitarism and the principles of constitutional republicanism which had been preserved by Union armies. Although a small, professional force continued to govern the South, its manpower had been purposefully slashed and its reach deliberately checked, revealing the limits, but not altogether the death, of military occupation during the Civil War era.[56]

9 | Military Reconstruction and the Fate of Union

In the spring of 1871, the *Nation,* a leading journal of political and cultural opinion, published an editorial that captured the condition of the post–Civil War South. Supporting biracial suffrage, black office-holding, African American male citizenship, and "possession of common civil rights," the author applauded the gains of Reconstruction, by which "the negroes and Unionists [are] guaranteed a voice in the Government, [and are] secured in the exclusive control of it." Another powerful force, however, threatened to impede this progress. The insurrectionary Ku Klux Klan, the essay cautioned, "have taken the field against the new regime," terrorizing black southerners and Republicans. The *Nation* thus called upon the Federal government to take decisive action, recognizing that such a call to arms raised important questions: Should the US Army, now composed only of several thousand regular troops stationed in the South, intervene on behalf of law, order, and moral decency, protecting the great social and racial revolutions of 1863, 1865, and 1868? Or, abiding by constitutional tradition, should the peacetime army instead remain relatively idle and demobilized?[1]

The editorialist explained that the national government no longer possessed "the duty of protecting life and property" once the individual states had been restored to their original place within the Union. Indeed, Congress in 1867 authorized the US Army to extend its war powers to administer the functions of state government and to oversee biracial constitutional conventions in order to strengthen states' ability to govern their own citizens with fairness and equity. By 1871, just as the *Nation* published its opinion, and in the wake of so-called "Military Reconstruction," the formerly rebellious states had complied with Congress's demands, creating new governments dominated by Republicans and strengthened by a sizable black constituency. Although remnants of the army remained in the South to maintain peace, the *Nation*'s editorialist warned that any situation in which the military assumed extra-constitutional authority, even for the purposes of combating white violence against African Americans and Republicans, might carry serious, unwanted consequences. European powers, "if dealing with the South," would deploy one hundred thousand soldiers to suppress the dissidents, "patrol[ling] the roads with clouds of cavalry, and fill[ing] the streets with swarms of police." Although some Americans clamored for a forcible restoration of order, the author remarked that, in contrast to the European model, "we [instead] vote a regiment of cavalry or two companies of infantry to put it in motion—that is, about enough men to make one county tolerable safe."[2]

While supportive of the improvements made in the South, the *Nation* remained guarded about the military intervention some said was required to protect those gains, conscious of implications that appeared to the writer even more troubling than the threat of the Klan. "If we once get into the habit of treating the Constitution as a mere expression of opinion, to be set aside whenever its observance seems inconvenient," the author resolved, "we have sown the seeds of anarchy." Preservation of the American tradition, in which citizens defined the scope of government, necessitated that black and white southerners, buttressed by local and state institutions, should independently solve the region's violent chaos. Thus, the US Army "cannot interfere effectively," the editorial concluded, "and had better not interfere at all."[3]

With these words, the *Nation* underscored the continuing tension between occupation and the republican tradition. Despite the Union's bold experiment in Military Reconstruction, in which the army assumed unprecedented "peacetime" authority over civil institutions and procedure, the republican critique of occupation, which dated to the Mexican-American War, continued to linger deep into the post–Civil War years. In their occupations of Mexico and the Confederacy, white volunteers argued that occupation undermined the citizen-soldier ideal. They chafed at the undesirable duties of governing "inferior" Mexicans and even white southerners, contending that occupation during the Civil War symbolized the powerful, corrupting influences of a standing army. These wartime fears of martial occupation blossomed further during the early years of Reconstruction when the army, still populated by a few volunteers, enforced domestic policy in the absence of active hostilities. And the presence of African American occupiers, who generally believed military coercion to be a useful tool in their struggle for freedom, only intensified the fears of white observers about the chaotic, destabilizing nature of a standing army.[4]

By 1867 professional US soldiers who remained in the South and managed the process and aftermath of Military Reconstruction brought the two-decade critique of occupation to its zenith. While many accepted the gravity and even

necessity of their tasks—subduing white southern violence, protecting biracial constitutional conventions, and safeguarding both emancipation and the
impending Fourteenth Amendment—some voiced the same apprehensions
that had been expressed by white citizen-soldiers during the war, claiming
that domestic occupation undermined national military custom. While regulars willingly performed their duties, they worried about the implications of
their service as agents of political change. Although mandated by Congress,
the Reconstruction Acts departed from the Union's traditionally limited constitutional system, assigning to the army civil duties that it had never before
assumed. Echoing the *Nation,* army regulars cited the tension between the
need to alter the political and social conditions of the South and the preservation of the tenets of limited government that had long defined American life.[5]

Regular soldiers, however, were not the only ones who sought to define
the meaning and worth of military occupation during the middle years of
Reconstruction. Across the South, veterans of the USCT, alongside scores of
black civilians, populated militia companies that attempted to stem the tide
of white terrorist violence in remote areas beyond the reach of Federal troops.
The black militia movement, a grassroots mobilization of informal military
force, grew to fill critical voids left by an increasingly ambivalent and legally
hamstrung United States army in the wake of Military Reconstruction. Filling roles similar to those undertaken by black regiments during the war, these
militias employed active force to shape the social and political landscape, underscoring the continued problem of "militarized freedom." Expanding the
definition and scope of occupation, they paraded and marched through their
communities, guarding freedpeople against the onslaught of violent intimidation. Black Reconstruction militias exemplified the continuity in African
American soldiers' defiance of white northern assumptions about the role of
domestic military force. They also reflected the lingering implications of the
Emancipation Proclamation's garrisoning clause, which had sought to limit
black soldiers' claims to full citizenship by placing them in auxiliary military
service. Instead of relegating them to the sidelines as intended, the proclamation had instead trained African American troops in the art of uncompro-
mising, active occupation. Such powerful approaches were adopted by black
militias in their quest to secure political and social equality.[6]

Doubts among regular soldiers about the efficacy of postwar military influence, together with the advent of African American militias, underscored
the Civil War era's continuing struggle between republicanism and race, a

dichotomy showcased by the ongoing in-the-ranks unease with occupation. As the first two years of Reconstruction had demonstrated, the project of postwar occupation inspired fierce debate between white and black participants about the military's natural limits in shaping civil life. As the United States negotiated the paths of Military Reconstruction, the process and aftermath of which further exposed the era's competing visions of occupation, the white perspective, grounded in republicanism, ultimately reigned. The army, as the *Nation* advocated, had to check its domestic influence if the limited constitutional principles of Union were to be preserved. In a tragic twist of fate, the army's manpower and influence purposely waned in the wake of Military Reconstruction, facilitating the rise of white southern terrorism and black militia resistance. Just as the *Nation* bemoaned the racial and political violence that threatened to undo the era's revolutionary nature, professional military officers ironically considered the weakness of sustained Federal power as a symbol of the Union's strength. The South, by the 1870s, had been reconstructed politically. The United States and its federal system, these same voices cautioned, could not be reconstructed ideologically through military interference in political self-determination, even if the quest for white southern sovereignty came at the expense of black suffering and even death.

* * *

Ascending to the presidency in the wake of Abraham Lincoln's death in April 1865, Andrew Johnson applied a seemingly lenient and conciliatory—but also terribly shortsighted and racist—worldview to the complicated processes of Reconstruction. Although he had long despised the South's slaveholding class, labeling secessionists as rebellious traitors, Johnson retained the racial sensibilities of a white southerner deeply hostile to a post-emancipation society. A Tennessee Democrat, Johnson instituted Reconstruction policies that largely exonerated the South. Issuing thousands of pardons, refusing to punish former Confederates, and standing in stark opposition to black suffrage and equality, Johnson helped devise "reconstructed" state governments that oddly resembled those of the antebellum era. Indeed, by late 1866 the South had reemerged as a society that closely resembled the Confederate nation that went to war in 1861: the old ruling establishment had been refashioned; southern partisans and many former Confederates won election to national and state office; and African Americans were segregated into second-class positions, governed by the Black Codes and bound to a restrictive, quasi-slave labor system.[7]

On the surface, the South had been reconstructed, at least according to Johnson's conservative visions. The Republican Congress, however, comprised a vocal element of so-called radicals who sought fundamental and permanent change in the South. They declared that Reconstruction meant not only reintegration of the states and southern congressmen. It also required, they argued, a reconstructed *ideology,* a belief that the South must shed its Confederate, slaveholding identity, accept the verdict of the war, and assist in creating a more inclusive democracy. The war for Union had been waged, in part, to eliminate the slaveholding aristocracy, which threatened liberty and the promise of free labor. Yet the very rebels who survived the war appeared stronger and more unified in defeat than during the conflict. Republicans thus wrested control of Reconstruction away from the president, especially after Johnson vetoed the Freedmen's Bureau reauthorization bill and the proposed Civil Rights Act of 1866, following the southern states' refusal to ratify the Fourteenth Amendment. Winning overwhelming majorities in the congressional elections of 1866, the Republicans neutered Johnson's power and aimed to transform the South into a new biracial polity.[8]

The US military expanded its role from the first two years of Reconstruction during this subsequent congressional phase. The army carried out the new Republican agenda, assisting the party of Union and emancipation to gain a substantial foothold in the South. The Reconstruction Acts of 1867—the legislative genesis of Military Reconstruction—embodied the Republican vision of renewed military government. Effectively ignoring all of the conservative Reconstruction requirements under Abraham Lincoln and Andrew Johnson, the Reconstruction Acts appointed the army to supervise the creation of a new southern political and racial order. The laws divided the South into five military districts to be governed by a general and supervised by the regular army. Over the next few years, the military oversaw free, fair, open elections in which African Americans voted and enjoyed the fruits of equal citizenship—guaranteed by the adoption of the Fourteenth Amendment—the establishment of Republican state governments, authorization of public education, protection of private property, and enforcement of civil law. This project of massive change, which materialized in a stunningly brief amount of time, would not have occurred without the army's central influence. Biracial voting rights and newly reformed state governments reflected a Republican consensus about the purpose of Reconstruction. By 1871 the former Confederate states had been readmitted to the Union under the banner of civil and political equality, due in large part to the army's participation.[9]

Recent scholars have acknowledged both the limited and revolutionary nature of Military Reconstruction. However, as Mark Wahlgren Summers writes, "Military rule was, on the whole, pretty mild stuff, not far removed from what had come before it." Rather than trampling the defeated South as ruthless military dictators, professional soldiers usually sprang into action to maintain order and stability only when petitioned by civil agents. "The use of military power," Summers avers, "provides two important points about the success and failure of Radical Reconstruction," each of which reflected the decades-long ambivalence about the army's role in shaping political and social affairs. First, officers governed their military districts with qualified restraint, lest their actions in matters of law, government, and even race relations start to resemble strong-armed despotism. Conversely, but also directly related, the army willingly assumed unprecedented responsibilities aimed at finally consolidating the preservation of the Union. The unparalleled authorization to reform once rebellious states into biracial constituencies emboldened the military's traditional function. Summers therefore concludes, "Nothing so contrasted with tyranny than the South's treatment. By the standards of free-born Americans' past, nothing resembled it so closely."[10]

Military Reconstruction departed greatly from national tradition by incorporating the army intimately into the South's political, economic, and social realms. Constitutional republicanism had long safeguarded individual liberty against the coercions of government, yet the Reconstruction Acts called upon the army—as an arm of that very government—to usher in a new era of self-determination in the South. Preservation of the Union now assumed central importance in Congress's remaking of Reconstruction. The Thirteenth, Fourteenth, and Fifteenth Amendments—respectively outlawing slavery; protecting biracial citizenship, guaranteeing due process of law, and preventing state-sanctioned discrimination; and safeguarding the right to vote—added necessary strength to a federal constitution that assured democratic participation and sheltered the individual's ability to advance economically. This "new birth of freedom" would have been impossible without a decisive military during the war and without the army's continued postwar participation.[11]

Military Reconstruction, however, antagonized the debate about the army's occupying influence, as many professional soldiers questioned their newly assigned duties. Yes, the military had helped create and protect the environment in which the Reconstruction amendments and the great biracial elections of 1868 took place. But that was the problem, at least according to the standards of professional military culture. Regular soldiers approached their duties under the Reconstruction Acts with skepticism and conceded the boundaries of military power. In the aftermath of the military's increased role in this admittedly special occasion, they argued, the army should be used as moderately as possible, masking any appearance of coercion and appearing not as a radical, intrusive institution.[12]

The diminishing number of military personnel in the South between 1867 and 1870 further testified to professionals' insistence on an inexpensive and moderate peacetime occupation. With the advent of Military Reconstruction between 1866 and 1867, approximately twenty thousand soldiers occupied the South, a number that trended downward over the next three years; by October 1870 only 9,050 soldiers remained.[13] Such a numerical decline accompanied a heightened ideological awareness about the military's role both during and after the states' readmission. Soldiers begrudgingly recognized that the Reconstruction amendments could not be secured without oversight by the US Army, which would need to integrate itself deeply into the southern states' social, political, and economic fabrics. Yet as George Gordon Meade explained to a fellow officer in 1867, "you have not only to be a soldier, but must play the politician, a part which I am sure both to you and me would be not only difficult but disagreeable." Such a strapping military presence during peacetime reflected a dramatic departure from national custom and gave meaning to the era's revolutionary nature.[14]

By 1871, when the southern states complied with Congress's conditions for readmission and self-government and democracy were ostensibly established, the military sought a return to standard procedure. Yet this desire did not account for seething tensions, bubbling underneath the southern landscape. White southern conservatives, clothed in the pale sheets of the Ku Klux Klan or the bright garments of the Red Shirts, rose to challenge the newly formed Republican state governments, often in horrendous ways. Violence had long plagued the postwar South, manifesting itself in racial massacres in New Orleans and Memphis in 1866 and, in a broader sense, reflecting the anger, humiliation, and fears associated with emancipation and Confederate defeat. Insurgent groups, wielding chaotic guerrilla tactics, roamed the countryside, harassing, threatening, and killing Unionists and African Americans. The process and aftermath of Military Reconstruction transformed white southern hostilities into organized political resistance, as "terrorist" bands hoped to overthrow the reconstructed governments.[15]

Reconstruction violence functioned as a series of small wars and insurgencies—irregular paramilitary actions that sought to alter political and social conditions through armed intimidation—in which white southerners, many of whom once hailed as Confederates, aimed to "redeem" their region from the clutches of Republicans and African Americans. Violence evolved from the clandestine, haphazard, and night-riding attacks of the Ku Klux Klan to more organized paramilitary units that waged a form of political warfare against freedpeople and their Republican allies, disrupting party meetings, political organizations, and elections. Ultimately, by the mid-1870s, white conservative militias unleashed counterrevolutions that toppled state governments in Louisiana, Arkansas, Mississippi, and South Carolina. Postwar violence sought to meet particular social and political ends. Those who waged the insurgent battles of Reconstruction thus did not seek to reestablish the Confederate nation, but instead to rebalance the white South's oppressive racial hierarchy and political oligarchy within the new postwar Union.[16]

United States soldiers cataloged the nature of Reconstruction violence, describing the various methods brandished by white southerners. A captain in the Twenty-fourth Infantry, stationed at Vicksburg, noted that the local Klan "roam around the country principally at night, for the purpose of redressing any wrong or grievance white people may have or concern they have against freedmen." Sometimes, the officer explained, whites had only to express their grievances against the new racial order "and summary punishment is inflicted upon the parties complained of—sometimes to the extent of murder." Patrick Hasson, a lieutenant in the Fourteenth Infantry, claimed that freedpeople near Murfreesboro, Tennessee, "say that if [the army] leave here many of them must go to Nashville; that it would be a risk of their lives to remain here longer." Military occupation had sought to maintain stability and order, an obligation on which African Americans relied to safeguard their freedom. Yet, Hasson wrote, some blacks admitted that "to give me any specific information, for instance the names of any men connected with the recent outrages or belonging to the bands of men that walk at night, or anything that would lead to those mens names becoming known would be as much, as the informants life would be worth."[17]

Although charged with combating violence, soldiers were generally ambivalent about the army's ability to thwart white southern terrorism. Part of the problem stemmed from a lack of manpower and resources, as the army occupied only strategic positions throughout the South, sometimes removed from immediate areas of political and racial intimidation. "The number of men left at this post," Lieutenant Charles Lovell wrote in response to the kind of violence Patrick Hasson reported from Murfreesboro, "is inadequate for the proper performance of duty." Concerned that "disturbances in this neighborhood" might require substantial military force, Lovell groused that "I should be embarrassed by reason of the small effective force at my disposal." W. H. Vinal, an officer in the Sixteenth Infantry, reported an additional challenge from Philadelphia, Mississippi. "The services of my Detachment have not been called upon since my arrival and if they were—I would respectfully suggest it would be worse than useless. Every man in the country has a horse or mule," he protested. "Infantry could not move two miles before the cry 'Yankees are coming' would be spread."[18]

Despite the apparent martial latitude afforded by the Reconstruction Acts, both Lovell and Vinal embodied the systemic problems of Military Reconstruction. On the one hand, the army functioned as the most important institution in guiding the wayward states back into the Union, while also protecting civil rights and curtailing white resistance. Without the efforts of most commanders to remove unruly southerners from political office, to call and oversee constitutional conventions, and to insist on the supremacy of Federal law, Reconstruction would have died in its infancy. Such responsibilities, on the other hand, mandated a substantial military presence, a luxury sometimes deprived to the district commanders. The army had to operate within a broader culture that looked askance, both ideologically and financially, at a large military establishment that involved itself in civil affairs in spite of the ominous reality that the former Confederate states still contested Federal authority. Thus, as Lovell explained, the army could rarely employ the number of soldiers required for day-to-day operations. And, as Vinal alluded to, once a state had been readmitted, the army could engage violent offenders only at the behest of civil authorities, a cumbersome, bureaucratic process that wasted time and resources.[19]

Congress responded to Klan violence, which had become so pronounced especially in South Carolina and Mississippi, by passing the Enforcement and Ku Klux laws of 1870–71. Granting Federal power to prosecute those who used violence to intimidate black voters, and also granting the president authority to declare a state of rebellion and suspend habeas corpus, the laws seemed to bestow broad discretion to the Federal government in assisting civil agents maintain peace and security. While the military did use the Enforcement laws to battle and even eliminate portions of the Klan, some army officers feared that they would overstep their authority even despite the obvious violence consuming their districts. William T. Gentry informed a captain in the Department of the Gulf "of the greatest importance that, in all cases where U.S. Troops are used, the necessity for it shall be made very clear, and the use to which they are put, not left in doubt." A month later he remarked, "troops can only be used in cases of this kind as a *posse comitatus* to aid said authorities when called upon in the proper manner: they are not expected to take the initiative."[20]

Gentry's perspective appears remarkably detached both from the purpose of the Enforcement laws and from the broader purpose of Reconstruction. He reflected, however, the continuity of opinion long voiced by US soldiers about the bounds of Federal military power. And the same people who endorsed the Enforcement laws—moderate and liberal Republicans—also criticized the acts' implications. Just as the *Nation* had done in 1871, those who spoke most favorably of the efforts to safeguard the Fourteenth and Fifteenth amendments also questioned the expansion of Federal and military power. "A lasting, possibly even a permanent military presence could hold equality's gains," Mark Summers writes. "But that," he counters, "was politically impossible, fiscally unsustainable," because most Republicans "had reached the limits of what they felt it safe for a republic to do, even for equal rights." The army indeed conducted several hundred expeditions under the authority of the Enforcement laws, assisting civil authorities to arrest violent dissidents. Yet the military suffered from a "lack of administrative machinery and personnel that a full enforcement required, as well as," Summers concludes, "by a military reduced to puny size."[21]

It is crucial to understand *why* and *how* regulars such as William Gentry remained wedded to concepts that had long defined the American character, despite the rampant injustices that plagued the Reconstruction landscape. Officers interpreted the era's political and racial conditions within a strict adherence to republicanism, a concept that seems frustratingly outmoded and obsolete to any twenty-first-century observer. They believed that they had already acted outside the boundaries of national tradition when securing and enforcing the Reconstruction amendments and Reconstruction Acts; any additional military involvement in state affairs, they argued, would carry potentially damaging consequences. They could discard national tradition and fundamentally alter the ideological nature of Union—recently preserved through a bloody war—by conducting a serious, indefinite military occupation of the South, using a standing army to enforce every aspect of social, political, and racial equality. Or, they could limit martial involvement in civil affairs, potentially risking the gains made through wartime victory, but also upholding the national tradition of limited government and abhorrence of standing armies.[22]

Although the answer seems obvious to modern observers, regular army soldiers remained devoted to the restraints of military involvement in the states, regardless of the growing chaos and racial violence in the South. Their attitudes confirmed the commentary of white Union soldiers who, during the war and early stages of Reconstruction, remarked consistently about the dangerous implications of military occupation. And the opinions expressed between 1867 and 1877 further highlighted why African American soldiers and civilians, fearing a loss of life and liberty, sought a marked alteration to what they considered the unnecessary constraints placed on occupation. In the end, the culture of American republicanism, born during the Revolution and secured during the Civil War, won the day. We must take seriously the reasons why white northerners remained so concerned about an imagined standing army and so fearful of long-term military occupation. Their beliefs, while seemingly irrelevant and antiquated today, were undertaken with great focus more than a century ago.[23]

Regular army officers underscored these beliefs about the restrained roles of the Federal government and military during the second half of Reconstruction. Brigadier General Samuel D. Sturgis, who served in Texas, referred bluntly to his occupation responsibilities as early as 1866 as "going entirely outside the duty of my profession." Nelson Miles, a volunteer officer during the war and colonel in the peacetime army agreed, welcoming a transfer to the West to regulate Indian affairs. "It was a pleasure to be relieved of the anxieties and responsibilities of civil affairs," he explained about his Reconstruction assignment in North Carolina, "to hear nothing of the controversies incident to race prejudice, and to be once more engaged in strictly military duties, a profession to which I was devoted." Sturgis, Miles, and their colleagues had not been trained to oversee political affairs or regulate a state's social structure. Indeed, they considered the complexity of Reconstruction beyond their obligations as professional soldiers. Such comments anticipated a growing concern among officers who believed that they served in very peculiar, extraordinary conditions. They were sent to the South to maintain order, yet were also expected to walk a fine line between military responsibility and local civilian affairs.[24]

The very nature of the Reconstruction acts necessitated that soldiers involve themselves in state matters, but fear of military usurpation checked most officers' actions. Observers, both in and out of the military, ironically believed that the army would be more likely than white southerners to incite chaos and instability. Troops in the Fourth Military District of Arkansas, for instance, incurred the wrath of their commanding general after entering a private home. "The military are the servants of the laws, and are for the benefit of the people," the general declared. "The assumption that a party of soldiers can, at their own option, forcibly destroy a citizen's property, and commit a gross violation of the public peace, would not be tolerated under a Napoleon." The fear of arbitrary military interference motivated other officers to maintain strict control of their men, even when white southerners perpetuated violence. Once state governments had been reestablished, officers were ordered "not to act at all in the matter unless called upon [by] the properly constituted Civil authorities and then only to protect them from violence while in the discharge of their duties."[25]

Federal military policy mirrored the concerns of army officers. Before a state was readmitted and a Republican government established—and especially thereafter—military officials were expected to maintain, at best, a "peacekeeping" presence, ordered into action only when civilian authorities requested assistance. Gen. George H. Thomas, the postwar commander of the Department of the Cumberland, received orders in 1868 outlining "the obligation of the military . . . in common with all citizens, to obey the summons of a marshal or sheriff must be held subordinate to their paramount duty as members of a permanent military body." Officers were expected to determine "whether the service required of him is lawful and necessary and compatible with the proper discharge of his ordinary military duties, and must limit his action absolutely to proper aid in execution of the lawful precept exhibited to him by the marshal or sheriff." Such murky, legalistic rhetoric fostered even deeper ambivalence among some officers who already questioned the limits of their duty. And despite the presence of garrisons across the South, depleted manpower and paltry financial resources underscored the army's inability to provide adequate protection to Republicans and African Americans on election days. Although soldiers participated in routine patrols of the countryside, arrested white terrorist insurgents, and prevented political coups from forming, the military largely remained in the background, on purpose, allowing civil authorities to govern daily affairs.[26]

Officers, who were generally conservative in nature, drew a clear distinction between military government and the maintenance of peace. Writing in the post-1867 environment, especially upon readmission of the southern states, some commanders explained that civil government *had* to function on its own, lest the entire experiment in republican democracy be threatened. They willingly employed martial law as a temporary measure because it supported civil government. Yet they stopped short of supplanting the state governments, fearing the prospect of military despotism. This did not mean that they neglected to employ troops to administer the Enforcement Acts against the Ku Klux Klan. But they continued to believe that they stood on shaky ground. In addition, many soldiers did not harbor the idealistic sensibilities of congressional radicals, leaning instead toward the conservative views of either the Democrats or Republicans. Thus, they possessed little ideological concern for the plight of freedpeople, and most certainly did not advocate unconditional military power to enforce racial equality.[27]

William T. Sherman especially despised the insurgency waged by white conservatives against Republican governments. But his devotion to republican *tradition,* despite the restraint it mandated, guided the bulk of his decisions. Although presumably naïve, Sherman genuinely insisted that the army remain apolitical, a position he had long advocated well prior to Reconstruction. Hesitant to employ his troops in a substantial fashion, as General of the Army he wrote in 1870, "I think the use of our soldiers should be limited to maintaining the peace." He endorsed arresting Ku Klux and other white southerners who threatened violence but firmly opposed entering the realm of political or social affairs.[28]

His position remained strikingly consistent throughout the entire Reconstruction era. "No matter what change we desire in the feelings and thoughts of people South," he wrote in September 1865, "we cannot accomplish it by force. Nor can we maintain there an army large enough to hold them in subjugation. All we can, or should, attempt is to give them rope, to develop in an honest way if possible, preserving in reserve enough military power to check any excesses if they attempt any." A decade later, he retained this attitude. "I have all along tried to save our officers and soldiers from the dirty work imposed on them," he informed his brother in 1875, "and may, thereby, have incurred the suspicion of the President that I did not cordially sustain his force."

He considered himself exonerated, though, believing, "I have always thought it wrong to bolster up weak State governments by our troops. We should keep the peace always; but not act as bailiff constables and catch thieves. That should be beneath a soldier's vocation."[29]

It appears that Sherman constructed a worldview divorced from the wartime preservation of the Union and the troubling realities of the postwar South. Yet his outlook ironically encapsulated the very definition of victory during the postwar period. Sherman and his contemporaries operated within an ideological context only one century removed from the Revolution; their experiences with long-term military occupation were only five to ten years old, practiced exclusively during wartime. Thus, Sherman deemed it inconceivable to use the military to refashion citizens' ideologies and governing structures, no matter how much he may have hated secession, the destructive war perpetuated by white southerners, or the chaotic defiance practiced by unrepentant insurgents. Employing the US Army as a tool of social and political change against white citizens, and for the benefit of African Americans, simply did not enter into his worldview. Limited government interference and a democratic South managed by local whites underscored Sherman's quest for postwar order and stability. Only arbitrary military interference could undermine such visions.[30]

Even Ulysses S. Grant, one of the principal architects of Military Reconstruction, embodied the tensions prompted by the army's continued presence in the South. Fully supportive of "peacetime" occupation, arguing that the former Confederate states remained in rebellion against Federal authority, Grant mandated the military to oversee the formal restoration process. While acting as general-in-chief, the position he held prior to Sherman's appointment, Grant advised Congress's drafting of the Reconstruction Acts. Guided by pragmatism and an innate ability to interpret conditions from a dispassionate, yet also judicious perspective, he believed that the army could pave the most efficient path to sectional reunion. Thus, he endorsed an active role for the military, advocating the removal of recalcitrant civil officials, while also sanctioning military guardedness against white southerners' violent racism and insolence.[31]

Grant also understood that the army had entered into an unprecedented role far removed from its traditional functions. In this recognition, Grant reflected the confusing, and sometimes contradictory nature of the Reconstruction Acts, which various army commanders had to negotiate for themselves.

"My views," he told Major General John Pope, chief of the Third Military District, "are that District Commanders are responsible for the faithful execution of the reconstruction Act of Congress, and that, in Civil matters, I cannot give them an order. I can give them my views however, for what they are worth." Stressing the limited extent to which officers could wield their power, a problem that plagued the army through most of Reconstruction, Grant explained to Philip Sheridan, commander of the First Military District, "the law contemplates that district commanders shall be their own judges of the meaning of its provisions." When engaging disobedient civil officials, Grant clarified, "you make no more removals than you find absolutely necessary. That you make none whatever, except it be for the gravest disregard of the law.... That you make up your mind fully as to the proper course to pursue, and pursue it, without fear, and take the consequences."[32]

Grant did not waver in his commitment to Military Reconstruction inasmuch as he attempted to define the scope of the army's role. Writing to Edward O. C. Ord, who commanded the Fourth Military District, Grant declared, "I am exceedingly anxious to see reconstruction effected and Military rule put an end to." Aware that the army had never before assumed civil responsibilities, Grant desired that the institution maintain a limited role. For the time being, though, he believed that the army had acted necessarily within the bounds of Federal law, never overstepping its powers. "Politicians should be perfectly satisfied with the temperate manner with which the Military have used authority thus far," he acknowledged. Alluding, however, to the potential consequences of an overly expansive military state, Grant cautioned, "If there is a necessity for continuing it too long there is great danger of a reaction against the Army. The best way," he concluded, "to secure a speedy termination of Military rule is to execute all the laws of Congress in the spirit in which they were conceived, firmly but without passion." For Ulysses S. Grant, the army could preserve the Union once and for all, but only within its legal allowances, divorced from the very "passion" that demanded its omnipresence across the violent, feverish, white South.[33]

Brevet Major General William H. Emory, commander of the Department of the Gulf during the early 1870s, articulated this problematic dichotomy between necessity and implications. Fearing in early 1871 an overthrow of Louisiana's Republican administration, Emory called upon Washington to provide guidelines on how best to avoid political turmoil. He received vague orders suggesting that military forces stationed in New Orleans should be employed only in a limited fashion. Attempting to forestall violence in New Orleans, Emory deployed several hundred soldiers throughout the city. He informed the various ringleaders "that if any violence is used it will be my duty to disperse them with grapeshot." However, he also advised Republican governor Henry C. Warmoth not to call upon the military to settle the political dispute. "You will use every means in your power to avoid the necessity of bringing the U.S. troops into the appearance of interfering in the legislative functions," Emory warned, "or, of making it necessary to shed the blood of our fellow citizens."[34]

A day later, Emory expanded on his beliefs, explaining that the present crisis ultimately threatened a particular political ideology. "In a conflict between the Executive and the Legislature of a State," he began, "where it is difficult to decide which is right, I have recognized throughout the necessity, in a Republican form of Government of not siding against the Legislature and the propriety of not interfering in its organization in any manner." He added, "I feel neither competent to decide this quarrel nor have I authority to do so." Emory did not yet conclude the letter, adding a peculiar postscript. "Both factions of the Legislature are," he opined, "making use of the presence of Troops here to keep up this agitation to the prejudice of the interests of this great city." With these words, William H. Emory encapsulated the essence of the Army's Reconstruction-era troubles, suggesting that the military, regardless of its limited, moderate presence, would inevitably become a source of social instability.[35]

* * *

Few events captured Emory's ambivalence about the role of Federal military power in the wake of Military Reconstruction better than the rise of local and state militia units populated by African Americans. The army's formal role largely ended once the rebellious states had complied with Congress's demands for restoration. The aftermath of reunion consolidated black and Republican activism, inspiring fierce, persistent backlashes from white southerners bent on redeeming their states through violent intimidation. Desperate for effective resistance against Klan-like groups, Republican state governments raised militia units composed primarily of African American volunteers to safeguard the revolutionary political and social changes across the South. "These forces were created," writes Otis A. Singletary, the principal historian of black militias, "to fill the power vacuum that resulted from the withdrawal of Federal troops when the states had complied with the conditions set forth in the Reconstruction acts."[36]

Maintaining the constitutional balance of federalism by limiting the influence of national institutions—that is, the army—militias, raised and deployed by the states, symbolized the ongoing quest to uphold the Union's republican balance. Designed to preserve peace, maintain stability, and ensure safety for black and loyal white voters, militias assumed the roles formerly undertaken by the army. The African Americans who overwhelmingly filled militia ranks embodied another purpose: employing localized martial authority to shape and strengthen the promises of emancipation and equality. Employing a direct outgrowth of their wartime and early postwar experiences, black Reconstruction militias expanded the definition and scope of military occupation, revealing the extent to which freedpeople relied on the active force of arms to protect their communities against white terror. Filling critical voids left by a shrinking and remote army, wielding the weapons of counterinsurgency, and once again standing as a body of occupiers, black militias represented the final, unintended outgrowth of the Emancipation Proclamation's garrisoning clause.

During the late 1860s and early 1870s, as reports of chaotic violence inundated statehouses throughout the Republican South, governors appealed to their legislatures to draft laws formally enrolling militias. When raised, the militias resembled the US Army both in their composition and purpose. Most governors, for example, functioned as commanders in chief and were given wide latitude in their control over these units, including the liberty to call troops whenever they deemed military force necessary. Although some states struggled to arm, equip, and fund their militias, the Federal government ultimately assisted in providing crucial financial and tangible resources. Congress approved the delivery of arms based on quotas, and even Ulysses S. Grant sanctioned the militia project. The president advised his general-in-chief, William T. Sherman, about the exigencies facing the North Carolina militia: "I want them to have the uniforms . . . and am willing to sign any legal order necessary to accomplish that purpose." Federal endorsements such as Grant's underscored one of the central aims of the militia system: maintaining an active military occupation of the South without employing national institutions to accomplish the task. Use of localized militias allowed Congress to supply critical resources and funding to the unstable southern states without subjecting the Federal army to extensive service in the region.[37]

African Americans who populated state militias considered their service to be an extension of the kind of occupation once performed by USCT regiments. As former soldiers, many of whom had served in garrisons, they had learned that military duty behind the lines, especially as a black occupation force, oftentimes mandated violent, irregular tactics to defend new social orders. When the era's revolutionary change came under attack, black militiamen, according to historian Steven Hahn, "understood that whatever success they might achieve [in defending the Fourteenth and Fifteenth amendments] would depend on their ability to do battle of a different sort." Engaging in unconventional types of warfare had long defined the black military experience, which challenged and reshaped American assumptions about the purpose of occupying forces. Now, as the informal manifestation of occupation, black militias once again wielded martial power against their adversaries in ways that had long raised concerns among white soldiers who were reared in the republican ethic. For African American militiamen, in the tradition of their USCT predecessors, the use of militias to preserve racial equality justified the potential violation of some of the most fundamental ideological tenets of Union.[38]

The enrollment of African American men into state militias embodied a powerful truth that the Emancipation Proclamation's call for black soldiers had failed to bestow fully: recognition of formal citizenship and inclusion in the body politic. Abraham Lincoln's wartime insistence on garrisoning service for black troops had seemingly conflicted with the more active military tradition cherished by white volunteers, limiting African American claims to full citizenship on the basis of their service. Now, in the midst of Reconstruction, which black southerners defined as an ongoing state of war, the culture of civic obligation demanded that citizens forsake their private interests and join the growing ranks of volunteers in the quest for racial justice. In a fitting twist of irony, the militia movement demonstrated how the black military experience had come full circle. Once deemed unfit to serve in volunteer armies, African American soldiers had been relegated behind the lines, where they used their service to reshape the culture of military occupation. The violent wake of Military Reconstruction further crystalized the concomitant relationship between military service, occupation, and black citizenship, a notion defined by the precariously balanced Fourteenth Amendment. Indeed, the rise of black militias confirmed that citizens *would* volunteer to occupy towns and engage in counterinsurgency against the hostile forces of white aggression.[39]

Thus, similar to most USCT regiments during the war, black militias were largely homegrown and sought to impose a formidable bulwark against the racial strife and coercion that infected the Reconstruction South. Cataloging the local abuses inflicted by the Klan, an army officer in Nashville reported that "the blacks are desperate, and want only a leader to make war at once on their oppressors." He acknowledged that "something decided must be done if a war of races is to be prevented," advocating "some means of punishing these cowardly men who go about in disguise to whip negroes and commit outrages upon them." Their service actually inverted the concept of occupation in which black troops stood as a local military presence, guarding their own communities and marching in their own streets. Moved into action because of the US Army's relative absence, and, according to the officer, because the "civil [officials] are utterly worthless," militias offered a crucial grassroots alternative to the fears of formal domestic occupation, which had paralyzed American military culture.[40]

Militias employed the tactics of occupation to legitimize their military appeal. Governors often petitioned a militia presence on election days, imploring the units to preserve order and maintain security at polling places. Black militias served a dual political purpose: they protected Republican candidates and voters, while symbolizing the political and racial revolutions of Reconstruction. At a governor's request, militias also enforced martial law, sometimes arresting dissident civilians who threatened order and stability, while at other times confiscating private property. And, as forces of counterinsurgency, black militias shaped conditions through unconventional means. Drilling throughout the day, shooting their muskets in the air, and pressing local whites off streets all proclaimed the unapologetic nature of black occupation. Indeed, a gathering of the Union League—a black grassroots political organization—near Franklin, Tennessee, "procured drums and a fife, and had been marching about the outskirts of the town," one observer wrote. A black paramilitary unit, which was even more informal than militias, grew in response to attacks committed by local whites, hoping to stem the tide of violence. "There is no doubt," the commentator noted, "that the conservatives viewed the marching and displays of the League as a military demonstration and feared that it might result in strife."[41]

The Franklin Union League embodied one of the central purposes of the black militia movement: subduing restive white southerners through violence. Black communities near Mobile, Alabama, for example, "were congregated in large numbers and armed," instilling local whites with "[terror] at the defiant and threatening attitude of the negroes." Tapping into black desires for strong military occupation, militias sought to engage white southerners with the same violence under which freedpeople had suffered. When militia companies occupied the streets of Camden, South Carolina, a brawl ensued with local police, resulting in the deaths of several black troops. Upon hearing the news, some militiamen "broke ranks and ran down, hooping and hallooing with great fury," arriving at the home of a local woman thought to be harboring the policeman suspected of the shooting. "They broke down the door with the butts of their muskets," an observer noted, "they bayonetted one gentleman in the hand, who was trying to keep them off." Much like the wartime experiences of black occupation, both the presence and deployment of active violence were sometimes the only tools that could curtail white insurgents.[42]

Responding to a similar incident elsewhere in South Carolina, a captain in the Eighth Infantry summarized what he considered to be the implications of black militia occupation: "The measure while it has given the colored man a feeling of self reliance, has also exited [*sic*] da[n]gerously his vanity. The whites regarding it as a menace have thoroughly and generally armed." Indeed, two infamous episodes at Colfax, Louisiana, and Hamburg, South Carolina, underscored the captain's belief in the foundations and purposes of black militias, while also exposing his ambivalence on their sustained ability to occupy and defend their communities. What grew from a dirty, disputed election in Louisiana, and what materialized from the real and imagined political power of African Americans in upcountry South Carolina, resulted in violent battles respectively in 1873 and 1876. Although black militias played an integral role in each event, bloody affairs portended the white South's violent political redemption. As the Eighth Infantry's captain suggested, the rise of black military power, just as it had during the war, inspired an equally potent resistance from former Confederates bent on maintaining their dream of white supremacy.[43]

Colfax, located in Grant Parish, Louisiana, named for the sitting vice president and president, respectively, was established in the late 1860s as a Republican Party stronghold in the formerly rich, slaveholding districts of the Red River Valley. A dubious election in 1872 yielded rival claimants to state and local offices, which threatened Radical Republicans' power, instigating efforts to remove black officials from office. Rather than relinquish his position, William Ward, a USCT veteran, local militia leader, and one of Grant Parish's recently elected state representatives, organized his militia and occupied the local courthouse to defy conservative efforts at removal. Exuding a "semi-military character," Ward and his men garrisoned their immediate community, establishing guards, organizing pickets, and drilling companies. The militia benefited from other former soldiers—some of whom had been enslaved in nearby locales before the war—who likely employed military tactics they had learned in the army. By April 1873, with Ward in New Orleans to petition the US Army for assistance, conservatives arrived at Colfax and demanded surrender of the fortified courthouse. The black militia refused, and a battle ensued between the opposing forces. While whites shot at black civilians who tried to escape, others set fire to the courthouse, forcing those inside to flee, only to be met with gunfire as they retreated outside. Those African Americans who surrendered were later executed, resulting in more than one hundred black deaths in one of the most notorious mass murders in US history.[44]

Events in Hamburg, South Carolina, unfolded similarly. A region that had long festered from paramilitary violence, the upcountry teemed with white rifle clubs and black militias, each bent on shaping local and state politics. For white South Carolinians, and, for that matter, many former Confederates, African American militias offered unwelcome reminders of emancipation and wartime black military service. South Carolina's black Reconstruction militias had garnered a particularly infamous reputation, at least among white conservatives, for exuding what was perceived as a cocky, militaristic persona that was tied directly to African American political power. Indeed, Hamburg boasted active militias commanded by Prince Rivers (a former slave) and Doc Adams, both of whom were USCT veterans and active members of the Union League. Each drilled their units with militant precision, striding through the streets of Hamburg with confident, armed authority.[45]

On July 4, 1876, as Adams drilled his company in downtown Hamburg, a buggy approached with two white men who insisted on their right to pass along the street guarded by the militia. Adams refused, even attempting to force the men off the road. He ultimately yielded, but not without complication. The two men sought a warrant for Adams's arrest, after which a trial date was established to weigh Adams's complicity in disturbing the peace. When he did not arrive for the trial, white conservative militias rose to pursue their own brand of justice. Meanwhile, Adams's militia occupied a local building, arming themselves and preparing to meet their adversaries. When the whites arrived, and Adams refused to surrender the building, fighting ensued between both groups, resulting in the capture of several dozen black militiamen. The next day, despite the successful escape of Adams and several others, five of the prisoners were executed, inaugurating a widespread campaign of terror throughout South Carolina as white paramilitary units targeted black militias. Although they deployed relatively effective counterinsurgency methods, black militias throughout the South either soon disbanded or were shattered altogether, leading, by 1877, to the South's redemption of white conservative rule.[46]

The Colfax and Hamburg massacres, as well as the broader black militia movement, reveal several implications about the contested nature of military occupation during the Civil War era. First, African American militias during Reconstruction sought to emulate the practices of occupation that USCT regiments had earlier used to defend the fate of emancipation. Indeed, black militarism, both during and after the Civil War, was tied intimately to freedom and equality, notions that troubled and intimidated some white Americans, instilling paranoia about possible race wars. Second, historian Otis A. Singletary suggests that fears of racial strife among moderate Republicans hampered black militias because some governors claimed that deploying black troops would intensify white conservative anger, thus perpetuating racial violence. This same charge was leveled against the USCT during the early years of postwar occupation, undermining the black martial vision. Finally, black militias came to be associated with the US Army, and both forces were held responsible for contributing to the violence that engulfed the South. Rather than bringing stability, the presence of military forces in domestic society, regardless of their state or Federal associations, were seen as the prime culprits of volatility and insecurity.[47]

* * *

Just as the *Nation* declared in 1871, and as William H. Emory argued in 1872, *Harper's Weekly*, a long-time supporter of racial equality and the Republican vision of Reconstruction, concluded in 1877 that "the presence of troops has not preserved the Republican party" in the South. "A State government," it continued, "which can be upheld only by the national army is not in the American sense a government of the people." *Harper's* blamed the violence and chaos of the 1870s on the military's presence, believing that southern garrisons helped nurture the region's instability. "To insist that the army shall be retained in a State so long as there is disorder or the chance of disorder, is to propose a military administration; and for the State authorities to appeal immediately to the general government on the outbreak of trouble, is to disregard the fundamental conditions of the American system." The white voters in southern states who perpetuated violence were merely acting in defiance of the military, the newspaper explained. If the army, or even black militias, were not there, this logic concluded, voters would abstain from violent protest, exercising their majority rights at the polls. "They may be ignorant, brutal, and corrupt," the author acknowledged. "But if they cast lawfully the majority of the votes, the government they establish is the lawful government, and the national government, if lawfully invoked, can not see it overthrown by domestic violence."[48]

The rhetoric in *Harper's* underscored and explained the US Army's consistent southern demobilization during the 1870s. It also suggested why the army was deployed on a moderate basis while increasing numbers of soldiers were sent to the West to battle Native Americans, opening the frontier to white settlement. Soldiers were employed to arrest white insurgents only at the behest of civil authorities; otherwise, they remained relatively idle. Indeed, their presence as forces of occupation functioned on the fringes of a southern world exploding with violence, which black militias attempted to quell. Contemporary observers, however, attributed the escalating deterioration of order in the South to the military's continued, and in their minds pointless, existence. White southerners, who sought a return to the old order, learned that they could enforce their belligerence with little fear of Yankee reprisal. As historian George C. Rable concluded, "Moderate force, such as that applied by the army in the South, is more likely to produce a violent response than more draconian measures or a laissez-faire policy."[49]

The white southern insurgency that rose in response to the advent of Republican state governments reflected long-held white American fears about the army's presence in domestic society. Observers suggested that the volatile political battles waged between black militias and the Ku Klux Klan, Knights of the White Camellia, the White Line, and the Red Shirts materialized because of the army's standing in the way of otherwise peaceful self-government. By the mid-to-late 1870s, Americans examined this troubling situation with even greater scrutiny, equating instability in the South with the destabilization of Latin America and western Europe. Both the latter regions, Americans warned, contained large standing armies that threatened to seize power, regulate social and political affairs, and overthrow civilian governments. The growing chaos of Reconstruction symbolized that the nation, and especially the military, failed to exert proper control of its territory. William H. Emory determined that the "duty which the army is called upon to perform . . . is of such a character and so closely interwoven with political matters that it has been not only a very delicate one, but embarrassing to those charged with its execution."[50]

Emory implied that Military Reconstruction and its violent aftermath were actually competing battles over the fate of Union. The problem of military occupation functioned at the heart of this competition, as it had through much of the Civil War era, exposing critical questions about the role of Federal force in domestic life. Professional soldiers suggested that the practice of reconstruction meant rebalancing the southern states within federalism's proper orbit, alongside the new and necessary promises of emancipation and equality. Yet in order to maintain the Union as it was understood, the army could not continually impose the national government's will. The army's purpose was to craft a *lasting* Union, not fashion a new one altogether through the unprecedented force of a standing army.[51]

These final phases of military occupation in Civil War America call into question the "lost moment" interpretation of Reconstruction, which suggests a costly departure from racial and social equality and condemns a national retreat from military support afforded to black southerners and white unionists in the wake of the Reconstruction Acts and amendments. Scholars sometimes translate the violence and chaos of the 1870s, and the relatively limited response such incidents provoked from the Federal government and military, as a failure to capitalize on the gains made in the Civil War and its aftermath. There is no question that there existed a disastrous, failed opportunity for African Americans to enjoy the fruits of postwar freedom and equality. Yet this interpretation misses a broader understanding of why such an environment of violent intimidation flourished. Recent literature sometimes overlooks the nineteenth-century context in which white northerners operated and how they interpreted the limited constitutional roles of the military and government. Military Reconstruction temporarily altered the relationship between citizen and government. Yet once the Fourteenth and Fifteenth amendments were secured and the wayward states assimilated in the Union, northerners believed that the conditions of liberty and democracy had been established, relegating the army's expansive scope to the margins of civil and political life. And herein lay the central irony of Reconstruction: the very principles for

which the United States went to war in 1861—preservation of the Union's republican ideals—were the very values that purposely hindered a robust, long-
term military occupation from reshaping the postwar nation.[52]

In many ways, the prospect of preserving African American freedom and
equality in the South had little chance of succeeding; by 1877, white northerners were focused more on preserving and maintaining the Union's republican foundations than on safeguarding the rights of freedpeople. Nineteenth-
century attitudes regarding the role of government and the military assumed
much loftier importance than a dedication to racial equality. Americans, both
moderate and radical, were fluent in the languages of liberty, self-government,
and individual opportunity, and also dedicated to a military establishment detached from societal and political affairs. Yet in a marked, transitory departure
from national tradition, Congress temporarily attached these qualities to race,
enforced temporarily by the army, during the era of Military Reconstruction.
It was never assumed, however, that a long-term military presence should be
used to enforce what citizens had always taken for granted, which contributed
to the rise, but ultimate fall, of black militias that sought to fill the precarious
voids left by the army.[53]

* * *

The United States' mid-nineteenth-century experiment in military occupation appeared, by 1876 and 1877, to be on its deathbed. The end of Reconstruction seemed to herald the triumph of military republicanism, a concept that
had influenced the evolution of American military occupations since the late
1840s. Although garrisons still dotted the southern landscape, they resembled tiny islands in a sea of white defiance. The military's once-formidable
presence dwindled throughout the 1870s, evolving into a symbol of diminishing hope for black and white Republicans and inspiring increasing boldness
from white southern insurgents. Whereas garrisons once stood as pillars of
strength, projecting the power of the Union army and victory over the Confederacy, they now tottered upon the weakest of foundations. The once mighty
and feared US Army had become drained of its former vigor, relegated once
again to the fringes of American life. The culture of republicanism, buttressed
by a fierce contemporary dedication to its survival, stood firm.[54]

Some Americans had long warned that the culture of military republicanism—in particular the citizen-soldier tradition and aversions to standing

armies—was simply incompatible with long-term military occupation, especially during the "peacetime" world of Reconstruction. If the United States' wars against Mexico and the Confederacy had been waged to prove the sanctity of majority rule, the superiority of the United States, and the supremacy of democracy, then Reconstruction, implemented according to these same tenets, somehow had to follow the same rubric. White northerners had, by 1877, made a purposeful calculation that the military's Reconstruction occupation of the South propped up unpopular governments, supported only the minority, and reeked of undemocratic corruption. In order to free the postwar United States from sectionalism's tight grip the nation must honor its heritage of civilian rule and its traditional suspicion of peacetime armies. Considerations of racial equality and equal protection under the law were conspicuously absent from this reckoning.[55]

Americans reaffirmed their adherence to republicanism in 1878 when Congress passed the Posse Comitatus Act. Underscoring an aversion to peacetime military occupation, the act prohibited the army from enforcing the law and regulating civil affairs unless approved by the US Constitution or prescribed by an act of Congress. State militias, which later evolved into the National Guard, would instead assume these responsibilities. Posse Comitatus, enforced through fines and imprisonment, seemed to seal American republicanism's final triumph over military occupation. It appeared that peacetime "nation building" at home, directed by the military, had once and for all proved incompatible with American ideals.[56]

The experience of military occupation during the Civil War era forced Americans to confront a host of troubling issues that had long plagued the nation: the relationship between the citizen and government; the proper function of the military in a free society; the racial components of volunteer service; and the bureaucratic, governing functions of the army, during both war and peace. In many ways, the experience of nineteenth-century occupation departed from national military tradition; in other ways, it laid the foundation for future American wars. Most important, the occupations during Reconstruction forced Americans to choose between faith in democratic majority rule and self-determination at the ballot box—however distasteful and violent—over the idealism of racial equality, competing forces that would have stunning consequences well into the twentieth and twenty-first centuries.[57]

NOTES

Abbreviations

BL	Bentley Historical Library, Michigan in the Civil War Collections, University of Michigan, Ann Arbor, Michigan
BME	Berlin, Ira, et al., eds. *A Documentary History of Emancipation, 1861–1867,* series 2, *The Black Military Experience.* New York: Cambridge University Press, 1985.
CWL	Basler, Roy P., ed. *Collected Works of Abraham Lincoln.* 9 vols. New Brunswick, NJ: Rutgers University Press, 1953–55.
CWLD	The American Civil War: Letters and Diaries (electronic database)
HNOC	Historic New Orleans Collection, Williams Research Center, New Orleans, Louisiana
JLNC	John L. Nau III Civil War Collection, Houston, Texas
LLMVC, LSU	Louisiana and Lower Mississippi Valley Collections, Hill Memorial Library, Louisiana State University
LOC	Library of Congress, Washington, DC
NARA	National Archives and Records Administration, Washington, DC
NMSUS	*The Negro in the Military Service of the United States, 1639–1886.* 5 microfilm reels. RG 94, National Archives and Records Administration
NYHS	New York Historical Society, Patricia D. Klingenstein Library, New York, New York
OR	War Department. *The War of the Rebellion: A Compilation of the Official Records of the Union and Confederate Armies.* 128 vols. Washington, DC: Government Printing Office, 1880–1901.
PAJ	Graf, LeRoy P., and Ralph W. Haskins, eds. *The Papers of Andrew Johnson.* 16 vols. Knoxville: University of Tennessee Press, 1967–2000.
PJD	Crist, Lynda L., et al., eds. *The Papers of Jefferson Davis.* 14 vols. Baton Rouge: Louisiana State University Press, 1971–2015.
PUSG	Simon, John Y., et al., eds. *The Papers of Ulysses S. Grant.* 32 vols. Carbondale: Southern Illinois University Press, 1967–present.
SCWC	James S. Schoff Civil War Collection, William L. Clements Library, University of Michigan, Ann Arbor, Michigan
SOR	*Supplement to the Official Records of the Union and Confederate Armies.* 100 vols. Wilmington, NC: Broadfoot Publishing Co., 1997–2001.
UA	University of Arkansas, Special Collections, David W. Mullins Library
UNC	Southern Historical Collection, Louis Wilson Round Special Collections Library, University of North Carolina, Chapel Hill

USAMHI   United States Army Military Heritage Institute, Carlisle Barracks, Carlisle,
         Pennsylvania
              CWMC (Civil War Miscellaneous Collection)
              CWTC (Civil War Times Collection)
              HCWRC (Harrisburg Civil War Roundtable Collection)
              SAWVC (Spanish American War Veterans Collection)
USCT   United States Colored Troops
VHS   Virginia Historical Society, Richmond, Virginia

Introduction | The Republican Tradition, Military Occupation, and Civil War History

1. *New York Herald,* June 30, 1846, quoted in Johannsen, *To the Halls of the Montezumas,* 48–49; James K. Polk, "First Annual Message to Congress," December 2, 1845, in Richardson, *Compilation of Messages and Papers of the Presidents,* vol. 4, pt. 3, pp. 405–13; Winders, *Mr. Polk's Army,* 70–72.

2. George L. Gaskell to Dearest Sister, March 10, 1862, Gaskell Papers, SAWVC, USAMHI; Fahs, *Imagined Civil War,* 61–92; Neely and Holzer, *Union Image,* 23–107; Higginbotham, "Martial Spirit in the Antebellum South," 3–26; Cunliffe, *Soldiers and Civilians,* 65–98; Gallagher, *Union War,* 3, 26–27, 54–71; McPherson, *For Cause and Comrades,* 18–21, 22–28, 35–36.

3. Henry Wilson Hubbell to My Dear Mother, May 1, 1861, Hubbell Papers, NYHS; Joseph F. Field to My Own Dear Kittie, October 5, 1862, Field Papers, SCWC; McPherson, *Battle Cry of Freedom,* 332–33; McPherson, *For Cause and Comrades,* 30–36; Mitchell, *Civil War Soldiers,* 1–23; Gallagher, *Union War,* 1–2, 33–36, 50–51, 53–54, 60, 66–67, 72–78, 104–9, 116–17; Hess, *Liberty, Virtue, and Progress,* 4–17.

4. Wood, *Radicalism of the American Revolution,* 8, 169, 233, 187–98, 253–54, 296, 322; Gallagher, *Union War,* 3–4, 6, 36–37, 45, 52, 62, 70, 73.

5. Pocock, *Machiavellian Moment,* 506–52; Bailyn, *Ideological Origins of the American Revolution,* 61–63, 281–84; Wood, *Radicalism of the American Revolution,* 215–20; Cunliffe, *Soldiers and Civilians,* 29–62; Bledsoe, *Citizen-Officers,* 1–6; Herrera, *For Liberty and the Republic,* 1–26.

6. Wood, *Radicalism of the American Revolution,* 215–20; Snyder, *Citizen-Soldiers and Manly Warriors,* 1–13; Bailyn, *Ideological Origins,* 301–19; Herrera, "Self-Governance and the American Citizen as Soldier," 21–52; Bledsoe, *Citizen-Officers,* xiii, 1–26, 55–56, 60–61.

7. Snyder, *Citizen-Soldiers and Manly Warriors,* 3 [quotations], 1–12, 79–101.

8. Bledsoe, *Citizen-Officers,* 1–24; Herrera, "Self-Governance and the American Citizen as Soldier," 21–52; Herrera, *For Liberty and the Republic,* 1–26; Hsieh, *West Pointers and the Civil War,* 1–33.

9. Herrera, "Self-Governance and the American Citizen as Soldier," 21–52; Higginbotham, *George Washington and the American Military Tradition;* Huntington, *Soldier and the State,* 203–4; Coffman, "Duality of the American Military Tradition," 973, 967–80; Cunliffe, *Soldiers and Civilians,* 53–54; Higginbotham, "Martial Spirit in the Antebellum South," 3–26; Laver, *Citizens More than Soldiers,* 67–69, 98–99, 139–42.

10. Adams quoted in Kohn, *Eagle and Sword,* 2; Coffman, *Old Army,* 3–41; Skelton, *American Profession of Arms,* 3–105; Bailyn, *Ideological Origins,* 36, 61–63, 112–19; Archer, *As if an Enemy's Country,* 123–43.

11. Royster, *Revolutionary People at War,* 35–43, 63–69, 73–74, 133–34; 260–66, 321–27, 338–40, 345–51, 354–60; Kohn, *Eagle and Sword,* 2–6, 9, 13, 37, 88, 127, 278, 282–83, 286; Cunliffe, *Soldiers and*

Civilians, 45–50; Coffman, *Old Army,* 38; Skelton, *American Profession of Arms,* xv, 1–86; Herrera, *For Liberty and the Republic,* 1–26; Hsieh, *West Pointers and the Civil War,* 1–33.

12. Kohn, *Eagle and Sword,* 2–6, 87–88, 272–73, 282–86; Bailyn, *Ideological Origins,* 62–65; Herrera, "Self-Governance and the American Citizen as Soldier," 21–52.

13. Herrera, *For Liberty and the Republic,* 17; Cunliffe, *Soldiers and Civilians,* 99–144; Hsieh, *West Pointers and the Civil War,* 1–53, 75–90; Coffman, *Old Army,* 137–38; Prucha, *Sword of the Republic;* Watson, *Jackson's Sword* and *Peacekeepers and Conquerors.*

14. Coffman, *Old Army,* 67, 81–82; Skelton, *American Profession of Arms,* 187, 184–90, 260–81.

15. Edmund Kirby Smith quoted in Skelton, *American Profession of Arms,* 187, 184–90, 260–81.

16. The phrase "dawning age of American wars of occupation" is used to show how white, nineteenth-century Americans interpreted the Mexican-American War, Civil War, and Reconstruction. The US Army had rarely ever been employed in similar and formal wartime military occupations before 1846. See, for example, Hsieh, *West Pointers and the Civil War,* 94–95. Native American lands and peoples, of course, had been occupied for centuries prior to the conflict with Mexico, oftentimes at the point of the bayonet, which justly complicates the historical narrative of American military occupations. Time, space, and interpretive focus, however, preclude a comprehensive treatment of this important literature. See Jennings, *Invasion of America;* Hietala, *Manifest Design;* Limerick, *Legacy of Conquest;* West, *Contested Plains;* Kelman, *Misplaced Massacre;* Osterhammel, *Transformation of the World,* 449–50. For interpretations about the formative aspects of US military government policy, see Justin Smith, "American Rule in Mexico," 287–302; Gabriel, "American Experience with Military Government," 630–43. Brody, *Visualizing American Empire;* Hoganson, *Fighting for American Manhood;* Hofstadter, "Cuba, the Philippines, and Manifest Destiny," 145–87; Renda, *Taking Haiti.*

17. Johannsen, *To the Halls of the Montezumas;* McCaffrey, *Army of Manifest Destiny;* Winders, *Mr. Polk's Army;* Foos, *Short, Offhand, Killing Affair;* Ash, *When the Yankees Came;* Blair, *With Malice toward Some;* Grimsley, *Hard Hand of War;* Browning, *Shifting Loyalties;* Danielson, *War's Desolating Scourge;* Smith, *Corinth, 1862;* Capers, *Occupied City;* Hearn, *When the Devil Came Down to Dixie;* Pierson, *Mutiny at Fort Jackson;* Maslowski, *Treason Must Be Made Odious;* Durham, *Nashville;* Durham, *Reluctant Partners;* Campbell, *When Sherman Marched North from the Sea;* Frank, *Civilian War;* Hess, *Civil War in the West;* Durrill, *War of Another Kind;* Fellman, *Inside War;* Sutherland, *Savage Conflict;* Downs, *After Appomattox.* For a study that directly engages the experiences of occupying Union soldiers, see Browning, "'I Am Not So Patriotic as I Was Once,'" 217–43, which adopts a local approach, focusing on the wartime occupations of Beaufort, and New Bern, North Carolina; Sheehan-Dean, "Long Civil War," 106–53. See also Frank, *With Ballot and Bayonet,* 18–39, 84–118.

18. For studies that have shaped the current field on Civil War soldiers, see Wiley, *Life of Johnny Reb;* Wiley, *Life of Billy of Yank;* Glatthaar, *March to the Sea and Beyond;* Barton, *Goodmen;* Mitchell, *Civil War Soldiers;* Linderman, *Embattled Courage;* Beringer et al., *Why the South Lost the Civil War;* McPherson, *What They Fought For,* and *For Cause and Comrades;* Hess, *Union Soldier in Battle;* Frank, *With Ballot and Bayonet;* Gallagher, *Confederate War;* Power, *Lee's Miserables;* Carmichael, *Last Generation;* Phillips, *Diehard Rebels;* Sheehan-Dean, *Why Confederates Fought;* Manning, *What This Cruel War Was Over;* Glatthaar, *General Lee's Army;* Noe, *Reluctant Rebels;* Clampitt, *Confederate Heartland;* Woodworth, *Nothing But Victory;* Foote, *Gentlemen and the Roughs;* Mitchell, *The Vacant Chair;* Gallagher, *Union War;* Ramold, *Across the Divide;* Bledsoe, *Citizen-Officers.*

19. This study reflects what Wayne E. Lee calls "the cultural analysis of war." Responses to armed conflict are based on how a particular culture understands war, the purpose of armies, the expectations of citizen-soldiers, and the scope of victory and defeat. Wars are thus not conducted by a universal set of principles to which all participants subscribe. Instead, individual societies wage war according to

their own established cultural ideals (Lee, "Mind and Matter," 1116–42). Phillips, *Diehard Rebels,* 2; Shy, "Cultural Approach to the History of War," 13–26; Lynn, "Embattled Future of Academic Military History," 777–89; Citino, "Military Histories Old and New," 1070–90; Grimsley, "Success and Failure in Civil War Armies," 115–41; Herrera, *For Liberty and the Republic,* 9–10. On the positioning of Civil War military history, see Vinovskis, "Have Social Historians Lost the Civil War?" 34–58; Glatthaar, "The 'New' Civil War History," 339–69; Gallagher and Meier, "Coming to Terms with Civil War Military History," 487–508; Hess, "Where Do We Stand?" 371–403.

20. Herrera, *For Liberty and the Republic,* 24 [quotation], 1–26, and "Self-Governance and the American Citizen as Soldier," 21–52, esp. 23; Gallagher and Meier, "Coming to Terms with Civil War Military History," 498–99. For scholarly challenges to republicanism as an analytical category, see Rodgers, "Republicanism," 11–38. Appleby, "Republicanism and Ideology," 461–73, "Republicanism in Old and New Contexts," 20–34, and *Liberalism and Republicanism in the Historical Imagination;* Smith, *Enemy Within,* 1–12; Berthoff, "From Republican Citizen to Free Enterprise," 131–54. For recent studies on the Civil War era that employ the republican paradigm, see Bledsoe, *Citizen-Officers;* Gallagher, *Union War;* Lang, "Republicanism, Race, and Reconstruction," 559–89; Smith, *Enemy Within;* Slap, *Doom of Reconstruction;* Summers, *Ordeal of the Reunion.*

21. Ash, *When the Yankees Came,* 77.

22. Browning, "'I Am Not So Patriotic as I Was Once,'" 217–43.

23. Johannsen, *To the Halls of the Montezumas,* 22–23, 167, 260, 264–65, 268, 278, 289–93; Foos, *Short, Offhand, Killing Affair,* 113–14, 129–30, 144–46; Neely, *Civil War and the Limits of Destruction,* 6–40; Winders, *Mr. Polk's Army,* 66–87; Levinson, *Wars within War.*

24. Warner, "Morale of Troops on Occupation Duty," 749–57; Browning, "'I Am Not So Patriotic as I Was Once,'" 217–43; Ash, *When the Yankees Came,* 24–27; Grimsley, *Hard Hand of War,* 1–66; Smith, *Enemy Within;* Frank, *With Ballot and Bayonet,* 83; Beringer et al., *Why the South Lost the Civil War,* 310. See chaps. 2, 8, and 9 for extended discussions of numbers.

25. Snyder, *Citizen-Soldiers and Manly Warriors,* 9.

26. *Statutes at Large,* 12:1269. Of the 166 USCT regiments, more than 100 (64 percent) performed exclusive garrison duty (Fox, *Regimental Losses in the American Civil War,* 17–22, 53; Gallagher, *Union War,* 92). On "garrisoning," I adopt the argument made in Freehling, *South vs. the South,* 119–20. Hahn, *Nation under Our Feet,* 91–102, 132–33, 265–313; Astor, *Rebels on the Border,* 121–67; Emberton, *Beyond Redemption,* 102–35. For major studies on African American soldiers during the Civil War, see Cornish, *Sable Arm;* McPherson, *Negro's Civil War;* Litwack, *Been in the Storm So Long;* Berlin et al., eds., *BME;* Glatthaar, *Forged in Battle;* Hollandsworth, *Louisiana Native Guards;* Trudeau, *Like Men of War;* John David Smith, ed., *Black Soldiers in Blue;* Wilson, *Campfires of Freedom;* Emberton, "'Only Murder Makes Men'"; Ash, *Firebrand of Liberty;* Dobak, *Freedom by the Sword;* Oakes, *Freedom National.*

27. Snyder, *Citizen-Soldiers and Manly Warriors,* 3 [quotation], 9, 85–92, 96.

28. For similar interpretations, see Hahn, *Nation under Our Feet,* 89–102; and Downs, *After Appomattox,* 1–10, 39–40, 44–46, 49–55, 58–60, 121–25.

29. For treatments of the military's role during Reconstruction, see Pfanz, "Soldiering in the South during the Reconstruction Period"; Sefton, *United States Army and Reconstruction;* Dawson, *Army Generals and Reconstruction;* Richter, *Army in Texas during Reconstruction;* Rable, *But There Was No Peace;* Zuczek, *State of Rebellion;* Bensel, *Yankee Leviathan;* Hogue, *Uncivil War;* Blair, "Use of Military Force to Protect the Gains of Reconstruction," 388–402; Downs, *After Appomattox;* Lang, "Republicanism, Race, and Reconstruction," 559–89; Summers, *Ordeal of the Reunion.*

30. Many Union soldiers cited in this study served in occupation and/or garrison capacities for at least one month, and in many cases much longer. Dyer's *Compendium,* the soldiers' writings,

manuscript-finding aids, regimental histories, and government documents provided the necessary information to determine the length of time spent on occupation duty.

1 | Conflicting Cultures and the Mexican-American War

1. Winders, *Mr. Polk's Army,* 66–87. This chapter owes intellectual and interpretive debts to Neely, *Civil War and the Limits of Destruction;* Foos, *Short, Offhand, Killing Affair;* and Winders, *Mr. Polk's Army,* which were also used to locate myriad published primary sources.

2. Johannsen, *To the Halls of the Montezumas,* 45–107; McCaffrey, *Army of Manifest Destiny;* Winders, *Mr. Polk's Army;* Foos, *Short, Offhand, Killing Affair,* 32; Guardino, "Gender, Soldiering, and Citizenship in the Mexican-American War of 1846–1848," 23–46.

3. Winders, *Mr. Polk's Army,* 70–71.

4. Johannsen, *To the Halls of the Montezumas,* 22–23, 167, 260, 264–65, 268, 278, 289–93; Foos, *Short, Offhand, Killing Affair,* 113–14, 129–30, 144–46; Neely, *Civil War and the Limits of Destruction,* 6–40.

5. Smith, "American Rule in Mexico," 287–302; Gabriel, "American Experience with Military Government," 630–43.

6. Hietala, *Manifest Design,* 173–214.

7. Diary entry, November 4, 1846, in Pace, ed., "Diary and Letters of William P. Rogers," 268; Foos, *Short, Offhand, Killing Affair,* 113–14, 129–30, 144–46; Johannsen, *To the Halls of the Montezumas,* 21–23.

8. Bauer, *Mexican War;* Wheelan, *Invading Mexico;* Henderson, *Glorious Defeat.*

9. Gabriel, "American Experience with Military Government," 630–43, esp. 631–33.

10. Johannsen, *To the Halls of the Montezumas,* 30–44; Foos, *Short, Offhand, Killing Affair,* 113–14; Smith, "American Rule in Mexico," 287–302, 293–94.

11. Johnson, *Winfield Scott,* 149–207; Peskin, *Winfield Scott and the Profession of Arms,* 132–93.

12. Scott, *Memoirs of Lieut.-General Scott,* 2:404; Johnson, *Winfield Scott,* 166–67; Weigley, *American Way of War,* 71–76.

13. Scott, *Memoirs,* 2:404; Johnson, *Winfield Scott,* 166–67; Weigley, *American Way of War,* 71–76.

14. Scott, *Memoirs,* 2:392–96; Gabriel, "American Experience with Military Government," 634–35; Levinson, "Occupation and Stability Dilemmas of the Mexican War," 6.

15. Upton, *Military Policy of the United States,* 210; Peskin, *Winfield Scott,* 159.

16. George G. Meade to Wife, October 27, 1846, in Meade, *Life and Letters of George Gordon Meade,* 1:148–49 [quotations]; Herrera, "Self-Governance and the American Citizen as Soldier," 37–38.

17. George G. Meade to Wife, May 27, 1846, in Meade, *Life and Letters,* 1:91 [quotations], 92, 94–95, 108, 152.

18. For studies of American perceptions of Mexico, Manifest Destiny, and race, see Hietala, *Manifest Design,* 1–9, 83–86, 152–66, 204–7, 239–40, 239–40; and Foos, *Short, Offhand, Killing Affair.*

19. Curtis diary entry, August 13, 1846, in Chance, ed. *Mexico under Fire,* 25; McCaffrey, *Army of Manifest Destiny,* 66–79. See also Neely, *Civil War and the Limits of Destruction,* ch. 1.

20. Hill diary entry, October 17, 1847, in Hughes and Johnson, eds., *Fighter from Way Back,* 137; Neely, *Civil War and the Limits of Destruction,* 12–40.

21. Tennery diary entry, November 21, 1846, in Livingston-Little, ed., *Mexican War Diary of Thomas D. Tennery,* 37–38.

22. Neely, *Civil War and the Limits of Destruction,* 28.

23. Levinson, "Occupation and Stability Dilemmas of the Mexican War," 1.

24. Zachary Taylor to Jefferson Davis, July 27, 1847, *PJD*, 3:203; Johannsen, *To the Halls of the Montezumas*, 36–38 [quotation, p. 36]; Henry Moses Judah diary entry, [June] 16, 1847, in Smith and Judah, eds., *Chronicles of the Gringos*, 400–3; Neely, *Civil War and the Limits of Destruction*, 88–89; Foos, *Short, Offhand, Killing Affair*, 110–37; Witt, *Lincoln's Code*, 117–30.

25. *House Exec. Docs.* #60, 30th Congress, 1st Session, 1847–49, p. 971; Levinson, *Wars within War*, 60–70; Smith, "American Rule in Mexico," 289–91; Coffman, "Duality of the American Military Tradition," 970–71; Kwasny, *Washington's Partisan War*, 273; Birtle, *U.S. Army Counterinsurgency and Contingency Operations Doctrine*, 16–17; Levinson, "Occupation Stability Dilemmas of the Mexican War," 1–10.

26. Letter extract, June 25, 1847, in Henshaw, *Recollections of the War with Mexico*, Kurutz, ed., 150; Johnson, *Gallant Little Army*, 116–18, 138–42, 147–48, 248–48, 251–53.

27. Thomas Barclay diary entry, September 14, 1847, in Peskin, ed., *Volunteers*, 181 [quotations], 180–86.

28. Ibid.

29. Donnavan, *Adventures in Mexico*, 24; Foos, *Short, Offhand, Killing Affair*, 142.

30. J. Jacob Oswandel, Diary entry, April 13, 1848, in Oswandel, *Notes on the Mexican War*, 529; Foos, *Short, Offhand, Killing Affair*, 113–14; Smith, "American Rule in Mexico," 289–91; Levinson, *Wars within War*, 61–70; McCaffrey, *Army of Manifest Destiny*, 127–28; Watson, *War on the Mind*, 244–45.

31. Foos, Short, *Offhand, Killing Affair*, 119–27; McCaffrey, *Army of Manifest Destiny*, 127–28.

32. Skelton, *American Profession of Arms*, 132, 252, 255–56, 318–25, 345–47; Hsieh, *West Pointers and the Civil War*, 1–74.

33. Ulysses S. Grant to Julia Dent, July 25, 1846, *PUSG*, 1:102.

34. Watson, "Manifest Destiny and Military Professionalism," 467–98; Hsieh, *West Pointers and the Civil War*, 54–74; Bledsoe, "Citizen-Officers," 43.

35. Winders, *Mr. Polk's Army*, 50–87.

36. Thomas Thorpe letter, September 28, 1846, in Thorpe, *Our Army at Monterey*, 120–21; Elliott, *Winfield Scott*, 448.

37. Diary entry, October 7, 1846, in Pace, ed., "Diary and Letters of William P. Rogers," 265; Meade, *Life and Letters*, 1:91–92, 108, 139, 162; Hughes and Johnson, eds., *Fighter from Way Back*, 43, 127–28, 132–33, 151; Cutrer, ed., *Mexican War Diary and Correspondence of George B. McClellan*, 38–39, 51–60, 119–21, 143–37; Skelton, *American Profession of Arms*, 132, 252, 255–56, 318–25, 345–47.

38. Winders, *Mr. Polk's Army*, 84–85.

39. Ibid., 81–87, 199–201.

40. Thomas Barclay diary entry, November 26, 1847, in Peskin, ed., *Volunteers*, 216; Diary entry, December 23–25, in Barringer, ed., "Mexican War Journal of Henry S. Lane," 408; Winders, *Mr. Polk's Army*, 198–99; Isaac Smith, *Reminiscences of a Campaign in Mexico*, 8–9, 93–95.

41. Franklin Smith diary entry, October 14, 1846, in Chance, ed., *Mexican War Journal of Captain Franklin Smith*, 48.

42. Diary entries, James Coulter diary, September 21, 1847, and Thomas Barclay diary, October 26, 1847, both in Peskin, ed., *Volunteers*, 192, 203.

43. Skelton, *American Profession of Arms*, 266.

44. Johnson, *Winfield Scott*, 192–93.

45. J. B. Duncan to Wife, April 23, 1847, in Henderson, ed., "Morgan County Volunteer in the Mexican War," 400.

46. Curtis diary entry, August 4, 1846, in Chance, ed., *Mexico under Fire*, 22. See also Gardner and

Simmons, eds., *Mexican War Correspondence of Richard Smith Elliott*, 186; George G. Meade to Wife, June 28, 1846, in Meade, *Life and Letters*, 1:110; Henry, *Campaign Sketches of the War with Mexico*, 124.

47. Foos, *Short, Offhand, Killing Affair*, chap. 5.

48. Ibid., 92; Billings, *Hardtack and Coffee*, 150.

49. Thomas Barclay diary entry, May 19, 1847, in Peskin, ed., *Volunteers*, 97; Neely, *Civil War and the Limits of Destruction*, 21.

50. McCaffrey, *Army of Manifest Destiny*, 127–28; Watson, *War on the Mind*, 118, 243–44; Warner, "Morale of Troops on Occupation Duty," 749–57.

51. Cooper, *Jefferson Davis*, 178–80.

52. "Remarks on the Ten Regiment Bill," January 3, 5, 1848, *PJD*, 3:255, 258.

53. Ibid., January 5, 1848, *PJD*, 3:258–59.

54. Ibid., 3:259.

55. Porter, *Review of the Mexican War*, 162–63, 175 [quotations], 161–84.

2 | Policy, Process, and the Landscape of Union Occupation during the Civil War

1. Gabriel, "American Experience with Military Government," 630–43, 637–38; Grimsley, *Hard Hand of War*, 1–66; Ash, *When the Yankees Came*, 1–75; Nelson and Sheriff, *People at War*, 85–104.

2. Gabriel, "American Experience with Military Government," 630–43, 637–38; Grimsley, *Hard Hand of War*, 1–66; Ash, *When the Yankees Came*, 1–75; Nelson and Sheriff, *People at War*, 85–104. For regional studies of wartime occupation, see Capers, *Occupied City*; Maslowski, *Treason Must Be Made Odious*; Durham, *Nashville, The Occupied City*, and *Reluctant Partners: Nashville and the Union*; Hearn, *When the Devil Came Down to Dixie*; Wills, *War Hits Home*; Pierson, *Mutiny at Fort Jackson*; Browning, *Shifting Loyalties*; Danielson, *War's Desolating Scourge*; Smith, *Corinth, 1862*; Clampitt, *Occupied Vicksburg*; Dilbeck, *More Civil War*. This chapter adopts the evolution of limited war to hard war outlined in Grimsley, *Hard Hand of War*; and Ash, *When the Yankees Came*.

3. Dew, *Apostles of Disunion*, 4–21, 74–82; Freehling, *Road to Disunion, Volume II*, 343–534; McClintock, *Lincoln and the Decision for War*, 50–51, 90–95, 124–25, 17–72, 187–90, 195–99, 241–51; Ash, *When the Yankees Came*, 13–37.

4. Ash, *When the Yankees Came*, 13–37; Grimsley, *Hard Hand of War*, 2–3, 23–35, 47–48, 54–66, 67–68, 75–80, 92–101; Hess, *Liberty, Virtue, and Progress*, 1–17, 23–30, 56–61; Paludan, *"A People's Contest,"* 1–14, 93–94, 224–25, 378, 381–82; Gallagher, *Union War*, 36–37, 45, 62, 70–118.

5. Abraham Lincoln, "Annual Message to Congress," December 3, 1861, *CWL*, 5:48–49; McClintock, *Lincoln and the Decision for War*, 149, 172–73, 181–82, 187–89, 205, 239, 247–52, 275; Ash, *When the Yankees Came*, 13–37, esp. 26; Grimsley, *Hard Hand of War*, 23–66; Danielson, *War's Desolating Scourge*, 33–35.

6. General Orders, No. 2, May 28, 1861, *OR*, ser. 1, vol. 2, p. 664; Irvin McDowell to E. D. Townsend, June 4, 1861, *OR*, vol. 2, pp. 664–65; General Orders, No. 13a, February 26, 1862, *OR*, ser. 1, vol. 7, pp. 669–70; Danielson, *War's Desolating Scourge*, 33–34; Ash, *When the Yankees Came*, 26–27.

7. Burnside, "Proclamation made to the People of North Carolina," February 16, 1862, *OR*, 9:363–64; Browning, *Shifting Loyalties*, 55–80; Durham, *Nashville*, 43–70; Danielson, *War's Desolating Scourge*, 34, 44–45; Ash, *When the Yankees Came*, 28.

8. Gallagher, *Confederate War*, 5–8, 63, 73, 75–80; Blair, *Virginia's Private War*, 9, 56, 77–80, 143; Campbell, *When Sherman Marched North from the Sea*, 71–74; Rubin, *Shattered Nation*, 1, 50–52, 84–85; Danielson, *War's Desolating Scourge*, 25–64; Ash, *When the Yankees Came*, 41–45; Grimsley, *Hard*

Hand of War, 67–95; Rable, *Civil Wars,* 154–80; Whites, *Civil War as a Crisis in Gender,* 101–5, 127, 148–49, 169–70; Faust, *Mothers of Invention,* 196–219; Ott, *Confederate Daughters,* 57–61; McCurry, *Confederate Reckoning,* 104–18.

9. Quotations in Staudenraus, "Occupied Beaufort, 1863," 140; Grimsley, *Hard Hand of War,* 31–35, 55–56, 67–68, 71–74; 98–105; Gallagher, *Union War,* 50–53.

10. Oakes, *Freedom National,* 87–90, 93, 95–96, 97–99, 172–74, 190–96, 252, 319–21.

11. McPherson, *Battle Cry of Freedom,* 355–56; Oakes, *Freedom National,* 93–99, 101–8; Berlin et al., eds., *Destruction of Slavery,* ser. 1 in *Freedom,* 1:70–75.

12. First Confiscation Act, August 6, 1861, *Statutes at Large,* 12:319; Second Confiscation Act, July 17, 1862, *Statutes at Large,* 12:568–92; *OR,* Series 3, 2:280–82 [Militia Act]; Oakes, *Freedom National,* 225, 248–54, 317, 321–24; Siddali, *From Property to Person;* Berlin, et al., eds., *Wartime Genesis of Free Labor,* ser. 1 in *Freedom,* 3:77–80.

13. *Statutes at Large,* 12:1269; Gallagher, *Union War,* 150 [quotation], 88–92, 141–50; Neely, "Lincoln and Theory of Self-Emancipation," 51, 45–60; McPherson, "Who Freed the Slaves?" 1–10; Grimsley, *Hard Hand of War,* 120–41; Oakes, *Freedom National,* 301–92. Brasher, *Peninsula Campaign,* demonstrates the relationships between the Union army and enslaved activism in shaping emancipation.

14. George B. McClellan to Abraham Lincoln, July 7, 1862, *OR,* ser. 1, vol. 11, pt. 1, pp. 73–74; Grimsley, *Hard Hand of War,* 31–35; Hattaway and Jones, *How the North Won,* 489–93; Stoker, *Grand Design,* 69–92, 107–18, 119–138, 346, 374, 384, 390, 411.

15. Ash, *When the Yankees Came,* 76–92; Hattaway and Jones, *How the North Won,* 489–93.

16. Ash, *When the Yankees Came,* 108–20, and *Middle Tennessee Society Transformed, 1860–1870;* Taylor, *Louisiana Reconstructed,* 13–52.

17. Ash, *When the Yankees Came,* 76–107.

18. Winfield Scott to William H. Seward, March 3, 1861, in Scott, *Memoirs of Lieut.-General Scott,* 2:627.

19. Kohn, *Eagle and Sword,* 2–6, 87–88, 272–73, 282–86; Bailyn, *Ideological Origins,* 62–65; Herrera, "Self-Governance and the American Citizen as Soldier," 21–52; Wood, *Empire of Liberty,* 7, 111, 149, 172.

20. Hattaway and Jones, *How the North Won,* 493–94.

21. William T. Sherman to Ellen Sherman, June 10, 1862, and Sherman to John Sherman, August 13, 1862, both in Simpson and Berlin, eds., *Sherman's Civil War,* 246, 273. See also Sherman to Henry W. Halleck, December 26, 1863, *OR,* vol. 31, pt. 3, pp. 497–98; Hess, *Civil War in the West,* 69–70.

22. Hattaway and Jones, *Why the North Won,* 489–96; Grimsley, *Hard Hand of War,* 162–70.

23. Hattaway and Jones, *Why the North Won,* 489–96; Grimsley, *Hard Hand of War,* 162–70; Ash, *When the Yankees Came,* 76–107.

24. The Twelfth Connecticut was the first regiment to land at New Orleans, on May 1, 1862, where it remained until October. The regiment then participated in various occupation duties in southeast Louisiana, expeditions into the Teche country, a foray into Texas, and in the Port Hudson campaign (Dyer, *Compendium,* 3:1012).

25. These figures encompass only soldiers who were considered "present for duty," and exclude those who had deserted, were in hospitals, or generally absent without leave. *OR,* vol. 14, p. 461; vol. 18, p. 733; vol. 22, pt. 2, pp. 299–300; vol. 23, pt. 2, pp. 378–80; vol. 24, pt. 3, pp. 370–71; vol. 25, pt. 2, pp. 320–21, 586–89; vol. 26, pt. 1, pp. 526–28. For similar returns and percentages from 1864, see *OR,* ser. 3, vol. 5, pp. 136–37, 496–47.

26. Ulysses S. Grant to Julia Dent Grant, March 1, 1862, *PUSG,* 4:305–6; Beringer et al., *Why the South Lost the Civil War,* 310.

27. Glatthaar, *Forged in Battle;* Hollandsworth, *Louisiana Native Guards;* Trudeau, *Like Men of War;* Smith, ed., *Black Soldiers in Blue;* Hahn, *Nation under Our Feet;* Manning, *What This Cruel War Was Over;* Dobak, *Freedom by the Sword;* Oakes, *Freedom National.*

28. Sherman, *Memoirs,* 2:15; *OR,* vol. 38, pt. 1, p. 115–17; and pt. 4, pp. 16–19, 359–62, 373–76; Weigley, *American Way of War,* 130.

29. Grant, *Personal Memoirs,* 563–64; Weigley, *American Way of War,* 131; Hess, *Civil War in the West,* 208–12, 217–20.

30. Weigley, *American Way of War,* 132; Hattaway and Jones, *How the North Won,* 685–88.

31. Gallagher, *Confederate War,* 17–59; Blair, *Virginia's Private War,* 6–7, 19–21, 52–56, 76–80, 131–32, 140–50; Rubin, *Shattered Nation,* 86–111; Campbell, *When Sherman Marched North from the Sea,* 71–74; Phillips, *Diehard Rebels,* 2–4, 25–26, 41–46, 53–60, 77, 80. Mark Grimsley defines "hard war" as "the erosion of the enemy's will to resist by deliberately or concomitantly subjecting the civilian population to the pressures of war" (Grimsley, *Hard Hand of War,* 5).

32. Futrell, "Federal Military Government in the South," 181–91; Nelson and Sheriff, *People at War,* 87; Ash, *When the Yankees Came,* 56–60, 76–92.

33. Grant to Henry W. Halleck, June, 24, 1862, *PUSG,* 5:149–52 (quotation, p. 149); Ash, *When the Yankees Came,* 56–61; Dilbeck, *More Civil War,* 41–68.

34. Ash, *When the Yankees Came,* 56–57; Freidel, "General Orders 100 and Military Government," 541–56; Grimsley, *Hard Hand of War,* 149–51, 178–79; Witt, *Lincoln's Code,* 109–219; "General Orders No. 100," *OR,* ser. 3, vol. 3, pp. 148–64; Dilbeck, *More Civil War,* 69–98.

35. "Proclamation," August 30, 1861, *OR,* vol. 3, pp. 466–67; McPherson, *Battle Cry of Freedom,* 352, 499; Capers, *Occupied City,* 48–49, 60; Hearn, *When the Devil Came Down to Dixie,* 134–38; Ash, *When the Yankees Came,* 57–60.

36. Circular, No. 3, Department and Army of the Tennessee," April 29, 1864, *OR,* vol. 32, pt. 3, pp. 538; "Police Regulations for the Army of the District of Arkansas," Headquarters, Provost Marshal General's Office, Helena, Arkansas, December 14, 1862, UA; Hess, *Civil War in the West,* 63; Blair, *With Malice toward Some,* 5–6, 100–101, 104–14, 123–28, 137–40, 143–46.

37. William H. Whitney to Dear Frank, August 30, 1863, in Laver, ed., "Where Duty Shall Call," 345.

38. Blake diary entry, February 20, 1862, Blake Diary, HNOC; Elihu P. Chadwick diary entry, August 20, 1864, Chadwick Papers, BL; Steers, ed., "Garrison Duty in Alexandria," 104–17.

39. Charles Francis Adams to Mother, May 12, 1861, in Ford, ed., *Cycle of Adams Letters,* 1:3–4.

40. Ash, *When the Yankees Came,* 92–107.

41. Ibid.; Hess, *Civil War in the West,* 62–70.

42. "No-man's-land" is adopted from Ash, *When the Yankees Came,* 99–107.

43. General Orders No. 19, Department of the Cumberland, November 19, 1862, *OR,* ser. 2, vol. 4, p. 737.

44. Grimsley, *Hard Hand of War,* 143.

45. Sherman to Grant, October 4, 1862, *OR,* vol. 17, pt. 2, p. 261 (first quotation); Sherman to Halleck, December 24, 1864, *OR,* vol. 44, p. 799; Grimsley, *Hard Hand of War,* 172–75; Royster, *Destructive War,* 89, 95, 106–7, 110, 117, 270–71, 352–56; Marszalek, *Sherman,* 293–96.

46. Grimsley, *Hard Hand of War,* 205–15.

47. Neely, "Was the Civil War a Total War?" 5–28; Grimsley, *Hard Hand of War;* Neely, *Civil War and the Limits of Destruction;* Hsieh, "Total War and the American Civil War Reconsidered," 393–408.

48. Rose, *Rehearsal for Reconstruction,* 141–168, 199–377; Dawson, *Army Generals and Reconstruction,* 5–45; Tunnell, *Crucible of Reconstruction;* Durham, *Reluctant Partners,* 174–97; Foner, *Reconstruction,* 1–123; Ash, *When the Yankees Came,* 50, 53, 171–76, 181–83, 234.

3 | Union Soldiers and the Symbol of a Standing Army of Occupation

1. Frank H. Peck to My Dear Mother, April 30, 1862 [first quotation], May 1862 [second and third quotations], Montgomery Family Papers, Peck Correspondence, LOC. For an interpretation of the challenges of occupation in New Orleans, see Scott, "'Glory of the City Is Gone,'" 45–69; Pierson, *Mutiny at Fort Jackson;* and Dilbeck, *More Civil War,* 41–55.

2. Peck to Dear David, June 17, 1862 [first quotation], Peck to My Dear Mother, October 20, 1862 [second, third, and fourth quotations], Montgomery Family Papers, Peck Correspondence, LOC.

3. Frank H. Peck to My Dear Mother, October 20, 1862 [first and second quotations], September 22, 1862 [third quotation], Montgomery Family Papers, Peck Correspondence, LOC; Smith, *Gallant Dead,* 358.

4. McPherson, *For Cause and Comrades;* Hess, *Union Soldier in Battle;* Linderman, *Embattled Courage;* Mitchell, *Civil War Soldiers.*

5. Warner, "Morale of Troops on Occupation Duty," 749–57; Browning, "'I Am Not So Patriotic as I Was Once,'" 217–43; Ash, *When the Yankees Came,* 24–27; Grimsley, *Hard Hand of War,* 1–66; Gallagher, *Union War,* 26–27, 64, 120, 124; Lang, "Soldiering on the Texas Coast and the Problem of Confederate Nationalism," 157–82.

6. Frank H. Peck to My Dear David, December 4, 1862, Montgomery Family Papers, Peck Correspondence, LOC.

7. Kohn, *Eagle and Sword,* 2–6, 87–88, 272–73, 282–86; Bailyn, *Ideological Origins,* 62–65; Herrera, "Self-Governance and the American Citizen as Soldier," 21–52.

8. Herrera, "Self-Governance and the American Citizen as Soldier," 21–52; Summers, *Ordeal of the Reunion,* 14, 17.

9. Zenas T. Haines letter, June 1, 1863 in Harris, ed., *"In the Country of the Enemy,"* 180; diary entry, November 28, 1863, in Clark, ed., *Downing's Civil War Diary,* 154. The provost marshal and subsequent provost guard functioned, in part, as the military police force in occupied towns and cities (Ash, *When the Yankees Came,* 84; Durham, *Nashville,* 239; Blair, *With Malice toward Some,* 5–6, 100–101, 104–14, 120–26).

10. Zenas T. Haines letter, June 1, 1863, in Harris, ed. *"In the Country of the Enemy,"* 180; diary entry, January 13, 1864, in Clark, ed., *Downing's Civil War Diary,* 162.

11. Zenas T. Haines letter, May 12, 1863, in Harris, ed. *"In the Country of the Enemy,"* 170; George Henry Bates to Dear Parents, April 8, 1863, Bates Letters, SCWC; George O. Jewett to Dear Deck, December 6, 1862, Jewett Papers, LOC; diary entry, February 18, 1863, in Hosmer, *The Color-Guard,* 74.

12. Ash, *When the Yankees Came,* 25–34.

13. Ibid., 14, 19–20, 42–44, 61–62, 197–202, 218–20; Blair, *With Malice toward Some,* 128–59.

14. William T. Shepherd to Dear Father and Mother, August 9, 1862, in Hackemer, ed., *To Rescue My Native Land,* 210; Rable, *Civil Wars,* 154–80; Whites, *Civil War as a Crisis in Gender,* 101–5, 127, 148–49, 169–70; Faust, *Mothers of Invention,* 196–219; Ott, *Confederate Daughters,* 57–61; McCurry, *Confederate Reckoning,* 104–18; Blair, *With Malice toward Some,* 128–59.

15. John Vreeland to Dear Parents, March 31, 1862, Vreeland-Warden Papers, USAMHI.

16. Henry C. Gilbert to My Dear Wife, April 1, 1864, Gilbert Papers, SCWC; Mitchell, *Vacant Chair,* 92–100.

17. Thomas Williams to Mary Neosho Bailey, June 13, 1862 [first quotation], in Williams, ed., "Letters of General Thomas Williams," 320; Minos Miller to Dear Mother, December 14, 1862 [second quotation], Minos Miller Papers, 1860–1866, UA; Charles G. Blake to My dear Judith, August 8, 1863 [third quotation], DL0603, Blake Letters, JLNC; Thomas N. Stevens to Carrie, June 2, 1863, in Blackburn, ed., *"Dear Carrie...,"* 108.

18. Butler, *Autobiography and Personal Reminiscences,* 417–18; Hearn, *When the Devil Came Down to Dixie,* 101–9, 130–32, 139, 219–20; Long, "(Mis)Remembering General Order No. 28," 17–32; Scott, "'Glory of the City Is Gone,'" 51–52.

19. Victor, ed., *Incidents and Anecdotes of the War,* 395; Thorne, ed., *Civil War Diary of Cyrus F. Boyd,* 97; Mitchell, *Vacant Chair,* 89–114; Royster, *Destructive War,* 86–87; Danielson, *War's Desolating Scourge,* 32, 38, 40–43, 63, 71, 75, 117–18, 157–58.

20. Long, "(Mis)Remembering General Order No. 28," 21; McCurry, *Confederate Reckoning,* 104–16.

21. Charles Francis Adams, Jr., to Charles Francis Adams, Sr., July 16, 1862, in Ford, ed., *Cycle of Adams Letters,* 1:164–65.

22. Thomas Williams to Mary Neosho Bailey, June 16, 1862, in Williams, ed., "Letters of General Thomas Williams," 321.

23. William T. Sherman to Major R. M. Sawyer, January 31, 1864, in Simpson and Berlin, eds., *Sherman's Civil War,* 598; Grimsley, *Hard Hand of War,* 117–18, 171–74, 213.

24. C. M. Duren to Dear Father, February 18, 1864, in Duren, "Occupation of Jacksonville," 267; Clement Abner to Boughton to Friends at Home, November 6, 1863, Boughton Papers, SCWC.

25. George H. Cadman to My dear Wife, June 3, 1863, Cadman Papers, UNC.

26. Ibid.

27. Diary entry, January 10 [first quotation], and January 19, 1863 [second quotation], Millspaugh Diary, BL; George H. Davis to Dear Father and Mother, March 12, 1863, Davis Letters, LLMVC, LSU.

28. Benjamin C. Lincoln to Dear Wife, December 22, 1862, Lincoln Papers, SCWC. See also, D. Leib Ambrose diary entry, December 22, 1862, in Sutherland, ed., *From Shiloh to Savannah,* 89. On "hard war" measures, see Grimsley, *Hard Hand of War,* 3–5, 60–61, 114–17, 142–44, 166–67, 178–79.

29. James W. Denver to My Dear Wife, November 29, 1862, Denver Letter, HCWRC, USAMHI. See also Ulysses S. Grant to Commanding General, Bethel, Tennessee, October 25, 1862, Letter 8, and Ulysses S. Grant to Maj. Genl. McPherson, October 25, 1862, Letter 10, Entry 4709, Department of the Tennessee, 1862–65, Letters Sent, RG 393, NARA; Grimsley, *Hard Hand of War,* 96–98.

30. Samuel Kerr to Dear Malvina, December 24, 1862, DL0522.56, Kerr Letters, JLNC; Gallagher, *Union War,* 67–69; Neely, *Civil War and the Limits of Destruction,* 6–40; Grimsley, *Hard Hand of War,* 222–25.

31. Summers, *Ordeal of the Reunion,* 14.

32. On the scholarly debate about when, how, and why Union soldiers came to support emancipation, see Manning, *What This Cruel War Was Over,* 86–90, 118–19, 121, 150–55, 191–92, 218–19; Gallagher, *Union War,* 40–41, 78–82, 101–10, 112–14, 142–45; Hess, *Liberty, Virtue, and Progress,* 96–102; Mitchell, *Civil War Soldiers,* 117–31; Jimerson, *Private Civil War,* 34–49; McPherson, *For Cause and Comrades,* 118–30; Grimsley, *Hard Hand of War,* 120–41; Ramold, *Across the Divide,* 55–86; Browning, "'I Am Not So Patriotic as I Was Once,'" 223–26; Luebke, "'Equal to Any Minstrel Concert I Ever Attended at Home,'" 509–32. Oakes, *Freedom National,* 143–44, 207–10, 213–14, 327–28, 345–92, 414–15, 419–22, 427–28, 438, 443, 475, 547, and Gallagher, *Union War,* 141–50, offer the best treatments of the Union army's role in "military emancipation."

33. Zenas T. Haines letter, May 23, 1863, in Harris, ed., *"In the Country of the Enemy,"* 174; William H. Root diary entry, May 19, 1863, in Root, ed., "Experiences of a Federal Soldier in Louisiana in 1863," 654; Charles Hill to My Dear Martha, November 5, 1862, Hill Letters, DL0283, JLNC; George W. Whitman to Mother, March 16, 1862, in Loving, ed., *Civil War Letters of George Washington Whitman,* 48; Gallagher, *Union War,* 101–10, 141–50; Ash, *When the Yankees Came,* 149–53.

34. On the loyal citizenry's views on slavery, see Gallagher, *Union War,* 2, 34, 40–46, 62–63, 67–69, 72–73.

35. Mitchell, *Civil War Soldiers,* 117; Andrew H. Minnick to Dear Father & Mother, December 11, 1862, Federal Soldiers' Letters Collection, Unit 3, #03185, UNC; William Thompson Lusk to Elizabeth Freeman Adams Lusk, November 13, 1861, Lusk, *War Letters of William Thompson Lusk,* 101; William H. Nichols, to Dear Friends, May 22, 1864, Nichols Papers, CWMC, USAMHI; Ash, *When the Yankees Came,* 31–33, 94, 101, 153–56.

36. Lawrence Van Alstyne, diary entry, October 19, 1863, Van Alstyne, *Diary of an Enlisted Man,* 197; Edward Lewis Sturtevant to Dear Mary, March 21, 1863, Sturtevant Letters, MSS 390, HNOC. For treatments of Union soldiers' attitudes about emancipation and social change, see Mitchell, *Civil War Soldiers,* 129–31; Browning, "'I am Not So Patriotic as I Was Once,'" 223–26; Ramold, *Across the Divide,* 55–86.

37. Charles Francis Adams Jr. to Henry Brooks Adams, April 6, 1862, in Ford, ed., *Cycle of Adams Letters,* 1:130.

38. Ibid., 1:130–31, 132–33.

39. Browning, "'I Am Not So Patriotic as I Was Once,'" 217–43.

40. Diary entry, July 29, 1862, Beatty, *Citizen-Soldier,* 161.

41. Thompson, *Recollections with the Third Iowa Regiment,* 187.

42. Luther F. Hale to John Sidney Andrews, July 10, 1862, John Sidney Andrews Papers, BL; Linderman, *Embattled Courage,* 11–15; McPherson, *For Cause and Comrades,* 23–25, 77–82, 168–70; Hess, *Union Soldier in Battle,* 73–109.

43. Samuel H. Root to My Affectionate Wife, November 20, 1862, Root Letters, CWMC, USAMHI; Adolphus P. Wolf to Dear Parents, February 9, 1863, Wolf Letters, CWTC, USAMHI; George W. Newcomb to My Dear Wife, November 24, 1862, George W. Newcomb Letters, CWMC, USAMHI.

44. Harrison Soule to Darling Mary, February 22, 1863, Soule Papers, BL; Orrin S. Allen to Dear Frank, January 24, 1863, in Rockwell, trans., "Dear Frank," VHS; Browning, "I Am Not So Patriotic as I Was Once,'" 217–18, 237–43.

45. Charles H. Smith to Dear wife, March 17, 1863, CWMC, USAMHI; Samuel Kerr to Dear Malvina, September 22, 1862, DL0522.44, JLNC; John Sidney Andrews to Dear Laura, March 25, 1862, Andrews Papers, BL. See also Augustus D. Ayling diary entry, May 19, 1863, in Herberger, ed., *Yankee at Arms,* 128.

46. Samuel H. Root to Dear Wife, June 12, 1863, Root Letters, CWMC, USAMHI; John Russell to Dear Sister, December 8, 1862, John Russell Letters, CWTC, USAMHI. See also Thomas N. Stevens to Carrie, June 14, 1863, in Blackburn, ed., *"Dear Carrie . . . ,"* 114.

47. Harry Beard to My Dear Father, November 4, 1864, Beard Family Papers, LOC.

48. Grant, *Personal Memoirs,* 198.

49. De Forest, *Volunteer's Adventures,* 25; King diary entry, February 10, 1863, in Swedburg, ed. *Three Years with the 92d Illinois,* 54.

50. James M. Willet to Dear Helen, November 22, 1862; to Darling Wife, November 30, 1862; and to My darling Wife, November 7, 1864, all in Willet Correspondence, NYHS.

51. Oliver Wilcox Norton to Dear Mother, April 14, 1864, and to Dear Sister L, July 23, 1864, in Norton, *Army Letters,* 210–11 [first two quotations], 219, 221–22 [remaining quotations].

52. Charles Musser to parents, [undated letter, probably February 3], 1863, in Popchuck, ed., *Soldier Boy,* 25.

53. Charles Musser to Sister Hester, April 24, 1863, and to Dear Father, June 12, 1864, in Popchuck, ed., *Soldier Boy,* 47, 135–36.

4 | Informal Economies and the Strains of Republican Disinterestedness

1. Hepworth, *Whip, Hoe, and Sword,* 244.

2. J. H. Wilson to [John A.] Rawlins, September 16, 1863, *OR,* vol. 30, pt. 3, p. 664.

3. Ibid.

4. Hess, *Liberty, Virtue, and Progress,* 9–14, 42–47, 49–54, 64–77.

5. Cunliffe, *Soldiers and Civilians,* 213–86; Royster, *Revolutionary People at War,* 72–73; Anderson, *People's Army,* 44, 48, 124–26, 127–31; Linderman, *Embattled Courage,* 34–60; Skelton, *American Profession of Arms,* 45–46, 149–50, 260–81; McCaffrey, *Army of Manifest Destiny,* 106–28; Winders, *Mr. Polk's Army,* 81, 85–87, 197; Herrera, "Self-Governance and the American Citizen as Soldier," 21–52; Carmichael, *Last Generation,* 149–78; Foote, "Rich Man's War, Rich Man's Fight," 269–287; Laver, *Citizens More than Soldiers,* 103–4; Mitchell, *Vacant Chair,* 12–13, 41–42; Foote, *Gentlemen and the Roughs;* Ramold, *Baring the Iron Hand;* Bledsoe, "Citizen-Officers," 1–54, 117–72.

6. Ultimately, this chapter reveals a wartime extension of the so-called "market revolution." Sellers, *Market Revolution,* 245–46, 250–52, 257–58, 268–73, 281; Rotundo, *American Manhood,* 10–30, 279–83; Bruegel, *Farm, Shop, Landing,* 1–12, 13–14, 32–34, 66–72, 187–215; Lamoreaux, "Rethinking the Transition to Capitalism in the Early American Northeast," 437–61; Luskey, *On the Make;* Howe, *What Hath God Wrought,* 35; Feller, "The Market Revolution Ate My Homework," 408–15; Currarino, "Toward a History of Cultural Economy," 564–85. Soldiers in campaigning armies and even those troops captured as prisoners of war engaged in informal economies. This chapter does not intend to minimize the role of informal economies elsewhere, but rather to highlight how they operated specifically within the realm of wartime occupation. For references to informal economies elsewhere, see Ramold, *Baring the Iron Hand,* 74–75; Gray, *Business of Captivity,* chaps. 7 and 8. On the relationship between work and nineteenth-century masculinity, see Rotundo, *American Manhood,* 167–74. On the problem of morality, masculinity, and individualism within the Union army, see Foote, *Gentlemen and the Roughs,* 1–16, 17–20, 25–29, 31, 33, 36–39, 176.

7. Warner, "Morale of Troops on Occupation Duty," 752 [quotation], 749–57; Ramold, *Baring the Iron Hand,* 54; Wiley, *Life of Billy Yank,* 220; Browning, *Shifting Loyalties,* 141.

8. Berthoff, "From Republican Citizen to Free Enterpriser," 131–54, and M. T. Smith, *Enemy Within,* both engage the problems of republicanism and corruption in the nineteenth-century market economy.

9. William T. Shepherd to Father, July 22, 1862, in Hackemer, ed., *To Rescue My Native Land,* 206; Frank Peck to Dear David, June 17, 1862, Montgomery Family Papers, Peck Correspondence, LOC.

10. Diary entry, June 1863, in Jackson, *Colonel's Diary,* 99; Courtland G. Stanton to wife, October 2, 1863, DL0011.063, Stanton Letters, JLNC. See also William Ward Orme to wife, November 3, 1862, Illinois State Historical Library Papers, UA.

11. Harrison Soule to Mary [Wife], May 8, and June 14, 1862, Soule Papers, BL; Mitchell, *Civil War Soldiers,* 98–102; Ash, *When the Yankees Came,* 171–75.

12. Clement Boughton to C[larence] E. Boughton, May 24, 1862, Boughton Papers, SCWC; McGehee, "Military Origins of the New South," 328–29; Ash, *When the Yankees Came,* 171–75.

13. Henry C. Gilbert to My Dear Daughter Grace, November 3, 1863, Gilbert Papers, SCWC; Ash, *When the Yankees Came,* 79–84.

14. Robert Stuart Finley to Friend Molly, March 7, 1862, Finley Papers, UNC.

15. Benjamin T. Wright to [unknown], February 27, 1864, Wright Letters, DL1126, JLNC. See also, Benjamin F. McIntyre diary entries, January 16 and March 11, 1863, in Tilley, ed., *Federals on the Frontier,* 100–101, 121; and diary entries January 12 and 16, 1865, Shumway Diary, UNC.

16. Courtland G. Stanton to Wife, June 1, 1863, Courtland G. Stanton Letters, DL0011.048, JLNC.

17. Denny, *Wearing the Blue*, 115.

18. Ibid., 116–17; Browning, *Shifting Loyalties*, 141.

19. Rankin P. McPheeters to Anne McPheeters, March 2, 1864, McPheeters Family Collection, USAMHI.

20. Wilder Dwight letters, July 31, 1861, and August 3, 1861, in Dwight, *Life and Letters of Wilder Dwight*, 61, 63, 66–67; Rudolph diary entry, August 27, 1862, in Roe, ed., *Civil War Soldier's Diary*, 112; Benjamin Harrison to Wife, October 15, 1863, in Sievers, *Benjamin Harrison: Hoosier Warrior*, 228; J. Henry Blakeman to mother, November 18, 1864, Blakeman Letters, CWMC, USAMHI.

21. William Augustus Walker to unknown, July 11, 1862, in Silber and Sievens, eds., *Yankee Correspondence*, 61; Samuel H. Root to Dear Wife, September 20, 1862, Root Papers, CWMC, USAMHI; Augustus D. Ayling diary entry, May 4, 1863, in Herberger, ed., *Yankee at Arms*, 124; Browning, "'I Am Not So Patriotic as I Was Once,'" 218–20, 234–35.

22. Luskey, *On the Make*, 21 [quotation], 1–20; Rotundo, *American Manhood*, 167–74; Foner, *Free Soil, Free Labor, Free Men*, 11–39. For an important critique of the free-labor ideal, see Glickstein, *American Exceptionalism, American Anxiety*.

23. T. F. Browne to Singer Mnf. Co., August 1864, Federal Occupation of New Orleans Collection, HNOC; Wiley, *Life of Billy Yank*, 48–49.

24. Luther M. Fairbanks to his sister, July 1, 1862, Fairbank letters, LLMVC, LSU; John C. Kinney to Friend Eliza, July 14, 1862, Kinney Papers, LLMVC, LSU; Samuel Root to My Dear Wife, February 16, 1863, Root Papers, CWMC, USAMHI. "Self-making" is borrowed from Luskey, *On the Make*, 1–5.

25. Ramold, *Baring the Iron Hand*, 75; Luskey, *On the Make*, 1–5. See, for example, Robert Stuart Finley to Friend Molly, March 7, 1862, Finley Papers, UNC; Benjamin T. Wright to [unknown], February 27, 1864, Wright Letters, DL1126, JLNC; and diary entries, January 12 and 16, 1865, Shumway Diary, UNC.

26. John M. Steward to Dear Abby, March 24, 1864, Steward Letters, CWMC, USAMHI.

27. Benjamin F. McIntyre diary entries, January 16 and March 11, 1863, in Tilley, ed., *Federals on the Frontier*, 100–101, 121.

28. Orrin S. Allen to Dear Frank [Francis E. Wade Allen], January 25, 1863, in Rockwell, trans., "Dear Frank," VHS.

29. Orrin S. Allen to Dear Frank, February 18 and 20, 1863, in Rockwell, trans., "Dear Frank," VHS; Hyde, *History of the Hundred and Twelfth N.Y. Volunteers*, 20.

30. Orrin S. Allen to Dear Frank, February 20, 1863, in Rockwell, trans., "Dear Frank," VHS.

31. Orrin S. Allen to Dear Frank, March 28, 1863 [quotation], February 20, April 6, November 1, 1863, in Rockwell, trans., "Dear Frank," VHS.

32. Orrin S. Allen to Dear Frank, April 27, and June 23, 1864, in Rockwell, trans., "Dear Frank," VHS.

33. Rankin P. McPheeters to Annie M. McPheeters, March 1, 1864, McPheeters Family Collection, USAMHI.

34. Brig. Gen. Benjamin Loan to Maj. Gen. Samuel Curtis, November 16, 1862, *OR*, vol. 13, pp. 798–99. See also General Orders, No. 6, Headquarters, Cavalry Division, Army of the Ohio, August 25, 1864, *OR*, vol. 38, pt. 5, p. 668.

35. Maj. Gen. Samuel R. Curtis to John T. Cox, June 6, 1864, *OR*, vol. 34, pt. 4, pp. 250–51.

36. Coulter, "Commercial Intercourse with the Confederacy in the Mississippi Valley," 377–95; Roberts, "Federal Government and Confederate Cotton," 262–75; Johnson, "Contraband Trade during the Last Year of the Civil War," 635–52; Parks, "Confederate Trade Center under Federal Occupation,"

289–314; Johnson, "Trading with the Union," 308–25; Ruminski, "'Tradyville,'" 511–37. In August 1861, Abraham Lincoln issued a proclamation that prohibited trade with the Confederacy, unless sanctioned by an official government permit (Richardson, ed., *Compilation of the Messages and Papers of the Presidents,* 6:37–38). The Confederate government issued a series of laws at the beginning of the war that outlawed trade of various goods, hoping to deprive the Union of such resources (*OR,* ser. 4, vol. 1, pp. 341–42, 529).

37. Surdam, "Traders or Traitors," 301–12; Leigh, "Trading with the Enemy."

38. Surdam, "Traders or Traitors," 301–12; Leigh, "Trading with the Enemy"; Smith, *Enemy Within,* 154–56; Ruminski, "'Tradyville,'" 511–37.

39. Hess, *Civil War in the West,* 70–73, 140–42.

40. L. Kent [provost marshal general, Vicksburg, Miss.] to Ulysses S. Grant, September 13, 1863, Entry 4709, Box 1, Department of the Tennessee, 1862–66, Letters Received, Part 1, RG 393, NARA. For additional examples, see Parks, "Confederate Trade Center under Federal Occupation," 289–314; Simpson, *Ulysses S. Grant,* 144–45.

41. S. A. Hurlbut to John A. Rawlins, March 7, 1863, *OR,* vol. 24, pt. 3, p. 92. See also John S. Phelps to Henry W. Halleck, August 17, 1862, *OR,* vol. 13, p. 577; General Orders, No. 31, Department of the Mississippi, June 6, 1862, *OR,* vol. 10, pt. 2, p. 632.

42. J. R. Paul to Samuel Sharp, May 4, 1862 [quotations], *OR,* vol. 10, pt. 2, p. 638; Danielson, *War's Desolating Scourge,* 59–62.

43. J. R. Paul to Samuel Sharp, May 4, 1862 [first quotation], *OR,* vol. 10, pt. 2, p. 638; J. R. Paul to Dear Brother, May 4, 1862 [second quotation], *OR,* vol. 10, pt. 2, p. 639; L. F. Ross to John A. McClernand, July 25, 1862 [third quotation], *OR,* vol. 17, pt. 2, 120. Even southern unionists, who wanted to sell their cotton, sought out Union soldiers' access to markets. See T. G. Newbill to Col. Richardson, February 1, 1863, *OR,* 24, pt. 3, pp. 177–78.

44. Gardner diary entries, October 14 [first quotation] and October 13 [second quotation], 1863, in Shewmaker and Prinz, eds., "Yankee in Louisiana," 290–91; Ramold, *Baring the Iron Hand,* 43–78; Foner, *Free Soil, Free Labor, Free Men,* 11–39.

45. Samuel H. Root to Dear Wife, September 20, 1862, Root Letters, CWMC, USAMHI; George Stanton Denison to Salmon P. Chase, October 10, 1862, in Dodson, comp., *Diary and Correspondence of Salmon P. Chase,* 325; Smith, *Enemy Within,* 46–47, 155, 160–61, 170–71; Hearn, *When the Devil Came Down to Dixie,* 56–57, 92–99, 145–60, 162–67, 181–96.

46. J. H. Wilson to [John A.] Rawlins, September 16, 1863, *OR,* ser. 1, vol. 30, pt. 3, p. 664.

47. General Orders, No. 66, August 7, 1862, *OR,* vol. 17, pt. 2, p. 158 [first two quotations]; William T. Sherman to David D. Porter, October 25, 1863, *OR,* vol. 31, pt. 1, p. 737 [third quotation]; General Orders, No. 23, Department of the Gulf, 19th Army Corps, March 20, 1863, vol. 15, pp. 1115–16 [fourth quotation].

48. General Orders, No. 23, Department of the Cumberland, November 27, 1862, *OR,* vol. 20, pt. 2, p. 104 [first two quotations]; "General Orders, No. 100, Instructions for the Government of the Armies of the United States in the Field," April 24, 1863, Sec. 2, Art. 46, *OR,* ser. 3, vol. 3, p. 153; General Orders, No. 15, District of Morganzia, April 1, 1865, *OR,* vol. 48, pt. 2, p. 3; General Orders No. 4, April 29, 1864, Huntsville, Alabama, April 29, 1864, vol. 32, pt. 3, pp. 537–38.

49. S. A. Hurlbut to J. C. Kelton, November 17, 1863, *OR,* vol. 31, pt. 3, p. 180; Lash, "'The Federal Tyrant at Memphis,'" 15–28 [final quotation, p. 25].

50. Charles A. Dana to Edwin M. Stanton, January 21, 1863, *OR,* vol. 52, pt. 1, p. 331; Ulysses S. Grant to William T. Sherman, July 21, 1863, *OR,* vol. 24, pt. 3, p. 539; Diary entry, November 3, 1862, Seaman Diary, CWTC, USAMHI.

51. Opal, *Beyond the Farm,* 1–16, 179–92.

52. Samuel Root to My Dear Wife, February 16, 1863, Root Letters, CWMC, USAMHI; David Hunter to Ulysses S. Grant, May 2, 1864, *OR,* vol. 34, pt. 3, p. 390. See also Julius Varney to Dearest Wife, January 19, 1863, Varney Letters, Lewis Leigh Collection, USAMHI; General Orders, No. 23, Department of the Gulf, 19th Army Corps, March 20, 1863, *OR,* vol. 15, pp. 1115–16; S. A. Hurlbut to John A. Rawlins, March 7, 1863, *OR,* vol. 24, pt. 3, p. 92.

5 | The Irregular War, Guerrilla Violence, and Counterinsurgency

1. George H. Thomas to Don Carlos Buell, August 7, 1862, *OR,* vol. 16, pt. 1, p. 839 [first and second quotations]; Keil, *Thirty-Fifth Ohio,* 84 [third and fourth quotations]; Report of Col. Ferdinand Van Derveer, August 9, 1862, *OR,* vol. 16, pt. 1, p. 841 [final quotation]; Mountcastle, *Punitive War,* 64–67; Danielson, *War's Desolating Scourge,* 72–73; Grimsley, *Hard Hand of War,* 78–85, esp. 81.

2. Mitchell, *Civil War Soldiers,* 134; Sutherland, *Savage Conflict.*

3. Fellman, *Citizen Sherman,* 140.

4. Birtle, *U.S. Army Counterinsurgency and Contingency Operations Doctrine,* 23. For a useful discussion of the place of guerrilla warfare in the American military tradition, see Hsieh, *West Pointers and the Civil War,* 1–10, 111–13, 123–24.

5. Fellman, *Inside War,* 149–66; Mitchell, *Civil War Soldiers,* 132–38; Ash, *When the Yankees Came,* 21–22, 47–50, 64–65, 63–67; Sutherland, ed., *Guerrillas, Unionists, and Violence on the Confederate Home Front;* Mackay, *Uncivil War;* McKnight, *Contested Borderland;* Burkhardt, *Confederate Rage, Yankee Wrath;* Mountcastle, *Punitive War;* Myers, *Executing Daniel Bright;* Sutherland, *Savage Conflict;* McKnight, *Confederate Outlaw.*

6. William T. Sherman to Salmon P. Chase, August 11, 1862, in Simpson and Berlin, eds., *Sherman's Civil War,* 269; Ash, *When the Yankees Came,* 34, 46–50; Sutherland, *Savage Conflict, passim.*

7. John M. King diary entry, February 10, 1863, in Swedburg, ed., *Three Years with the 92d Illinois,* 52.

8. W. S. Rosecrans to Sterling Price, October 16, 1862, *OR,* ser. II, vol. 4, p. 627; John Pope, "General Orders, No. 7," July 10[?], 1862, *OR,* vol. 12, pt. 2, p. 51; Birtle, *U.S. Army Counterinsurgency and Contingency Operations Doctrine,* chap. 2.

9. Charles Harding Cox to My dear Sister, February 13, 1863, in Sylvester, ed., "Civil War Letters of Charles Harding Cox," 48; diary entry, February 26, 1862, Henry J. Seaman Diary, CWTC, USAMHI; Samuel Kerr to Dear Malvina, December 26, 1862, DL0522.57, Kerr Letters, JLNC. See also Frank Marcotte to Dear Mother, July 25, 1862, in Marcotte, ed., *Private Osborne, Massachusetts 23rd Volunteers,* 92–93; diary entry, July 22, 1862, Dexter Ladd Diary, CWMC, USAMHI.

10. Jerome Spilman to Dear Wife, July 23 [1862], Spilman Letters, CWTC, USAMHI; Courtland G. Stanton to wife, [March or April] 5, 1863, DL0011.032, Stanton Letters, JLNC; Browning, "'I Am Not So Patriotic as I Was Once,'" 230.

11. Frank Twitchell to [unknown], April 3, 1864, Twitchell Letter, LLMVC, LSU.

12. Charles O. Musser to Dear Father, February 12, 1863, in Popchuck, ed., *Soldier Boy,* 27; Faust, *This Republic of Suffering,* 6–17, 28–31.

13. Frank H. Peck to mother, August 3, 1862, Montgomery Family Papers, Peck Correspondence, LOC.

14. John Vreeland to Dear Parents, July 23, 1861, Vreeland Letters, Vreeland-Warden Collection, USAMHI; Report of Brig. Gen. Thomas Williams, June 10, 1862, Entry 1756, Department of the Gulf, Letters Received, Box 1, Part 1, RG 393, NARA; William S. Rosecrans, "To the Loyal Citizens of Western Virginia," August 20, 1861, *OR,* vol. 5, p. 576; Sutherland, *Savage Conflict,* 28–29, 47–52.

15. Downs, "Mexicanization of American Politics," 387–409; Sutherland, *Savage Conflict,* 28–29, 47–52.

16. Lisa M. Brady has recently called for historians to consider "how ideas about what is wild and what is civilized affected conduct during war," especially in the realm of guerrilla conflict. ("The Future of Civil War Studies: Environmental Histories," http://journalofthecivilwarera.org/forum-the-future -of-civil-war-era-studies/the-future-of-civil-war-era-studies-environmental-histories. Accessed October 15, 2015).

17. Charles Wright Wills, diary entries, June 9, 1862, in Kellogg, comp., *Army Life of an Illinois Soldier,* 100; Stephen F. Fleharty letters, May 3, and June 19, 1863, in Reyburn and Wilson, ed., *"Jottings from Dixie,"* 111, 121. See also Charles W. Porter, diary entry, April 4, 1863, in Porter, *In the Devil's Dominions,* 89. For a study that engages the military and environmental dimensions of guerrilla warfare, see Stith, *Extreme Civil War.*

18. David Millspaugh, diary entry, April 21, 1863, Millspaugh Diary, BL; William H. Whitney to Dear Brother Frankie, January 21, 1864, in Laver, ed., "'Where Duty Shall Call,'" 361.

19. Fellman, *Inside War,* 149–66.

20. Charles Wright Wills diary entry, August 14, 1862, in Kellogg, comp., *Army Life of an Illinois Soldier,* 125.

21. Wills diary entry, December 12, 1862, in Kellogg, comp., *Army Life of an Illinois Soldier,* 136.

22. Mitchell, *Civil War Soldiers,* 135.

23. William T. Sherman to Salmon P. Chase, August 11, 1862, in Simpson and Berlin, eds., *Sherman's Civil War,* 269.

24. Birtle, *U.S. Army Counterinsurgency and Contingency Operations Doctrine,* 23–47; Noe, "Exterminating Savages," in Noe and Wilson, eds., *Civil War in Appalachia,* 104–30.

25. Birtle, *U.S. Army Counterinsurgency and Contingency Operations Doctrine,* 23–47; Noe, "Exterminating Savages," in Noe and Wilson, eds., *Civil War in Appalachia,* 104–30; Grimsley, *Hard Hand of War,* 111–19, 184–85.

26. Edward F. Noyes to R. H. Stephenson, September 21, 1861, quoted in Sutherland, *Savage Conflict,* 59; Mountcastle, *Punitive War,* 66–67; Fellman, *Citizen Sherman,* 140; Grimsley, *Hard Hand of War,* 7–66.

27. John A. Keith to Benjamin Butler, May 22, 1862, Entry 1756, Department of the Gulf, Letters Received, Box 1, Part 1, RG 393, NARA (thanks to Aaron Sheehan-Dean for sharing a transcript of this source).

28. Ibid.

29. Addison McPheeters, Jr., to R. P. McPheeters, November 25, 1862, McPheeters Family Papers, USAMHI; Charles Wright Wills, diary entry, June 4, 1863, in Kellogg, comp., *Army Life of an Illinois Soldier,* 178; Ash, *When the Yankees Came,* 13–75; Grimsley, *Hard Hand of War,* 67–170; Mountcastle, *Punitive War,* 1, 6–7, 24–25, 59, 71–72, 106–8, 126–28; Danielson, *War's Desolating Scourge,* 45–91.

30. James A. Connolly, diary entry, November 26, 1864, in Connolly, *Three Years in the Army of Cumberland,* 324; Frank, *With Ballot and Bayonet,* 79–80; Mitchell, *Civil War Soldiers,* 138; Gallagher, *Union War,* 54–71.

31. John Beatty diary entry, May 2, 1862, in Beatty, *Citizen-Soldier,* 138–39; Sutherland, *Savage Conflict,* 124–25, 153, 178, 234–35; Mountcastle, *Punitive War,* 56–84; Grimsley, *Hard Hand of War,* 78–119; Birtle, *U.S. Army Counterinsurgency and Contingency Operations Doctrine,* 36–40.

32. Special Order No. 211, May 6, 1863, Entry 1756, Department of the Gulf, Letters Received, Box 3, Part 1, RG 393, NARA (thanks to Aaron Sheehan-Dean for sharing a transcript of this source). See also Circular, No. 1, Department of Arkansas, March 23, 1864, *OR,* vol. 34, pt. 2, p. 705; J. Holt to Edward M. Stanton, August 5, 1864, *OR,* ser. 3, vol. 4, p. 577–79.

33. Fellman, *Inside War*, 186–89.

34. Dudley to Davis, September 6, 1862, Entry 1756, Department of the Gulf, Letters Received, Box 1, Part 1, RG 393, NARA (thanks to Aaron Sheehan-Dean for sharing a transcript of this source); Henry C. Gilbert to My Dear Wife, July 18, and November 4, 1863, Gilbert Papers, SCWC.

35. Charles O. Musser to Dear Father, November 9, 1864, in Popchuck, ed., *Soldier Boy*, 161; Letter of C. C. Marsh, August 10, 1861, *OR*, vol. 3, p. 449; William D. Whipple to John Bell Hood, February 1, 1865, *OR*, ser. 2, vol. 8, p. 164; Sutherland, *Savage Conflict*, 113.

36. Taylor Peirce to Dear Catherine, February 16, 1863, in Kiper, ed., *Dear Catherine, Dear Taylor*, 80.

37. Mann, *History of the Forty-fifth Regiment Massachusetts Volunteer Militia*, 219.

38. Ibid., 219–20; Browning, "'I Am Not So Patriotic as I Was Once,'" 231. Northerners commonly practiced the feminization of their wartime political and military opponents. See, for example, Silber, "Intemperate Men, Spiteful Women, and Jefferson Davis," 614–35.

39. The hunting paradigm is best articulated in Fellman, *Inside War*, 176–84.

40. Diary entry, May 29, 1863, Kellogg, comp., *Army Life of an Illinois Soldier*, 177. See also Charles W. Porter, diary entry, April 4, 1863, in Porter, *In the Devil's Dominions*, 54–55; Fellman, *Inside War*, 176–84.

41. Frank Peck to Dear David, August 10, 1862, Montgomery Family Papers, Peck Correspondence, LOC.

42. Henry C. Gilbert to Dear Wife, March 23, 1864, Gilbert Papers, SCWC. Roualeyn George Gordon-Cumming was a Scottish traveler, sportsman, and author who spent much of the mid-nineteenth century hunting big game in Africa. He wrote of his exploits in *Five Years of a Hunter: Life in the Far Interior of South Africa* (1850). Jules Gérard, known popularly during the nineteenth century as "the lion hunter," was a French sportsman and author who wrote *Lion Hunting and Sporting Life in Algeria* (1856).

43. Circular, No. 2, District of Central Missouri, March 1, 1864, *OR*, vol. 34, pt. 2, pp. 478–79.

44. R. B. Marcy to Maj. O. D. Greene, March 29, 1864, *OR*, vol. 34, pt. 2, pp. 775–76; Fellman, *Inside War*, 87.

45. R. B. Marcy to Maj. O. D. Greene, March 29, 1864, *OR*, vol. 34, pt. 2, p. 776; Fellman, *Inside War*, 87.

46. Francis Lieber, "Guerrilla Parties Considered with Reference to the Laws and Usages of War," *OR*, ser. 3, vol. 2, pp. 308, 307 [first and second quotations], 301–9; Henry W. Halleck to Francis Lieber, August 6, 1862, *OR*, ser. 3, vol. 2, p. 301; Freidel, *Francis Lieber*; Becker, "Lieber's Place in History," in Mack and Lesesne, eds., *Francis Lieber and the Culture of the Mind*, 1–7; Dilbeck, "'Genesis of This Little Tablet with My Name,'" 231–53; Sutherland, *Savage Conflict*, 126–28.

47. General Orders, No. 100, "Instructions for the Government of Armies of the United States in the Field," April 24, 1863, *OR*, ser. 3, vol. 3, pp. 148–64, 150 [quotation]; Grimsley, *Hard Hand of War*, 148–51; Freidel, "General Orders 100 and Military Government," 541–56; Gabriel, "American Experience with Military Government," 637–39; Mancini, "Francis Lieber, Slavery, and the 'Genesis' of the Laws of War," 325–48; Witt, *Lincoln's Code*, 170–96.

48. General Orders, No. 100, *OR*, ser. 3, vol. 3, p. 150; Grimsley, *Hard Hand of War*, 150.

49. Hogue, "Lieber's Military Code and Its Legacy," in Mack, ed., *Francis Lieber and the Culture of the Mind*, 51–61.

50. F. A. Roe to Henry W. Morris, September 11, 1862, *OR*, vol. 15, p. 569; Mountcastle, *Punitive War*, 71.

51. Charles Henry Moulton to Dear Bro and Sister, October 31, 1862, Moulton Papers, BL.

52. Charles O. Musser, undated letter fragment [probably February 3, 1863; first and second quo-

tations], Musser to Dear Father and Mother, April 29, 1863 [third and fourth quotations], and Musser letter fragment [probably June 1863], in Popchuck, ed., *Soldier Boy,* 25, 49, 54.

53. Stephen F. Fleharty letter, December 31, 1862, in Reyburn and Wilson, eds., *Jottings from Dixie,* 88.

54. Robert Gould Shaw to My Dearest Annie, June 9, 1863, in Duncan, ed., *Blue-Eyed Child of Fortune,* 343.

55. Robert Gould Shaw to My Dearest Annie, June 6, 1863, in Duncan, ed., *Blue-Eyed Child of Fortune,* 339.

56. Shaw to My Dearest Annie, June 9, 1863, in Duncan, ed., *Blue-Eyed Child of Fortune,* 343 [all quotations].

57. Ibid., 343–44.

58. Ibid., 343.

59. Hsieh, "Total War and the American Civil War Reconsidered," 393–408; Neely, *Civil War and the Limits of Destruction,* 198–219.

60. Grimsley, *Hard Hand of War,* 223–25; Neely, *Civil War and the Limits of Destruction.*

61. Mitchell, *Civil War Soldiers,* 138; Grimsley, *Hard Hand of War,* 184–85, 224; Neely, *Civil War and the Limits of Destruction,* 5.

6 | Lincoln's Proclamation and the White Racial Assumptions of Wartime Occupation

1. Garland H. White to Edwin M. Stanton, May 7, 1862, *BME,* 82.

2. Douglass, "Address for the Promotion of Colored Enlistments," July 6, 1863, in Foner, ed., *Life and Writings of Frederick Douglass,* 3:365; John David Smith, *Lincoln and the U.S. Colored Troops,* 3, 5–6, 10–23.

3. The federal government authorized a conscription act in March 1863 to address the manpower shortage caused by military occupation, battlefield deaths, disease, and a shortage of volunteers (McPherson, *Battle Cry of Freedom,* 600–601). Gallagher, *Union War,* 2, 54–55, 77.

4. *Statutes at Large,* 12:1269; Gallagher, *Union War,* 77, 92–118; Fox, *Regimental Losses in the American Civil War,* 17–22, 53; Freehling, *South vs. the South,* 119–20.

5. Cornish, *Sable Arm;* McPherson, *Negro's Civil War;* Litwack, *Been in the Storm So Long;* Berlin et al., eds., *BME;* Glatthaar, *Forged in Battle,* and "Black Glory," 133–62; Hollandsworth, *Louisiana Native Guards;* Trudeau, *Like Men of War;* John David Smith, ed., *Black Soldiers in Blue;* Wilson, *Campfires of Freedom;* Hahn, *Nation under Our Feet;* Manning, *What This Cruel War Was Over;* Dobak, *Freedom by the Sword;* Emberton, "'Only Murder Makes Men'"; Oakes, *Freedom National;* John David Smith, *Lincoln and the U.S. Colored Troops;* Luke and Smith, *Soldiering for Freedom;* Humphreys, *Intensely Human;* Reid, *Freedom for Themselves.*

6. Franklin, *Emancipation Proclamation;* Guelzo, *Lincoln's Emancipation Proclamation;* Holzer, Medford, and Williams, *Emancipation Proclamation;* Blair and Younger, *Lincoln's Proclamation;* Gallagher, *Union War,* 50–53, 75–76, 79–81, 82–86, 106–9, 116–18; Fredrickson, *Big Enough to be Inconsistent,* 99–103, 107, 114, 119; Oakes, *Freedom National,* 340–92; Masur, *Lincoln's Hundred Days;* Foner, *Fiery Trial,* 216–21; 240–49, 265, 268–74, 288, 292, 299, 301, 314, 333.

7. Emberton, "'Only Murder Makes Men,'" 372; Berry, *Military Necessity and Civil Rights Policy;* Sternhell, "Revisionism Reinvented?" 245–46; Freehling, *South vs. the South,* 119–20. For an interpretation of garrisoning in the Confederate military context, see Lang, "Soldiering on the Texas Coast and the Problem of Confederate Nationalism," 157–82.

8. Sternhell, "Revisionism Reinvented?" 245–46; Freehling, *South vs. the South,* 119–20.

9. Berlin, "Who Freed the Slaves?" 105–22; McPherson, "Who Freed the Slaves?" 1–10; Gallagher, *Union War*, 50–53, 75–76, 88–89; Berlin et al., eds., *BME*, 1–6.

10. Freehling, *South vs. the South*, 119; Manning, *What This Cruel War Was Over*, 118–19, 121, 150–55, 191–92; Gallagher, *Union War*, 40–41, 72–78, 80–82, 101–6, 113–14; Foner, *Fiery Trial*, 249–55.

11. *Statutes at Large*, 12:319 [First Confiscation Act]; *Statutes at Large*, 12:568–92 [Second Confiscation Act]; Siddali, *From Property to Person*, 52–53, 61, 64, 79, 95, 107, 115–16, 176; Freehling, *South vs. the South*, 119–20.

12. Freehling, *South vs. the South*, 119–20.

13. Fleming, ed., *Life and Letters of Alexander Hays*, 53; Skelton, *American Profession of Arms*, 184–90, 260–81; Coffman, *Old Army*, 67, 81–82.

14. P. W. Jackson to Truman Seymour, March 11, 1863, Entry 4109, Department of the South, Letters Received, Pt. 1, Box 3, RG 393, NARA; Charles O. Musser to Dear Father, September 12, 1864, in Popchuck, ed., *Soldier Boy*, 152–53; Francis Skillin to Dear Brother, July 13, 1862, Skillin Letters, Mss. 4667, LLMVC, LSU; Courtland G. Stanton to Wife, April 15, 1864, DL0011.070, Stanton Letters, JLNC; Joseph Emery Fiske to My dear Parents, February 19, 1864, in Fiske, *War Letters of Capt. Joseph E. Fiske*, 47; George W. Newcomb to My dear little Wife, May 11, 1864, Newcomb Letters, CWMC, US-AMHI; George Hovey Cadman to My dear wife, March 21, 1863, Cadman Papers, UNC; George Hawley to Brother, June 20, 1865, Hawley Letters, DL0806.3, JLNC; diary entry, July 8, 1864, Cox, "Civil War Diary of Jabez T. Cox,":48–49; George O. Jewett to Dear Deck, August 16, 1863, Jewett Collection, LOC; diary entries, January 12 and March 1, 1863, in Swedburg, ed., *Three Years with the 92d Illinois*, 23, 57; Jonas Denton Elliott to My Dear Wife, May 8, 1864, Elliott Letters, CWMC, USAMHI; Benjamin Harrison to Wife, October 15, 1863, and Harrison to W. P. Fishback, September 7, 1862, in Sievers, *Benjamin Harrison*, 228, 195, 220; Henry C. Gilbert to My Dear Wife, October 29, 1862, and October 30, 1863, Gilbert Papers, SCWC; Skelton, *American Profession of Arms*, 260–81; Browning, *Shifting Loyalties*, 141–42; Mitchell, *Vacant Chair*, 39–54.

15. Skelton, *American Profession of Arms*, 260–81.

16. Revised Militia Act, July 17, 1862, *OR*, ser. 3, vol. 2, pp. 281, 280; *Congressional Globe*, Senate, 37th Congress, 2nd Session, 3197–3203; Oakes, *Freedom National*, 361, 378.

17. *CWL*, Speech at Peoria, Illinois, October 16, 1854, 2:256, 247–83; Fredrickson, *Big Enough to be Inconsistent*, 84, 43–84; Foner, *Fiery Trial*, 63–144; Escott, *Lincoln's Dilemma*, 18–20, 44–50.

18. Fredrickson, *Big Enough to Be Inconsistent*, 85–126; Gallagher, *Union War*, 50–52, 75–76, 79–81, 82–88, 90–95, 101–9, 116–19; Escott, *Lincoln's Dilemma*, 48, 73.

19. Address on Colonization, August 14, 1862, and Annual Message to Congress, December 1, 1862, both in *CWL*, 5:372, 535–36; Neely, "Colonization and the Myth that Lincoln Prepared the People for Emancipation," 45–74, esp. 64–65; Escott, *Lincoln's Dilemma*, 100–101, 110–14, 116–21.

20. Magness and Page, *Colonization after Emancipation*, 3–18, 24–27, 42, 78, 104–9, 117–22, 124–28; Escott, *Lincoln's Dilemma*, 142, 178, 189–90.

21. Wendell Phillips quoted in Paludan, *Presidency of Abraham Lincoln*, 189; and in Freehling, *South vs. the South*, 119; Masur, *Lincoln's Hundred Days*, 197–99, 219.

22. Bates, *Opinion*, 12; Oakes, *Freedom National*, 357–60; Vorenberg, "Abraham Lincoln's 'Fellow Citizens,'" 154–56.

23. Oakes, *Freedom National*, 360–62.

24. Bates, *Opinion*, 23, 21–24; Emberton, "'Only Murder Makes Men,'" 387.

25. Vorenberg, "Abraham Lincoln's 'Fellow Citizens,'" 157 [quotation], 158.

26. Lincoln to John A. Dix, January 14, 1863, and Lincoln to Andrew Johnson, March 26, 1863, both in *CWL*, 6:56, 149–50; John David Smith, *Lincoln and the U.S. Colored Troops*, 75.

27. Lincoln to James C. Conkling, August 26, 1863, CWL 6:408–9; John David Smith, *Lincoln and the U.S. Colored Troops,* 35.

28. Lincoln to Grant, August 9, 1863, *CWL,* 6:374; Grant to Henry W. Halleck, July 24, 1863, *PUSG,* 9:110; Cornish, *Sable Arm,* 266–67; Freehling, *South vs. the South,* 150–51; Lowe, "Battle on the Levee," 107–135.

29. Abraham Lincoln, Third Annual Message to Congress, December 8, 1863, *OR,* ser. 3, vol. 3, pp. 1153, 1144–55.

30. Interview with Alexander W. Randall and Joseph T. Mills, August 19, 1864, *CWL,* 7:507.

31. Lincoln to Michael Hahn, March 13, 1864, *CWL,* 7:243; Final Public Address, April 11, 1865, *CWL,* 8:403; Masur, *Lincoln's Last Speech.*

32. Fredrickson, *Big Enough to be Inconsistent,* 117–20; Vorenberg, "Abraham Lincoln's 'Fellow Citizens,'" 158–62.

33. Butler, *Butler's Book,* 902–8; Fredrickson, "Man but Not a Brother," 39–58; Neely, "Abraham Lincoln and Black Colonization," 77–83; Vorenberg, "Abraham Lincoln's 'Fellow Citizens,'" 161–62; Foner, *Fiery Trial,* 401–2, fn. 52.

34. David Hunter to Edwin M. Stanton, June 23, 1862, *BME,* 52 [first Hunter quotation]; General Orders, No. 17, Department of the South, March 6, 1863, *OR,* vol. 14, p. 1021 [second Hunter quotation]; Edward F. Hall to My dear Susan and Eddy, July 15, 1862, in Silber and Sievens, eds., *Yankee Correspondence,* 91; Henry W. Halleck to Ulysses S. Grant, March 30, 1863, *PUSG,* 8:93. See also *New York Times,* April 9, 1862; John W. DeForest Letters, October 10, 1862, in DeForest, *Volunteer's Adventures,* 50; Higginson, *Army Life,* 42; Thomas N. Stevens to Carrie, May 22, 1863, in Blackburn, ed., *"Dear Carrie . . . ,"* 103.

35. David Hunter to Edwin M. Stanton, June 23, 1862, *BME,* 52; *New York Times,* January 9, 1863; Voelz, *Slave and Soldier,* 33–58, 85–88, 161–92.

36. William Winthrop to Frederick Seward, August 25, 1863, *NMSUS,* reel 2, vol. 3, pp. 1528–30; Johnson, "Race, Foreign Armies and United States Colored Troops," accessed June 2015.

37. Ulysses S. Grant to Henry W. Halleck, July 24, 1863, *PUSG,* 9:110; General Orders, No. 40 [Banks], Department of the Gulf, May 1, 1863, *OR,* vol. 15:717. See also John McClernand to U.S. Grant, February 17 and 18, 1862, 4:242, Grant to Halleck, April 19, 1863, 8:91–92, and Theodore S. Bowers to James B. McPherson, July 22, 1863, 9:112—all in *PUSG;* John S. Chatfield to Charles G. Halpine, May 19, 1863, *BME,* 490; John S. Chatfield to Charles G. Halpine, May 26, 1863, Entry 4109, Department of the South, Letters Received, Part 1, Box 2, RG 393, NARA; William T. Sherman to James B. McPherson, September 4, 1863, and Sherman to John A. Logan, January 20, 1864, both in Simpson and Berlin, eds., *Sherman's Civil War,* 535, 588–89; Berlin et al., eds., *BME,* chap. 10.

38. Record of Events, 50th USCT, *SOR,* vol. 78, pt. 2, pp. 131–32; Capt. Edward R. Fowler to Lieut. Col. A. G. Bennett, August 3, 1863, *BME,* 492. See also Cyrus A. Gray to James T. Rusling, May 14, 1864, Entry 57c, U.S. Colored Troops Regimental Papers, 15th USCT, Letters Received, Box 17, RG 94, NARA; Hess, *Civil War in the West,* 164–65, 241–44.

39. William T. Sherman to John A. Spooner, July 30, 1864, *OR,* vol. 38, pt. 5, p. 306; Freehling, *South vs. the South,* 151, 153.

40. William T. Sherman to John A. Spooner, July 30, 1864, *OR,* vol. 38, pt. 5, p. 306; Freehling, *South vs. the South,* 151, 153; Marszalek, *Sherman,* 270–71; Freehling, *South vs. the South,* 151, 153. See also Officer of the 9th Army Corps, "Notes on Colored Troops," 7–8.

41. George Hawley to Dear Sister Henrietta, July 17, 1864, DL0806.2, Hawley Letters, JLNC; Julian E. Bryant to William Cullen Bryant, January 22, 1864, in Murray and Rodney, "Colonel Julian E. Bryant," 276–77; Lt. Col. David Branson to Lt. Col. R. B. Irwin, July 7, 1864, *BME,* 505.

42. Col. James C. Beecher to Brig. Gen. Edward A. Wild, September 13, 1863, and Lieut. Col. Thomas J. Morgan to Capt. R. D. Mussey, December 6, 1863, both in *BME,* 493, 499. See also Longacre, ed., "Letters from Little Rock of Captain James M. Bowler," 235–48; Inspection Report, 58th USCT, July 15, 1864, *OR,* vol. 39, pt. 2, 188; Brig. Gen. Daniel Ullman to Hon. Henry Wilson, December 4, 1863, and Capt. O. J. Wright to Brig. Gen. Lorenzo Thomas, November 3, 1864, both in *BME,* 496–98, 504; Trudeau, *Like Men of War,* 91–93, 252–55; Berlin et al., eds., *BME,* 362–68.

43. Humphreys, *Intensely Human,* 12 [quotation], 10–11, 80–83, 104–18; "Causes of Death and Discharge in Three Black Regiments," and Daniel Ullman to Lt. Col. C. T. Christensen, October 29, 1864, both in *BME,* 514, 513; Daniel Ullman to Henry Wilson, December 4, 1863, reel 2, vol. 3, p. 1784, and Daniel Ullman to Lorenzo Thomas, April 16, 1864, reel 3, vol. 4, pp. 2486–87, both in *NMSUS*; Reid, *Freedom for Themselves,* 382, fn. 10; Wilson, *Campfires of Freedom,* 38–41.

44. Adj. Gen. Lorenzo Thomas to Edwin M. Stanton, April 1, 1863, *BME,* 489 [quotation], 484–85; John David Smith, *Lincoln and the U.S. Colored Troops,* 37–38.

45. Grant to Lincoln, August 23, 1863, and Grant to Halleck, July 11, 1863, both in *PUSG,* 9:196–97, 23–24; Grant to Sherman, March 4, 1864, and Grant to Sherman, April 4, 1864, both in *PUSG,* 10:190, 255. See also Grant to Halleck, July 24, 1863, *OR,* vol. 24, pt. 3, pp. 546–47; Grant to Halleck, April 19, 1863, *PUSG,* 8:91–92; Grant to Stanton, January 6, 1865, *PUSG,* 13:237–38. Simpson, "Quandaries of Command," 123–49.

46. B. Field to Edwin M. Stanton, March 20, 1863, *NMSUS,* reel 2, vol. 3, pp. 1128–31; Higginson, *Army Life,* 42–43; Dobak, *Freedom by the Sword,* 167–68, 198–99.

47. Glatthaar, *Forged in Battle,* 108–20, 221–22; Wilson, *Campfires of Freedom,* 17–25, 30–35, 120–23; Berlin et al., eds., *BME,* 433–79.

48. Ulysses S. Grant to Henry W. Halleck, July 24, 1863, *OR,* vol. 24. pt. 3, p. 547; Higginson, *Army Life,* 23; Simpson, *Ulysses S. Grant,* 87–88, 91, 93, 104, 144–45; *New York Times,* January 9, 1863; Officer of the 9th Army Corps, *Notes on Colored Troops,* 6–7; Emberton, "'Only Murder Makes Men,'" 376–78; Wilson, "In the Shadow of John Brown," 315.

49. F. H. Pierpont to Edwin M. Stanton, January 27, 1864, *OR,* vol. 33, pp. 433; Emberton, "'Only Murder Makes Men,'" 378–79.

50. Higginson, *Army Life,* 14; "Negro Emancipation," *Harper's Weekly,* January 10, 1863, quoted in Emberton, "'Only Murder Makes Men,'" 380; Daniel Ullman to Henry Wilson, December 4, 1863, *NMSUS,* reel 2, vol. 3, pp. 1784. See also Report of Thomas Smith, Chaplain, 53rd USCT, May 31, 1864, Entry 57c, U.S. Colored Troops Regimental Papers, 53rd USCT, Letters Received, Box 36, RG 94, NARA; General Orders, No. 17, Department of the South, March 17, 1863, *OR,* vol. 14, pp. 1020–21; Wilson, *Campfires of Freedom,* 20–22, 19–28; Glatthaar, *Forged in Battle,* 84–85; Emberton, "'Only Murder Makes Men,'" 379–80.

51. Glatthaar, *Forged in Battle,* 113 [quotation], 114–20; Berlin et al., eds., *BME,* 433–42; Capers, *Occupied City,* 221.

52. Of the 27,976 Union soldiers occupying the Mississippi River Valley from Columbus, Kentucky, to Forts Jackson and St. Philip, Louisiana, 18,299 were African American soldiers (*OR,* vol. 48, pt. 1, 1108–1110; Cornish, *Sable Arm,* 265–66).

53. For recent interpretations of white soldiers' views of the USCT, see Browning, "'I Am Not So Patriotic as I Was Once,'" 225–26; Manning, *What This Cruel War Was Over,* 95–96, 147–48, 153–57, 220.

54. Minos Miller to Dear Mother, January 9, 1863, Miller Papers, UA; Charles Hill to My Very Dear Martha, April 19, 1863, DL0383, Hill Letters, JLNC; John C. Myers diary entry, October 28, 1864, in Myers, *Daily Journal of the 192d Reg't,* 128. See also Harrison Soule to Dear Mary, August 30, 1863,

Soule Papers, BL; Reuben J. Wells to [Wife], June 4, 1863, Wells Letters, Gladstone Collection, US-AMHI; Amos S. Collins to Wife, March 23, 1864, DL0534.5, Collins Letters, JLNC; Peter H. Yawyer to Dear Brother, January 1, 1863, Yawyer Letters, LLMVC, LSU; George M. Turner to My dear aunt Susan, May 2, 1864, in Silber and Sievens, eds., *Yankee Correspondence,* 87; DeForest, *Volunteer's Adventures,* 50–51; Thomas N. Stevens to Carrie, April 12 and May 2, 1863, in Blackburn, ed. *"Dear Carrie . . . ,"* 90, 96.

55. Charles Harding Cox to Katie, August 28, 1863, in Sylvester, ed., "Civil War Letters of Charles Harding Cox," 64; Silas Doolittle to Sister Sarah, March 22, 1865, DL0525.019, JLNC. See also Charles Boothby to Father, January 15, 1863, Boothby Letters, LLMVC, LSU; Charles Bennett to Dear Parents, May 8, 1863, Bennett Letters, HNOC; "Townsend" to Dear Brother, December 15, 1863, Federal Soldier's Letters from Port Hudson Collection, HNOC; Jimerson, *Private Civil War,* 103–4.

56. General Orders No. 12, Headquarters, U.S. Forces at Port Hudson, July 30, 1863, *OR,* vol. 26, pt. 1, pp. 663–64; diary entry, January 28, 1863, Linscott Diary, CWMC, USAMHI; Capers, *Occupied City,* 220–21; James C. Beecher to Brig. Gen. Edward A. Wild, Berlin et al., eds., *BME,* 112–13; Reid, *Freedom for Themselves,* 130–31; Col. H. N. Frisbie to Lieut. O. A. Rice, September 24, 1864, *BME,* 510–12.

57. Henry Brown diary entry, June 13, 1863, Brown Diary, LOC; Testimony of Joseph Walker, September 11, 1863, *OR,* vol. 28, pt. 1, p. 330.

58. Harrison Soule to Dear Father, January 26, 1864, Soule Papers, BL. See also William A. Sabin to Friend Benjamin, May 5, 1863, in Silber and Sievens, eds., *Yankee Correspondence,* 102; Chelsey A. Mosman diary entry, April 21, 1865, in Gates, ed., *Rough Side of War,* 353.

59. Benjamin F. McIntyre diary entry, August 6, 1863, in Tilley, ed., *Federals on the Frontier,* 202.

60. Benjamin F. McIntyre diary entries, November 6, 1863, and April 9, 1864, in Tilley, ed., *Federals on the Frontier,* 253, 326; Gallagher, *Union War,* 105.

61. Daniel W. Sawtelle to Dear Sister, February 22, 1863, in Buckingham, ed., *All's For the Best,* 221–22; Charles Francis Adams, Jr. to Charles Francis Adams, Sr., July 28, 1862, in Ford, ed., *Cycle of Adams Letters,* 169–70; Unknown to Brother, March 16, 1863, Soldiers Letters, 115th New York Infantry, Lewis Leigh Collection, USAMHI; Julius Varney to Wife, January 19, 1863, Varney Papers, Lewis Leigh Collection, USAMHI; Samuel Root to My Dear Wife, March 9, 1863, Root Papers, CWMC, USAMHI; Charles H. Smith to Wife, May 22, 1863, Smith Letters, CWMC, USAMHI; Henry M. Newhall to Sister, September 27, 1862, Newhall Papers, UA; Franklin M. Rose to Mr. Frost, August 12 and September 30, 1863, DL0795.2 and DL0795.3, Rose Letters, JLNC; George Hawley to Dear Sister Henrietta, July 17, 1864, DL0806.2, Hawley Letters, JLNC; Gallagher, *Union War,* 105, 110.

7 | Racial Authority, Cultural Change, and Black Wartime Military Occupation

1. James Henry Gooding to Abraham Lincoln, in Berlin et al., eds., September 28, 1863, *BME,* 386–87.

2. James Henry Gooding to Abraham Lincoln, September 28, 1863, *BME,* 386–87.

3. James F. Jones Letter, May 8, 1864, in Redkey, ed., *Grand Army of Black Men,* 141–43; Chenery, *Fourteenth Regiment Rhode Island Heavy Artillery,* 94–143.

4. Hahn, *Nation under Our Feet,* 91–102, 132–33, 265–313; Astor, *Rebels on the Border,* 121–67; Emberton, *Beyond Redemption,* 102–35; Freehling, *South vs. the South,* 119–20.

5. Quoted in Litwack, *Been in the Storm So Long,* 90; Trudeau, *Like Men of War,* 171; Ash, *When the Yankees Came,* 158–59; Astor, *Rebels on the Border,* 129, 135, 142; Hahn, *Nation under Our Feet,* 100.

6. Quotes in Wilson, *Black Phalanx,* 291–93; Hahn, *Nation under Our Feet,* 100.

7. Quotes in Wilson, *Black Phalanx*, 291–93; Hahn, *Nation under Our Feet*, 100.

8. Rufus Sibb Jones Letter [8th USCT], April 13, 1864, and "Rufus" Letter [7th USCT], May 17, 1864, both cited in Redkey, ed., *Grand Army of Black Men*, 50, 54–55.

9. John C. Brock Letter, July 30, 1864, in Redkey, ed., *Grand Army of Black Men*, 100–101.

10. Mary Semmes to Sallie Hoxton, March 3, [1863], Randolph Family Papers, VHS.

11. Diary entry, July 3, 1863, Harriet Ellen Moore Diary, UNC; diary entry, October 24, 1864, Mahala Perkins Harding Eggleston Roach Diary, VHS [final quotation]; A. W. Blair to Montgomery Blair, September 11, 1863, in Berlin et al., eds., *BME*, 209; Mitchell, ed., *Maryland Voices of the Civil War*, 408, 411, 413; J. Blake to unknown, October 18, [1864], Blake Letters, DL1029, JLNC; Ash, *When the Yankees Came*, 159; Marshall, *Creating a Confederate Kentucky*, 26–31; Reid, *Freedom for Themselves*, 127; Cornish, *Sable Arm*, 158; Myers, *Executing Daniel Bright*, 57–58.

12. Rumley diary entries, March 25, 1863 [first quotation], June 18, 1863 [second quotation], June 11, 1865 [third quotation], and June 5, 1865 [final quotation], in Browning, ed., *Southern Mind under Union Rule*, 59, 73, 179, 177, and *Shifting Loyalties*, 80, 96–100, 169.

13. Higginson, *Army Life*, 83, 178 [final quotation].

14. H. N. Frisbie to O. A. Rice, September 24, 1864, *OR*, vol. 41, pt. 1, p. 810; J. Blake to unknown, October 18, [1864], Blake Letters, DL1029, JLNC; Henry Gilbert to My Dear Wife, September 26, 1863, Gilbert Papers, SCWC. See also Charles Enslow Calvin to Wife, December 14, 1864, Calvin Letters, LOC; [Unknown] to Dear Wife and Mother, September 27, 1864, B. F. Trail Letters, 28th USCT, Gladstone Collection, USAMHI; Minos Miller to Dear Mother, April 14, 1865, Miller Papers, UA; [Unknown] to Miss Cynthia, October 17, 1863, Black Soldiers in Louisiana Collection, HNOC; Ulysses S. Grant to Henry W. Halleck, September 30, 1863, *OR*, vol. 30, pt. 3, p. 944.

15. J. Blake to unknown, October 18, [1864], Blake Letters, DL1029, JLNC; Burkhardt, *Confederate Rage, Yankee Wrath*, 38–42; Astor, *Rebels on the Border*, 121–35.

16. George L. Andrews to J. L. Logan, August 5, 1863, *OR*, ser. 2, vol. 6, p. 177; diary entry, June 1863, in Jackson, *The Colonel's Diary*, 96. See also L. Kent to John A. Rawlins, September 24, 1863, *OR*, vol. 24, pt. 3, p. 590; Report of J. Holt, October 8, 1864, *OR*, ser. 2, vol. 7, p. 949; George L. Andrews to G. Norman Lieber, September 14, 1863, Entry 1756, Department of the Gulf, Letters Received, Part 1, Box 2, RG 393, RG 393, NARA; Sutherland, *Savage Conflict*, 229–31; Berlin, et al., eds., *BME*, 568; Myers, *Executing Daniel Bright*, 114.

17. Stark A. W. Peighton to Jefferson Davis, August 7, 1863 [quotations], A. E. Bovay to John A. Dix, July 11, 1863, and J. Holt to Abraham Lincoln, August 19, 1863, all in *OR*, ser. 2, vol. 6, p. 188 [quotations], 106, 216–18; Glatthaar, *Forged in Battle*, 69.

18. J. Holt to Abraham Lincoln, August 19, 1863, *OR*, ser. 2, vol. 6, p. 217; Henry F. Gladding to Dear Mother, October 26, 186[3], Gladding Letter, VHS.

19. Jefferson Davis to Thomas Bragg, September 1, 1863, and James A. Seddon Indorsement, both in *OR*, ser. 2, vol. 6, pp. 245, 188.

20. [B. F. Trail] to Dear Wife and Mother, September 27, 1864, Trail Correspondence, Gladstone Collection, USAMHI.

21. General Orders, No. 7, District of Vicksburg, May 18, 1864, *OR*, vol. 39, pt. 2, p. 38. See also N. B. Buford to W. D. Green, March 23, 1864, *OR*, vol. 34, pt. 2, p. 705; Unknown to My Ever dear Relatives, February 14, [1864], Pickett Family Papers, Gladstone Collection, USAMHI.

22. F. H. Pierpont to Edwin M. Stanton, January 27, 1864, *OR*, vol. 33, pp. 432–33; General Orders, No. 7, District of Vicksburg, *OR*, vol. 39, pt. 2, p. 38.

23. Emberton, *Beyond Redemption*, 102–6.

24. "Militarized freedom" is adopted from Emberton, *Beyond Redemption*, 102–35; Grimsley, *Hard Hand of War*, 162–70; Myers, *Executing Daniel Bright*, 111–14, 131–32.

25. Edward M. McCook to Edwin M. Stanton, June 3, 1863, *NMSUS,* reel 2, vol. 3, pt. 1, pp. 1285–86.

26. Rufus Saxton to Edwin M. Stanton, November 12, 1862, and Thomas Wentworth Higginson to Rufus Saxton, February 1, 1863, both in *OR,* vol. 14, p. 190 [Saxton], p. 198 [Higginson]; Higginson, *Army Life,* 48–73; Wilson, "In the Shadow of John Brown," 313–15; Dobak, *Freedom by the Sword,* 34–40.

27. William T. Sherman to James B. McPherson, February 1, 1864, *OR,* vol. 32, pt. 2, p. 310; Dobak, *Freedom by the Sword,* 199–201. See also Report of Charles A. Gilchrist, March 9, 1864, *OR,* vol. 32, pt. 1, pp. 395–400; Report of Henry W. Bowers, August 6, 1864, *OR,* vol. 35, pt. 1, pp. 405–6; Hess, *Civil War in the West,* 242; Dobak, *Freedom by the Sword,* 61–62, 138–39.

28. James W. Anderson Letter, January 14, 1865, in Redkey, ed., *Grand Army of Black Men,* 126. See also Report of James S. Brisben, October 20, 1864, *OR,* vol. 39, pt. 1, pp. 556–57; Mays, "Battle of Saltville," 200–226. For similar examples, see H. N. Frisbie to O. A. Rice, September 24, 1864, *OR,* vol. 41, pt. 1, pp. 808–10; Report of I. J. Wistar, December 17, 1863, *OR,* vol. 29, pt. 1, pp. 974–76.

29. Thomas Ewing Jr. to C. W. Marsh, August 3, 1863, in Berlin et al., eds., *BME,* 229; Thirteenth USCT quoted in Trudeau, *Like Men of War,* 336. See also J. Holt to Edwin M. Stanton, July 31, 1864, and John L. Bullis to Maj. Gen. Burbridge, September 17, 1864, both in Berlin et al., *BME,* 264, 267; Fellman, *Inside War,* 211–13; Reid, *Freedom for Themselves,* 111–15; Marshall, *Creating a Confederate Kentucky,* 20–30; Astor, *Rebels on the Border,* 120–35; Sutherland, *Savage Conflict,* 229.

30. Wilson, "In the Shadow of John Brown," 317–20 [Higginson quotation, p. 320].

31. First, third, and final quotations in Duncan, *Blue-Eyed Child of Fortune,* 343, 44; Second Shaw quotation in Wilson, "In the Shadow of John Brown," 323, 321–22; Rose, *Rehearsal for Reconstruction,* 252–53.

32. For an important interpretation of the antebellum roots of a black military tradition, see Kerr-Ritchie, "Rehearsal for War," 1–34; and Rael, *Black Identity and Black Protest,* 54–81.

33. Report of Edward A. Wild, December 28, 1863, *OR,* vol. 29, pt. 1, p. 911 [first quotation], 911–17; *New York Times* correspondent quoted in Trudeau, *Like Men of War,* 115, 112–18; Dobak, *Freedom by the Sword,* 318, 320–23.

34. Report of Edward A. Wild, December 28, 1863, *OR,* vol. 29, pt. 1, pp. 912 [first four quotations], 915 [remaining quotations]; Myers, *Executing Daniel Bright,* 76–98.

35. Milton M. Holland Letter, January 19, 1864, in Redkey, ed., *Grand Army of Black Men,* 94.

36. Roland, *Louisiana Sugar Plantations,* 72–73, 101–14; Frazier, "'Out of Stinking Distance,'" 151–70.

37. Report of A. Watson Webber, September 1, 1864, *OR,* vol. 41, pt. 1, p. 295; William T. Sherman to James B. McPherson, February 1, 1864, *OR,* vol. 32, pt. 2, p. 310. See also Report of Charles A. Chapin, August 31, 1864, and Report of John G. Hudson, September 4, 1864, both in *OR,* vol. 41, pt. 1, pp. 295–96, 302–3; Lorenzo Thomas to William T. Sherman, March 30, 1864, and Sherman to Thomas, April 12, 1864, both in *OR,* ser. 3, vol. 4, 210–11, 225–26; Frazier, "'Out of Stinking Distance,'" 168.

38. Joseph E. Williams Letter, June 23, 1863, in Redkey, ed., *Grand Army of Black Men,* 90–91.

39. Milton M. Holland Letter, January 1, 1864, in Redkey, ed., *Grand Army of Black Men,* 94–95; "Gen. Butler's Department; Invasion of North Carolina by Gen. Wild's Colored Battalions," *New York Times,* January 9, 1864 [remaining quotations]; Report of Edward A. Wild, December 21, 1863, *OR,* vol. 29, pt. 1, pp. 910–17; Dobak, *Freedom by the Sword,* 320–23.

40. George L. Davis to James Bowen, August 21, 1863, Entry 1845, Provost Marshal General Records, Department of the Gulf, Letters Received, Part 1, Box 1, RG 393, NARA (thanks to Aaron Sheehan-Dean for sharing a transcript of this source).

41. James M. Jones Letter, May 28, 1864, in Redkey, ed., *Grand Army of Black Men,* 142; Testimony from Captain Joseph L. Coppoc, July 18, 1863, and Edward F. Brown to Col. Scofield, July 18, 1863, both in Entry 4720, Department of the Tennessee, Letters Received, Part 1, Box 1, RG 393, NARA.

42. George W. Hatton Letter, May 28, 1864, in Redkey, ed., *Grand Army of Black Men,* 95–96.

43. H. G. O. Weymouth to A. G. Draper, May 3, 1864, Entry 57c, U.S. Colored Troops Regimental Papers, 35–36th USCT, Box 29, RG 94, NARA [quotation]; *OR,* ser. 2, vol. 7, pp. 163–66; Reid, *Freedom for Themselves,* 126–37.

44. Quoted in Dobak, *Freedom by the Sword,* 332; Glatthaar, *Forged in Battle,* 201–2.

45. Joseph E. Williams Letter, July 18, 1863, in Redkey, *Grand Army of Black Men,* 92. See also Edward W. Belt to Governor Bradford, March 15, 1864, in Berlin et al., *BME,* 216–17.

46. Thomas J. Morgan to Davis Tilson, March 7, 1864, 14th USCT Inf., Regimental Letter and Order Book, vol. 1, RG 94, NARA; Edward M. McCook to Edwin M. Stanton, June 3, 1863, *NMSUS,* reel 2, vol. 3, pt. 1, pp. 1285–86.

47. Report of Rufus Saxton, November 30, 1863, *OR,* vol. 28, pt. 1, p. 745 [first quotation]; Report of Henry S. Bowers, August 6, 1864, *OR,* vol. 35, pt. 1, p. 406 [second quotation]; H. N. Frisbie to O. A. Rice, September 24, 1864, *OR,* vol. 41, pt. 1, p. 809 [third quotation]; S. C. Armstrong to Lt. Lyon, April 20, 1865, in Berlin et al., *BME,* 566 [final quotation].

48. Milton Holland Letter, January 19, 1864, in Redkey, ed., *Grand Army of Black Men,* 95.

8 | Republicanism, Race, and the Problem of Postwar Occupation

1. Ulysses S. Grant to Andrew Johnson, December 18, 1865, *PUSG,* 15:435; Simpson, *Let Us Have Peace,* 112, 122–24; Blair, "Use of Military Force to Protect the Gains of Reconstruction," 394.

2. Grant to Johnson, December 18, 1865, *PUSG,* 15:434; Downs, *After Appomattox;* Sefton, *United States Army and Reconstruction;* Dawson, "US Army in the South," 39–64.

3. Downs, *After Appomattox,* 11 [quotation], 1–10, 104–10; Gallagher, *Union War,* 124–25; Sefton, *United States Army and Reconstruction,* 261.

4. Newell and Shrader, "U.S. Army's Transition to Peace," 867–94.

5. Ibid.

6. Summers, *Ordeal of the Reunion,* 1–5, 13–14, 17–21; Benedict, "Preserving the Constitution," 65–90; Gallagher, *Union War,* 124–28, 151–53; Downs, "Anarchy at the Circumference," 98–121, esp. 108–9; Holberton, *Homeward Bound;* Jordan, *Marching Home,* 23–25.

7. Franklin, *Reconstruction after the Civil War,* 36; Pfanz, "Soldiering in the South," 127–59; Litwack, *Been in the Storm So Long,* 267–74; Fletcher, "Negro Volunteer in Reconstruction," 124–31; Berlin et al., eds., *BME,* 733–64; Glatthaar, *Forged in Battle,* 207–30; Redkey, ed., *Grand Army of Black Men,* 159–204; Zalimas, "Black Union Soldiers in the Postwar South"; Hahn, *Nation under Our Feet,* 133, 254–55; Reid, *Freedom for Themselves,* 255–98; Dobak, *Freedom by the Sword,* 457–96; Astor, *Rebels on the Border,* 121–45; Ash, *Massacre in Memphis,* 71, 77, 86–87; Downs, *After Appomattox,* 13

8. Grant to Johnson, December 18, 1865, *PUSG,* 435; Simpson, "Quandaries of Command," 138–49.

9. Gallagher, *Union War,* 124–28; Holberton, *Homeward Bound,* 8–9, 151; Pfanz, "Soldiering in the South," 10; Sefton, *United States Army and Reconstruction,* 261–62; Bradley, *Bluecoats and Tar Heels,* 42–43. For several interpretations of the end of the war at Appomattox see Rubin, *Shattered Nation,* 4–7, 117, 126–38, 163; Varon, *Appomattox,* 115–80; and Waugh, "'I Only Knew What Was in My Mind,'" 307–336.

10. Edward Rolfe to My Dear Boy, July 4, 1865, in Lillibridge, ed., *Hard Marches, Hard Crackers, and Hard Beds,* 173; Charles O. Musser to Dear Father, July 15, 1865, in Popchuck, ed., *Soldier Boy,* 215; Madison Bowler to Dear Lizzie, May 16, and June 3, 1865, in Foroughi, ed., *Go If You Think It Your Duty,* 288, 296.

11. Wilber Fisk letter, May 19, 1865, in Rosenblatt, eds., *Hard Marching Every Day,* 326–27; diary entry, April 9, 1865, in Herberger, ed., *Yankee at Arms,* 230; Elisha Hunt Rhodes diary entry, April 9, 1865, in Rhodes, ed., *All for the Union,* 221–22; Downs, *After Appomattox,* 1–10; Gallagher, *Confederate War,* 63, 85.

12. Charles O. Musser to Dear Father, May 14, 1865, in Popchuck, ed., *Soldier Boy,* 205; John F. Brobst to Dear Mary, May 27, 1865, in Roth, ed., *Well, Mary,* 143.

13. Thomas N. Stevens to Dear Carrie, June 15, 1865, in Blackburn, ed., *"Dear Carrie . . . ,"* 328; Elisha Hunt Rhodes diary entries, May 2 and May 10, 1865, in Rhodes, ed., *All for the Union,* 227, 230; Benjamin B. Sanborn to Dear Jane, May 20 and June 5, 1865, in Fry, ed., *As Ever Your Own,* 197, 200; M. S. Crowell to Brother, October 5, 1865, Crowell Letters, UA; Gallagher, *Union War,* 125, 127–28.

14. J. Henry Blakeman to Mina, June 23, 1865, Blakeman Letters, Lewis Leigh Collection, USAMHI; Jethro Ayers Hatch to Dear Father, June 5, 1865, DL0985.13, Hatch Letters, JLNC; Jordan, *Marching Home,* 71–72.

15. Wilber Fisk letter, June 4, 1865, in Rosenblatt, eds., *Hard Marching Every Day,* 330–31.

16. Downs, *After Appomattox,* 90–108, 262–63; Sefton, *United States Army and Reconstruction,* 261; Downs, "Anarchy at the Circumference," 98–121.

17. Sefton, *United States Army and Reconstruction,* 5–59; Pfanz, "Soldiering in the South," 21–126; Richter, "'Outside My Profession,'" 5–21; Greenough, "Aftermath at Appomattox," 5–23; Wade, "'I Would Rather Be among the Comanches,'" 45–64; Richter, "'It Is Best to Go in Strong-Handed,'" 113–42.

18. Madison Bowler to Dear Lizzie, July 26, 1865, in Foroughi, ed., *Go If You Think It Your Duty,* 303; Quincy A. Gilmore to Bvt. Brig. Gen. Molineux, June 5, 1865, *OR,* vol. 47, pt. 3, pp. 629–30; Downs, *After Appomattox,* 39–45.

19. Hannibal Augustus Johnson, July 14, 1865, Johnson Letters, UNC; Henry Gay to Dear Father and Mother, August 11, 1865, Gay Letters, CWMC, USAMHI.

20. James Sykes to Agnes [May 1865], Sykes Letters, Butler Center; Danford D. Cole to Emma, August 3, 1865, Cole Letters, UA; Rable, *But There Was No Peace,* 1–15; Carter, *When the War Was Over,* 6–23; Phillips, *Diehard Rebels,* 178–90; Sutherland, *Savage Conflict,* 276–77; Bradley, *Bluecoats and Tar Heels,* 39–42.

21. H. Matson, "Early Days of Reconstruction in Northeastern Arkansas," in Neill, ed., *Glimpses of the Nation's Struggle,* 322–23; J. H. Wilson to George H. Thomas, June 16, 1865, *OR,* vol. 49, pt. 2, p. 1002; General Orders, No. 59, Division of West Mississippi, May 25, 1865, *OR,* vol. 48, pt. 2, p. 592; Bradley, *Bluecoats and Tar Heels,* 30–33.

22. Woodruff diary entry, November 7, 1865, in Boney, ed., *Union Soldier in the Land of the Vanquished,* 58–59.

23. Alvin C. Voris letters, May 28 and June 4, 1865, in Mushkat, ed., *Citizen-Soldier's Civil War,* 262, 263.

24. Alvin C. Voris letter, May 30, 1865, in Mushkat, ed., *Citizen-Soldier's Civil War,* 264.

25. Alvin C. Voris letter, June 18, 1865, in Mushkat, ed., *Citizen-Soldier's Civil War,* 264.

26. Sefton, *United States Army and Reconstruction,* 6–7; Downs, *After Appomattox,* 73–74; Cimbala, *Under the Guardianship of the Nation,* 25–28.

27. Henry Adams to Charles Francis Adams, Jr., September 5, 1862, in Ford, ed., *Cycle of Adams Letters,* 1:182–83.

28. Ibid.

29. John C. Gill to My dear Mother, June 21 and July 7, 1865, in Lupold, ed., "Union Medical Officer Views the 'Texians,'" 484, 485–86; Carter, *When the War Was Over,* 6–23; Phillips, *Diehard Rebels,* 178–90.

30. Report of Lieut. Col. H. C. Forbes, in Edward Hatch to Brig. Gen. W. D. Whipple, June 22, 1865, *OR*, vol. 49, pt. 2, p. 1024; Carter, *When the War Was Over*, 179.

31. Report of Lieut. Col. H. C. Forbes, in Edward Hatch to Brig. Gen. W. D. Whipple, June 22, 1865, *OR*, vol. 49, pt. 2, p. 1025; Carter, *When the War Was Over*, 179.

32. Croushore and Potter, eds., *Union Officer in the Reconstruction*, 153.

33. Ibid., 4–5; Downs, *After Appomattox*, 94–100.

34. Ulysses S. Grant to Edwin M. Stanton, May 16, 1866, *PUSG*, 16:199–200; Sefton, *United States Army and Reconstruction*, 261–62.

35. Summers, *Ordeal of the Reunion*, 36–37 [quotation], 42–43; "General Grant and His Advisors," *Harper's Weekly*, November 2, 1867, p. 690; Gallagher, *Union War*, 124.

36. Franklin, *Reconstruction after the Civil War*, 36; Pfanz, "Soldiering in the South," 127–59; Litwack, *Been in the Storm So Long*, 267–74; Fletcher, "Negro Volunteer in Reconstruction," 124–31; Berlin et al., eds., *BME*, 733–64; Glatthaar, *Forged in Battle*, 207–30; Redkey, ed., *Grand Army of Black Men*, 159–204; Zalimas, "Black Union Soldiers in the Postwar South"; Hahn, *Nation under Our Feet*, 133, 254–55; Reid, *Freedom for Themselves*, 255–98; Dobak, *Freedom by the Sword*, 457–96; Astor, *Rebels on the Border*, 121–45; Ash, *Massacre in Memphis*, 71, 77, 86–87.

37. Berlin et al., eds., *BME*, 734; Work, "United States Colored Troops in Texas during Reconstruction," 337–58; Downs, *After Appomattox*, 108–10; Bradley, *Bluecoats and Tar Heels*, 47–48.

38. Calvin Holly to O. O. Howard, December 16, 1865, in Berlin et al., eds., *BME*, 755–56 [quotations], 735, 742, 743; S. H. Birdsall to J. H. Hindman, July 15, 1865, Entry 57c, U.S. Colored Troops Regimental Papers, 1st–2nd USCT, Box 11, RG 94, NARA; Josiah T. White to James C. Beecher, June 20, 1865, Entry 57c, U.S. Colored Troops Regimental Papers, 35th–36th USCT, Box 29, RG 94, NARA; Dobak, *Freedom by the Sword*, 464, 466–68; Astor, *Rebels on the Border*, 146–67; Carter, *When the War Was Over*; Bradley, *Bluecoats and Tar Heels*, 58–63.

39. James H. Payne letter, August 19, 1865, in Redkey, ed., *Grand Army of Black Men*, 171.

40. Pvt. Calvin Holly to Maj. Gen. O. O. Howard, December 16, 1865, and H. M. Turner to Edwin M. Stanton, both in Berlin et al., eds., *BME*, 755, 757.

41. N. B. Sterrett letter, July 8, 1865, and Garland H. White letter, October 23, 1865, both in Redkey, ed., *Grand Army of Black Men*, 173; Pfanz, "Soldiering in the South," 129, 201.

42. For examples, see Fletcher, "Negro Volunteer in Reconstruction," 126–27; Glatthaar, *Forged in Battle*, 215–16; Dobak, *Freedom by the Sword*, 458–96; Astor, *Rebels on the Border*, 121–67; Emberton, *Beyond Redemption*, 102–35; Berlin et al., eds., *BME*, 734–35.

43. L. Johnson to J. Hampton, February 1, 1866, Entry 57c, U.S. Colored Troops Regimental Papers, 44th–46th USCT, Box 34, RG 94, NARA; Charles L. Norton to Wickham Hoffman, July 25, 1865, Entry 57c, U.S. Colored Troops Regimental Papers, 98th–101st USCT, Box 50, RG 94, NARA; Edwin O. Latimer to A. G. Chamberlain, June 27, 1865, in Berlin et al., eds., *BME*, 738; Dobak, *Freedom by the Sword*, 465; Bradley, *Bluecoats and Tar Heels*, 65–66.

44. William B. Johnson letter, July 8, 1865, and George Thomas letter, July 18, 1865, both in Redkey, ed., *Grand Army of Black Men*, 179, 190; A. J. Willard to George W. Hooker, November 19, 1865, in Berlin et al., eds., *BME*, 752–54.

45. A. J. Willard to George W. Hooker, November 19, 1865, and John Ely to H. S. Brown, April 9, 1866, both in Berlin et al., eds., *BME*, 752–54, 761–62.

46. Carl Schurz to Andrew Johnson, August 29, 1865, in *PAJ*, 8:671–72.

47. William H. Holden to Andrew Johnson, June 26, 1865, and S. R. Rodgers to Andrew Johnson, November 22, 1865, in *PAJ*, 8:293, 9:417–18; Hahn, *Nation under Our Feet*, 133; Fletcher, "Negro Volunteer in Reconstruction," 126–27; Berlin et al., eds., *BME*, 735–37; Bradley, *Bluecoats and Tar Heels*,

58–63; Ash, *Massacre in Memphis,* 4, 34–42, 104–5; Alexander, *North Carolina Faces the Freedmen,* 9–12, 137–39.

48. Alexander, *North Carolina Faces the Freedmen,* 137–39.

49. Hugh P. Kennedy to Andrew Johnson, July 21, 1865, and William L. Sharkey to Andrew Johnson, August 25, 1865, both in *PAJ,* 8:445, 653; E. G. Baker to Messrs. Irby, Ellis, and Mosely, October 22, 1865, in Berlin et al., eds., *BME,* 747–49.

50. Andrew Johnson to William L. Sharkey, August 25, 1865 [quotation], and Johnson to George H. Thomas, September 4, 8, 1865, both in *PAJ,* 8:653–54, 9:26, 48–49; Zalimas, "Black Union Soldiers in the Postwar South," 37; Carter, *When the War Was Over,* esp. chaps. 2 and 3.

51. George H. Thomas to Andrew Johnson, September 9, 1865, *OR,* vol. 49, pt. 2, pp. 1111–12; L. Johnson to J. Hampton, February 1, 1866, Entry 57c, U.S. Colored Troops Regimental Papers, 44th–46th USCT, Box 34, RG 94, NARA; John Glenn testimony, May [29], 1865, and George G. Meade to Edwin M. Stanton, September 20, 1865, both in Berlin et al., eds., *BME,* 418–19, 746–47.

52. Ulysses S. Grant to William T. Sherman, October 31, 1865 [first quotation], and Grant to George H. Thomas, November 4, 1865 [second quotation], *PUSG,* 15:377, 390. See also Grant to John Pope, October 14, 1865, *PUSG,* 15:337–38; Grant to Sherman, March 3, 14, 1866, *PUSG,* 16:93, 116–17; Simpson, "Quandaries of Command," 136–49.

53. Simpson, *Let Us Have Peace,* 113; U. S. Grant to George H. Thomas, March 28, 1866, and Grant to Edwin M. Stanton, July, 1866, both *PUSG,* 16:139–40, 233. For an excellent narrative and interpretative treatment of white attitudes toward the USCT, see Ash, *Massacre in Memphis,* 4, 34–42, 104–5.

54. U. S. Grant to Edwin M. Stanton, May 16, 1866, *PUSG,* 199–200; Simpson, "Quandaries of Command," 146–47.

55. Charles J. Jenkins to Andrew Johnson, February 15, 1866, in Berlin et al., eds., *BME;* Ely Parker to Theodore S. Bowers, January 27, 1866, *PUSG,* 16:459; Bailyn, *Ideological Origins,* 61–70.

56. Reid, *Freedom for Themselves,* 487–96; Downs, "Anarchy at the Circumference," 98–121; Summers, *Ordeal of the Reunion;* Gallagher, *Union War,* 124–25.

9 | Military Reconstruction and the Fate of Union

1. "The Problem at the South," *Nation,* March 23, 1871, p. 192. See Zuczek, *State of Rebellion,* 88–117, esp. 93–94, for the specific context in which the *Nation* remarked on the problem of Klan violence in South Carolina.

2. "The Problem at the South," *Nation,* March 23, 1871, pp. 192–93; Summers, *Ordeal of the Reunion,* 103–6; Downs, *After Appomattox,* 161–63; Birtle, *U.S. Army Counterinsurgency and Contingency Operations Doctrine,* 55–56.

3. "The Problem at the South," *Nation,* March 23, 1871, pp. 192–93.

4. Sefton, *United States Army and Reconstruction,* 109–85; Foner, *Reconstruction,* 271–91; Blair, "Use of Military Force to Protect the Gains of Reconstruction," 395–97; Summers, *Ordeal of the Reunion,* 103–20; Downs, *After Appomattox,* 161–210.

5. Sefton, *United States Army and Reconstruction,* 253; Dawson, "US Army in the South," 39–64; Hsieh, *West Pointers and the Civil War,* 75–76, 94–95.

6. "Militarized freedom" is borrowed from Emberton, *Beyond Redemption,* chap. 4; Singletary, *Negro Militia and Reconstruction;* Astor, *Rebels on the Border,* 171, 186, 240; Hahn, *Nation under Our Feet,* 265–313; Egerton, *Wars of Reconstruction,* 94, 112, 120, 210, 240, 280, 285, 292, 297–98, 305, 307, 313–15.

7. Foner, *Reconstruction*, 176-227; Carter, *When the War Was Over.*

8. Rubin, *Shattered Nation*, 141-248; Foner, *Reconstruction*, 228-80.

9. Foner, *Reconstruction*, 176-227, 271-91; Sefton, *United States Army and Reconstruction*, 109-85; Dawson, "US Army in the South," 43-45; Blair, "Use of Military Force to Protect the Gains of Reconstruction," 395-97; Downs, *After Appomattox*, 161-210.

10. Summers, *Ordeal of the Reunion*, 109, 116 [quotations].

11. Gallagher, *Union War*, 2, 152-53; Downs, *After Appomattox*, 164-66, 202-3, 248-49.

12. Summers, *Ordeal of the Reunion*, 110-12; Bradley, *Bluecoats and Tar Heels*, 5-6, 159-88.

13. Sefton, *United States Army and Reconstruction*, 261. Not accounting for troops stationed in Texas, which comprised more soldiers than any other southern state, approximately 15,000 were positioned throughout the rest of the former Confederacy in October 1867; in October 1870, approximately 4,000 troops occupied the South, excluding Texas.

14. George G. Meade to Regis de Trobriand, August 28, 1867, in Post, *Life and Memoirs of Comte Regis de Trobriand*, 347 [quotation]; Sefton, *United States Army and Reconstruction*, 261-62; Rable, *But There Was No Peace*, 109.

15. Rable, *But There Was No Peace*, xi-xiii, 1-15, 33-58, 188-89; Budiansky, *Bloody Shirt*, 1-8, 140, 165-67, 170, 221-22, 236-37, 241-45; Hogue, *Uncivil War*, 1-13; Fellman, *In the Name of God and Country*, 97-102; Summers, *Ordeal of the Reunion*, 79-80, 96-97, 147-50, 255-58, 263-66, 356-68; Hahn, *Nation under Our Feet*, 265-313.

16. Grimsley, "Wars for the American South," 6-22, 34-36; Hogue, *Uncivil War*, 1-4, 9-13, 131, 199; Rubin, *Shattered Nation*, 4,7, 163; Hsieh, "Total War and the American Civil War Reconsidered," 399-400; Gallagher, *Confederate War*, 157-58, 206-7, fn. 1; Boyle, *Violence after War*, 5-7; Boot, *Savage Wars of Peace*, xvii-xxi; Blair, "Finding the End of America's Civil War," 1753-66; Rable, *But There Was No Peace.*

17. [Capt. S. C. Greene] to Brvt. Maj. John [Tyler], November 5, 1868, Entry 316, Department of Arkansas and 7th Army Corps and 4th Military District, Office of the Inspector, Letters Sent, Part 1, RG 393, NARA; Report of Lt. Patrick Hasson, September 6, 1869, Entry 4406, Division of the South, Letters Received, Part 1, Box 1, RG 393, NARA.

18. Col. Charles Lovell to Lt. E. Davis, March 18, 1870, Entry 926, Department of the Cumberland, Letters Received, Part 1, Box 10, RG 393, NARA; W. H. Vinal quoted in Sefton, *United States Army and Reconstruction*, 223-24.

19. Summers, *Ordeal of the Reunion*, 107-16; 213-35; Downs, "Anarchy at the Circumference," 98-121, and *After Appomattox*, 179-80, 188-97.

20. W. Gentry to Capt. Thomas E., January 9 and February 5, 1872, Entry 1962, Department of the Gulf, Letters Sent, Part 1, Vol. 1, RG 393, NARA; Zuczek, *State of Rebellion*, 95-100, 105-6; Summers, *Ordeal of the Reunion*, 267-72; Sefton, *United States Army and Reconstruction*, 222-23; Blair, "Use of Military Force to Protect the Gains of Reconstruction," 396; Downs, *After Appomattox*, 224-25, 238.

21. Summers, *Ordeal of the Reunion*, 270-71 [quotations]; Blair, "Use of Military Force to Protect the Gains of Reconstruction," 397.

22. Rable, *But There Was No Peace*, 81-185; Emberton, *Beyond Redemption, passim*; Lemann, *Redemption;* Budiansky, *Bloody Shirt;* Keith, *The Colfax Massacre.*

23. Gallagher, *Union War*, 152, 199, fn. 3.

24. S. D. Sturgis to R. F. Halsted, April 13, 1866, *House Exec. Docs.*, 40th Cong., 2nd Sess., 1867-68, Doc. No. 57, p. 123; Miles, *Serving the Republic*, 111. See also Richter, "'Outside My Profession,'" 5-21; *Harper's Weekly*, November 9, 1867, p. 706; March 20, 1875, p. 230; and April 7, 1877, p. 262.

25. Quotations in Pfanz, "Soldiering in the South," 485, 488-89.

26. J. C. Kelton to George H. Thomas, August 25, 1868, Entry 926, Department of the Cumberland, Letters Received, Part 1, Box 1, RG 393, NARA; Rable, *But There Was No Peace,* 108–9; Blair, "Use of Military Force to Protect the Gains of Reconstruction," 396.

27. Dawson, "US Army in the South," 46–50; Rable, *But There Was No Peace,* 109.

28. William T. Sherman to Alfred A. Terry, January 12, 1870, *Sen. Exec. Docs.,* 41st Cong., 2nd Sess., Doc. No. 41, p. 6.

29. William T. Sherman to John Sherman, September 21, 1865, and William to John, January 7, 1875, in Thorndike, ed., *Sherman Letters,* 256, 342.

30. Marszalek, *Sherman,* 364–76; Fellman, *Citizen Sherman,* 255–56, 292–93, 296.

31. Simpson, *Let Us Have Peace,* 170–88.

32. Ulysses S. Grant to John Pope, April 21, 1867, and Grant to Philip Sheridan, April 5, 1867, both in *PUSG,* 17:117, 96; Simpson, *Let Us Have Peace,* 180–82; Downs, *After Appomattox,* 182–84.

33. Ulysses S. Grant to Edward O. C. Ord, September 22, 1867, *PUSG,* 17:354.

34. William H. Emory to Henry C. Warmoth, January 13, 1872, Entry 1962, Department of the Gulf, Letters Sent, Part 1, Vol. 1, RG 393, NARA; Dawson, *Army Generals and Reconstruction,* 117, 121–28, 132–34, 137–38.

35. Emory to Warmoth, January 14, 1872, Entry 1962, Department of the Gulf, Letters Sent, Part 1, Vol. 1, RG 393, NARA.

36. Singletary, *Negro Militia in Reconstruction,* 4 [quotation], 3–16; Hahn, *Nation under Our Feet,* 283–85; Zuczek, *State of Rebellion,* 50–53; Kerr-Ritchie, "Rehearsal for War," 1–34.

37. Ulysses S. Grant to William T. Sherman, June 17, 1870, *PUSG,* 20:175–76; House Misc. Doc. 191, 42nd Cong., 2nd Sess., pp. 1–8; Singletary, *Negro Militia in Reconstruction,* 17–33; Zuczek, *State of Rebellion,* 74–76.

38. Hahn, *Nation under Our Feet,* 266.

39. Kerr-Ritchie, "Rehearsal for War," 1–34.

40. W. P. Carlin to George H. Thomas, June 19, 1868, RG 393, Entry 926, Department of the Cumberland, Letters Received, Part 1, Box 14, NARA.

41. Report of W. P. Carlin, July 15, 1867, Entry 926, Department of the Cumberland, Letters Received, Part 1, Box 11, RG 393, NARA; Singletary, *Negro Militia and Reconstruction,* 34–49.

42. T. C. English to AAG, Department of the South, August 30, 1869, Entry 4406, Division of the South, Letters Received, Part 1, Box 1, RG 393, NARA; Testimony of James Chesnut, July 8, 1871, U.S. Congress, *Joint Select Committee to Inquire into Condition of Affairs in the Late Insurrectionary States,* 1:450.

43. H. M. Lazelle to J. H. Taylor, September 26, 1870, Entry 4406, Division of the South, Letters Received, Part 1, Box 2, NARA.

44. Hahn, *Nation under Our Feet,* 294 [quotation], 292–95; Keith, *Colfax Massacre,* 77–79, 88–110; Lane, *Day Freedom Died,* 54–59, 90–109.

45. Hahn, *Nation under Our Feet,* 304–10; Singletary, *Negro Militia in Reconstruction,* 139–44; Rable, *But There Was No Peace,* 166–76; Zuczek, *State of Rebellion,* 163–74.

46. Hahn, *Nation under Our Feet,* 304–10; Singletary, *Negro Militia in Reconstruction,* 139–44; Rable, *But There Was No Peace,* 166–76; Zuczek, *State of Rebellion,* 163–74.

47. Singletary, *Negro Militia and Reconstruction,* 49, 145–52.

48. *Harper's Weekly,* "The Army and the States," April 7, 1877, p. 262.

49. Rable, *But There Was No Peace,* 110; Trelease, *White Terror,* 370.

50. William H. Emory to A.A.G., Department of the South, September 25, 1873, Entry 1962, Department of the Gulf, Letters Sent, Part 1, Vol. 1, RG 393, NARA; Downs, "Mexicanization of American Politics," 395–96; Grimsley, "Wars for the American South," 6–25.

51. Summers, *Ordeal of the Reunion,* 1–6.

52. Benedict "Preserving the Constitution," 65–90; Gallagher, *Union War,* 152, 199, fn. 3. For examples of "lost moment" scholarship, see Stampp, *Era of Reconstruction;* Gillette, *Retreat from Reconstruction;* Foner, *Reconstruction;* Fitzgerald, *Splendid Failure;* Cimbala and Miller, eds., *Great Task Remaining before Us,* ix–xiv. For studies that respond to the "lost moment" interpretation, see Summers, *Ordeal of the Reunion;* and Slap, *Doom of Reconstruction.*

53. Benedict, "Preserving the Constitution," 65–90; Santis, "Rutherford B. Hayes and the Removal of Troops at the End of Reconstruction," 417–50.

54. Gillette, *Retreat from Reconstruction,* 170–71.

55. Ibid., 172.

56. Dawson, "US Army in the South, 53; Glatthaar, "Civil War: New Definition of Victory," 123; Downs, *After Appomattox,* 241.

57. Blair, "The Use of Military Force to Protect the Gains of Reconstruction," 399.

BIBLIOGRAPHY

Manuscript and Archival Sources

Bentley Historical Library, Michigan in the Civil War Collections, University of
  Michigan, Ann Arbor, Michigan
    Charles Oscar Adams Papers
    Calvin Ainsworth Papers
    George Washington Alford Papers
    John Sidney Andrews Papers
    J. M. Bagley Papers
    Harold James Bartlett Papers
    Adelbert D. Baughman Papers
    Buchanan Family Papers
    William B. Calkins Papers
    Elihu Chadwick Papers
    Putnam H. Child Papers
    Thomas Jefferson Conely Papers
    George D. Converse Papers
    Sullivan Cook Papers
    Henry G. Cooley Papers
    John Corden Papers
    Henry M. Enos Papers
    Ferry Family (William Montague Ferry) Papers
    John S. Griffis Papers
    Griswold Family Papers
    Sidney H. Herriman Papers
    Edward Jelley Papers
    David Millspaugh Diary
    Orlando Moore Records and Papers
    Charles Henry Moulton Papers
    Jessie Phelps
    Curtis Z. Pratt Papers
    Slayton Family Papers
    Harrison Soule Papers

Butler Center for Arkansas Studies, Little Rock, Arkansas
  James Sykes Letters

Historic New Orleans Collection, Williams Research Center, New Orleans, Louisiana
  James C. Batchelor Letters
  Charles Bennett Letters
  Henry Bier Correspondence
  Black Soldiers in Louisiana Collection
  Charles H. Blake Diary
  Johnson Kelley Duncan Letters
  Federal Occupation of New Orleans Collection
  Federal Soldier's Letters from Port Hudson
  Forts Jackson and St. Philip Collection
  Michael Guinan Letters
  John Hart Diary
  Samuel B. Jones Letter
  A. D. Land Letter
  Henry M. Posey Letters
  Gilbert Shaw Letters
  Charles F. Sherman Letters
  B. Shuler Letter
  Edward Lewis Sturtevant Letters
  Melvan Tibbetts Letters
  Frankling S. Twitchell Letter
  Walton-Glenny Family Papers
  Union Soldier Letter
  Varnem V. Vaughan Papers
  Clark S. Willy Letter
  J. A. Wilson Letter

John L. Nau III Civil War Collection, Houston, Texas
  William B. Alexander Papers
  Henry C. Baldwin Papers
  Romaine A. Barnes Papers
  John Bartell Papers
  James M. Billings Papers
  Charles G. Blake Papers
  J. Blake Papers
  John Brown Papers
  George W. Browning Papers
  Amos S. Collins Papers
  Samuel W. Corliss Papers

Warren F. Dodge Papers
Silas Doolittle Papers
Henry R. Dunham Papers
Daniel Webb Ellis Papers
Horace A. Garrigus Papers
Amos Garrison Papers
Edward Gilbert Papers
Francis "Frank" M. Guernsey Papers
George Hawley Papers
Charles Hill Papers
Samuel J. Keller Papers
Harden G. Keplinger Papers
Stephen A. Matthews Papers
George J. Nash Papers
William L. Norton Papers
Samuel C. Pierce Papers
Joseph H. Prime Papers
Joe W. Richardson Papers
Martin V. B. Richardson Papers
Franklin M. Rose Papers
William L. Savage Papers
Phillip A. Simpson Papers
Robert D. Slayton Papers
George Snell Papers
Courtland G. Stanton Papers
Sylvester Strong Papers
John Warner Sturtevant Papers
Jacob Ulch Papers
William B. Whitney Papers
Benjamin W. Wilder Papers
William Wilson Papers
Richard Kirtland Woodruff Papers
Charles S. Worth Papers
Benjamin T. Wright Papers

Library of Congress, Washington, DC
Orra Bailey Collection
Ballou Family Papers
Daniel Carter Beard Papers
John R. Brinckle Papers
Henry Brown Diary
Charles Enslow Calvin Papers

Cass Gilbert Papers
George O. Jewett Collection
Montgomery Family Papers
William Franklin Patterson Papers
John Thomas Lewis Preston Diary
Patrick Ryan Diary
William Wrenshall Smith Diary

Louisiana and Lower Mississippi Valley Collections, Hill Memorial Library, Louisiana
   State University, Baton Rouge, Louisiana
    Thomas Alsop Letters
    Henry Anderson Letter
    Anonymous Civil War Letter
    Charles W. Boothby Papers
    Silas H. Brown Letter
    Joseph Burt, Jr. Papers
    William J. Christie Letters
    Civil War Officer Letter
    Civil War Soldiers Letters Collection
    John Calvin Curtis Letter
    E. Dane Letter
    George H. Davis Letters
    Richard Davis Letter
    Ned Doyle Letter
    Luther Fairbank Letters
    B. G. Farrar Papers
    John H. Guild Letters
    Richard Alexander Hall Letters
    John Hawkes Letter
    Calvin S. Hendrick Letter
    Union Soldier, Henry, Letter
    Henry Johnston Letter
    Charles L. Keyes Letters
    John C. Kinney Letters
    W. W. Leake Letter
    J. M. Little Letter
    Edward N. Marsh Letter
    E. L. Nickerson Letters
    Occupied New Orleans Collection
    Jessie Osgood Letters
    Eugene B. Payne Letters
    Edwards Pierrepont Papers

John Pitts Letter
F. D. Redfield Letter
Harai Robinson Papers
Sam (Union Soldier) Letter
P. N. Seely Letter
William Shelly Diary
Francis M. Skillin Letters
Joseph W. Smith Letter
Franklin S. Twitchell Letter
Robert A. Tyson Diary
Union Sailor Civil War Letter
Union Soldier, Oscar, Civil War Letter
William H. Whitney Letters
George Wilbor Letter
Josiah C. Witt Letter
U. S. Wyman Letter
Peter H. Yawyer Letter
William Zackman Letters

New-York Historical Society, Patricia D. Klingenstein Library, New York, New York
Henry Wilson Hubbell Correspondence and Papers
Samuel L. Merrell Correspondence
Miller Family Papers
Fordham Morris Papers
Charles E. Odell Diary
John Wagner Correspondence
James W. Willet Correspondence

James S. Schoff Civil War Collection, William L. Clements Library, University of
Michigan, Ann Arbor, Michigan
William L. Aughinbaugh Journal
Charles Barnett Journal
George Henry Bates Papers
Clement Abner Boughton Papers
Milton H. Boullemet Papers
Elliot N. and Henry M. Bush Papers
John S. Corliss Papers
Levi B. Downs Papers
Andrew J. Duncan Journal
John T. Durang Papers
Joseph F. Field Papers
Lyman Gardiner Papers

Henry C. Gilbert Papers
Henry Hayes Journal
Levi Hines Papers
Christopher Howser Keller Papers
Benjamin C. Lincoln Papers
Calvin Mehaffey Papers
Frederic S. Olmstead Journal
John Pierson Papers
Samuel Taylor Journal
Martin S. Webster Journals

Southern Historical Collection, Louis Round Wilson Special Collections Library,
   University of North Carolina, Chapel Hill
   William B. Alexander Letters
   Romeyn Beck Ayres Diary
   Macon Bonner Papers
   Gregory Hovey Cadman Papers
   Thomas Carey Diary
   Herbert Arthur Cooley Letters
   W. W. H. Davis Papers
   J. M. Drennan Diaries
   Federal Soldiers' Letters Collection
   Robert Stuart Finley Papers
   Horace K. Ford Papers
   Hannibal Augustus Johnson Letters
   Harriet Ellen Moore Diary
   Charles B. Quick Correspondence
   D. M. Ransdell Diary
   Ira Russell Papers
   Samuel A. Shumway Diary
   Jeremiah Stetson Papers

University of Arkansas Special Collections, David W. Mullins Library, Fayetteville,
   Arkansas
   Milton P. Chambers Papers
   Danford D. Cole Letters
   M. S. Crowell Letters
   Ellsworth Family Papers
   Fordyce Family Papers
   Haney Family Papers
   Roy G. Hutcheson Collection
   Illinois State Historical Library, Selected Arkansas Manuscripts

    Henry M. Newhall Letters
    William Ward Orme Letters
Andrew Johnston Letter
Elihu G. Martin Letter
Minos Miller Papers
James S. Moose Papers
William Ward Orme Letters
Police Regulations for the Army U.S. District of Eastern Arkansas, 1862
Ira Russell Letters
John B. Scotton Letter
Samuel Sprague Letters
United States Army Colored Infantry Regiment, 81st
Arabella Lanktree Wilson Papers

United States Army Military Heritage Institute, Carlisle Barracks, Carlisle, Pennsylvania
    Civil War Miscellaneous Collection
        Alvin H. Alexander Papers
        G. E. Andrews Papers
        William J. Barber
        J. Henry Blakeman
        William H. Davis Papers
        Edward Dean Papers
        John M. Eaton Papers
        Jonas Denton Elliott Papers
        James A. P. Fancher Papers
        Henry Gay Papers
        John B. Green Papers
        Joshua G. Hamlin Papers
        Jairus T. Hammond Papers
        Alfred Holcomb Papers
        George Hotchkiss Papers
        Henry R. Hoyt Papers
        Owen D. Ivins Letter
        John Joraleman Papers
        Carroll E. Kingsley Papers
        Dexter B. Ladd Papers
        Melville C. Linscott Papers
        Charles H. Lutz Papers
        Daniel Mead Papers
        Harvey M. Miller Papers
        Joseph K. Nelson Papers
        George W. Newcomb Papers

Elias Peck Letter
James A. Price Papers
William H. H. Reed Papers
Alfred P. Rockwell Papers
Samuel H. Root Papers
Francis M. Skillin Papers
Charles H. Smith Papers
John M. Steward Papers
Charles Stowe Papers
James C. Whitehill Papers

Civil War Times Illustrated Collection
George A. Breckinridge Papers
William H. Brown Papers
William H. Croop Papers
Francis A. Dawes Papers
Saxton DeWolf Papers
Eleazer B. Doane Papers
William E. Dunn Papers
George W. Peck Papers
Lewis F. Phillips Papers
John Russell Papers
Joseph Scroggs Diary
William H. Seagrave Papers
Henry J. Seaman Papers
Norman D. Smith Papers
L. H. Spencer Papers (Chesson Collection)
Jerome Spilman Papers
Isaiah G. W. Steedman Papers
Charles Stewart Papers
Demeritt W. Stone, Jr., Papers
Benjamin Thompson Papers
Adolphus P. Wolf Papers

William Gladstone Collection
Pickett Family Papers
B. F. Trail Correspondence

Harrisburg Civil War Roundtable Collection
James W. Denver Papers
John Hammond Papers
Daniel Himes Papers

Andrew Knox Papers
George W. and Jefferson O. McMillen Papers
John Meredith Papers
Edmund O'Dwyer Papers
Joseph H. Smith Papers
Oakley H. Smith Papers
James Stahle Papers

Lewis Leigh Collection
John Albright Papers
J. Henry Blakeman Papers
Hiram N. Childs Papers
William H. Harrison Papers
William H. Noble Papers
Stephen A. Stebbins Papers
William N. Thompson Papers
Julius Varney Papers
Wellington Wood Papers

McPheeters Family Papers
Addison W. and Rankin P. McPheeters Correspondence

Northwest Civil War Roundtable Collection
Alexander Adams Letters

Spanish American War Veterans Survey Collection
George L. Gaskell Papers

Vreeland Collection
Vreeland-Warden Papers

Virginia Historical Society, Richmond, Virginia
Orrin Sweet Allen Letters
Rockwell, William L., trans. "'Dear Frank': The War Years, 1862–1865: The Civil
War Letters of Orrin S. Allen to his Wife Francis E. Wade Allen and Family."
Charles H. Ashton Papers
Bagby Family Papers
Edward Charles Bates Papers
William Thomas Casey Papers
The Cavalier, 1863 (regimental newspaper, 5th Pennsylvania Cavalry)
Chester F. Channel Letters
Crenshaw Family Papers

William G. Ferris Papers
Henry F. Gladding Letter
Guerrant Family Papers
Heinrich Hohn Papers
Oscar D. Morhous Diary
Randolph Family Papers
Mahala Perkins Harding Roach Diary
Franz Wilhem von Schilling Papers
U.S. Army Provost Marshall Records
Weddell Family Papers
John A. Williams Letters

Government Documents

Congressional Globe, 37th Congress, 1862.
National Archives, Washington, DC
    RG 94: Records of the Adjutant General's Office
        Entry 57C, United States Colored Troops Regimental Papers
        The Negro in the Military Service of the United States, 1639–1886. 5 microfilm reels.
      Regimental Descriptive Books
        Fourteenth USCT
      Regimental Order Books
        Nineteenth USCT, Forty-ninth USCT, Fifty-second USCT
    RG 393, Part 1: Records of U.S. Army Continental Commands, 1821–1920
        Entry 316: Letters Sent, 1865–68, Office of the Inspector, Department of Arkansas and Seventh Army Corps, and Fourth Military District, 1862–70
        Entry 926, Letters Received, 1867–70, Department of the Cumberland
        Entry 1756, Letters Received, 1862–1865 and 1866–67, Department of the Gulf
        Entry 1845, Letters Received, 1863, Provost Marshal, Department of the Gulf
        Entry 1962, Letters Sent, 1871–78, Department of the Gulf
        Entry 1969, Letters Received, 1873–77, Department of the Gulf
        Entry 2433, Letters Received, 1864–68, Department of Mississippi
        Entry 3290, Letters Received, 1865–67, Department of North Carolina and Army of the Ohio
        Entry 4109, Letters Received, 1862–67, Department of the South
        Entry 4277, Letters Received, 1862–65, Provost Marshal, Department of the South
        Entry 4399, Letters Sent, 1869–76, Division of the South
        Entry 4406, Letters Received, 1869–76, Division of the South

Entry 4709, Letters Sent, 1862–65, Department of the Tennessee

Entry 4720, Letters Received, 1862–1866, Department of the Tennessee

Statutes at Large of the United States Congress, 37th Congress, March 1861–1863.

Statutes at Large of the United States Congress, 38th Congress, March 1863–1865.

Supplement to the Official Records of the Union and Confederate Armies. 100 vols. Wilmington, NC: Broadfoot Publishing Co., 1997–2001.

US Congress. *Testimony Taken by the Joint Select Committee to Inquire into the Condition of Affairs in the Late Insurrectionary States.* 13 vols. Washington, DC: Government Printing Office, 1872.

US House of Representatives. Executive Documents, 30th Congress, Sess. 1, 1847–1849.

——. Executive Documents, 39th Congress, Sess. 1, 1865–1866.

——. Executive Documents, 40th Congress, Sess. 2, 1867–1868.

——. Executive Documents, 41st Congress, Sess. 2, 1869–1870.

War Department. *The War of the Rebellion: A Compilation of the Official Records of the Union and Confederate Armies.* 128 vols. Washington, DC: Government Printing Office, 1880–1901.

——. *The 1863 Laws of War: Articles of War, General Orders No. 100, Army Regulations.* Reprint; Mechanicsburg, PA: Stackpole Books, 2005.

Newspapers and Periodicals

Harper's Weekly
The Nation
New York Times

Electronic Database

The American Civil War: Letters and Diaries: http://solomon.cwld.alexanderstreet.com.

Published Primary Sources

Ambrose, Stephen E., ed. *A Wisconsin Boy in Dixie: The Selected Letters of James K. Newton.* Madison: University of Wisconsin Press, 1961.

Ashkenazi, Elliott, ed. *The Civil War Diary of Clara Solomon: Growing Up in New Orleans, 1861–1862.* Baton Rouge: Louisiana State University Press, 1995.

Barden, John R., ed. *Letters to the Home Circle: The North Carolina Service of Pvt. Henry A. Clapp, Company F, Forty-fourth Massachusetts Volunteer Militia, 1862–1863.* Raleigh: Division of Archives and History, North Carolina Department of Cultural Resources, 1998.

Barringer, Graham A., ed. "The Mexican War Journal of Henry S. Lane." *Indiana Magazine of History* 53 (December 1957): 383–434.

Basler, Roy P., ed. *Collected Works of Abraham Lincoln.* 9 vols. New Brunswick, NJ: Rutgers University Press, 1953–55.

Bates, Edward. *Opinion of Attorney General Bates on Citizenship.* Washington, DC: Government Printing Office, 1862.

Bauer, Jack K., ed. *Soldiering: The Civil War Diary of Rice C. Bull, 123rd New York Volunteer Infantry.* San Rafael, California: Presidio Press, 1977.

Beatty, John. *The Citizen-Soldier; or, Memoirs of a Volunteer.* Cincinnati: Wilstach, Baldwin & Co., 1879.

Becker, Carl M., and Ritchie Thomas, eds. *Knapsack and Hearth: The Ladley Letters, 1857–1880.* Athens: Ohio University Press, 1988.

Berlin, Ira, et al., eds. *Freedom: A Documentary History of Emancipation, 1861–1867,* series 1, *The Destruction of Slavery.* New York: Cambridge University Press, 1985.

——. *Freedom: A Documentary History of Emancipation, 1861–1867,* series 1, *The Wartime Genesis of Free Labor: The Upper South.* New York Cambridge University Press, 1985.

——. *Freedom: A Documentary History of Emancipation, 1861–1867,* series 2, *The Black Military Experience.* New York: Cambridge University Press, 1985.

Billings, John D. *Hardtack and Coffee; or, The Unwritten Story of Army Life.* Boston: George M. Smith, & Co., 1888.

Blackburn, George M., ed. *"Dear Carrie...": The Civil War Letters of Thomas N. Stevens.* Mount Pleasant, Mich.: Clarke Historical Library, Central Michigan University, 1984.

Blegen, Theodore C., ed. *The Civil War Letters of Colonel Hans Christian Heg.* Northfield, Minn.: Norwegian-American Historical Association, 1936.

Bohrnstedt, Jennifer Cain, ed. *Soldiering with Sherman: The Civil War Letters of George F. Cram.* DeKalb: Northern Illinois Press, 2000.

Boney, F. N., ed. *A Union Soldier in the Land of the Vanquished: The Diary of Sergeant Mathew Woodruff, June–December, 1865.* Tuscaloosa: University of Alabama Press, 1969.

Browning, Judkin, ed. *The Southern Mind under Union Rule: The Diary of James Rumley, Beaufort, North Carolina, 1862–1865.* Gainesville: University Press of Florida, 2009.

Buckingham, Peter H., ed. *All's for the Best: The Civil War Reminiscences and Letters of Daniel W. Sawtelle.* Knoxville: University of Tennessee Press, 2001.

Burkhardt, George S., ed. *Double Duty in the Civil War: The Letters of Sailor and Soldier Edward W. Bacon.* Carbondale: Southern Illinois University Press, 2009.

Butler, Benjamin F. *Autobiography and Personal Reminiscences of Major-General Benj. F. Butler.* Boston: A. M. Thayer & Co., 1892.

——. *Private and Official Correspondence of Gen. Benjamin F. Butler, during the Period of the Civil War.* 5 vols. Norwood, MA: Plimpton Press, 1917.

Byrne, Frank L., ed. *Your True Marcus: The Civil War Letters of a Jewish Colonel.* Kent, OH: Kent State University Press, 1985.

Carter, Gari, ed. *Troubled State: Civil War Journals of Franklin Archibald Dick.* Kirksville, MO: Truman State University, 2007.

Chamberlain, Dick and Judy, eds. *Civil War Letters of an Ohio Soldier: S. O. Chamberlain and the 49th Ohio Volunteer Infantry.* Red Bluff, CA: Walker Lithograph, Inc., 1990.

Chance, Joseph E., ed. *The Mexican War Journal of Captain Franklin Smith.* Jackson: University Press of Mississippi, 1991.

———. *Mexico under Fire: Being the Diary of Samuel Ryan Curtis, 3rd Ohio Volunteer Regiment, during the American Military Occupation of Northern Mexico, 1846–1847.* Fort Worth: Texas Christian University Press, 1994.

Chenery, William H. *The Fourteenth Regiment Rhode Island Heavy Artillery (Colored) in the War to Preserve the Union, 1861–1865.* Providence: Snow & Farnham, 1898.

Clancy, Anne Robinson, ed. *A Yankee in a Confederate Town: The Journal of Calvin L. Robinson.* Sarasota, FL: Pineapple Press, 2002.

Clark, Olynthus B., ed. *Downing's Civil War Diary.* Des Moines: Historical Department of Iowa, 1916. (Accessed at CWLD, http://solomon.cwld.alexanderstreet.com, February 2012.)

Coffin, Charles Carleton. *The Boys of '61; or, Four Years of Fighting.* Boston: Estes & Lauriat, 1885.

Collier, John S., and Bonnie B., eds. *Yours for the Union: The Civil War Letters of John W. Chase.* New York: Fordham University Press, 2004.

Connolly, James Austin. *Three Years in the Army of the Cumberland: The Letters and Diary of Major James A. Connolly.* Bloomington: Indiana University Press, 1959.

Cooke, Chauncey Herbert. *Soldier Boy's Letters to his Father and Mother, 1861–5.* Independence, WI: News-Office, 1915. (Accessed at CWLD, http://solomon.cwld.alexanderstreet.com, February 2012.)

Cox, Jabez T. "Civil War Diary of Jabez T. Cox." *Indiana Magazine of History* 28 (March 1932): 40–54.

Crist, Lynda L., et al., eds. *The Papers of Jefferson Davis.* 14 vols. Baton Rouge: Louisiana State University Press, 1971–2015.

Croushore, James H., and David Morris Potter, eds. *A Union Officer in the Reconstruction.* New Haven, CT: Yale University Press, 1948.

Cutrer, Thomas W., ed. *The Mexican War Diary and Correspondence of George B. McClellan.* Baton Rouge: Louisiana State University Press, 2009.

Davidson, Garber A. *The Civil War Letters of the Late 1st Lieut. James J. Hartley, 122nd Ohio Infantry Regiment.* Jefferson, N.C.: McFarland, 1998.

Day, David L. *My Diary of Rambles with the 25th Mass. Volunteer Infantry: With Burnside's Coast Division; 18th Army Corps, and Army of the James.* Milford, MA: King & Billings, 1884. (Accessed at CWLD, http://solomon.cwld.alexanderstreet.com, February 2012.)

DeForest, John W. *A Volunteer's Adventures: A Union Captain's Record of the Civil War.* Baton Rouge: Louisiana State University Press, 1996.

DeRosier, Arthur H., Jr. ed. *Through the South with a Union Soldier.* Johnson City: East Tennessee State University, 1969.

Denny, J. Waldo. *Wearing the Blue in the Twenty-Fifth Mass. Volunteer Infantry, with Burnside's Coast Division, 18th Army Corps, and Army of the James.* Worcester, MA: Putnam & Davis, 1879.

Dodson, S. H., comp. *Diary and Correspondence of Salmon P. Chase.* Washington, DC: Government Printing Office, 1903.

Donnavan, Corydon. *Adventures in Mexico.* Cincinnati: Robinson & Jones, 1847.

Duncan, Russell, ed. *Blue-Eyed Child of Fortune: The Civil War Letters of Colonel Robert Gould Shaw.* Athens: University of Georgia Press, 1992.

Dupree, Stephen A., ed. *Campaigning with the 67th Indiana, 1864: An Annotated Diary of Service in the Department of the Gulf. William A. McMillan, Diarist.* New York: iUniverse, Inc., 2006.

Duren, C. M. "The Occupation of Jacksonville, February 1864 and the Battle of Olustee: Letters of Lt. C. M. Duren, 54th Massachusetts Regiment, U.S.A." *Florida Historical Quarterly* 32 (April 1954): 262–87.

Dwight, Wilder. *Life and Letters of Wilder Dwight, Lieut-Col. Second Mass. Inf. Vols.* Boston: Little, Brown & Co., 1891. (Accessed at CWLD, http://solomon.cwld.alexander street.com, February 2012.)

Dyer, Frederick H. *A Compendium of the War of the Rebellion: After Compiled and Arranged from Official Records of the Federal and CSA Armies, Reports of the Adjutant Generals of the Several States, the Army Registers and other Reliable Documents and Sources,* 3 vols. Des Moines: Dyer Publishing Co., 1908.

East, Charles. *The Civil War Diary of Sarah Morgan.* Athens: University of Georgia Press, 1991.

Eby, Cecil D., Jr., ed. *A Virginia Yankee in the Civil War: The Diaries of David Hunter Strother.* Chapel Hill: University of North Carolina Press, 1961.

Fiske, Joseph E. *War Letters of Capt. Joseph E. Fiske.* Wellesley, MA: Maugus Press, 1900. (Accessed at CWLD, http://solomon.cwld.alexanderstreet.com, February 2012)

Fleming, George Thornton, ed. *Life and Letters of Alexander Hays.* Pittsburgh: N.p., 1919. (Accessed at CWLD, http://solomon.cwld.alexanderstreet.com, February 2012.)

Foner, Philip S., ed. *The Life and Writings of Frederick Douglass.* 5 vols. New York: International Publishers, 1950–59.

Ford, Worthington Chauncey, ed. *A Cycle of Adams Letters, 1861–1865.* 2 vols. Boston: Houghton Mifflin Co., 1920. (Accessed at CWLD, http://solomon.cwld.alexanderstreet.com, February 2012.)

Foroughi, Andrea R. *Go If You Think It Your Duty: A Minnesota Couple's Civil War Letters.* St. Paul: Minnesota Historical Society, 2008.

Fry, Laurie, ed. *As Ever Your Own: The Civil War Letters of B. B. Sanborn.* Arlington, VA: Naptime Publishing, 1997.

Gardner, Mark L., and Marc Simmons, eds. *The Mexican War Correspondence of Richard Smith Elliott.* Norman: University of Oklahoma Press, 1997.

Gates, Arnold, ed. *The Rough Side of War: The Civil War Journal of Chelsey A. Mosman 1st Lieutenant, Company D 59th Illinois Volunteer Infantry Regiment.* Garden City, NY: Basin Publishing, 1987.

Gordon, George H. *A War Diary of Events in the War of the Great Rebellion, 1863–1865.* Boston: Houghton, Mifflin, & Co., 1885.

Graf, LeRoy P., and Ralph W. Haskins, eds. *The Papers of Andrew Johnson.* 16 vols. Knoxville: University of Tennessee Press, 1967–2000.

Grant, Ulysses S. *Personal Memoirs of U. S. Grant*. 1885; New York: De Capo Press, 1982.

Gray, John Chipman. *War Letters, 1862–1865, of John Chipman Gray and John Codman Ropes*. Boston: Houghton Mifflin, 1927.

Grimsley, Mark, and Todd D. Miller, eds. *The Union Must Stand: The Civil War Diary of John Quincy Adams Campbell, Fifth Iowa Infantry*. Knoxville: University of Tennessee Press, 2000.

Hackemer, Kurt H., ed. *To Rescue My Native Land: The Civil War Letters of William T. Shepherd, First Illinois Light Artillery*. Knoxville: University of Tennessee Press, 2005.

Harris, William C., ed. *"In the Country of the Enemy": The Civil War Reports of a Massachusetts Corporal*. Gainesville: University Press of Florida, 1999.

Hatch, Carl E., ed. *Dearest Susie: A Civil War Infantryman's Letters to His Sweetheart*. New York: Exposition Press, 1971.

Hauptman, Laurence M. *A Seneca Indian in the Union Army: The Civil War Letters of Sergeant Isaac Newton Parker, 1861–1865*. Shippensburg, PA: Burd Street Press, 1995.

Henderson, Alfred J., ed. "A Morgan County Volunteer in the Mexican War." *Journal of the Illinois State Historical Society* 41 (December 1948): 383–99.

Henry, W. S. *Campaign Sketches of the War with Mexico*. New York: Harper, 1847.

Henshaw, John Corey. *Recollections of the War with Mexico*. Ed. Gary Kurutz. Columbia: University of Missouri Press, 2008.

Hepworth, George H. *The Whip, Hoe, and Sword; or, The Gulf-Department in '63*. Boston: Walker, Wise, 1864.

Herberger, Charles F., ed. *A Yankee at Arms: The Diary of Lieutenant Augustus D. Ayling, 29th Massachusetts Volunteers*. Knoxville: University of Tennessee Press, 1999.

Higginson, Thomas Wentworth. "Regular and Volunteer Officers." *Atlantic Monthly* 14 (September 1864): 348–57.

——. *Army Life in a Black Regiment and Other Writings*. 1870; New York: Penguin, 1997.

Hoffman, Mark, ed. *Among the Enemy: A Michigan Soldier's Civil War Journal*. Detroit: Wayne State University Press, 2013.

Hosmer, James K. *The Color-Guard: Being a Corporal's Note of Military Service in the Nineteenth Army Corps*. Boston: Walker, Wise, & Co., 1864. (Accessed at CWLD, http://solomon.cwld.alexanderstreet.com, February 2012.)

Howe, Henry Warren. *Passages from the Life of Henry Warren Howe: Consisting of Diary and Letters Written during the Civil War, 1816–1865*. Lowell, MA: Courier-Citizen Co., 1899. (Accessed at CWLD, http://solomon.cwld.alexanderstreet.com, February 2012.)

Hughes, Nathaniel Cheairs, Jr., and Timothy Johnson, eds. *A Fighter from Way Back: The Mexican War Diary of Lt. Daniel Harvey Hill, 4th Artillery, USA*. Kent, OH: Kent State University Press, 2002.

Hyde, William Lyman. *History of the One Hundred and Twelfth N. Y. Volunteers*. Fredonia, NY: W. McKinstry, 1866.

Jackson, Joseph Orville, ed. *Some of the Boys . . . : The Civil War Letters of Isaac Jackson, 1862–1865*. Carbondale: Southern Illinois University Press, 1960.

Jackson, Oscar Lawrence. *The Colonel's Diary: Journals Kept before and during the Civil War by the Late Oscar L. Jackson . . . of the 63rd Regiment O. V. I*. Privately published,

1922. (Accessed at CWLD, http://solomon.cwld.alexanderstreet.com, February 2012.)

Johnson, Charles F. *The Long Roll: Being a Journal of the Civil War, as Set Down during the Years 1861–1863*. East Aurora, NY: The Roycrofters, 1911.

Jones, Jenkin Lloyd. *An Artilleryman's Diary*. Madison: Wisconsin History Commission, 1914. (Accessed at CWLD, http://solomon.cwld.alexanderstreet.com, February 2012.)

"Journal of Melville Cox Robertson." *Indiana Magazine of History* 28 (June 1932): 116–37.

Kamphoefner, Walter D., and Wolfgang Helbich, eds., *Germans in the Civil War: The Letters They Wrote Home*. Trans. Susan Carter Vogel. Chapel Hill: University of North Carolina Press, 2006.

Keil, Frederick W. *Thirty-Fifth Ohio: A Narrative of Service from August, 1861 to 1864*. Fort Wayne, IN: Archer, Housh & Co., 1894.

Kellogg, Mary E., comp. *Army Life of an Illinois Soldier*. Washington, DC: Globe Printing Co., 1906.

Kiper, Richard L., ed., and Donna B. Vaughn, trans. *Dear Catherine, Dear Taylor: The Civil War Letters of a Union Soldier and His Wife*. Lawrence: University Press of Kansas, 2002.

Laver, Tara Z. "'Where Duty Shall Call': The Baton Rouge Civil War Letters of William H. Whitney." *Louisiana History* 46 (Fall 2005): 333–70.

Leslie, James W., ed. "Arabella Lanktree's Wilson's Civil War Letter." *Arkansas Historical Quarterly* 47 (Autumn 1988): 257–72.

Lillibridge, Laurence F., ed. *Hard Marches, Hard Crackers, and Hard Beds, and Picket Guard in a Desolate Country: The Edward Rolfe Civil War Letters and Diaries*. Prescott Valley, AZ: Lillibridge Publishing Co., 1993.

Lind, Henry C. *The Long Road for Home: The Civil War Experiences of Four Farmboy Soldiers of the Twenty-Seventh Massachusetts Regiment of Volunteer Infantry as Told by Their Personal Correspondence, 1861–1864*. Rutherford, N.J.: Fairleigh Dickinson University Press, 1992.

Livingston-Little, D. E., ed. *The Mexican War Diary of Thomas D. Tennery*. Norman: University of Oklahoma Press, 1970.

Longacre, Edward G., ed. "Letters from Little Rock of Captain James M. Bowler, 112th United States Colored Troops." *Arkansas Historical Quarterly* 40 (Autumn 1981): 235–48.

Looby, Christopher, ed. *The Complete Civil War Journal and Selected Letters of Thomas Wentworth Higginson*. Chicago: University of Chicago Press, 2000.

Loving, Jerome M., ed. *Civil War Letters of George Washington Whitman*. Durham, NC: Duke University Press, 1975.

Lupold, Harry F., ed. "A Union Medical Officer Views the 'Texians.'" *Southwestern Historical Quarterly* 77 (April 1974): 481–86.

Lusk, William Thompson. *War Letters of William Thompson Lusk: Captain, Assistant Adjutant-General, United States Volunteers, 1861–1863*. Privately published, 1911.

Lynch, Charles H. *The Civil War Diary, 1862–1865, of Charles H. Lynch, 18th Connecticut Vols*. Hartford: Case, Lockwood & Brainard, 1915. (Accessed at CWLD, http://solomon.cwld.alexanderstreet.com, February 2012.)

Mann, Albert William. *History of the Forty-fifth Regiment Massachusetts Volunteer Militia.* Boston: W. Spooner, 1908.

Mannis, Jedediah, and Galen R. Wilson, eds. *Bound to Be a Soldier: The Letters of Private James T. Miller.* Knoxville: University of Tennessee Press, 2001.

Marcotte, Frank B., ed. *Private Osborne, Massachusetts 23rd Volunteers: Burnside Expedition, Roanoke Island, Second Front against Richmond.* Jefferson, NC: McFarland & Company, 1999.

Marshall, Elizabeth Hulsey, ed. "Watch on the Chattahoochee: A Civil War Letter." *Georgia Historical Quarterly* 43 (December 1959): 427–28.

Matson, H. "Early Days of Reconstruction in Northeastern Arkansas." Edward D. Neill, ed., *Glimpses of the Nation's Struggle, Second Series, Military Order of the Loyal Legion of the United States.* St. Paul, MN: St. Pau Book and Stationary Co., 1890.

McDonald, Hunter, ed. *A Diary with Reminiscences of the War and Refugee Life in the Shenandoah Valley, 1860–1865 [by] Mrs. Cornelia McDonald.* Nashville: Cullom & Ghertner Co., 1935.

McPherson, James M., ed. *The Negro's Civil War: How American Negroes Felt and Acted during the War for the Union.* New York: Pantheon Books, 1965.

Meade, George Gordon. *The Life and Letters of George Gordon Meade, Major-General United States Army.* New York: Charles Scribner's Sons, 1913.

Miles, Nelson A. *Serving the Republic: Memoir of the Civil and Military Life of Nelson A. Miles.* New York: Harper & Brothers, 1911.

Mitchell, Charles W., ed. *Maryland Voices of the Civil War.* Baltimore: Johns Hopkins University Press, 2007.

Mushkat, Jerome, ed. *A Citizen-Soldier's Civil War: The Letters of Brevet Major General Alvin C. Voris.* DeKalb: Northern Illinois University Press, 2002.

Myers, John C. *A Daily Journal of the 192d Reg't Penn'a Volunteers.* Philadelphia: Crissy & Markley Printers, 1864. (Accessed at CWLD, http://solomon.cwld.alexanderstreet.com, March 2014.)

Norton, Oliver Wilcox. *Army Letters, 1861–1865.* Privately published, 1903. (Accessed at CWLD, http://solomon.cwld.alexanderstreet.com, February 2012.)

An Officer of the 9th Army Corps. "*Notes on Colored Troops and Military Colonies on Southern Soil.* New York: N.p., 1863.

Oswandel, J. Jacob. *Notes on the Mexican War, 1846–47–48.* Philadelphia: N.p., 1885.

Pace, Eleanor Damon, ed. "The Diary and Letters of William P. Rogers, 1846–1862." *Southwestern Historical Quarterly* 32 (April 1929): 259–99.

Palladino, Anita, ed. *Diary of a Yankee Engineer: The Civil War Diary of John Henry Westervelt, Engineer, 1st New York Volunteer Engineer Corps.* New York: Fordham University Press, 1997.

Pelka, Fred, ed. *The Civil War Letters of Colonel Charles F. Johnson, Invalid Corps.* Amherst: University of Massachusetts Press, 2004.

Peskin, Allan, ed. *Volunteers: The Mexican War Journals of Private Richard Coulter and Sergeant Thomas Barclay, Company E, Second Pennsylvania Infantry.* Kent, OH: Kent State University Press, 1991.

Popchuck, Barry, ed. *Soldier Boy: The Civil War Letters of Charles O. Musser, 29th Iowa.* Iowa City: University of Iowa Press, 1995.

Porter, Charles T. *Review of the Mexican War.* Auburn, NY: Alden & Parsons, 1849.

Porter, Charles W. *In the Devil's Dominions: A Union Soldier's Adventures in "Bushwhacker Country."* Ed. Patrick Brophy. Nevada, MO: Vernon County Historical Society, 1998.

Post, Marie Caroline. *The Life and Memoirs of Comte Regis de Trobriand.* New York: E. P. Dutton & Co., 1910.

Priest, John Michael, et al., eds. *From New Bern to Fredericksburg: Captain James Wren's Civil War Diary.* Shippensburg, PA: White Mane Publishing Co., 1990.

Rankin, David C., ed. *Diary of a Christian Soldier: Rufus Kinsley and the Civil War.* New York: Cambridge University Press, 2004.

Redkey, Edwin S., ed. *A Grand Army of Black Men: Letters from African-American Soldiers in the Union Army, 1861–1865.* New York: Cambridge University Press, 1992.

Reyburn, Philip J., and Terry L. Wilson, eds. *"Jottings from Dixie": The Civil War Dispatches of Sergeant Major Stephen F. Fleharty, U.S.A.* Baton Rouge: Louisiana State University Press, 1999.

Rhodes, Robert Hunt, ed. *All for the Union: The Civil War Diary and Letters of Elisha Hunt Rhodes.* New York: Vintage Books, 1992.

Richardson, James D. *A Compilation of the Messages and Papers of the Presidents, 1789–1897.* 10 vols. Washington, DC: Government Printing Office, 1896–99.

Roe, David D., ed. *A Civil War Soldier's Diary: Valentine C. Robinson, 39th Illinois Regiment.* DeKalb: Northern Illinois University Press, 2006.

Root, L. Carroll, ed. "The Experiences of a Federal Soldier in Louisiana in 1863." *Louisiana Historical Quarterly* 19 (July 1936): 635–67.

Rosenblatt, Emil, and Ruth Rosenblatt, eds., *Hard Marching Every Day: The Civil War Letters of Private Wilbur Fisk, 1861–1865.* Lawrence: University Press of Kansas, 1992.

Roth, Margaret Brobst, ed. *Well, Mary: Civil War Letters of a Wisconsin Volunteer.* Madison: University of Wisconsin Press, 1960.

Rowland, Kate Mason, and Mrs. Morris L. Croxall, eds. *The Journal of Julia LeGrand: New Orleans, 1862–1863.* Richmond: Everett Waddey Co., 1911.

Ryan, Harriet Fitts, ed. "The Letters of Harden Perkins Cochrane, 1862–1864." *Alabama Review* 7 (October 1954): 277–94.

Scott, Winfield. *Memoirs of Lieut.-General Scott, LL.D.* 2 vols. New York: Shelden & Co., 1864.

Sherman, William T. *Memoirs of General William T. Sherman.* 2 vols. Bloomington: Indiana University Press, 1957.

Shewmaker, Kenneth E., and Andrew K. Prinz, eds. "A Yankee in Louisiana: Selections from the Diary and Correspondence of Henry R. Gardner." *Louisiana History* 5 (Summer 1964): 271–95.

Silber, Nina, and Mary Beth Sievens, eds. *Yankee Correspondence: Civil War Letters between New England Soldiers and the Home Front.* Charlottesville: University Press of Virginia, 1996.

Simon, John Y., et al., eds. *The Papers of Ulysses S. Grant.* 32 vols. Carbondale: Southern Illinois University Press, 1967–present.

Simpson, Brooks D., and Jean V. Berlin, eds. *Sherman's Civil War: Selected Correspondence of William T. Sherman, 1860–1865.* Chapel Hill: University of North Carolina Press, 1999.

Smith, George Gilbert. *Leaves from a Soldier's Diary: The Personal Record of Lieutenant George G. Smith, Co. C., 1st Louisiana Regiment Infantry Volunteers [White] during the War of the Rebellion.* Putnam, CT: G. G. Smith, 1906. (Accessed at CWLD, http:// solomon.cwld.alexanderstreet.com, February 2012.)

Smith, George Winston, and Charles Judah, eds. *Chronicles of the Gringos: The U.S. Army in the Mexican War, 1846–1848.* Albuquerque: University of New Mexico Press, 1968.

Smith, Isaac. *Reminiscences of a Campaign in Mexico.* Indianapolis: Chapmans & Spann, 1848.

Smith, W. F., ed. "The Yankees in New Albany: Letter of Elizabeth Jane Beach, July 29, 1864." *Journal of Mississippi History* 2 (January 1941): 42–48.

Staudenraus, P. J., ed. "A War Correspondent's View of St. Augustine and Fernandina: 1863." *Florida Historical Quarterly* 41 (July 1962): 60–65.

——. "Occupied Beaufort, 1863: A War Correspondent's View." *South Carolina Historical Magazine* 64 (July 1963): 136–44.

Steers, Ed, ed. "Garrison Duty in Alexandria: The Red River Campaign Letters of Lt. Charles W. Kennedy, 156th New York Volunteer Infantry." *Civil War Regiments* 4, no. 2 (1994): 104–17.

Strong, Robert Hale, ed. *A Yankee Private's Civil War.* Chicago: Henry Regnery Co., 1961.

Sutherland, Daniel E., ed. *From Shiloh to Savannah: The Seventh Illinois Infantry in the Civil War.* DeKalb: Northern Illinois University Press, 2003.

Swedberg, Claire E., ed. *Three Years with the 92nd Illinois: The Civil War Diary of John M. King.* Mechanicsburg, PA: Stackpole Books, 1999.

Swint, Henry L., ed. *Dear Ones at Home: Letters from Contraband Camps.* Nashville: Vanderbilt University Press, 1966.

Sylvester, Lorna Lutes, ed. "The Civil War Letters of Charles Harding Cox." *Indiana Magazine of History* 68 (March 1972): 24–78; (September 1972): 181–239.

Thompson, S. D. *Recollections with the Third Iowa Regiment.* Cincinnati: privately published, 1864.

Thorndike, Rachel Sherman, ed. *The Sherman Letters: Correspondence between General and Senator Sherman from 1837 to 1891.* New York: Charles Scribner's Sons, 1894.

Thorne, Mildred, ed. *The Civil War Diary of Cyrus F. Boyd, Fifteenth Iowa Infantry, 1861–1863.* Baton Rouge: Louisiana State University Press, 1998.

Thorpe, T. B. *Our Army at Monterey.* Philadelphia: Carey & Hart, 1847.

Tilley, Nannie M., ed. *Federals on the Frontier: The Diary of Benjamin F. McIntyre.* Austin: University of Texas Press, 1963.

Torrey, Rodney Webster. *War Diary of Rodney W. Torrey, 1862–1863.* Place and publisher not identified. (Accessed at CWLD, http://solomon.cwld.alexanderstreet.com, February 2012.)

Van Alstyne, Lawrence. *Diary of an Enlisted Man.* New Haven, CT: Tuttle, Morehouse, & Taylor Co., 1910.

Victor, Orville J. *Incidents and Anecdotes of the War; Together with Life Sketches of Eminent Leaders, and Narratives of the Most Memorable Battles for the Union.* New York: James D. Torrey, 1862.

Volwiler, A. T., ed. "Letters from a Civil War Officer." *Mississippi Valley Historical Review* 14 (March 1928): 508–29.

Weaver, C. P., ed. *Thank God My Regiment an African One: The Civil War Diary of Colonel Nathan W. Daniels.* Baton Rouge: Louisiana State University Press, 1998.

Wescott, M. Ebenezer. *Civil War Letters, 1861 to 1865.* Mora, MN: privately published, 1909. (Accessed at CWLD, http://solomon.cwld.alexanderstreet.com, February 2012.)

Williams, G. Mott. "Letters of General Thomas Williams, 1862." *American Historical Review* 14 (January 1909): 304–28.

Wilson, Joseph T. *The Black Phalanx: A History of the Negro Soldiers of the United States in the War of 1775–1812, 1861-'65.* Hartford: American Publishing Co., 1888.

Winschel, Terrence J., ed. *The Civil War Diary of a Common Soldier: William Wiley of the 77th Illinois Infantry.* Baton Rouge: Louisiana State University Press, 2001.

Secondary Sources

Adams, Kevin. *Class and Race in the Frontier Army: Military Life in the West, 1870–1890.* Norman: University of Oklahoma Press, 2009.

Alexander, Roberta Sue. *North Carolina Faces the Freedmen: Race Relations during Presidential Reconstruction, 1865–1867.* Durham, NC: Duke University Press, 1985.

Anderson, Fred. *A People's Army: Massachusetts Soldiers and Society in the Seven Years' War.* Chapel Hill: University of North Carolina Press, 1996.

Appleby, Joyce. "Republicanism and Ideology." *American Quarterly* 37 (Autumn 1985): 461–73.

——. "Republicanism in Old and New Contexts." *William and Mary Quarterly* 43 (January 1986): 20–34.

——. *Liberalism and Republicanism in the Historical Imagination.* Cambridge, MA: Harvard University Press, 1992.

Archer, Richard. *As If an Enemy's Country: The British Occupation of Boston and the Origins of Revolution.* New York: Oxford University Press, 2010.

Ash, Stephen V. *Middle Tennessee Society Transformed, 1860–1870: War and Peace in the Upper South.* Baton Rouge: Louisiana State University Press, 1988.

——. "Poor Whites in the Occupied South, 1861–1865." *Journal of Southern History* 57 (February 1991): 39–62.

——. *When the Yankees Came: Conflict and Chaos in the Occupied South, 1861–1865.* Chapel Hill: University of North Carolina Press, 1995.

——. *Firebrand of Liberty: The Story of Two Black Regiments That Changed the Course of the Civil War.* New York: W. W. Norton & Co., 2008.

———. *A Massacre in Memphis: The Race Riot That Shook the Nation One Year after the Civil War.* New York: Hill & Wang, 2013.

Astor, Aaron. *Rebels on the Border: Civil War, Emancipation, and the Reconstruction of Kentucky and Missouri.* Baton Rouge: Louisiana State University Press, 2012.

Ayers, Edward L. *What Caused the Civil War? Reflections on the South and Southern History.* New York: W. W. Norton, 2005.

Bailyn, Bernard. *Ideological Origins of the American Revolution.* Cambridge, MA: Harvard University Press, 1967.

Ball, Durwood. *Army Regulars on the Western Frontier, 1848–1861.* Norman: University of Oklahoma Press, 2001.

Ballard, Michael B. *Vicksburg: The Campaign That Opened the Mississippi.* Chapel Hill: University of North Carolina Press, 2004.

Barton, Michael. *Goodmen: The Character of Civil War Soldiers.* University Park: Pennsylvania State University Press, 1981.

———. *The Civil War Soldier: A Historical Reader.* New York: New York University Press, 2002.

Bauer, K. Jack. *The Mexican War, 1846–1848.* New York: Macmillan, 1974.

Becker, Peter W. "Lieber's Place in History." In *Francis Lieber and the Culture of the Mind,* ed. Charles R. Mack and Henry H. Lesesne, 1-7. Columbia: University of South Carolina Press, 2005.

Bell, Andrew McIlwaine. *Mosquito Soldiers: Malaria, Yellow Fever, and the Course of the American Civil War.* Baton Rouge: Louisiana State University Press, 2010.

Belz, Herman. *Reconstructing the Union: Theory and Policy during the Civil War.* Ithaca, NY: Cornell University Press, 1969.

Benedict, Michael Les. "Preserving the Constitution: The Conservative Basis of Radical Reconstruction." *Journal of American History* 61 (June 1974): 65–90.

Bensel, Richard Franklin. *Yankee Leviathan: The Origins of Central State Authority in America, 1859–1877.* New York: Cambridge University Press, 1990.

Bergeron, Arthur W., Jr. *Confederate Mobile.* Jackson: University Press of Mississippi, 1991.

Beringer, Richard E., et al., *Why the South Lost the Civil War.* Athens: University of Georgia Press, 1986.

Berlin, Ira. "Who Freed the Slaves? Emancipation and Its Meaning." In *Union and Emancipation: Essays on Politics and Race in the Civil War Era,* ed. David W. Blight and Brooks D. Simpson, 105–22. Kent, OH: Kent State University Press, 1997.

Berlin, Ira D. *Slaves No More: Three Essays on Emancipation and the Civil War.* Cambridge: Cambridge University Press, 1992.

Berry, Mary Frances. *Military Necessity and Civil Rights Policy: Black Citizenship and the Constitution, 1861–1868.* Port Washington, NY: Kennikat Press, 1977.

Berry, Stephen. "Forum: The Future of Civil War Era Studies." *Journal of the Civil War Era* 2 (March 2012): online at http://journalofthecivilwarera.org/forum-the-future-of-civil-war-era-studies.

Berthoff, Rowland. "From Republican Citizen to Free Enterpriser, 1787–1837." In *Republic of the Dispossessed: The Exceptional Old-European Consensus in America,* by Rowland Berthoff, 137–54. Columbia: University of Missouri Press, 1997.

Birtle, Andrew J. *U.S. Army Counterinsurgency and Contingency Operations Doctrine, 1860–1941*. Washington, DC: United States Army Center of Military History, 2009.

Blair, William A. *Virginia's Private War: Feeding Body and Soul in the Confederacy, 1861–1865*. New York: Oxford University Press, 1998.

———. "The Use of Military Force to Protect the Gains of Reconstruction." *Civil War History* 51 (December 2005): 388–402.

———. *With Malice toward Some: Treason and Loyalty in the Civil War Era*. Chapel Hill: University of North Carolina Press, 2014.

———. "Finding the Ending of America's Civil War." *American Historical Review* 120 (December 2015): 1753–66.

Blair, William A., and Karen Fisher Younger. *Lincoln's Proclamation: Emancipation Reconsidered*. Chapel Hill: University of North Carolina Press, 2009.

Bledsoe, Andrew Scott. *Citizen-Officers: The Union and Confederate Volunteer Junior Officer Corps in the American Civil War*. Baton Rouge: Louisiana State University Press, 2015.

Blight, David W. *Race and Reunion: The Civil War in American Memory*. Cambridge, MA: Harvard University Press, 2002.

Binkin, Martin, and Mark J. Eitelberg. *Blacks and the Military*. Washington, DC: Brookings Institution, 1982.

Boot, Max. *The Savage Wars of Peace: Small Wars and the Rise of American Power*, rev. ed. New York: Basic Books, 2014.

Boritt, Gabor S., ed. *Why the Confederacy Lost*. New York: Oxford University Press, 1992.

Boyle, Michael J. *Violence after War: Explaining Instability in Post-Conflict States*. Baltimore: Johns Hopkins University Press, 2014.

Bradley, Mark L. *Bluecoats and Tar Heels: Soldiers and Civilians in Reconstruction North Carolina*. Lexington: University Press of Kentucky, 2009.

Brady, Lisa M. "The Future of Civil War Studies: Environmental Histories." *Journal of the Civil War Era* 2 (March 2012): online at http://journalofthecivilwarera.org/forum-the-future-of-civil-war-era-studies/the-future-of-civil-war-era-studies-environmental-histories.

Brandt, Dennis W. *From Home Guards to Heroes: The 87th Pennsylvania and Its Civil War Community*. Columbia: University of Missouri Press, 2006.

Brasher, Glenn David. *The Peninsula Campaign and the Necessity of Emancipation: African Americans and the Fight for Freedom*. Chapel Hill: University of North Carolina Press, 2012.

Brody, David. *Visualizing Empire: Orientalism and Imperialism in the Philippines*. Chicago: University of Chicago Press, 2010.

Brown, Christopher Leslie, and Philip D. Morgan, eds. *Arming Slaves: From Classical Times to the Modern Age*. New Haven, CT: Yale University Press, 2006.

Browning, Judkin. "Removing the Mask of Nationality: Unionism, Racism, and Federal Military Occupation in Eastern North Carolina." *Journal of Southern History* 71 (August 2005): 589–620.

———. "'I Am Not So Patriotic as I Was Once': The Effects of Military Occupation on the Occupying Soldiers during the Civil War." *Civil War History* 55 (June 2009): 217–43.

———. *Shifting Loyalties: The Union Occupation of Eastern North Carolina.* Chapel Hill: University of North Carolina Press, 2011.

Bruce, Susannah U. *The Harp and the Eagle: Irish-American Volunteers and the Union Army, 1861–1865.* New York: New York University Press, 2006.

Brugel, Martin. *Farm, Shop, Landing: The Rise of a Market Society in the Hudson Valley, 1780–1860.* Durham, NC: Duke University Press, 2002.

Budiansky, Stephen. *The Bloody Shirt: Terror after the Civil War.* New York: Viking Press, 2008.

Buker, George E. *Blockaders, Refugees, and Contrabands: Civil War on Florida's Gulf Coast, 1861–1865.* Tuscaloosa: University of Alabama Press, 1993.

Burkhardt, George S. *Confederate Rage, Yankee Wrath: No Quarter in the Civil War.* Carbondale: Southern Illinois University Press, 2007.

Campbell, Jacqueline Glass. *When Sherman Marched North from the Sea: Resistance on the Confederate Home Front.* Chapel Hill: University of North Carolina Press, 2003.

Capers, Gerald M. *Occupied City: New Orleans under the Federals, 1862–1865.* Lexington: University of Kentucky Press, 1965.

Carmichael, Peter S. *The Last Generation: Young Virginians in Peace, War and Reunion.* Chapel Hill: University of North Carolina Press, 2005.

Carrigan, Jo Ann. "Yankees versus Yellow Jack in New Orleans, 1862–1866." *Civil War History* 9 (1963): 248–60.

Carter, Dan T. *When the War Was Over: The Failure of Self-Reconstruction in the South, 1865–1867.* Baton Rouge: Louisiana State University Press, 1985.

Cash, W. J. *The Mind of the South.* New York: Alfred A. Knopf, 1941.

Cimbala, Paul A. *Under the Guardianship of the Nation: The Freedmen's Bureau and the Reconstruction of Georgia, 1865–1870.* Athens: University of Georgia Press, 1997.

Cimbala, Paul A., and Randall M. Miller, eds. *Union Soldiers and the Northern Home Front: Wartime Experiences and Postwar Adjustments.* New York: Fordham University Press, 2002.

———. *The Great Task Remaining before Us: Reconstruction as America's Continuing Civil War.* New York: Fordham University Press, 2010.

Citino, Robert M. "Military Histories Old and New: A Reintroduction." *American Historical Review* 112 (October 2007): 1070–90.

Clampitt, Bradley R. *The Confederate Heartland: Military and Civilian Morale in the Western Confederacy.* Baton Rouge: Louisiana State University Press, 2011.

———. *Occupied Vicksburg.* Baton Rouge: Louisiana State University Press, 2016.

Clark, Christopher. *The Roots of Rural Capitalism: Western Massachusetts, 1780–1860.* Ithaca, NY: Cornell University Press, 1990.

Clinton, Catherine, ed. *Southern Families at War: Loyalty and Conflict in the Civil War South.* New York: Oxford University Press, 2000.

Coffman, Edward M. *The Old Army: A Portrait of the American Army in Peacetime, 1784–1898.* New York: Oxford University Press, 1986.

———. "The Duality of the American Military Tradition." *Journal of Military History* 64 (October 2000): 967–80.

Cooper, William J., Jr. *Jefferson Davis, American.* New York: Vintage, 2001.

Cornell, Saul. *A Well-Regulated Militia: The Founding Fathers and the Origins of Gun Control in America.* New York: Oxford University Press, 2006.

Cornish, Dudley Taylor. *The Sable Arm: Negro Troops in the Union Army, 1861–1865.* New York: W. W. Norton & Co., 1966.

Cotham, Edward T., Jr. *Battle on the Bay: The Civil War Struggle for Galveston.* Austin: University of Texas Press, 1998.

Coulter, E. Merton. "Commercial Intercourse with the Confederacy in the Mississippi Valley, 1861–1865." *Mississippi Valley Historical Review* 5 (March 1919): 377–95.

Crawford, Martin. *Ashe County's Civil War: Community and Society in the Appalachian South.* Charlottesville: University Press of Virginia, 2001.

Cunliffe, Marcus. *Soldiers and Civilians: The Martial Spirit in America, 1776–1865.* Boston: Little Brown, 1968.

Currarino, Rosanne. "Toward a History of Cultural Economy." *Journal of the Civil War Era* 2 (December 2012): 564–85.

Currie, James T. *Enclave: Vicksburg and Her Plantations, 1863–1870.* Jackson: University Press of Mississippi, 1980.

Danielson, Joseph W. *War's Desolating Scourge: The Union's Occupation of North Alabama.* Lawrence: University Press of Kansas, 2012.

Dawson, Joseph G., III. *Army Generals and Reconstruction: Louisiana, 1862–1877.* Baton Rouge: Louisiana State University Press, 1982.

———. "The US Army in the South: Reconstruction as Nation Building." In *Armed Diplomacy: Two Centuries of American Campaigning,* 39–63. Fort Leavenworth, KS: Combat Studies Institute Press, 2003.

Dew, Charles B. *Apostles of Disunion: Southern Secession Commissioners and the Causes of the Civil War.* Charlottesville: University Press of Virginia, 2001.

Dilbeck, D. H. "'The Genesis of This Little Tablet with My Name': Francis Lieber and the Wartime Origins of General Orders No. 100." *Journal of the Civil War Era* 5 (June 2015): 231–53.

———. *A More Civil War: How the Union Waged a Just War.* Chapel Hill: University of North Carolina Press, 2016.

Dobak, William A. *Freedom by the Sword: The U.S. Colored Troops, 1862–1877.* Washington, DC: United States Army Center of Military History, 2011.

Donald, David, ed. *Why the North Won the Civil War.* Baton Rouge: Louisiana State University Press, 1960.

Downs, Gregory P. "The Mexicanization of American Politics: The United States' Transnational Path from War to Stabilization." *American Historical Review* 117 (April 2012): 387–409.

——. "Anarchy at the Circumference: Statelessness and the Reconstruction of Authority in Emancipation North Carolina." In *After Slavery: Race, Labor, and Citizenship in the Reconstruction South,* ed. Bruce E. Baker and Brian Kelly, 98–121. Gainesville: University Press of Florida, 2013.

——. *After Appomattox: Military Occupation and the Ends of War.* Cambridge, MA: Harvard University Press, 2015.

Dubbs, Carol Kettenburg. *Defend This Old Town: Williamsburg during the Civil War.* Baton Rouge: Louisiana State University Press, 2002.

Dunkelman, Mark H. *Brothers One and All: Esprit de Corps in a Civil War Regiment.* Baton Rouge: Louisiana State University Press, 2004.

Dupree, Stephen A. *Planting the Union Flag in Texas: The Campaigns of Major General Nathaniel P. Banks in the West.* College Station: Texas A&M University Press, 2008.

Durham, Walter T. *Nashville, the Occupied City: The First Seventeen Months—February 16, 1862, to June 30, 1863.* Nashville: Tennessee Historical Society, 1985.

——. *Reluctant Partners: Nashville and the Union, July 1, 1863, to June 30, 1865.* Nashville: Tennessee Historical Society Press, 1987.

Durrill, Wayne K. *War of Another Kind: A Southern Community in the Great Rebellion.* New York: Oxford University Press, 1990.

Dyer, John Percy. "Northern Relief for Savannah during Sherman's Occupation." *Journal of Southern History* 19 (1953): 457–72.

Egerton, Douglas R. *The Wars of Reconstruction: The Brief, Violent History of America's Most Progressive Era.* New York: Bloomsbury Press, 2014.

Eisenhower, John S. D. *So Far from God: The U.S. War with Mexico, 1846–1848.* New York: Random House, 1989.

Elliott, Charles Winslow. *Winfield Scott: The Soldier and the Man.* New York: Macmillan, 1937.

Emberton, Carole. "'Only Murder Makes Men': Reconsidering the Black Military Experience." *Journal of the Civil War Era* 2 (September 2012): 369–93.

——. *Beyond Redemption: Race, Violence, and the American South after the Civil War.* Chicago: University of Chicago Press, 2013.

Escott, Paul D. *Lincoln's Dilemma: Blair, Sumner, and the Republican Struggle over Racism and Equality in the Civil War Era.* Charlottesville: University of Virginia Press, 2014.

Fahs, Alice. *The Imagined Civil War: Popular Literature of the North and South, 1861–1865.* Chapel Hill: University of North Carolina Press, 2001.

Faust, Drew Gilpin. *Mothers of Invention: Women of the Slaveholding South in the American Civil War.* Chapel Hill: University of North Carolina Press, 1996.

——. "'We Should Grow Too Fond of It': Why We Love the Civil War." *Civil War History* 50 (December 2004): 368–83.

——. *This Republic of Suffering: Death and the American Civil War.* New York: Alfred A. Knopf, 2008.

Feller, Daniel. "The Market Revolution Ate My Homework." *Reviews in American History* 25 (September 1997): 408–15.

Fellman, Michael. *Inside War: The Guerrilla Conflict in Missouri during the Civil War.* New York: Oxford University Press, 1989.

———. *Citizen Sherman: A Life of William Tecumseh Sherman.* New York: Random House, 1995.

———. *In the Name of God and Country: Reconsidering Terrorism in American History.* New Haven, CT: Yale University Press, 2010.

Fitzgerald, Michael W. *Splendid Failure: Postwar Reconstruction in the American South.* New York: Ivan R. See, 2007.

Fletcher, Marvin E. "The Negro Volunteer in Reconstruction, 1865–1866." *Military Affairs* 32 (December 1968): 124–31.

Foner, Eric. *Free Soil, Free Labor, Free Men: The Ideology of the Republican Party before the Civil War.* New York: Oxford University Press, 1970.

———. *Reconstruction: America's Unfinished Revolution, 1863–1877.* New York: Harper & Row, 1988.

———. *The Fiery Trial: Abraham Lincoln and American Slavery.* New York: W. W. Norton, 2010.

Foos, Paul. *A Short, Offhand, Killing Affair: Soldiers and Social Conflict during the Mexican-American War.* Chapel Hill: University of North Carolina Press, 2002.

Foote, Lorien. "Rich Man's War, Rich Man's Fight: Class, Ideology, and Discipline in the Union Army." *Civil War History* 51 (September 2005): 269–87.

———. *The Gentlemen and the Roughs: Violence, Honor, and Manhood in the Union Army.* New York: New York University Press, 2010.

Fox, William F. *Regimental Losses in the American Civil War.* Albany, NY: Albany Publishing Co., 1893.

Frank, Joseph Allan. *With Ballot and Bayonet: The Political and Socialization of American Civil War Soldiers.* Athens: University of Georgia Press, 1998.

Frank, Lisa Tendrich. *The Civilian War: Confederate Women and Union Soldiers during Sherman's March.* Baton Rouge: Louisiana State University Press, 2015.

Franklin, John Hope. *The Militant South, 1800–1860.* Boston: Beacon Press, 1956.

———. *Reconstruction after the Civil War.* Chicago: University of Chicago Press, 1961.

———. *The Emancipation Proclamation.* Garden City, NY: Doubleday, 1963.

Frazier, Donald S. "'Out of Stinking Distance': The Guerrilla War in Louisiana." In *Guerrillas, Unionists, and Violence on the Confederate Home Front.* Ed. Daniel E. Sutherland. Fayetteville: University of Arkansas Press, 1999.

———. *Fire in the Cane Field: The Federal Invasion of Louisiana and Texas, January 1861–January 1863.* Buffalo Gap, TX: State House Press, 2009.

Fredrickson, George M. "A Man but Not a Brother: Abraham Lincoln and Racial Equality." *Journal of Southern History* 41 (February 1975): 39–58.

———. *Big Enough to Be Inconsistent: Abraham Lincoln Confronts Slavery and Race.* Cambridge, MA: Harvard University Press, 2008.

Freehling, William W. *The South vs. the South: How Anti-Confederate Southerners Shaped the Course of the Civil War.* New York: Oxford University Press, 2001.

———. *The Road to Disunion, Volume II: Secessionists Triumphant, 1854–1861.* New York: Oxford University Press, 2007.

Freidel, Frank. "General Orders 100 and Military Government." *Mississippi Valley Historical Review* 32 (March 1946): 541–56.

———. *Francis Lieber: Nineteenth-Century Liberal.* Baton Rouge: Louisiana State University Press, 1947.

Futrell, Robert F. "Federal Military Government in the South, 1861–1865." *Military Affairs* 15 (Winter 1951): 181–91.

Gabriel, Ralph H. "American Experience with Military Government." *American Historical Review* 49 (July 1944): 630–43.

Gallagher, Gary W. *The Confederate War.* Cambridge, MA: Harvard University Press, 1997.

———. *The Union War.* Cambridge, MA: Harvard University Press, 2011.

Gallagher, Gary W., and Kathryn Shively Meier. "Coming to Terms with Civil War Military History." *Journal of the Civil War Era* 4 (December 2014): 487–508.

Gerteis, Louis S. *From Contraband to Freedman: Federal Policy toward Southern Blacks, 1861–1865.* Westport, CT: Greenwood Press, 1973.

Gillette, William. *Retreat from Reconstruction, 1869–1879.* Baton Rouge: Louisiana State University Press, 1979.

Glatthaar, Joseph T. *The March to the Sea and Beyond: Sherman's Troops in the Savannah and Carolinas Campaign.* New York: Free Press, 1985.

———. *Forged in Battle: The Civil War Alliance of Black Soldiers and White Officers.* New York: Free Press, 1990.

———. "The 'New' Civil War History: An Overview." *Pennsylvania Magazine of History and Biography* 98 (April 1990): 339–69.

———. "Black Glory: The African-American Role in Union Victory." In *Why the Confederacy Lost,* ed. Gabor S. Borritt, 133–62. New York: Oxford University Press, 1992.

———. *General Lee's Army: From Victory to Collapse.* New York: Free Press, 2008.

———. "The Civil War: A New Definition of Victory." In *Between War and Peace: How America Ends Its Wars,* ed. Col. Matthew Moten, 107–28. New York: Free Press, 2011.

Glickstein, Jonathan A. *American Exceptionalism, American Anxiety: Wages, Competition, and Degraded Labor in the Antebellum United States.* Charlottesville: University of Virginia Press, 2002.

Gray, Michael P. *The Business of Captivity: Elmira and Its Civil War Prison.* Kent, OH: Kent State University Press, 2001.

Greenough, Mark K. "Aftermath at Appomattox: Federal Military Occupation of Appomattox County, May–November, 1865." *Civil War History* 31 (1985): 5–23.

Grimsley, Mark. *The Hard Hand of War: Union Military Policy toward Southern Civilians.* New York: Cambridge University Press, 1995.

———. "Success and Failure in Civil War Armies: Clues from Organizational Culture." In *Warfare and Culture in World History,* ed. Wayne E. Lee, 115–41. New York: New York University Press, 2011.

———. "Wars for the American South: The First and Second Reconstructions Considered as Insurgencies." *Civil War History* 58 (March 2012): 24–36.

Grivas, Theodore. *Military Governments in California, 1846–1850.* Glendale, CA: Arthur H. Clark Co., 1963.

Gross, Robert A. *The Minutemen and Their World.* New York: Hill & Wang, 1976.

Guardino, Peter. "Gender, Soldiering, and Citizenship in the Mexican-American War of 1846–1848." *American Historical Review* 119 (February 2014): 23–46.

Guelzo, Allen C. *Lincoln's Emancipation Proclamation: The End of Slavery in America.* New York: Simon & Schuster, 2004.

Hahn, Steven. *A Nation under Our Feet: Black Political Struggles in the Rural South from Slavery to the Great Migration.* Cambridge, MA: Harvard University Press, 2003.

Hattaway, Herman, and Archer Jones. *How the North Won: A Military History of the Civil War.* Urbana: University of Illinois Press, 1991.

Hearn, Chester G. *Six Years of Hell: Harpers Ferry during the Civil War.* Baton Rouge: Louisiana State University Press, 1996.

———. *When the Devil Came Down to Dixie: Ben Butler in New Orleans.* Baton Rouge: Louisiana State University Press, 1997.

Henderson, Timothy J. *A Glorious Defeat: Mexico and Its War with the United States.* New York: Hill & Wang, 2007.

Herrera, Ricardo A. "Self-Governance and the American Citizen as Soldier, 1775–1861." *Journal of Military History* 65 (January 2001): 21–52.

———. *For Liberty and the Republic: The American Citizen as Soldier, 1775–1861.* New York: New York University Press, 2015.

Hess, Earl J. *Liberty, Virtue, and Progress: Northerners and Their War for the Union.* New York: New York University Press, 1988.

———. *The Union Soldier in Battle: Enduring the Ordeal of Combat.* Lawrence: University Press of Kansas, 1997.

———. *The Civil War in the West: Victory and Defeat from the Appalachians to the Mississippi.* Chapel Hill: University of North Carolina Press, 2012.

———. "Where Do We Stand? A Critical Assessment of Civil War Studies in the Sesquicentennial Era." *Civil War History* 60 (December 2014): 371–403.

Hewitt, Lawrence Lee. *Port Hudson, Confederate Bastion on the Mississippi.* Baton Rouge: Louisiana State University Press, 1987.

Hietala, Thomas R. *Manifest Design: American Exceptionalism and Empire.* Ithaca, NY: Cornell University Press, 2003.

Higginbotham, Don. *George Washington and the American Military Tradition.* Athens: University of Georgia Press, 1985.

———. "The Martial Spirit in the Antebellum South: Some Further Speculations in a National Context." *Journal of Southern History* 58 (February 1992): 3–26.

Hofstadter, Richard. "Cuba, the Philippines, and Manifest Destiny." In *The Paranoid Style in American Politics,* by Richard Hofstadter, 145–87. Cambridge, MA: Harvard University Press, 1964.

Hoganson, Kristin L. *Fighting for American Manhood: How Gender Politics Provoked the Spanish-American and Philippine-American War.* New Haven, CT: Yale University Press, 1998.

Hogue, James K. *Uncivil War: Five New Orleans Street Battles and the Rise and Fall of Radical Reconstruction.* Baton Rouge: Louisiana State University Press, 2006.

Holberton, William B. *Homeward Bound: The Demobilization of the Union & Confederate Armies, 1865–1866*. Mechanicsburg, PA: Stackpole, 2001.

Hollandsworth, James G., Jr. *The Louisiana Native Guards: The Black Military Experience during the Civil War*. Baton Rouge: Louisiana State University Press, 1995.

Holzer, Harold, Edna Greene Medford, and Frank J. Williams. *The Emancipation Proclamation: Three Views*. Baton Rouge: Louisiana State University Press, 2006.

Houge, L. Lynn. "Lieber's Military Code and Its Legacy." In *Francis Lieber and the Culture of the Mind,* ed. Charles R. Mack and Henry H. Lesesne, 51–60. Columbia: University of South Carolina Press, 2005.

Howe, Daniel Walker. *What Hath God Wrought: The Transformation of America, 1815–1848*. New York: Oxford University Press, 2007.

Hsieh, Wayne Wei-Siang. *West Pointers and the Civil War: The Old Army in War and Peace*. Chapel Hill: University of North Carolina Press, 2009.

———. "Total War and the American Civil War Reconsidered: The End of an Outdated 'Master Narrative.'" *Journal of the Civil War Era* 1 (September 2011): 394–408.

Humphreys, Margaret. *Intensely Human: The Health of the Black Soldier in the American Civil War*. Baltimore: Johns Hopkins University Press, 2008.

Huntington, Samuel P. *The Soldier and the State: The Theory and Politics of Civil-Military Relations*. Cambridge, MA: Harvard University Press, 1957.

Hyman, Harold M. *A More Perfect Union: The Impact of the Civil War and Reconstruction on the Constitution*. New York: Alfred A. Knopf, 1973.

Jennings, Francis. *The Invasion of America: Indians, Colonialism, and the Cant of Conquest*. Chapel Hill: University of North Carolina Press, 1975.

Jimerson, Randall C. *The Private Civil War: Popular Thought during the Sectional Conflict*. Baton Rouge: Louisiana State University Press, 1988.

Johannsen, Robert W. *To the Halls of the Montezumas: The Mexican War in the American Imagination*. New York: Oxford University Press, 1985.

Johnson, James E. "Race, Foreign Armies and United States Colored Troops." *New York Times* "Disunion" Blog, February 23, 2015. http://opinionator.blogs.nytimes.com/2015/02/23/race-foreign-armies-and-united-states-colored-troops/?_r=0.

Johnson, Ludwell H. "Contraband Trade during the Last Year of the Civil War." *Mississippi Valley Historical Review* 49 (March 1963): 635–52.

———. "Trading with the Union: The Evolution of Confederate Policy." *Virginia Magazine of History and Biography* 78 (July 1970): 308–25.

Johnson, Timothy D. *Winfield Scott: The Quest for Military Glory*. Lawrence: University Press of Kansas, 1998.

———. *A Gallant Little Army: The Mexico City Campaign*. Lawrence: University Press of Kansas, 2007.

Jones, Jacqueline. *Saving Savannah: The City and the Civil War*. New York: Alfred A. Knopf, 2008.

Jones, James Boyd, Jr. "A Tale of Two Cities: The Hidden Battle against Venereal Disease in Civil War Nashville and Memphis." *Civil War History* 31 (1985): 270–76.

Jordan, Brian Matthew. *Marching Home: Union Veterans and Their Unending Civil War.* New York: W. W. Norton, 2014.

Keith, LeeAnna. *The Colfax Massacre: The Untold Story of Black Power, White Terror, and the Death of Reconstruction.* New York: Oxford University Press, 2008.

Kelman, Ari. *A Misplaced Massacre: Struggling over the Memory of Sand Creek.* Cambridge, MA: Harvard University Press, 2013.

Kerby, Robert L. *Kirby Smith's Confederacy: The Trans-Mississippi South, 1863–1865.* New York: Columbia University Press, 1972.

Kerr-Ritchie, Jeffrey R. "Rehearsal for War: Black Militias in the Atlantic World." *Slavery and Abolition* 26 (April 2005): 1–34.

Knouff, Gregory T. *The Soldiers' Revolution: Pennsylvanians in Arms and the Forging of Early American Identity.* University Park: Pennsylvania State University Press, 2004.

Kohn, Richard H. *Eagle and Sword: The Federalists and the Creation of the Military Establishment in America, 1783–1802.* New York: Free Press, 1975.

Kousser, J. Morgan, and James M. McPherson, eds. *Region, Race, and Reconstruction: Essays in Honor of C. Vann Woodward.* New York: Oxford University Press, 1982.

Kwasney, Mark V. *Washington's Partisan War, 1775–1783.* Kent, OH: Kent State University Press, 1996.

Lamoreaux, Naomi R. "Rethinking the Transition to Capitalism in the Early American Northeast." *Journal of American History* 90 (September 2003): 437–61.

Lane, Charles. *The Day Freedom Died: The Colfax Massacre, the Supreme Court, and the Betrayal of Reconstruction.* New York: Henry Holt & Co., 2008.

Lang, Andrew F. "Soldiering on the Texas Coast and the Problem of Confederate Nationalism." In *This Corner of Canaan: Essays on Texas in Honor of Randolph B. Campbell,* ed. Richard B. McCaslin et al., 157–84. Denton: University of North Texas Press, 2013.

———. "Republicanism, Race, and Reconstruction: The Ethos of Military Occupation in Civil War America." *Journal of the Civil War Era* 4 (December 2014): 559–89.

Lash, Jeffrey N. "'The Federal Tyrant at Memphis': General Stephen A. Hurlbut and the Union Occupation of West Tennessee, 1862–64." *Tennessee Historical Quarterly* 48 (Spring 1989): 15–28.

Laver, Harry S. *Citizens More than Soldiers: The Kentucky Militia and Society in the Early Republic.* Lincoln: University of Nebraska Press, 2007.

Lawson, Melinda. *Patriot Fires: Forging a New American Nationalism in the Civil War North.* Lawrence: University Press of Kansas, 2002.

Lee, Wayne E. "Mind and Matter—Cultural Analysis in American Military History." *Journal of American History* 93 (March 2007): 1116–42.

Leigh, Phil. "Trading with the Enemy." *New York Times* "Disunion" Blog, October 28, 2012; http://opinionator.blogs.nytimes.com/2012/10/28/trading-with-the-enemy/?_r=0.

Lemann, Nicholas. *Redemption: The Last Battle of the Civil War.* New York: Farrar, Straus, & Giroux, 2006.

Levine, Bruce. *Confederate Emancipation: Southern Plans to Free and Arm Slaves during the Civil War.* New York: Oxford University Press, 2006.

Levinson, Irving W. "Occupation and Stability Dilemmas of the Mexican War: Origins and Solutions." In *Armed Diplomacy: Two Centuries of American Campaigning*, 1–16. Fort Leavenworth, KS: Combat Studies Institute Press, 2003.

———. *Wars within War: Mexican Guerrillas, Domestic Elites, and the United States of America, 1846–1848*. Fort Worth: Texas Christian University Press, 2005.

Limerick, Patricia Nelson. *The Legacy of Conquest: The Unbroken Past of the American West*. New York: W. W. Norton, 1987.

Linderman, Gerald F. *Embattled Courage: The Experience of Combat in the American Civil War*. New York: Free Press, 1989.

Litwack, Leon F. *Been in the Storm So Long: The Aftermath of Slavery*. New York: Alfred A. Knopf, 1979.

Livermore, Thomas L. *Numbers and Losses in the Civil War in America, 1861–1865*. Boston: Houghton, Mifflin & Co., 1900.

Logue, Larry. *To Appomattox and Beyond: The Civil War Soldier in War and Peace*. Chicago: Ivan R. Dee, 1996.

Long, Alecia P. "(Mis)Remembering General Order No. 28: Benjamin Butler, the Woman Order, and Historical Memory." In *Occupied Women: Gender, Military Occupation in the American Civil War*, ed. LeeAnn Whites and Alecia P. Long, 17–32. Baton Rouge: Louisiana State University Press, 2009.

Lowe, Richard. "Battle on the Levee: The Fight at Milliken's Bend." In *Black Soldiers in Blue: African American Troops in the Civil War Era*, ed. John David Smith, 107–35. Chapel Hill: University of North Carolina Press, 2002.

Luebke, Peter C. "'Equal to Any Minstrel Concert I Ever Attended at Home': Union Soldiers and Blackface Performance in the Civil War South." *Journal of the Civil War Era* 4 (December 2014): 509–32.

Luke, Rob, and John David Smith. *Soldiering for Freedom: How the Union Army Recruited, Trained, and Deployed the U.S. Colored Troops*. Baltimore: Johns Hopkins University Press, 2014.

Luskey, Brian P. *On the Make: Clerks and the Quest for Capital in Nineteenth-Century America*. New York: New York University Press, 2010.

Lynn, John A. "The Embattled Future of Academic History." *Journal of Military History* 61 (October 1997): 777–89.

Mackay, Robert R. *The Uncivil War: Irregular Warfare in the Upper South, 1861–1865*. Norman: University of Oklahoma Press, 2004.

Magness, Phillip W., and Sebastian N. Page. *Colonization after Emancipation: Lincoln and the Movement for Black Resettlement*. Columbia: University of Missouri Press, 2011.

Mancini, Matthew J. "Francis Lieber, Slavery, and the 'Genesis' of the Laws of War." *Journal of Southern History* 77 (May 2011): 325–48.

Manning, Chandra. *What This Cruel War Was Over: Soldiers, Slavery, and the Civil War*. New York: Alfred A. Knopf, 2007.

Marshall, Anne E. *Creating a Confederate Kentucky: The Lost Cause and Civil War Memory in a Border State*. Chapel Hill: University of North Carolina Press, 2010.

Marszalek, John F. *Sherman: A Soldier's Passion for Order*. New York: Free Press, 1993.

Martin, Richard A. "Defeat in Victory: Yankee Experience in Early Civil War Jacksonville." *Florida Historical Quarterly* 53 (1974): 1–32.

Maslowski, Peter. "A Study of Morale in Civil War Soldiers." *Military Affairs* 34 (December 1970): 122–26.

———. *Treason Must Be Made Odious: Military Occupation and Wartime Reconstruction in Nashville, Tennessee*. Millwood, NY: KTO Press, 1978.

Masur, Louis P. *Lincoln's Hundred Days: The Emancipation Proclamation and the War for the Union*. Cambridge, MA: Harvard University Press, 2012.

———. *Lincoln's Last Speech: Wartime Reconstruction and the Crisis of Reunion*. New York: Oxford University Press, 2015.

Mays, Thomas D. "The Battle of Saltville." In *Black Soldiers in Blue: African American Troops in the Civil War Era*, ed. John David Smith, 200–26. Chapel Hill: University of North Carolina Press, 2002.

McCaffrey, James M. *Army of Manifest Destiny: The American Soldier in the Mexican War, 1846–1848*. New York: New York University Press, 1992.

McClintock, Russell. *Lincoln and the Decision for War: The Northern Response to Secession*. Chapel Hill: University of North Carolina Press, 2008.

McCurry, Stephanie. *Confederate Reckoning: Power and Politics in the Civil War South*. Cambridge, MA: Harvard University Press, 2010.

McFeely, William S. *Grant: A Biography*. New York: W. W. Norton, 1981.

McGehee, C. Stuart. "Military Origins of the New South: The Army of the Cumberland and Chattanooga's Freedmen." *Civil War History* 34 (December 1988): 323–43.

McKnight, Brian D. *Contested Borderland: The Civil War in Appalachian Kentucky and Virginia*. Lexington: University Press of Kentucky, 2006.

———. *Confederate Outlaw: Champ Ferguson and the Civil War in Appalachia*. Baton Rouge: Louisiana State University Press, 2011.

McPherson, James M. *Battle Cry of Freedom: The Civil War Era*. New York: Oxford University Press, 1988.

———. *What They Fought For, 1861–1865*. Baton Rouge: Louisiana State University Press, 1994.

———. "Who Freed the Slaves?" *Proceedings of the American Philosophical Society* 139 (March 1995): 1–10.

———. *For Cause and Comrades: Why Men Fought in the Civil War*. New York: Oxford University Press, 1998.

———. "Antebellum Southern Exceptionalism: A New Look at an Old Question." *Civil War History* 50 (December 2004): 418–33.

Miller, Edward. *The Black Civil War Soldiers of Illinois: The Story of the Twenty-Ninth U.S. Colored Infantry*. Columbia: University of South Carolina Press, 1998.

Mitchell, Reid. *Civil War Soldiers: Their Expectations and Their Experiences*. New York: Viking Press, 1988.

———. *The Vacant Chair: The Northern Soldier Leaves Home*. New York: Oxford University Press, 1993.

Mountcastle, Clay. *Punitive War: Confederate Guerrillas and Union Reprisals.* Lawrence: University Press of Kansas, 2009.

Murray, Donald M., and Robert M. Rodney. "Colonel Julian E. Bryant: Champion of the Negro Soldier." *Journal of the Illinois State Historical Society* 56 (Summer 1963): 257–81.

Myers, Barton A. *Executing Daniel Bright: Race, Loyalty, and Guerrilla Violence in a Coastal Carolina Community 1861–1865.* Baton Rouge: Louisiana State University Press, 2009.

Neely, Mark E., Jr. "Abraham Lincoln and Black Colonization: Benjamin Butler's Spurious Testimony." *Civil War History* 25 (March 1979): 77–83.

——. "Lincoln and the Theory of Self-Emancipation." In *The Continuing Civil War: Essays in Honor of the Civil War Round Table of Chicago,* ed. John Y. Simon and Barbara Hughett, 45–60. Dayton, OH: Morningside Press, 1992.

——. "Was the Civil War a Total War?" *Civil War History* 50 (December 2004): 434–58.

——. *The Civil War and the Limits of Destruction.* Cambridge, MA: Harvard University Press, 2007.

——. "Colonization and the Myth That Lincoln Prepared the People for Emancipation." In *Lincoln's Proclamation: Emancipation Reconsidered,* ed. William A. Blair and Karen Fisher Younger, 45–74. Chapel Hill: University of North Carolina Press, 2009.

Neely, Mark E., Jr., and Harold Holzer. *The Union Image: Popular Prints of the Civil War North.* Chapel Hill: University of North Carolina Press, 2000.

Nelson, Scott Reynolds, and Carol Sheriff. *A People at War: Civilians and Soldiers in America's Civil War, 1854–1877.* New York: Oxford University Press, 2007.

Newell, Clayton R., and Charles R. Shrader, "The U.S. Army's Transition to Peace, 1865–66." *Journal of Military* 77 (July 2013): 867–94.

Noe, Kenneth W. "Exterminating Savages: The Union Army and Mountain Guerrillas in Southern West Virginia, 1861–1862." In *The Civil War in Appalachia: Collected Essays,* ed. Kenneth W. Noe and Shannon H. Wilson, 104–30. Knoxville: University of Tennessee Press, 1997.

——. *Reluctant Rebels: The Confederates Who Joined the Army after 1861.* Chapel Hill: University of North Carolina Press, 2010.

Nosworthy, Brent. *The Bloody Crucible of Courage: Fighting Methods and Combat Experience of the Civil War.* New York: Basic Books, 2005.

Oakes, James. *Freedom National: The Destruction of Slavery in the United States, 1861–1865.* New York: W. W. Norton, 2013.

Opal, J. M. *Beyond the Farm: National Ambitions in Rural New England.* Philadelphia: University of Pennsylvania Press, 2008.

Osterhammel, Jürgen. *The Transformation of the World: A Global History of the Nineteenth Century,* trans. Patrick Camiller. Princeton, NJ: Princeton University Press, 2014.

Ott, Victoria E. *Confederate Daughters: Coming of Age during the Civil War.* Carbondale: Southern Illinois University Press, 2008.

Paludan, Phillip Shaw. *Victims: A True Story of the Civil War.* Knoxville: University of Tennessee Press, 1981.

——. *"A People's Contest": The Union and Civil War.* New York: Harper & Row, 1988.

——. *The Presidency of Abraham Lincoln.* Lawrence: University Press of Kansas, 1994.

Papke, David Ray. *The Pullman Case: The Clash of Labor and Capital in Industrial America.* Lawrence: University Press of Kansas, 1999.

Paret, Peter, ed. *Makers of Modern Strategy: From Machiavelli to the Nuclear Age.* Princeton, NJ: Princeton University Press, 1986.

Parks, Joseph H. "A Confederate Trade Center under Federal Occupation: Memphis, 1862 to 1865." *Journal of Southern History* 7 (August 1941): 289–314.

Pearce, George F. *Pensacola during the Civil War: A Thorn in the Side of the Confederacy.* Gainesville: University Press of Florida, 2000.

Peskin, Allan. *Winfield Scott and the Profession of Arms.* Kent, OH: Kent State University Press, 2003.

Phillips, Jason. *Diehard Rebels: The Confederate Culture of Invincibility.* Athens: University of Georgia Press, 2007.

Pierson, Michael D. *Mutiny at Fort Jackson: The Untold Story of the Fall of New Orleans.* Chapel Hill: University of North Carolina Press, 2008.

Pocock, J. G. A. *The Machiavellian Moment: Florentine Political Thought and the Atlantic Republican Tradition.* Princeton, NJ: Princeton University Press, 1975.

Potter, David M. *The South and the Sectional Conflict.* Baton Rouge: Louisiana State University Press, 1968.

Power, J. Tracy. *Lee's Miserables: Life in the Army of Northern Virginia from the Wilderness to Appomattox.* Chapel Hill: University of North Carolina Press, 1998.

Prokopowicz, Gerald J. *All for the Regiment: The Army of the Ohio, 1861–1862.* Chapel Hill: University of North Carolina Press, 2001.

Prucha, Francis Paul. *The Sword of the Republic: The United States Army on the Frontier, 1783–1846.* New York: Macmillan, 1968.

Rable, George C. *But There Was No Peace: The Role of Violence in the Politics of Reconstruction.* Athens: University of Georgia Press, 1984.

——. *Civil Wars: Women and the Crisis of Southern Nationalism.* Urbana: University of Illinois Press, 1989.

Rael, Patrick. *Black Identity and Black Protest in the Antebellum North.* Chapel Hill: University of North Carolina Press, 2002.

Ramold, Steven J. *Baring the Iron Hand: Discipline in the Union Army.* DeKalb: Northern Illinois University Press, 2009.

——. *Across the Divide: Union Soldiers View the Northern Home Front.* New York: New York University Press, 2013.

Reardon, Carol. *With a Sword in One Hand and Jomini in the Other: The Problem of Military Thought in the Civil War North.* Chapel Hill: University of North Carolina Press, 2012.

Reid, Richard M. *Freedom for Themselves: North Carolina's Black Soldiers in the Civil War Era.* Chapel Hill: University of North Carolina Press, 2008.

Renda, Mary A. *Taking Haiti: Military Occupation and the Culture of U.S. Imperialism, 1915–1940.* Chapel Hill: University of North Carolina Press, 2001.

Rice, Charles. "The Bullwhip Mutiny." *Civil War Times Illustrated* 40 (February 2002): 38–43, 62.

Richter, William L. "'Outside My Profession': The Army and Civil Affairs in Texas Reconstruction." *Military History of Texas and the Southwest* 9 (1971): 5–21.

———. "'It Is Best to Go in Strong-Handed': Army Occupation of Texas, 1865–1866." *Arizona and the West* 27 (Summer 1985): 113–42.

———. *The Army in Texas during Reconstruction, 1865–1870.* College Station: Texas A&M University Press, 1987.

Ripley, C. Peter. *Slaves and Freedmen in Civil War Louisiana.* Baton Rouge: Louisiana State University Press, 1976.

Roberts, A. Sellew. "The Federal Government and Confederate Cotton." *American Historical Review* 32 (January 1927): 262–75.

Robertson, James I., Jr. *Soldiers Blue and Gray.* Columbia: University of South Carolina Press, 1988.

Rodgers, Daniel T. "Republicanism: The Career of a Concept." *Journal of American History* 79 (June 1992): 11–38.

Roland, Charles P. *Louisiana Sugar Plantations during the American Civil War.* Leiden: E. J. Brill, 1957.

Rose, Willie Lee. *Rehearsal for Reconstruction: The Port Royal Experiment.* Indianapolis: Bobbs-Merrill, 1964.

Rotundo, E. Anthony. *American Manhood: Transformations in Masculinity from the Revolution to the Modern Era.* New York: Basic Books, 1993.

Rousey, Dennis C. *Policing the Southern City: New Orleans, 1805–1889.* Baton Rouge: Louisiana State University Press, 1996.

Royster, Charles. *A Revolutionary People at War: The Continental Army and American Character, 1775–1783.* Chapel Hill: University of North Carolina Press, 1979.

———. *The Destructive War: William Tecumseh Sherman, Stonewall Jackson, and the Americans.* New York: Alfred A. Knopf, 1991.

Rubin, Anne Sarah. *A Shattered Nation: The Rise and Fall of the Confederacy, 1861–1868.* Chapel Hill: University of North Carolina Press, 2005.

Ruminski, Jarret. "'Tradyville': The Contraband Trade and the Problem of Loyalty in Civil War Mississippi." *Journal of the Civil War Era* 2 (December 2012): 511–37.

Santis, Vincent de. "Rutherford B. Hayes and the Removal of Troops at the End of Reconstruction." In *Region, Race, and Reconstruction: Essays in Honor of C. Vann Woodward,* ed. J. Morgan Kousser and James M. McPherson, 417–46. New York: Oxford University Press, 1982.

Scott, Sean A. "'The Glory of the City Is Gone': Perspectives of Union Soldiers on New Orleans during the Civil War." *Louisiana History* 57 (Winter 2016): 45–69.

Sefton, James E. *The United States Army and Reconstruction, 1865–1877.* Baton Rouge: Louisiana State University Press, 1967.

Sellers, Charles. *The Market Revolution: Jacksonian America, 1815–1846.* New York: Oxford University Press, 1991.

Shannon, Fred Albert. *The Organization and Administration of the Union Army, 1861–1865.* 2 vols. Cleveland: Arthur Clark Company, 1928.

Sheehan-Dean, Aaron. *Why Confederates Fought: Family and Nation in Civil War Virginia.* Chapel Hill: University of North Carolina Press, 2007.

———. "The Long Civil War: Recent Writing on the Outcomes of the U.S. Civil War." *Virginia Magazine of History and Biography* 119 (June 2011): 107–53.

———, ed. *The View from the Ground: Experiences of Civil War Soldiers.* Lexington: University Press of Kentucky, 2007.

Shy, John. *A People Numerous and Armed: Reflections on the Military Struggle for American Independence.* New York: Oxford University Press, 1976.

———. "The Cultural Approach to the History of War." *Journal of Military History* 57 (October 1993): 13–26.

Siddali, Silvana R. *From Property to Person: Slavery and the Confiscation Acts, 1861–1862.* Baton Rouge: Louisiana State University Press, 2005.

Sievers, Harry. *Benjamin Harrison: Hoosier Warrior, 1833–1865.* Chicago: Regnery, 1952.

Silber, Nina. "Intemperate Men, Spiteful Women, and Jefferson Davis: Northern Views of the Defeated South." *American Quarterly* 41 (December 1989): 614–635.

Simpson, Brooks D. *Let Us Have Peace: Ulysses S. Grant and the Politics of War and Reconstruction, 1861–1868.* Chapel Hill: University of North Carolina Press, 1991.

———. "Quandaries of Command: Ulysses S. Grant and Black Soldiers." In *Union and Emancipation: Essays on Politics and Race in the Civil War Era,* ed. David W. Blight and Brooks D. Simpson, 123–50. Kent, OH: Kent State University Press, 1997.

———. *Ulysses S. Grant: Triumph over Adversity, 1822–1865.* New York: Houghton Mifflin Co., 2000.

Singletary, Otis A. *Negro Militia and Reconstruction.* Austin: University of Texas Press, 1957.

Skeen, C. Edward. *Citizen Soldiers in the War of 1812.* Lexington: University Press of Kentucky, 1999.

Skelton, William B. *An American Profession of Arms: The Army Officer Corps, 1784–1815.* Lawrence: University Press of Kansas, 1992.

Slap, Andrew L. *The Doom of Reconstruction: The Liberal Republicans in the Civil War Era.* New York: Fordham University Press, 2010.

Smith, Derek. *The Gallant Dead: Union and Confederate Generals Killed in the Civil War.* Mechanicsburg, PA: Stackpole Books, 2005.

Smith, Jean Edward. *Grant.* New York: Simon & Schuster, 2001.

Smith, John David. *Lincoln and the U.S. Colored Troops.* Carbondale: Southern Illinois University Press, 2013.

———, ed. *Black Soldiers in Blue: African American Troops in the Civil War Era.* Chapel Hill: University of North Carolina Press, 2002.

Smith, John David, and J. Vincent Lowery, eds. *The Dunning School: Historians, Race, and the Meaning of Reconstruction.* Lexington: University Press of Kentucky, 2013.

Smith, Justin H. "American Rule in Mexico." *American Historical Review* 23 (January 1918): 287–302.

Smith, Michael Thomas. *The Enemy Within: Fears of Corruption in the Civil War North.* Charlottesville: University of Virginia Press, 2011.

Smith, Timothy B. *Corinth, 1862: Siege, Battle, Occupation.* Lawrence: University Press of Kansas, 2012.

Snyder, R. Claire. *Citizen-Soldiers and Manly Warriors: Military Service and Gender in the Civic Republican Tradition.* Lanham, MD: Rowman & Littlefield, 1999.

Stampp, Kenneth M. *The Era of Reconstruction, 1865–1877.* New York: Vintage Books, 1965.

Sternhell, Yael A. "Revisionism Reinvented? The Antiwar Turn in Civil War Scholarship." *Journal of the Civil War Era* 3 (June 2013): 239–56.

Stith, Matthew M. *Extreme Civil War: Guerrilla Warfare, Environment, and Race on the Trans-Mississippi Frontier.* Baton Rouge: Louisiana State University Press, 2016.

Stoker, Donald. *The Grand Design: Strategy and the U.S. Civil War.* New York: Oxford University Press, 2010.

Summers, Mark Wahlgren. *A Dangerous Stir: Fear, Paranoia and the Making of Reconstruction.* Chapel Hill: University of North Carolina Press, 2009.

———. *The Ordeal of the Reunion: A New History of Reconstruction.* Chapel Hill: University of North Carolina Press, 2014.

Surdam, David G. "Traders or Traitors: Northern Cotton Trading during the Civil War." *Business and Economic History* 28 (Winter 1999): 301–12.

Sutherland, Daniel E. *Seasons of War: The Ordeal of a Confederate Community, 1861–1865.* New York: Free Press, 1995.

———. *A Savage Conflict: The Decisive Role of Guerillas in the American Civil War.* Chapel Hill: University of North Carolina Press, 2009.

Sutherland, Daniel E., ed. *Guerrillas, Unionists, and Violence on the Confederate Home Front.* Fayetteville: University of Arkansas Press, 1999.

Taylor, Joe Gray. *Louisiana Reconstructed, 1863–1877.* Baton Rouge: Louisiana State University Press, 1974.

Thomas, Benjamin P., and Harold M. Hyman. *Stanton: The Life and Times of Lincoln's Secretary of War.* New York: Alfred A. Knopf, 1962.

Townsend, Stephen A. *The Yankee Invasion of Texas.* College Station: Texas A&M University Press, 2005.

Trelease, Allen W. *White Terror: The Ku Klux Klan Conspiracy and Southern Reconstruction.* New York: Harper & Row, 1971.

Trudeau, Noah Andre. *Like Men of War: Black Troops in the Civil War, 1862–1865.* Boston: Little Brown, 1998.

Tunnell, Ted. *Crucible of Reconstruction: War, Radicalism, and Race in Louisiana, 1862–1877.* Baton Rouge: Louisiana State University Press, 1984.

Upton, Emory. *The Military Policy of the United States.* Washington: Government Printing Office, 1912.

Urwin, Gregory J. W., ed. *Black Flag over Dixie: Racial Atrocities and Reprisals in the Civil War.* Carbondale: Southern Illinois University Press, 2004.

Varon, Elizabeth R. *Appomattox: Victory, Defeat, and Freedom at the End of the Civil War.* New York: Oxford University Press, 2014.

Vinovskis, Maris A. "Have Social Historians Lost the Civil War? Some Preliminary Demographic Speculations." *Journal of American History* 76 (June 1989): 34–58.

Voelz, Peter M. *Slave and Soldier: The Military Impact of Blacks in the Colonial Americas.* New York: Garland Publishing, 1993.

Vorenberg, Michael. "Abraham Lincoln's 'Fellow Citizens'—before and after Emancipation." In *Lincoln's Proclamation: Emancipation Reconsidered,* ed. William A. Blair and Karen Fisher Younger, 151–69. Chapel Hill: University of North Carolina Press, 2009.

Wade, Michael G. "'I Would Rather Be among the Comanches': The Military Occupation of Southwest Louisiana, 1865." *Louisiana History* 39 (Winter 1998): 45–64.

Warner, Nathaniel. "The Morale of Troops on Occupation Duty." *American Journal of Psychiatry* 102 (May 1946): 749–57.

Watson, Peter. *War on the Mind: The Military Uses and Abuses of Psychology.* New York: Basic Books, 1978.

Watson, Samuel J. "Manifest Destiny and Military Professionalism: Junior U.S. Army Officers' Attitudes toward War with Mexico, 1844–1846." *Southwestern Historical Quarterly* 99 (April 1996): 467–98.

——. *Jackson's Sword: The Army Officer Corps on the American Frontier, 1810–1821.* Lawrence: University Press of Kansas, 2012.

——. *Peacekeepers and Conquerors: The Army Officer Corps on the American Frontier, 1821–1846.* Lawrence: University Press of Kansas, 2013.

Waugh, Joan. "'I Only Knew What Was in My Mind': Ulysses S. Grant and the Meaning of Appomattox." *Journal of the Civil War Era* (September 2012): 307–336.

Weigley, Russell F. *The American Way of War: A History of United States Military Strategy and Policy.* Bloomington: Indiana University Press, 1977.

West, Elliott. *The Contested Plains: Indians, Goldseekers, and the Rush to Colorado.* Lawrence: University Press of Kansas, 1998.

Westwood, Howard C. "The Cause and Consequence of a Union Black Soldier's Mutiny and Execution." *Civil War History* 31 (September 1985): 222–36.

——. *Black Troops, White Commanders, and Freedmen during the Civil War.* Carbondale: Southern Illinois University Press, 1992.

Wheelan, Joseph. *Invading Mexico: America's Continental Dream and the Mexican War, 1846–1848.* New York: Carroll & Graf, 2007.

Whites, LeeAnn. *The Civil War as a Crisis in Gender: Augusta, Georgia, 1860–1890.* Athens: University of Georgia Press, 1995.

Wiley, Bell Irvin. *The Life of Johnny Reb: The Common Soldier of the Confederacy.* Indianapolis: Bobbs-Merrill, 1943.

——. *The Life of Billy Yank: The Common Soldier of the Union.* Indianapolis: Bobbs-Merrill, 1952.

Wills, Bryon Steel. *The War Hits Home: The Civil War in Southeastern Virginia.* Charlottesville: University Press of Virginia, 2001.

Wilson, Keith P. *Campfires of Freedom: The Camp Life of Black Soldiers during the Civil War.* Kent, OH: Kent State University Press, 2002.

———. "In the Shadow of John Brown: The Military Service of Colonels Thomas Higginson, James Montgomery, and Robert Shaw in the Department of the South." In *Black Soldiers in Blue: African American Troops in the Civil War Era,* ed. John David Smith, 306–35. Chapel Hill: University of North Carolina Press, 2002.

Winders, Richard Bruce. *Mr. Polk's Army: The American Military Experience in the Mexican War.* College Station: Texas A&M University Press, 1997.

Witt, John Fabien. *Lincoln's Code: The Laws of War in American History.* New York: Free Press, 2012.

Wood, Gordon S. *The Radicalism of the American Revolution.* New York: Alfred A. Knopf, 1991.

———. *Empire of Liberty: A History of the Early Republic, 1789–1815.* New York: Oxford University Press, 2009.

Woodward, C. Vann. *Reunion and Reaction: The Compromise of 1877 and the End of Reconstruction.* Boston: Little, Brown & Co., 1951.

Woodworth, Steven E. *While God Is Marching On: The Religious World of Civil War Soldiers.* Lawrence: University of Kansas Press, 2001.

———. *Nothing but Victory: The Army of the Tennessee, 1861–1865.* New York: Alfred A. Knopf, 2005.

———, ed. *The Art of Command in the Civil War.* Lincoln: University of Nebraska Press, 1998.

———, ed. *The Loyal, True, and Brave: America's Civil War Soldiers.* Wilmington, DE: Scholarly Resources, 2002.

Wooster, Robert. *Soldiers, Sutlers, and Settlers: Garrison Life on the Texas Frontier.* College Station: Texas A&M Press, 1987.

Work, David. "United States Colored Troops in Texas during Reconstruction, 1865–1867." *Southwestern Historical Quarterly* 109 (January 2006): 337–58.

Wyatt-Brown, Bertram. *Southern Honor: Ethics and Behavior in the Old South.* New York: Oxford University Press, 1982.

———. *The Shaping of Southern Culture: Honor, Grace, and War, 1760s–1880s.* Chapel Hill: University of North Carolina Press, 2001.

Zuczek, Richard. *State of Rebellion: Reconstruction in North Carolina.* Columbia: University of South Carolina, 1996.

Dissertations and Theses

Beall, Jonathan A. "'Won't We Never Get Out of This State?' Western Soldiers in Post-Civil War Texas, 1865–1866." M.A. thesis. Texas A&M University, 2004.

Bledsoe, Andrew Scott. "Citizen-Officers: The Union and Confederate Volunteer Junior Officer Corps in the American Civil War, 1861–1865." Ph.D. dissertation, Rice University, 2012.

Herrera, Ricardo A. "Guarantors of Liberty and Republic: The American Citizen as Soldier and the Military Ethos of Republicanism, 1775–1861." Ph.D. dissertation, Marquette University, 1998.

Kirkland, John Robert. "Federal Troops in the South Atlantic States during Reconstruction, 1865–1877." Ph.D. dissertation, University of North Carolina at Chapel Hill, 1967.

Pfanz, Harry W. "Soldiering in the South during the Reconstruction Period, 1865–1877." Ph.D. dissertation, Ohio State University, 1958.

Wilson, Spencer. "Experiment in Reunion: The Union Army in Civil War Norfolk and Portsmouth, Virginia." Ph.D. dissertation, University of Maryland, 1973.

Zalimas, Robert J., Jr. "Black Union Soldiers in the Postwar South, 1865–1866." M.A. thesis, Arizona State University, 1993.

INDEX